The numbers of children living in poverty in the Unit
during the 1980s and remains high. Why are so ma
families? What are the effects of poverty on children
emotional development? What role can public pol.
preventing or alleviating the damaging effects of poverty on children?

Children in Poverty examines these questions, focusing on the child rather than on
parents' income or self-sufficiency. The contributors come from diverse fields – economics, sociology, public health, psychology, child development, and education –
affording depth and wide coverage of the topic.

Children in poverty

Children in poverty
Child development and public policy

Edited by

ALETHA C. HUSTON
University of Kansas

 CAMBRIDGE
UNIVERSITY PRESS

Published by the Press Syndicate of the University of Cambridge
The Pitt Building, Trumpington Street, Cambridge CB2 1RP
40 West 20th Street, New York, NY 10011-4211, USA
10 Stamford Road, Oakleigh, Melbourne 3166, Australia

© Cambridge University Press 1991

First published 1991
First paperback edition 1994

Printed in the United States of America

Library of Congress Cataloging-in-Publication Data is available

A catalog record for this book is available from the British Library

ISBN 0-521-39162-8 hardback
ISBN 0-521-47756-5 paperback

Contents

Contributors

NAN MARIE ASTONE is a sociologist and an assistant professor of population dynamics at the Johns Hopkins School of Hygiene and Public Health.

FRANCES A. CAMPBELL is coordinator of psychological assessment at the Frank Porter Graham Child Development Center, University of North Carolina at Chapel Hill.

GREG J. DUNCAN is a research scientist at the Survey Research Center, University of Michigan, and codirector of the Panel Study on Income Dynamics.

ALETHA C. HUSTON is a professor of human development and psychology at the University of Kansas and codirector of the Center for Research on the Influences of Television on Children (CRITC).

LORRAINE V. KLERMAN is a professor of public health in the Department of Epidemiology and Public Health, School of Medicine, Yale University.

HENRY M. LEVIN is a professor of education, director of the Center for Educational Research, and an affiliated faculty member of the Department of Economics at Stanford University.

SARA S. MCLANAHAN is a professor of sociology and public affairs at Princeton University.

VONNIE C. MCLOYD is an associate professor of psychology and a research associate in the Center for Human Growth and Development at the University of Michigan.

NADINE F. MARKS is a sociologist and doctoral candidate in sociology at the University of Wisconsin–Madison.

DEBORAH A. PHILLIPS is an associate professor of psychology at the University of Virginia and a former mid-career Fellow in the Bush Foundation Program in Child Development and Social Policy at Yale University.

CRAIG T. RAMEY is a professor of psychology and pediatrics, codirector of the Curtan International Research Center, and codirector of the Sparks Center for Developmental and Learning Disorders at the University of Alabama at Birmingham.

vii

Lisbeth Bamberger Schorr is a lecturer in the Department of Social Medicine at Harvard Medical School.

Leon Wilson is an assistant professor in the Department of Sociology and the Center for Urban, Labor, and Metropolitan Affairs at Wayne State University.

Preface

Any casual consumer of news is aware that the numbers of children living in poverty in the United States increased dramatically during the 1980s and remained high into the early 1990s. Editorial writers and news commentators offer the statistics on the percentage of children living in poverty with depressing regularity. In fact, the mass media discovered the trend about 15 years after it began. The percentage of U.S. children living in poor families has been increasing since about 1970.

When information about children's poverty began to surface in the mid-1980s, I, like many others, reacted with concern and alarm but with little sense of what to do about the problem. Most of my research career as a developmental psychologist had been devoted to issues with social importance: the effects of mass media on children and sex-role development throughout the life span. My work on sex roles has a strong feminist perspective, and it is by now commonplace knowledge that poverty increasingly has become the plight of females as well as of children. It followed fairly naturally, therefore, for me to move more explicitly into the study of public policy and children's poverty.

Psychologists and child-development specialists often discuss social or public policy, and a small group have devoted major efforts to the topic. But policy studies have been centered in other disciplines: political science, economics, sociology, and social welfare. Thanks to an internal sabbatical program at the University of Kansas designed to promote interdisciplinary study, I spent a year in the Department of Political Science learning about a wide variety of approaches to public policy. This experience made me acutely aware of the fundamental differences in perspective arising from the fact that psychologists conceptualize human behavior at the level of the individual, whereas political scientists and those in related disciplines conceptualize at an aggregate societal level. Equally important was the realization that although children are central to child developmentalists' interests, they have relatively little importance in most other disciplines studying public policy. Children are discussed in connection with welfare policy primarily as economic burdens of adults. The major content subdivisions of public policy texts typically do not include an entry for "child policy" or even "family policy."

This book is an effort to bring to the topic of children in poverty the strengths and wisdom of the various disciplines devoted to policy analysis. Scholars who take a developmental view and those who use a socioeconomic perspective are represented. Their chapters, however, are not simply a collection of different disciplinary perspectives; they each integrate their work with those in other disciplines. The book is designed to shed light on basic questions and to provide a better understanding of policies affecting children's welfare. It is based on a working conference, "Children and Poverty," held at the University of Kansas in June 1988.

The contributors, representing disciplines that analyze societal and economic influences (economics, sociology, and public health) and disciplines dealing at the individual level with children's development and welfare (psychology, child development, and education), presented earlier versions of the chapters in this book at the conference. We spent three days in the lively discussion reflected throughout the book, particularly in the introductory and concluding chapters.

Several books about poverty have been published in recent years, but most of them treat children as economic adjuncts to parents. In this volume, we take the perspective of the child and evaluate policies on the basis of their effects on the health and welfare of children. Unlike many policy analysts, we do not assume that the economic or psychological welfare of children necessarily coincides with that of parents. Rather than focusing solely on family income or parents' participation in the labor force as indicators, we ask about the effects of economic conditions and public policies on children's health, cognitive development, education, and emotional well-being.

Our intended audiences are policy makers and scholars. We provide a data-oriented approach, but it is communicated in an accessible style that will be readable for a range of people interested in policy issues. Our goal is not just to assemble and integrate what we know but to clarify what we need to know. The creative tension between research and action runs throughout *Children in Poverty*. Contributors are not afraid to argue that we know enough to act. At the same time, one of our goals is to articulate questions that require research, to identify areas in which there is a distinct need for more knowledge.

The conference from which this book arose was generously supported by the Foundation for Child Development and the Ford Foundation. Yvonne Caldera, Alison Dishinger, Tiffany Merkel, Suwatchara Piemyet, Michelle St. Peters, and Rosemarie Truglio provided invaluable help in recording and transcribing the discussions at the conference. Vicki Hamlin and Shelley Marcotte aided in the typing and final printing of the manuscript. Colleagues too numerous to mention individually gave encouragement, critiques, and commentary that were helpful in refining the ideas.

1 Children in poverty: Developmental and policy issues

Aletha C. Huston

Until recently, 7-year-old Justin Coles received little treatment for recurring ear infections that might create permanent hearing loss. Justin's mother works part-time as a nurse's aide, and her husband, a laid-off steelworker, paints houses. Their combined income of $13,000 falls below the federal poverty level for a family of five, but it is too high for the family to qualify for Medicaid in Pennsylvania. Mrs. Coles described their dilemma as a choice between medical treatment for Justin and having food on the table or a roof over their heads. Justin is fortunate to be covered by a privately sponsored health insurance program for children of the working poor, but many of the 37 million people in the country without health insurance are not so lucky (Dunn, 1989).

Alain Cooper spent his childhood in his native Harlem living "most of the time" with his mother and several of his eight brothers and sisters. When he was about 7 years old, his mother was imprisoned, and there was no one to care for the family. Finally, Connie, a 20-year-old friend, and her boyfriend took in five of the boys and one pregnant girl, attempting to support them. Ultimately, the boyfriend left, and Connie became a "street girl." The children were left alone for days at a time, and there was no money for food or rent even though their father and mother both sent money to Connie. Alain began working in the back of a bar at age 11, but he was never paid so he learned to help himself to the contents of the cash register (Williams & Kornblum, 1985, pp. 17–19).

Alma is a 9-year-old Mexican-American girl who is in foster care with an Anglo foster mother. She was referred for therapy "after she had been severely physically abused by her stepfather, Javier, a Nicaraguan exile who lived with the family for one year. . . . He punished her brutally over a period of three days, breaking an arm and ribs and burning her palms by holding them over a stove burner. . . . [Her] hands were severely scarred, and she wore mittens throughout her therapy to keep scar tissue from constricting the extension of her fingers." Alma sometimes denied that she was Hispanic, identifying her mother and Javier as Hispanic and "bad." After a year of therapy, she was more comfortable with her ethnicity, and her fear and anger seemed to be at manageable levels (Ramirez, 1989, pp. 243–244).

1

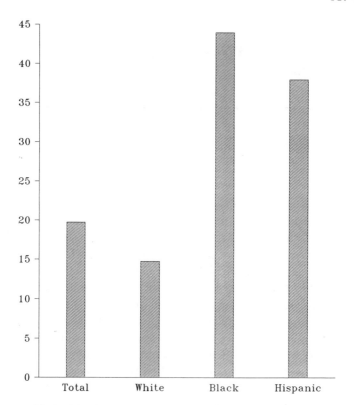

Figure 1.1a. Percentage of children living in families with incomes below the poverty line by ethnic group. From "Poverty Drops Slightly in 1988 but Continues to Rise for Young Children and Young Families" by the Children's Defense Fund, December 1989, *CDF Reports, 11*(5), pp. 1, 4.

These children represent a few of the many faces of poverty in the contemporary United States. Even a casual consumer of the mass media is aware that their numbers are high. During much of the last two decades, poverty among U.S. children has been on the rise, reversing the downward trend that had occurred from the 1950s to the early 1970s. In 1985, 20% of all children lived in families with incomes below the official poverty level; 41% of all black children and 37% of all Hispanic children lived in poverty (Burtless, 1986; Duncan, this volume; Moynihan, 1986; U.S. Department of Education, 1988). By 1988, the rate had dropped to 19.2% for all children; among children under age 3, it was 23.3% (Children's Defense Fund, 1989). These trends are illustrated in Figure 1.1. Children now experience higher rates of poverty than do elderly adults or adults in general. Poverty is also more prevalent for children in the United States than for those in most other industrialized nations (Duncan, this volume; Smeeding & Torrey, 1988).

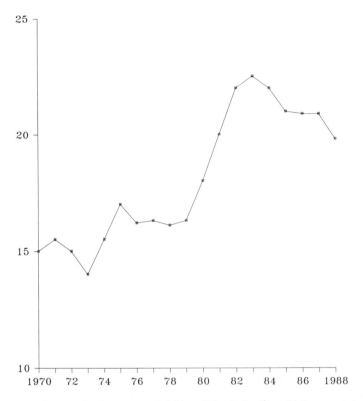

Figure 1.1b. Percentage of children living in families with incomes below the poverty line from 1970 to 1988. From "Poverty Drops Slightly in 1988 but Continues to Rise for Young Children and Young Families" by the Children's Defense Fund, December 1989, *CDF Reports, 11*(5), pp. 1, 4.

Why, how, and what can be done?

This book addresses three sets of questions. First, why are so many children growing up in poor families? How and why has the economic status of families with children deteriorated in the last 20 years? What social and economic forces account for the high rates of children's poverty (and by implication might be altered to reduce poverty)?

Second, what are the effects of poverty on children's physical, cognitive, social, and emotional development? Why do these effects occur? How do these effects vary (or remain the same) for children in persistent and transitory poverty?

Third, what role can public policy and policy research play in preventing or alleviating the damaging effects of poverty on children? What are the goals of public policies affecting families, and how do they mesh with predominant social values? When is it most effective to raise family income, and when are such intensive human services as educational programs, health centers, or family support required to help children overcome the negative effects of poverty? Where do we need more research to provide information guiding policy, and where do we know enough to act? How are policies evaluated? What criteria make sense in evaluating policies for children?

Child-centered policy analysis

Unlike many other recent analysts of poverty, the authors in this book take a child-centered approach to understanding poverty and to evaluating the possible solutions to children's poverty. Most policy analyses of U.S. poverty either implicitly or explicitly include children as a major target for antipoverty policies. For the most part, however, these discussions, ranging from Murray (1984) to Ellwood (1988) and Wilson (1987), analyze and recommend policies for adults who may also be parents. Mainstream policy analysis, based primarily in economics and political science, usually occurs at a social-economic level dealing with aggregates of adults. Such scholars make the assumption that policies that reduce parents' poverty will also solve the problems of poor children. Although such an assumption is undoubtedly justified in many cases, the interests of children are not always identical to those of their parents.

Children as individuals in their own right are virtually absent from many policy discussions. Commonly used policy categories include such headings as welfare, education, and family policy, but rarely child policy. Gilbert Steiner (1981) observed several years ago that family policy is not child policy. His point is illustrated in a symposium on "family policy" in a 1989 issue of *Policy Studies Review* (Anderson & Hula, 1989). Although children are discussed in several of the articles, even the feminist analyses proceed from the vantage point of the adults who are responsible for children. One result is that policy proposals are often directed primarily to changing parental circumstances (i.e., income) or behavior. Important issues are obscured. For instance, when the family rather than the child is the target such issues as foster care or homelessness among adolescents easily can be neglected.

In this book, we take the child rather than the parent as the focal point of analysis. A child-centered analysis grows naturally out of developmental psychology, child development, and education, disciplines that until recently have been minor voices in the policy arena. Children's healthy development is conceived as a primary goal in its own right. Child-centered analysis leads one to ask about the direct outcomes of policies for children, not just for their parents. It leads one to examine a broad range of developmental outcomes that go well beyond the typical economic criteria of dollars earned or hours worked.

The child-centered point of view is illustrated in Schorr's (1988) *Within Our Reach* and in edited volumes on such topics as child care, family support, parental leave, and educational interventions (e.g., Lande, Scarr, & Gunzenhauser, 1989; Stevenson & Siegel, 1984; Yogman & Brazelton, 1986; Zigler & Frank, 1988). They begin with what we know about the conditions that promote children's development and proceed to ask how policy can assure that children's basic needs are met.

These two orientations – social-economic and child-developmental – often lead to different questions about policy and different criteria for evaluating policy. Policy analysts and policy makers stress *economic* rationales for policies and programs affecting poor children. The short-term economic goal is to encourage parents to enter and remain in the labor force so that they can generate income by working. For example, welfare reform and child care programs are promoted because they permit mothers to work for pay outside their homes (Phillips, this volume). Conversely, cash or in-kind benefits are criticized on the grounds that they reduce parents' incentives to work.

The bulk of research on welfare reform and income maintenance is devoted almost exclusively to evaluating success in attaining such short-term economic goals. Parental labor force participation and earnings are the primary or sole criteria for success. In the 1980s, welfare reform experiments in different localities defined success or failure almost entirely on the basis of parents' economic self-sufficiency (Gueron, 1987). The debate surrounding the federal welfare reform legislation passed in 1988 was couched in a framework weighing the costs of welfare against the costs of education and training that could lead to employment.

The income maintenance experiments of the 1960s and 1970s were among the most extensive and expensive social experiments ever conducted. Many of the volumes generated by those experiments are devoted to analyzing the effects of income supplements on adults' labor force participation. In some groups, work hours declined, especially among women with children. Interpretations of these patterns dwelt almost entirely on the negative implications of reduced work hours for family income and for the health of the economy. They rarely asked whether there were benefits of reduced maternal employment for the family or for the children (Haveman, 1986; Institute for Research on Poverty, 1976; Kershaw & Fair, 1976; Robins & West, 1980).

A child-centered analysis leads to different questions. For example, do income supplements improve quality of life, particularly for children? Do they improve nutrition, parent–child relations, school motivation, neighborhood safety, or physical health? Some of the findings are suggestive. For example, families often spent their increased income on improving their housing (Kershaw & Fair, 1976). Better housing probably means better schools and safer neighborhoods, both of which could have important consequences for children. People also bought appliances and durable consumer goods, clothes, and in some instances, more food.

Economic assumptions also underlie the view of children as human capital in whom we should invest for the future. Using this rationale, the goal of public policies that reduce poverty is to produce a healthy, educated work force prepared for the economic challenges of a competitive world in the next generation. Early interventions to promote health and education are justified by their long-term economic payoffs in larger earnings, less welfare dependence, lower prison populations, and other benefits. For instance, preschool education is sometimes evaluated by calculating the increased earnings that will result from higher rates of high school graduation. One result is that an extreme burden of proof is placed on programs for young children; they must achieve more than most other social programs because their outcomes are so far in the future.

Developmental psychologists, educators, and professionals in the human services take a fundamentally different perspective based on *humanitarian, moral, human rights, and social equity* principles. Antipoverty policies are justified on the grounds that children have a right not to be poor, that is, a right to grow up with reasonable levels of physical and emotional protection and comfort. Children have basic rights to quality of life; they have inherent value as individuals at any point in their lives, not simply as future adults. The welfare of children is taken as a given in a society that values social equity and justice. Early childhood education, health care, and quality child care are advocated in order to provide for the current developmental needs of children and not simply as adjuncts to parents' labor force participation or as investments in future workers. Policies and programs are evaluated by examining such developmental outcomes as health status, school progress, intellectual development, and social behavior. One example is an analysis of the income maintenance experiments showing some improvements in health, nutrition, school performance, and fertility control when families received income supplements (Salkind & Haskins, 1982). It is significant, however, that the quality and quantity of the data collected about these outcomes was sparse.

Economic and developmental rationales do not necessarily conflict, but achieving one set of goals does not always result in reaching the others. Policies aimed at the short-term economic goal of getting a mother into the labor force and raising her income may not benefit her child if that child is left in unsuitable child care or is unsupervised after school. Increased family income may not always be used for the benefit of children. In the chapter by McLanahan, Astone, and Marks (this volume), family income increased dramatically when single mothers married, but children in stepfamilies had many of the same problems as those in single-mother families. In many cases, of course, increased income does produce direct benefits for children's development. The point of these counterexamples is that evaluators should measure developmental variables directly rather than rely solely on parent labor force participation as *the* index of policy success.

Nature of poverty for children

Defining poverty

The official poverty level established by the U.S. government is the most widely used index of poverty. It was originally based on the estimated cost of an "economy food budget" multiplied by 3 on the assumption that food should constitute one-third of a family's budget. It is adjusted for family size, the age of the head of the household, and the number of children under age 18. Annual adjustments to the poverty index are made for the cost of living based on the Consumer Price Index (Danziger, Haveman, & Plotnick, 1986).

Several criticisms of this index are common. Some critics argue that it overestimates poverty because it includes only cash income. It does not include such in-kind transfers as food stamps or medical care. This argument in part has been answered by analyses showing that although adding the market or cash value of in-kind transfers to family incomes reduces the percentage of children living below the poverty line, a substantial number remain. For example, in 1983, 22.2% of all children under age 18 lived in families with cash incomes below the poverty level; 15.6% remained below the poverty level when in-kind transfers were counted as income (Danziger et al., 1986). Moreover, there are serious questions about equating the market value of such commodities as medical care to cash transfers (Hill, 1988).

Some critics argue that a cut-off level underestimates the severity of poverty because it does not indicate variations in family income below that level. The *poverty gap* is the total dollar amount by which the incomes of the poor fall below the poverty level. In 1986, it was $49.2 billion, an increase of more than 50% from 1977 (Greenstein, 1988).

Critics also contend that poverty is relative rather than absolute; therefore, it ought to be defined relative to the median income in the population. The official poverty level changed relative to median income from .46 in 1965 to .38 in 1979 and to .41 in 1983 (Danziger et al., 1986). Therefore, the trends over time based on the poverty level may be underestimates of the change in relative poverty. Hernandez (1989) examined trends in incomes of families with children, defining deprivation as incomes below 50% of the "prevailing family standard" (the median income for two-parent families with an employed father). The percentages are higher than those based on the poverty level, but the trends over time are similar (see Figure 1.2). These analyses also show changes in economic circumstances in the range just above the poverty level. As the percentage of children in deprivation increased during the 1970s and 1980s, the proportion living in "comfortable circumstances" (incomes ranging from 67% to 150% of the prevailing family standard) declined.

Finally, as the examples at the beginning of this chapter illustrate, many

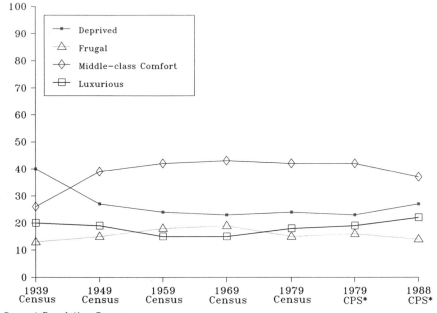

Figure 1.2. Proportions of children age 0 to 17 living in deprived, frugal, comfortable, or luxurious economic circumstances for selected years from 1939 to 1987. From "The Changing Needs of America's Children from the Great Depression to the 21st Century" by D. J. Hernandez, April 1989. Paper presented at the Biennial Meeting of the Society for Research in Child Development, Kansas City, MO.

children are essentially without families and are by definition without income. The many children in institutions, foster care, or other placements outside their families are not included when families are counted as the units in poverty statistics.

All of these approaches to defining poverty are consistent in showing trends over time – declining rates of poverty until the early 1970s, increases through the early 1980s, and a leveling off in the late 1980s. Analyses of family incomes by the Congressional Budget Office (1988) show a similar pattern for families with children. Moreover, they demonstrate an increase in income inequality from 1970 to 1986. Families at the top of the income distribution became relatively more affluent; those at the bottom became relatively poorer (see Figure 1.3).

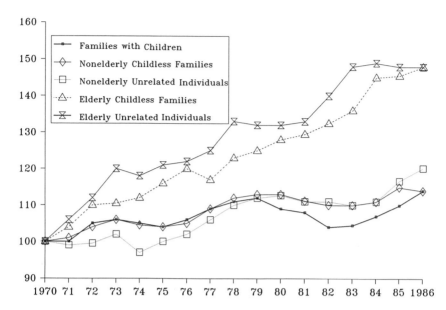

Figure 1.3a. Mean adjusted family income, relative to 1970 value (set at 100), by family type, from 1970 to 1986. From *Trends in Family Income: 1970–1988* by the Congressional Budget Office, 1988, Washington, DC: Author.

Persistent and transitory poverty

Taking a cross section of poverty at one point in time can obscure distinctions between children whose poverty is relatively transitory and those who live in persistent poverty. The Panel Study of Income Dynamics followed a nationally representative sample of families over a period of 15 years. Slightly over half of all the children in the sample lived in poverty or near poverty (less than 150% of the official poverty level) at some time between ages 4 and 18. In many cases, however, poverty lasted only a year or two. About 12% of the sample lived in poverty for more than 4 years of their childhood (Duncan, 1984; Duncan, this volume).

Race is the most striking and disturbing distinction between families whose poverty is persistent and those for whom it is transitory. Black children have a much higher risk of living in chronic poverty than do white children. The *average* black child in the Panel Study on Income Dynamics spent 5.5 years in poverty; the average nonblack child spent 0.9 years in poverty. Many chronically poor children also live in single-mother families. Mothers who are either unmarried or in their teen years at the child's birth and who are poorly educated have children who are at risk for long-term poverty (Duncan, this volume; Furstenberg, Brooks-Gunn, & Morgan, 1987).

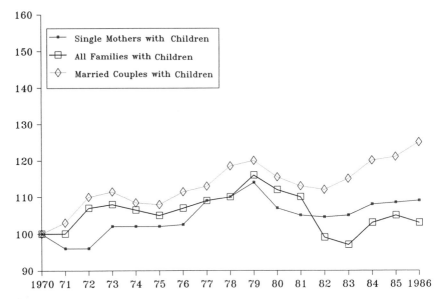

Figure 1.3b. Mean adjusted family income, relative to 1970 value (set at 100), for families with children, from 1970 to 1986. From *Trends in Family Income: 1970–1988* by the Congressional Budget Office, 1988, Washington, DC: Author.

Transitory poverty for children often results from parental unemployment or divorce. Although transitory poverty probably entails fewer social and environmental risks than chronic poverty does, it nonetheless can have a lasting impact on children's development. Large fluctuations in family income may force the family to change neighborhoods and schools and to forgo "extras" such as recreational activities, lessons, and new clothes. Moreover, income volatility is likely to create emotional stress for parents, which, in turn, leads some of them to be less nurturant and more punitive to their children (Emery, Hetherington, & DiLalla, 1984; McLoyd, 1989).

Urban and rural poverty

Mention poverty to most Americans, and they will probably conjure up an image of an all-black ghetto in a deteriorated area of a large city. Black children in urban ghettos live not only with poverty in their own families but also with the burdens of racism that can result in inferior educational systems and perceived lack of opportunity (Ogbu, 1988). Some large urban ghettos have high concentrations of adults who are poor and chronically unemployed with virtually no attachment to the labor market. This pattern increased dramatically in a few of the largest cities during the 1980s as middle- and working-class blacks took advantage of opportunties to leave impoverished urban neighborhoods (Wacquant & Wilson, 1989; Wilson, 1987). Children living in these ghetto neighborhoods have few models of conventional success and are isolated from the norms and opportunities in the larger society. Instead, they live in an environment where criminal activity succeeds and where the threat of violence is ever present.

Although the rates of poverty in rural parts of the United States are as high as those in central cities (Jensen, 1988), rural poverty in the 1980s was almost invisible to the public and to policy analysts. It seems strange to recall that the standard media image of poverty in the 1960s was an underfed white family in rural Appalachia. Compared to poor people in urban areas, the poor in rural areas are more often married and have a working head of the family, and they are less often nonwhite and less often have children. On the whole, rural poor families receive fewer welfare benefits and more often live in states that do not provide Aid to Families with Dependent Children (AFDC) for two-parent families (Jensen, 1988). Single women with children in small towns and rural areas are employed in lower-level jobs than comparable women in urban and suburban areas; their poverty often is due to the low wages that are common in rural areas (Cautley & Slesinger, 1988).

The distinction between persistent and transitory poverty forms an important theme in many of the papers that follow. Duncan sets the stage in chapter 2 by describing the result of longitudinal analyses of family incomes, and several other contributors follow his lead in their discussions of the settings, circumstances, and problems associated with poverty. In her earlier work, Schorr (1988) made a strong argument that specific policies and programs are needed for children experiencing the multiple risks of persistent poverty. By contrast, like others in the field, we have given little attention to the distinction between urban and rural poverty. In the conclusion, we suggest the need for more attention to the needs of rural poor children.

Summary of chapters

The authors in this book represent a wide spectrum of disciplines, including economics, public health, sociology, psychology, and education. They bring both social-economic and child-developmental orientations to their chapters, but the book is not a confrontation between these views. Instead, each author integrates these perspectives in a discussion of policy issues and questions.

Each author was asked to address the three major questions, discussed earlier in this chapter, that guide this book: Why are so many children living in poverty? What are the effects of poverty on children's physical, intellectual, and social development? What role can public policy play in preventing or alleviating the damaging effects of poverty on children? Some chapters emphasize the causes of children's poverty and some are concerned primarily with its effects, but none of them is restricted to one set of questions. Every author addresses issues of the antecedents and the consequences of children's poverty, and every author considers the role of public policy and policy research.

In chapter 2, Duncan delineates some of the reasons for the increase in children's poverty from 1970 to the late 1980s. He identifies three major factors: changes in family structure (increasing percentages of mother-only families), changes in the labor market (low wages and unemployment), and reductions in such government transfers as Aid to Families with Dependent Children. He distinguishes the factors associated with persistent poverty and income volatility. Blacks are not only at high risk for persistent poverty; they also have a higher probability than whites of sudden income loss, and they are less likely to have savings to buffer that loss. Unemployment is the most common reason for sudden income loss for men. Divorce is the most common reason for women and children to experience sudden income loss; men's incomes are not reduced substantially by divorce.

Duncan demonstrates clear effects of family income on children's long-term attainments and on their physical and mental health. Although the effects of persistent and transitory poverty are different, both conditions have some deleterious consequences for children. Family income has effects on children's later attainments that are independent of family education and occupational prestige. *Why* such effects occur is much less clear than *that* they occur. Duncan suggests that we need longitudinal studies of children's development to investigate the mechanisms by which family incomes affect children and to understand the influence of such intervening variables as social support, stress, coping behavior, and perceptions of economic strain. Answers to these questions would inform policy choices. If income per se is the problem, then policies directed at providing minimum incomes are indicated; if psychological and social factors associated with poverty are critical, then policies providing services that address these factors are also needed.

In chapter 3, McLanahan, Astone, and Marks examine the relative importance of income and psychological and social factors as influences on adolescents' attainment. They address one important correlate of children's poverty – single-mother family structure. Children in single-mother families have lower educational attainment and a higher probability of early child-bearing than children in two-parent families. Earlier research suggested that single mothers' low income is one important reason, but patterns of parent socialization (e.g., parent–child communication, supervision) and neighborhood factors (e.g., school quality, peer-group attainment) could also account for differences between children of single mothers and those with two resident parents. Using three national surveys of adolescents, these authors examine three outcomes: dropping out of school, teen pregnancy, and nonmarital pregnancy.

Their findings are consistent. Although single-mother families differ from intact two-parent families on many of the socialization and neighborhood characteristics, these variables do not account for their children's higher frequency of school dropouts, teen pregnancy, or unmarried pregnancy. Low income remains the major factor accounting for the effects of single-mother family structure. However, children in stepfamilies show patterns similar to those in single-mother homes, even though their family incomes are relatively high. Clearly, there is more to be learned about the reasons for family structure differences.

Whatever else may contribute to outcomes for children of single mothers, low income is clearly one important factor. Therefore, McLanahan et al. recommend policies that would reduce the economic insecurity of single-mother families and increase their incomes. They offer suggestions on three fronts: increasing mothers' earnings by improving job possibilities and making child care available, increasing private transfers from nonresident parents, and increasing public transfers.

Adolescent childbearing is both a consequence and a cause of childhood poverty. In chapter 4, Klerman examines the reasons why adolescent parenting contributes to poverty. She points out that social concern about adolescent pregnancy has increased during the last 20 years while the rates of teenage childbearing have declined. Why the fuss? Probably the most important reason is that most adolescent mothers are unmarried and poor. The fathers of their children, who are often young and poor themselves, provide little financial support for their children. Adolescent mothers have low earning power primarily because they leave school early and ultimately have low levels of educational attainment. Their original families often are poor and cannot provide much financial help. The remaining option, welfare support, leaves young mothers with incomes well below the poverty line.

Klerman then asks what leads to early childbearing. The answers are poverty in their original families, lower-class and ghetto neighborhoods, nonintact families, and lax parental control – all correlates of poverty. Clearly, the reasons for childhood poverty are to some degree circular; growing up poor leaves young people vulnerable to the very conditions that perpetuate poverty in the next generation.

Children of adolescent mothers are at risk for health problems, low intellectual performance beginning in preschool and continuing into the school years, and high rates of behavior problems. Whether these child outcomes are due to poverty and its associated variables or to maternal age per se is difficult to determine. Whatever the reasons, adolescent mothers provide less supportive and more punitive child rearing than older mothers.

Klerman considers a wide range of programs for the prevention of adolescent pregnancy and for alleviating the effects of adolescent childbearing. The most successful prevention programs provide access to contraception; programs emphasizing knowledge and attitudes or enhancing life options also have demonstrated effectiveness in some cases. Although abortion often is not easily available to teenagers, it nevertheless is used by them extensively. Ameliorative programs need to focus on reducing poverty, providing services such as prenatal care, and involving fathers. Klerman concludes with the observation that programs to prevent adolescent pregnancy are more effective than are programs to support adolescent parents, yet they are more difficult to establish because they are socially controversial.

These three chapters establish that childhood poverty and its associated family and social conditions have deleterious effects on children's development. In chapter 5, McLoyd and Wilson pursue an in-depth analysis of the environmental stresses and family processes that mediate the effects of urban ghetto poverty on children's mental health. Children in economically deprived families are at high risk for depression, low self-confidence, peer conflict, and conduct disorders, in part because they live with violence, deteriorated housing, and frequent moves from one dwelling to another (or to no home at all) that result in shifting schools and neighborhoods. Adults in urban ghettos also have high rates of mental health problems. Single mothers live with especially high levels of stress and isolation, which can lead to depression and nonsupportive parenting (McAdoo, 1986). Earlier studies of families who experienced major income loss in the Great Depression of the 1930s demonstrated that many of the effects on children were mediated by their parents' reactions to financial stress. Parental depression and nonsupportive parenting may also mediate some of the effects of persistent poverty on children in urban ghettos.

McLoyd and Wilson report the results of a study of children and mothers who were receiving Aid to Families with Dependent Children. Measures of psychological functioning, modes of coping with financial problems, financial stress, and support systems outside the family were included. Maternal feelings of environmental stress and psychological distress were associated with less nurturant parenting, which was in turn related to children's psychological distress. Even more important, however, mothers who shared their personal and financial problems had children who reported high levels of distress. Distressed children worried about the future and, surprisingly, had more social supports among peers and adults outside the family than less distressed children. Variation in the amount of economic hardship experienced by different families was only slightly related to children's psychological well-being, but, of course, all these families were quite poor.

Family process analyses of poverty are rare in the literature, perhaps because of the fear that they will be interpreted as a way of blaming the victim – that is, of blaming the parent(s), the family structure, or the "culture" for the negative outcomes of poverty. Yet, as McLoyd and Wilson demonstrate, it is reasonable to suppose that the stresses of living in poverty will take their toll on parents as well as on children. Moreover, if parents mediate some of the effects of poverty, then interventions to help parents by giving them economic, social, and psychological support may alleviate some of the mental health problems experienced by their children.

Poor children are at risk for problems of physical as well as mental health. In chapter 6, Klerman describes the health status of poor children, analyzes the reasons for their health problems, and suggests means of improving their health. She begins with the grim facts. Children living in poverty are at risk of illness and dying from a wide range of causes. Infant mortality is high because of short gestation periods, low birth weight, and sudden infant death syndrome. These problems are in turn related to low maternal weight gain, obstetrical complications, infections, smoking, drugs, and the lack of adequate prenatal care. Poor children do not have higher rates of congenital anomalies than other children. During childhood, poor children have relatively high rates of infectious diseases, chronic conditions, and injuries from accidents and child abuse.

All of these health problems are related to the living conditions of poverty, particularly of persistent poverty. The poor lack money to buy goods and services that would help them avoid infection, accidents, and injury. They often feel a loss of control over their lives and low levels of self-esteem. Many have unhealthy life-styles, which include smoking and alcohol and drug abuse, and lack such safety precautions as smoke detectors and seat belts. The poor sometimes underuse personal health services, primarily because of cost, barriers to access, problems of transportation, language, and hours of operation.

The health problems of poor children have long-range effects on their cognitive, social, and emotional development. Low birth weight children are at risk for developmental delays, particularly when they live in stressful environments. Common and easily treated problems of childhood can create important barriers to development if untreated. Otitis media, for instance, can lead to temporary or permanent hearing loss and delayed language development. Measles and other childhood diseases, for which immunizations are available, can produce permanent damage to sensory organs and neurological functioning.

Klerman identifies four major domains for policy change. The first is to improve living conditions, primarily through improving family income. The second is to increase prevention through such universal programs as mandatory seat belt legislation and such targeted programs as lead removal. The third is to improve access to personal health services, primarily through increasing eligibility for Medicaid, nutritional supplements for women and children (WIC), and Head Start. Finally, she proposes a reorientation of the nation's personal health services system to provide universal health care.

The next three chapters deal more specifically with services to children and families: child care, early intervention, and education. In chapter 7, on child care, Phillips highlights the distinction between social-economic and developmental orientations. For some policy makers, child care is an adjunct to the welfare system; its goal is to release mothers to enter the work force so that they will not be dependent on public assistance. For others, the goal is child care that will enhance children's physical, cognitive, and social development. The justification for the developmental view is sometimes ultimately economic; it is designed to prevent intergenerational cycles of poverty and welfare by giving the next generation a better chance of economic self-sufficiency. Child care does serve both of these goals. Availability of child care increases mothers' work hours and earnings, and developmentally oriented child care leads to improved health and cognitive development and to long-term school success.

Phillips reviews the data on child care use and cost and on federal programs serving low-income children during the 1980s. Poor families with employed mothers spend 20% to 30% of their incomes on child care. Federal programs based primarily in the welfare system tend to provide minimal funding, and their total allocation dropped during the 1980s. Head Start is the major developmentally oriented program, and despite its higher per-child cost, it was the only federal program that received increases in funding in the 1980s. The total spent on both kinds of programs for the poor, however, was considerably less than the federal expenditure on tax credits for child care – a benefit that serves affluent families more than poor families.

The late 1980s and early 1990s are a period ripe for new child care policies as women become more active in the labor market and as government agencies increasingly feel the pressures for welfare reform. Concern about children as human capital is also surfacing as analysts recognize the need for a skilled, educated labor force to maintain the nation's economic well-being in the future. A notable step occurred when a major child care funding bill became law in 1990.

Phillips cautions us about the dangers of allowing policies that treat child care only as an adjunct to the welfare system. Such policies emphasize low cost rather than quality of care; they could satisfy the short-term goal of reduced welfare costs while leading to long-term social problems of school failure and delinquency for children who experience unsafe and inadequate care during their early years.

Ramey and Campbell (chapter 8) document the importance and potential value of high-quality developmentally oriented interventions in their discussion of their own Abecedarian experiment and other experimental programs for very young children. In the Abecedarian experiment, high-risk children from poor families attended developmental day-care from infancy until they entered school. Throughout the preschool years, their performance on general tests of cognitive development was superior to that of a well-matched control group who received health services but did not take part in the experimental day-care program.

The preschool findings from this project are well-known; what is new in this paper is a follow-up at age 8. Half of the children in the preschool day-care group and half of the control group received an additional intervention program between ages 5 and 8 in which special teachers taught parents to carry out educational activities at home to supplement the school curriculum. Children who had had the preschool intervention continued to perform better than the control group on tests of overall cognitive development through the third grade; school-age intervention did not add to the preschool effect. However, for indices of academic achievement – performance on tests of reading and math as well as the probability of being retained in a grade – both preschool and school-age interventions made a difference. Half of the children who received no intervention were held back in kindergarten, first grade, or second grade; only 16% of those who received both interventions were held back.

The Abecedarian experiment is one of several demonstrations of the power of early intervention. Two major conclusions are warranted. First, evaluations of educational interventions should go beyond IQ to examine indices of school performance and school success. School is, after all, the major avenue out of poverty for most children.

Second, infancy and early childhood are important periods for establishing the basic foundations of healthy intellectual and behavioral development. Ramey and Campbell argue that programs begun in infancy have more profound effects than those begun at age 3 or 4, and preschool programs in turn prevent some of the disadvantages with which many poor children enter school. For instance, children who attended Head Start–type preschool interventions in several locations in the 1960s and 1970s had a long-term advantage in school performance. Throughout the school years, children who experienced preschool intervention were less likely to experience school failure (i.e., placement in a special class, retention in grade, or dropping out of school) than were control groups (Lazar & Darlington, 1982).

Early childhood is important, but preschool intervention should not be viewed as a permanent "fix." Once children enter school, the qualities of the educational program are critically important. In chapter 9, Levin describes an experimental program of educational acceleration for at-risk students. This program addresses the major dilemma of special education: If students who enter school without basic skills and knowledge are given a separate curriculum that is less demanding than the normal curriculum, they will get farther and farther behind. Remedial education can lead to low expectations and to stigma, and it often emphasizes the dullest, most repetitive drill-and-practice learning tasks.

Accelerated schools for high-risk students avoid these problems by incorporating timetables and the explicit goal that children will perform at grade level in basic subjects. They are designed to induce high expectations of success and to offer stimulating, interesting instruction that deals with concepts and problem solving rather than drill. Like most successful interventions, they involve parents and community resources; teachers also take a major role in decisions about curriculum. Basic decisions in these schools are made by steering committees composed of administrators, teachers, parents, and community representatives. Task and policy committees are a part of the school organization. Levin provides a detailed description of schools that are qualitatively different from most present schools in their governance and in their emphasis on educational results, that is, on children's academic performance.

Accelerated schools are sufficiently new that no long-term summative evaluation has been conducted yet. The initial outcomes, however, are positive: reduced discipline problems, improved attendance, increased parent participation, increased student achievement, and reduced grade repetition and placement in special classes. Similar programs in various parts of the country have met with similar successes.

Quality child care, early intervention, and accelerated schools were selected as examples for this volume, but there are many more services and interventions with demonstrated effectiveness in combating some of the disadvantages of poverty. Schorr (1988) described successful programs for providing prenatal care, health care, family support, and family planning, to name only a few. What, then, are the barriers to policies that would reduce poverty and provide effective interventions for children in poverty? The final two chapters in this volume deal with two major issues in policy formation and implementation: cost-benefit analysis and principles for effective intervention.

One major barrier to many interventions is cost. It is almost a truism to point out that public policies depend heavily on cost as well as effectiveness. Cost-benefit and cost-effectiveness analyses are widely used economic tools for making informed decisions about allocation of resources in the policy arena, but they are rarely used systematically in programs for children. In chapter 10, Levin discusses principles for the use of these techniques to evaluate interventions for children. One major difficulty in such evaluations is finding an appropriate way to quantify the benefits or outcomes of an intervention. Changes in children's health, cognitive functioning, school performance, quality of life, psychological distress, or self-esteem are often difficult to quantify. They rarely translate directly into dollars.

It may be surprising to some readers that estimating costs is fraught with almost as many difficulties as determining outcomes. Levin describes the steps required to identify the ingredients of an intervention and to determine and analyze their costs. For instance, volunteered personnel time, donated facilities, and contributed supplies may not entail direct monetary payments, but they need to be included in an inventory of costs.

Levin illustrates cost-effectiveness analysis in a comparison of four alternatives for raising reading and mathematics achievement of elementary school children. It highlights the point that an intervention producing small effects may be worthwhile if its costs are low; that is, the conclusion that one draws from a cost-effectiveness analysis is not based solely on the magnitude of effects but on the quantity of effect per unit of cost.

Although Levin demonstrates a wide range of topics in which cost-benefit and cost-effectiveness analyses provide useful information, three major obstacles to using these tools for policy decisions need to be overcome. First, decision makers need to be educated about these forms of analysis so that they are not easily misled by biased or badly constructed analyses. Second, social scientists who evaluate social programs need to become more sophisticated so that economic analyses can be incorporated in evaluation studies. Finally, standard methods for constructing such studies need to be established so that results are comparable across studies and across investigators.

Economic analyses are useful and important means of affecting policy decisions, but in chapter 11, Schorr introduces a caution: Relying exclusively on quantifiable outcomes may lead to a proliferation of single-problem, quick-fix strategies that are easily measured and demonstrated. Schorr points out that many interventions and programs are effective or ineffective as a result of the organizational structures used to implement them. She devotes her analysis to extracting principles for successful implementation by examining a wide range of effective programs. They are comprehensive, placing the child in the context of family and surroundings (e.g., involving parents in schools). They offer a broad spectrum of services that are integrated and allow service providers to cross conventional professional boundaries. The professionals are caring and respected. The services are designed to reduce barriers of distance, time, and money for the participants (e.g., placing health clinics for adolescents in or near schools).

These components of successful programs sound reasonable, yet ineffective programs predominate in part because they try to use one-shot, single-problem remedies. Bureaucracies and professional boundaries interfere with the flexibility and fluidity that characterize successful programs. Demonstration programs that succeed are often watered down when they are adopted for large numbers of people. In order to have successful interventions, we need to expand programs that are already working on a large scale (e.g., Head Start, WIC, and Medicaid), remove some of the obstacles and disincentives to successful programs, and find ways of encouraging large-scale implementation of successful demonstrations like the Abecedarian project.

Schorr begins her chapter with an observation that is widely supported in research on children's development. Risk factors interact. Their effects multiply. A child already at risk because of low birth weight, prenatal exposure to alcohol or drugs, or poor nutrition is especially vulnerable to a damaging environment. A child who is at risk because of being unwanted, in too large a family, or abused by a highly stressed parent is especially vulnerable to the damaging effects of a school that expects little and provides little. A child who sees few role models of success, has little hope for a better future, or fails in school is especially vulnerable to early sexual activity and pregnancy. If risks multiply one another, then interventions that reduce one risk factor can have relatively large effects by removing a multiplier. For example, improved prenatal care that reduces the number of low birth weight babies could have relatively large effects by reducing the number of highly vulnerable children.

Summary

Childhood poverty is endemic in the United States. It increased considerably during the 1970s and early 1980s and continues at a high rate into the 1990s. This book addresses three major questions: Why are so many children living in poverty? What are the effects of poverty on children's physical, intellectual, and social development? What role can public policy play in preventing or alleviating the damaging effects of poverty on children?

We take a child-centered approach to policy analysis. Mainstream policy analysis is dominated by social-economic concepts and methods in which parents' income is the principal focus. Policy proposals are usually concerned with income and labor force participation, and evaluations of such new policies as income maintenance or of welfare reforms are typically based primarily on changes in parental earnings and labor force participation. Social-economic assumptions also lead to the view of children as human capital in whom the society should invest to promote their future economic productivity.

In developmental psychology and education, children's welfare is the major goal. Policy proposals are derived from information about those economic and environmental conditions that affect children's development, and they are evaluated by examining such indices of child development as physical and mental health, academic performance, and behavior problems. Children's welfare is taken as a valued goal in and of itself.

Social-economic and child-developmental rationales do not necessarily conflict. For instance, increasing family income by improving parent earnings has demonstrably positive effects on children's development. However, they sometimes lead to different policies and goals. For instance, providing inexpensive and inadequate child care may succeed in getting single mothers into the labor force but may have deleterious effects on their children's development.

Poverty is not a homogeneous condition; it comes in different levels of severity, for varying lengths of time, and in different ecological and cultural contexts. Poverty is usually defined by the official government poverty level, but some analysts prefer to describe the poverty gap (how much below the poverty level incomes fall) or family income relative to the median income. These indices produce different estimates of the numbers of poor children, but they all show the same trends over time. All define children's poverty by examining families; they do not take into account the many children who have tenuous family connections.

In this book, we distinguish between persistent and transitory poverty. Black children and children of single mothers are at especially high risk for persistent poverty. We also point out that recent analyses have been devoted primarily to urban poverty; rural poverty is common and receives relatively little attention from policy makers or policy analysts.

The authors in this book represent several disciplines, including economics, public health, sociology, psychology, and education. They each attempt to integrate social-economic and child-developmental perspectives as they address the issues of why children are poor, how poverty affects children, and what public policy can do about it.

References

Anderson, E., & Hula, R. C. (Eds.).(1989). Symposium: Family policy. *Policy Studies Review*, 8, 573–736.

Burtless, G. (1986). Public spending for the poor: Trends, prospects, and economic limits. In S. H. Danziger & D. H. Weinberg (Eds.), *Fighting poverty: What works and what doesn't* (pp. 18–49). Cambridge, MA: Harvard University Press.

Cautley, E., & Slesinger, D. P. (1988). Labor force participation and poverty status among rural and urban women who head families. *Policy Studies Review, 7*, 795–809.

Children's Defense Fund. (1989, December). Poverty drops slightly in 1988 but continues to rise for young children and young families. *CDF Reports, 11*(5), pp. 1, 4.

Congressional Budget Office. (1988). *Trends in family income: 1970–1986*. Washington, DC: Author.

Danziger, S. H., Haveman, R. H., & Plotnick, R. D. (1986). Antipoverty policy: Effects on the poor and the nonpoor. In S. H. Danziger & D. H. Weinberg (Eds.), *Fighting poverty: What works and what doesn't* (pp. 50–77). Cambridge, MA: Harvard University Press.

Duncan, G. (1984). *Years of poverty, years of plenty: The changing economic fortunes of American workers and families*. Ann Arbor, MI: University of Michigan, Survey Research Center.

Dunn, M. (1989, November 21). The caring program: Health services reach children of working poor. *Lawrence Journal World*, p. 6A.

Ellwood, D. T. (1988). *Poor support: Poverty in the American family*. New York: Basic Books.

Emery, R. E., Hetherington, E. M., & DiLalla, L. F. (1984). Divorce, children, and social policy. In H. W. Stevenson & A. E. Siegel (Eds.), *Child development research and social policy* (Vol. 1, pp. 189–266). Chicago: University of Chicago Press.

Furstenberg, F. F., Jr., Brooks-Gunn, J., & Morgan, S. P. (1987). *Adolescent mothers in later life*. Cambridge: Cambridge University Press.

Furstenberg, F. F., Jr., Peterson, J. L., Nord, C. W., & Zill, N. (1983). The life course of children after divorce: Marital disruption and parental contact. *American Sociological Review, 48*, 656–658.

Greenstein, R. (1988, February 25). Testimony. In *Children and families in poverty: The struggle to survive*. Hearing before the Select Committee on Children, Youth, and Families, U.S. House of Representatives, Washington, DC.

Gueron, J. M. (1987). Welfare to work programs: Lessons on recent state initiatives. *Policy Studies Review, 6*, 733–743.

Haveman, R. H. (1986). Review of social experimentation. *Journal of Human Resources, 21*, 586–603.

Hernandez, D. J. (1989, April). *The changing needs of America's children from the Great Depression to the 21st century.* Paper presented at the Biennial Meeting of the Society for Research in Child Development, Kansas City, MO.

Hill, R. B. (1988). Cash and noncash benefits among poor black families. In H. P. McAdoo (Ed.), *Black families.* (2nd ed., pp. 306–323). Newbury Park, CA: Sage.

Institute for Research on Poverty. (1976). *The rural income maintenance experiment.* Madison, WI: University of Wisconsin, Author.

Jensen, L. (1988). Rural–urban differences in the utilization and ameliorative effects of welfare programs. *Policy Studies Review, 7,* 782–794.

Kershaw, D., & Fair, J. (1976). *The New Jersey income-maintenance experiment* (Vol. 1). New York: Academic Press.

Lande, J. S., Scarr, S., & Gunzenhauser, N. (Eds.). (1989). *Caring for children: Challenge to America.* Hillsdale, NJ: Erlbaum.

Lazar, I., & Darlington, R. (1982). Lasting effects of early education: A report from the Consortium for Longitudinal Studies. *Monographs of the Society for Research in Child Development, 47*(2–3, Serial No. 195).

McAdoo, H. P. (1986). Strategies used by black single mothers against stress. In M. C. Simms & J. Malveaux (Eds.), *Slipping through the cracks: The status of black women* (pp. 153–166). New Brunswick, NJ: Transaction Books.

McLoyd, V. C. (1989). Socialization and development in a changing economy: The effects of paternal job and income loss on children. *American Psychologist, 44,* 293–302.

Moynihan, D. P. (1986). *Family and nation.* San Diego: Harcourt Brace Jovanovich.

Murray, C. (1984). *Losing ground: American social policy, 1950–1980.* New York: Basic Books.

Ogbu, J. U. (1988). Cultural diversity of human development. In D. T. Slaughter (Ed.), *New directions in child development: Vol. 42. Black children and poverty: A developmental perspective* (pp. 11–28). San Francisco: Jossey-Bass.

Ramirez, O. (1989). Mexican American children and adolescents. In J. T. Gibbs, L. N. Huang, & Associates (Eds.), *Children of color: Psychological interventions with minority youth* (pp. 224–250). San Francisco: Jossey-Bass.

Robins, P. K., & West, R. W. (1980). Program participation and labor-supply response. *Journal of Human Resources, 15,* 499–523.

Salkind, N. J., & Haskins, R. (1982). Negative income tax: The impact on children from low-income families. *Journal of Family Issues, 3,* 165–180.

Schorr, L. B. (1988). *Within our reach: Breaking the cycle of disadvantage.* New York: Anchor Press.

Smeeding, T. M., & Torrey, B. B. (1988). Poor children in rich countries. *Science, 236,* 873–877.

Steiner, G. (1981). *The futility of family policy.* Washington, DC: Brookings.

Stevenson, H. W., & Siegel, A. E. (Eds.). (1984). *Child development research and social policy* (Vol. 1). Chicago: University of Chicago Press.

U.S. Department of Education. (1988). *Youth indicators 1988: Trends in the well-being of American youth.* Washington, DC: Author, Office of Educational Research and Improvement.

Wacquant, L. J. D., & Wilson, W. J. (1989). The cost of racial and class exclusion in the inner city. *The Annals of the American Academy of Political and Social Science, 501,* 8–25.

Williams, T. M., & Kornblum, W. (1985). *Growing up poor.* Lexington, MA: D. C. Heath.

Wilson, W. J. (1987). *The truly disadvantaged: The inner city, the underclass, and public policy.* Chicago: University of Chicago Press.

Yogman, M. W., & Brazelton, T. B. (Eds.). (1986). *In support of families.* Cambridge, MA: Harvard University Press.

Zigler, E. F., & Frank, M. (Eds.). (1988). *The parental leave crisis: Toward a national policy.* New Haven, CT: Yale University Press.

2   The economic environment of childhood

Greg J. Duncan

Certainly the average child growing up in a middle-class family is more likely to complete high school or college and to enjoy a higher paying and higher status job than a child raised in a poor family. To be sure, the correlation between the success of parent and child is far from perfect: Many very successful adults have come from impoverished families, and many children from well-to-do families fail to match the accomplishments of their parents. Nonetheless, the intergenerational transmission of social status is strong enough to lead one to wonder just what accounts for this correlation.

A plausible albeit as yet insufficiently tested assumption of this chapter is that the economic component of childhood – the income and assets of the family throughout childhood – matters a great deal in shaping the life chances of children. Furthermore, advantages provided by higher incomes are presumed to persist even after accounting for the effects of other characteristics associated with more affluent families. It follows from these assumptions that we should be concerned with the distribution of family economic incomes, in particular with regard to the subset of children raised in impoverished families whose insufficient incomes place them at risk of a range of developmental and health problems often associated with poverty.

This chapter summarizes what has been learned about the economic context of childhood. It begins with an examination of trends in the average level of family economic resources available to children, with special emphasis on the number and characteristics of children whose families' incomes are below the poverty line. About one in five children in the United States in the mid-1980s was poor, a rate that was much higher than in other advanced Western countries. Although varying widely across ethnic groups, poverty rates for each group were higher than estimated in either the 1970 or the 1980 census, although lower than in 1950 or 1960. The dramatic increase in the prevalence of single-parent families, a sluggish labor market, and declining benefit levels in transfer programs all played a role in the increased prevalence of poverty.

Preparation of this chapter was supported by the Ford Foundation. Sheldon Danziger and John Palmer made helpful comments on earlier drafts.

23

Rates of poverty given for children show percentages of children in the midst of poverty spells when the survey "snapshot" picture is taken but provide no direct information on dynamic aspects of poverty among children. This chapter's section on patterns of childhood poverty over 15 years examines the prevalence of poverty over the entire period of childhood and finds that much childhood poverty is short-lived, although long-term poverty, especially among black children, is by no means unimportant.

Apart from the average level of economic resources during childhood, another aspect of economic status is of interest – income volatility. Research on sharp income drops during the Great Depression and in more recent periods has found that there were long-lasting adverse effects on the mental and physical health of the individuals involved. In the section on income volatility the evidence on its prevalence during childhood and its links to important life events, such as divorce or unemployment, is reviewed.

Evidence on the role of parental income in affecting children's life chances is discussed in the section that asks if parental income matters. The few studies that have measures of both parental income and other background characteristics typically find important income effects, even after adjusting for the effects of other characteristics. Subsequent sections present some implications for needed research as well as a discussion of some policy implications of the findings.

The incidence of childhood poverty across time

Despite its prosperous economy, the United States in 1980 had the dubious distinction among advanced Western nations of having the highest fraction of its children living in poverty (Table 2.1, row 1).[1] Indeed, the only country included in the comparisons with a similar rate was Australia, which had a per capita national income only three-quarters as large as the United States. If anything, the U.S poverty rate is higher in the late 1980s than in 1980 (Table 2.2, row 1) and certainly is higher now than 20 years ago.

A longer-run view shows that the period since the end of World War II has seen remarkable economic growth and concomitant reductions in the fraction of children living in households with incomes below the poverty line. In 1949, one out of every two children was poor; for black children the rate was seven of eight (Table 2.2, rows 1 and 3). Poverty rates for all

---

1 Poverty is defined in the United States by a comparison of total family income and a poverty threshold based primarily on family size. The poverty threshold for a family of four in 1988 was about $12,000. Figures in Table 2.1 for other countries are based on an identical set of thresholds, with incomes converted to dollars with a multiyear average exchange rate (see Smeeding, 1988).

Table 2.1. *Poverty rates and transfer payments for children and their families by country, 1979–1982*

	United States	Australia	Canada	Germany	Norway	Sweden	Switzerland	United Kingdom
Poverty rates for children	17%	17%	10%	8%	8%	5%	5%	11%
Government transfers to families with children who were poor before taxes and transfers (in thousands of 1979 U.S.$)	$2.4	$2.8	$2.9	$3.0	$3.9	$6.4	$2.3	$3.2
Reduction in poverty of families with children due to transfers	17%	15%	37%	13%	47%	58%	7%	40%
Fraction of families with children poor before taxes and transfers who did not receive transfers	27%	1%	1%	0%	2%	0%	66%	1%

Source: Smeeding (1988), based on data from the 1979 U.S. Current Population Survey and other data sets in the Luxembourg Income Study.

Table 2.2. *Poverty rates for children across time by ethnic group*

	1949	1959	1969	1979	1985
All children	48%	26%	16%	17%	20%
White, not Hispanic	41	19	10	12	13
Black, not Hispanic	87	63	41	36	41
Hispanic	73	53	33	28	37

Note: For 1949–1979, children 0–14; for 1985, children 0–18.
Source: Danziger (1989b), based on data from the 1950, 1960, 1970, and 1980 dicennial censuses and the 1986 U.S. Current Population Survey.

ethnic groups fell by about 20 percentage points between 1949 and 1959 and by 10 to 20 percentage points during the 1960s. Poverty rates generally have risen since the early 1970s, rising during recessions and falling only moderately – or holding steady – during the periods of economic expansion. By the mid-1980s, after several years of recovery from the severe recession of 1981–1982, childhood poverty was still more prevalent than at the time of the 1970 census.

What accounts for the frustrating increase in childhood poverty during the 1970s and 1980s? Many culprits have been suggested, including a sluggish macroeconomic environment that lowered the real incomes of families in all economic strata; an increased inequality in the distribution of income; the increasing number of families headed by women; stagnant wages for young workers; decreases unrelated to business cycles in the labor force involvement of men, especially of minority men; and a decline in the value of transfer benefits available to low-income families. In varying degrees, almost all of these factors played a role.

Assembled in Table 2.3 is evidence on trends in a number of these factors as they relate to the incidence of poverty among families with children.[2] Data are presented for three years – 1970, 1978, and 1986 – that span the period of interest and avoid years of unusually good or bad economic conditions. The rate of poverty for families with children rose during this period by an average of about one percentage point every four years (Table 2.3, row 1), with much of the growth occurring during the recessions of the mid-1970s and early 1980s and the sharp inflation of the late 1970s. In contrast to earlier periods, the times of economic expansion, especially during the 1980s, were

2 The poverty rates of families with children shown in Table 2.3 differ from those for the children themselves that were shown in Table 2.2. Table 2.3 counts each family once whereas Table 2.2 effectively counts each family by the number of children it contains. Because poverty rates among families with large numbers of children are higher than rates for families with fewer children, poverty rates for children exceed those of families with children.

Table 2.3. *Characteristics of families with children, 1970–1986*

	1970	1978	1986
Poverty rate for families with children[a]	11%	12%	15%
Income inequality			
"Adjusted" family income for families with children, relative to 1970			
Median[b]	100	113	114
Poorest 20%[b]	100	103	88
Richest 20%[b]	100	116	127
Head under age 25[c]	100	100	82
Family structure			
Percentage of families with children headed by single mothers[d]	11	17	20
Poverty rate for families with children living with:			
Married couples[a]	6	5	7
Single mothers[a]	45	41	46
Poverty rate for families with children if families had 1970 composition patterns[e]	11	12	12
Labor market			
Median earnings of full-year, full-time male workers (in thousands of 1986 dollars)[f]			
Age 20–24	$17.5	$16.7	$14.2
Age 25–34	24.0	25.8	22.7
Percentage of families in bottom 20% of income distribution with one or more full-time workers[g]	38	29	24
Married couples[g]	58	55	54
Single mothers[g]	5	3	3
Cash transfers			
Average cash transfers received by pre-transfer poor (in thousands of 1984 dollars)[h]			
Married couples	$ 4.0	$ 3.8	$ 2.9
Single mothers	5.2	4.1	3.3

[a]CBO (1988), Table C–2. Poverty thresholds are adjusted with the CPI–X1 price index.
[b]CBO (1988), Table A–4. Adjustments to family income are made for family size and inflation as measured by the CPI–X1 price index.
[c]CBO (1988), Table A–10.
[d]CBO (1988), Table A–1.
[e]Calculations by the author based on CBO (1988).
[f]U.S. Bureau of the Census, Current Population Reports, Series P-60, various issues, adjusted with the CPI–X1 price index.
[g]CBO (1988), Table A–12.
[h]Danziger & Gottschalk (1985). Figures in the "1970" column are for 1973; figures in the "1978" column are for 1979, and figures in the "1986" column are for 1984. Dollar amounts have been adjusted by the conventional Consumer Price Index.

not of sufficient benefit to low-income families to allow the poverty rates to retreat to their prerecession levels.

Income inequality

At the heart of the phenomenon of increasing childhood poverty is the striking contrast between the changing economic fortunes of families at the top, middle, and bottom of the income distribution since the beginning of the 1970s. Income inequality increased sharply over the period, reversing a modest egalitarian trend that had prevailed since the end of World War II (Danziger & Gottschalk, 1985). The increasing inequality more than offset modest improvements in average living standards, producing an increase in childhood poverty.

Families in the middle of the income distribution enjoyed a modest improvement in their economic status. When, as in Table 2.3, family incomes are adjusted for family size, and using an inflation index that treats housing costs in a more reasonable way than the conventional Consumer Price Index, the resulting increase in the economic well-being of families at the middle of the distribution was about 14% between 1970 and 1986 (Table 2.3, row 2).[3] Had the distribution of income remained unchanged, then we would have observed an identical 14-percentage-point income increase for families at the top and bottom of the income distribution. Instead, families in the bottom one-fifth of the 1986 income distribution had adjusted incomes that were only 88% of what their counterparts had received in 1970 (row 3). Families in the top fifth enjoyed living standards that were 27% higher in 1986 than in 1970 (row 4).[4] Thus incomes for families with children became much less equally distributed over this period.

An increasingly unequal income distribution produced more childhood poverty in 1986 than in 1970 despite a general increase in living standards. This rules out one item from our list of suspected culprits – a disastrous economic environment shared by families at all income levels – and shifts the emphasis to factors that caused families at the bottom of the distribution to fall even further behind other families.

3 The poverty rates listed in the top row of Table 2.3 are also based on the revised Consumer Price Index. Without adjustments for family size and using the conventional Consumer Price Index, Danziger & Gottschalk (1985) found that mean family income rose by only 4% between 1967 and 1984 and actually fell by over 8% between 1973 and 1984. Although affecting the measures of trend in average family economic status, these adjustments make virtually no difference in the extent of the measured increase in income inequality during the 1970s and 1980s.

4 Put another way, in 1970 families with children at the point of entry into the top fifth of the income distribution enjoyed living standards that were 2.7 times higher than families at the point of entry into the bottom fifth. By 1986, this ratio had risen to 3.8, an increase of over 40%.

Family structure

Roughly twice as many families with children were headed by women in 1986 than in 1970 (20% versus 11%, Table 2.3, row 6), and the incidence of poverty among female-headed families consistently has been seven to eight times as high as among married-couple families (row 7). These two factors combined to account for virtually all of the increased prevalence of poverty among families with children and to shift the majority of poor families from the "married couples" category to the "single mothers" category. Had the 1986 families shown the same proportions of married-couple and mother-only families that prevailed in 1970, the 1986 poverty rate would have been 12% rather than 15% (row 9). In contrast, similar calculations for earlier periods show no role for family structure changes in child poverty for the decade between 1950 and 1960 and a very modest role between 1960 and 1970.

There are several reasons to treat these calculations cautiously, the most important of which is that these simulations assume that two-parent families switching to one-parent status originally had poverty rates that were the same as unchanging two-parent families (Bane, 1986). If, as is probable, they were more likely to be poor to begin with, then the simulations overstate the effect of family structure change. Despite these cautions, however, family structure changes during the 1970s and 1980s have to be considered among the key factors producing higher rates of childhood poverty.

Labor market conditions

There is little doubt that the economic growth of the 1950s and 1960s was primarily responsible for the large drops in poverty during that time. Nor is there any doubt that the business cycles of the 1970s and 1980s, especially the recessions in the mid-1970s and early 1980s, produced corresponding changes in the prevalence of poverty. However, the labor market of the 1970s and 1980s was shaped by a number of massive and seemingly contradictory changes. Despite the severe recessions, the economy employed some 30 million more workers in 1986 than in 1970, enabling large numbers of baby boomers and women of all ages to find work. At the same time, however, unemployment increased substantially, and the earnings of those finding work often failed to keep pace with inflation.

The disappointing earning trends were not limited to the more marginal members of the labor force. Shown on Table 2.3, rows 10 and 11, are earnings of full-time, full-year male workers. Inflation-adjusted earnings of both 20- to 24-year-old and 25- to 34-year-old men were higher in 1970 than they were 16 years later, in 1986, a situation that was without precedent in the postwar period (Levy, 1988). Earnings for other workers generally fared as badly, making it increasingly difficult for low-wage workers to earn their way out of poverty.

Despite the employment boom, certain subgroups of working-age individuals, especially minority men, were much less attached to the labor market in 1986 than in 1970. As shown in Table 2.3, rows 12 to 14, families with children at the bottom of the income distribution were much less likely to have one or more full-time earners in 1986 than in 1970. Part of this trend could be attributed to the increased prevalence of low-income female-headed families, for whom labor force participation rates were exceedingly low.[5] Taken together, sluggish wages and a falling labor force attachment reduced the importance of income from the labor market in the income packages of low-income families with children and brought more of these families into poverty.

Transfers

Cash benefits paid by the programs most likely to benefit families with children – in particular, Aid to Families with Dependent Children (AFDC) – generally lost ground to inflation during this period (Table 2.3, rows 15 and 16). In 1986 dollars, the median state paid nearly $600 per month to a qualifying AFDC family of four in 1970 and $400 per month in 1986 – a loss of 33%. Gottschalk and Danziger (1985) estimated that transfer income changes were about as important as labor market changes in accounting for changes in the overall poverty rate between 1967 and 1979. Noncash transfers, in particular Medicaid, fared much better during this period, making the total effect of trends in transfers on childhood poverty considerably more benign than implied by Table 2.3.

Its relatively low cash-transfer programs benefit levels go a long way in explaining why the poverty rate for children is so much higher in the United States than in other Western countries. When compared to other industrialized countries, it is clear that the United States spends less on transfers per poor family with children (Table 2.1, row 2), brings fewer such families out of poverty with those transfers (row 3), and has more holes in its "safety net" than almost any other country (row 4).

In sum, the rising poverty rate for children during the 1970s and 1980s was the product of a number of factors. Despite a modest increase in the living standards of the median family, growing family income inequality, fueled by stagnant wages for young workers, increasing numbers of families headed by

---

5 The reductions in the labor force participation of low-income families with children ran contrary to changes taking place at other points in the income distribution. Both middle-income married-couple families and, especially, middle-income mother-only families were more likely to have full-time labor market participants in the 1980s than in the 1970s.

Table 2.4 *Distribution of poor whites and poor blacks living in the 50 largest central cities, by poverty rate in the census tract of residence, 1970 and 1980*

Percentage in poverty in the census tract	Poor whites		Poor blacks	
	1970	1980	1970	1980
Under 20	64%	66%	20%	16%
20–29	18	17	26	21
30–39	10	9	27	27
40 and over	8	8	27	36

Source: Ellwood (1988), based on data from the 1970 and 1980 censuses.

women, reduced labor force attachment of prime-age, especially minority, men, and falling transfer program benefit levels, pushed increasing numbers of children into poverty.

Trends in the concentration of urban poverty

One final, and also troubling, recent trend is that of an increased geographic concentration of the urban poor between 1970 and 1980 (Table 2.4). Although not focused solely on children, the figures in Table 2.4 show that substantially higher numbers of black poor lived in neighborhoods in which many of their neighbors were also poor. If, as Wilson (1987) and others believe, the resulting social isolation of poor children raised in high-poverty neighborhoods is detrimental to their life chances, then the trend is particularly disturbing.[6]

Patterns of 15-year childhood poverty[7]

Rates of poverty revealed at different times by Census Bureau "snapshots" show the extent of childhood poverty at the times when those pictures are taken. However, they fail to measure the persistence of poverty across an individual's childhood. Finding that one-fifth of all children are poor in each of five consecutive years is consistent with two very different scenarios: one of high turnover, in which all children were poor in one and only one year, and another of great persistence, in which the same children were poor all five years and the remaining 80% of children experienced no poverty what-

6 As shown by Jargowsky & Bane (1991), the increased geographic concentration of poverty does not characterize all large cities and is instead concentrated among the very largest cities in the Northeast and Midwest, especially New York, Philadelphia, Detroit, and Chicago.
7 This section draws heavily from Duncan & Rodgers (1988) and Hill (1983).

ever. Bane and Ellwood (1986) found considerable turnover in the larger population but did not make separate estimates for children.

Duncan and Rodgers (1988) used data from the Panel Study of Income Dynamics (PSID) to analyze 15-year poverty patterns of children who were under the age of four in 1968, the first year of the study, and for whom data were available covering the family economic conditions of their childhood for 15 years. They distinguished six categories of economic status: family income below the poverty level for (1) 1 to 4 years, (2) 5 to 9 years, (3) 10 to 14 years, or (4) all 15 years; (5) family income never below the poverty level but below 150% of it for at least 1 year; and (6) family income always at least 150% of the poverty level.

In line with the analysis of poverty spells conducted by Bane and Ellwood (1986), they found that many more children come into contact with poverty than experience persistent poverty (Table 2.5). Whereas one-third of all children experienced poverty in at least 1 year, only about one child in twenty experienced poverty over 10 or more years of his or her childhood. However, persistent childhood poverty is far from insignificant; an estimated 4.8% of all children experienced poverty during at least two-thirds of their childhood years, and an additional 7% were poor for between 5 and 9 of the 15 years.

Duncan and Rodgers found a number of differences in these patterns across various demographic subgroups. Most striking are the racial differences, also shown in Table 2.5: Fewer than one in seven black children lived comfortably above the poverty line throughout the 15-year period, and more than one-quarter were poor for at least 10 of the 15 years. Blacks accounted for nearly 90% of the children who were poor during at least 10 out of 15 years.

Using an increment–decrement method applied to a much larger subsample of PSID children, Duncan and Rodgers estimated the prevalence of childhood poverty for various subgroups in the population. As shown in Table 2.6, many of these characteristics have substantial effects on the estimated prevalence of poverty, effects that often differ by race. Disability has the most powerful and consistent effects across both racial subgroups. Black children living in families where the household head was disabled during the entire 15-year period could expect to be poor in almost 11 of the 15 years; the comparable figure for whites was 3.3 years.

Several of the family structure measures had powerful effects on the expected amount of childhood poverty. The largest differential effect for the two racial subgroups is linked with the marital status of the mother at the time of the child's birth. White children born to never-married mothers, a relatively small group, can expect to spend more than one-third of their first 15 years in poverty – a figure that is considerably higher than any other in Table 2.6 for whites and the only one that is as high for whites as for blacks. For blacks, birth to a never-married mother increases the expected prevalence of poverty only slightly – from 5.4 to 6.0 of the first 15 years of childhood.

Table 2.5. *Fifteen-year poverty experiences of children under the age of 4 in 1968 by race*

	Distribution of poverty categories within racial groups (rows add to 100%)							Mean number of years poor	Unweighted number of observations
	Always above 150% of poverty line	Never poor, but not always above 150% of poverty line	Poor 1–4 years	Poor 5–9 years	Poor 10–14 years	Poor 15 years	All		
Nonblack	55.7%	19.3	19.8	4.6	0.6	0.0	100.0%	0.9	531
Black	13.0%	8.0	32.3	17.7	24.0	4.9	100.0%	5.5	493
All	48.4%	17.7	22.1	7.0	4.1	0.7	100.0%	1.5	1,075

Source: Duncan & Rodgers (1988), based on data from the Panel Study of Income Dynamics.

Table 2.6. *Expected years of childhood poverty out of 15 associated with various household characteristics*

	Expected years of poverty	
	White and other	Black
All households	0.8	5.4
Household at birth of child		
Never-married mother	6.2	6.0
Mother teenager	1.2	5.4
Education of head		
8 years	1.2	5.6
12 years	0.7	5.3
Household during all of childhood[a]		
Head disabled	3.3	10.9
Lives in South	0.8	6.4
Lives out of South	0.7	4.3
Lives in large city	0.7	3.9
Lives in rural area	1.1	8.1
Lives with 1 parent	3.2	7.3
Lives with 2 parents	0.5	3.0

[a] The expected years are estimated from the proportion of children in households with the specified characteristic who were born in poverty and from the observed transition probabilities for children in such households.
Source: Duncan & Rodgers (1988), based on data from the Panel Study of Income Dynamics.

In general, family structure patterns were powerful determinants of the economic fates of both white and black children. Living with one rather than two parents throughout childhood increases the expected years of childhood poverty for white children from 0.5 to 3.2 years. The comparable increase for blacks is relatively smaller – from 3.0 to 7.3 years – but larger than that for whites in absolute terms. These figures reveal the surprising fact that the expected prevalence of poverty among black children living in continuously two-parent families is about as high as the expected amount of poverty for white children who spend their entire childhood in single-parent families. Family structure differences between black and white families are obviously not the sole reason for the discrepancy between the amounts of poverty experienced by the two groups of children.

Locational measures have stronger effects for blacks than for whites, with a much higher prevalence of poverty among blacks in rural and Southern areas and a considerably lower prevalence in large urban areas. Apart from disability of the household head, rural location is the most powerful factor associated with black childhood poverty.

The final characteristic examined, the educational attainment of the household head, has surprisingly modest effects on the prevalence of childhood poverty, especially for blacks. Even black children living in households where the head is a high school graduate can expect to spend over 5 of their first 15 years below the poverty line.

Income volatility

The various measures of childhood poverty we have examined thus far properly focus our attention on the children with the fewest material resources available to them. The mixture of transitory and persistent poverty for children, shown in Table 2.5, suggests that family incomes exhibit substantial instability. This is potentially important because a growing body of evidence suggests that sharp losses of income, even if they do not reduce income to below-poverty levels, may produce long-lasting effects on the mental and possibly physical health of the adults experiencing them. Apart from parenting behavior, we know virtually nothing about corresponding effects on children.

The most extensive studies of the effects of income loss were conducted by Elder and Liker and their colleagues. They collected longitudinal data over several decades from a sample of Berkeley-area married couples with children as part of the Berkeley Guidance Study and used the data to perform a series of sophisticated analyses of the long-term consequences of income loss.[8] Couples experiencing a drop of one-third or more in family income between 1929 and the early 1930s were compared on a range of subsequent outcomes – marital and parent–child relationships and mental and physical health – with couples whose depression incomes did not fall as much, with some of the outcomes measured several decades later.

The researchers found that for married men the income losses produced uniformly harmful effects on marital and parenting behavior, apparently not so much because of the loss of income per se as because of the stress caused by the loss of status as breadwinner. For married women, living in families left badly off by the income losses, there were also harmful effects on their marriages, parenting, and subsequent health. For these working-class women, the income loss itself appeared to be the culprit, leaving them with too few resources to perform properly their functions as homemakers. It is of interest that women with pre-depression middle-class backgrounds who experienced such income losses did *better* subsequently than did otherwise similar women who had escaped such adversity. Their resources for coping were apparently adequate, and the economic hardship actually made them better able to handle subsequent problems.

8 Elder, 1974; Elder, 1979; Elder & Liker, 1983; Elder, Liker, & Cross, 1984; Elder, Liker, & Jaworski, 1984; Liker & Elder, 1984. Longitudinal evidence linking adverse income change to mental health is also presented in Perlin, Liberman, Menaghan, & Mullan, 1986

Table 2.7. *Various indicators of income volatility for children and individuals of all ages*

Age and race in 1969	Percentage with income/needs falling by more than 50% at least once, 1969–79	Of those with income/needs falling by more than 50%	
		Percentage living in families expecting the loss	Percentage living in families with substantial savings prior to loss
Individuals less than 5 years old			
All	27%	6%	42%
White	26	7	48
Black	35	4	16
Individuals of all ages	31	14	56

Source: Duncan (1988), based on data from the Panel Study of Income Dynamics.

Dramatic income losses were found to have quite diverse effects on children. In general, these effects were more detrimental for boys than they were for girls and for income losses occurring early in childhood as opposed to those occurring during the adolescent years. Ties between fathers and sons suffered the most; ties between mothers and daughters appeared to be strengthened by the economic losses. Virtually none of these effects persisted very far into the adult years.

The prevalence of dramatic drops in living standards during the 1969 to 1979 period were analyzed in Duncan (1988) and Burkhauser and Duncan (1988). Their measure of income volatility consisted of instances in which income to needs fell by more than 50% in consecutive years and is thus similar to that employed by Elder and Liker. The first column of Table 2.7 shows that the risk of this occurrence is substantial: More than one-quarter of white children and one-third of black children are estimated to have experienced such a drop at least once during the 11-year period. Virtually all of these decreases left the individuals involved in them with at best modest incomes. Some 87% of the individuals experiencing the decreases saw their family incomes fall to less than $25,000 (data not shown in Table 2.7), and more than one-third fell into poverty. Compounding the potential problems caused by these losses was the fact that the families containing children were much less likely than other families to have predicted the losses before they occurred and much less likely to have had savings available to cope with their financial consequences. Savings cushions were especially unlikely in black families with children.

An examination of the linkages between the events and the incidence of major income losses showed that divorce or separation was the most important family composition event associated with an income-to-needs drop and could be linked to one-seventh of the losses for white children and one-fifth of the losses for black children. A major spell of unemployment is the most frequent labor market change, followed by reductions in labor supply due to illness of the family head (Duncan, 1988).

Anatomy of income losses: The case of divorce

Events such as divorce or unemployment have rather different patterns of effects on family income across time. Most unemployment losses appear to be short-term (Corcoran & Hill, 1979; Sider, 1985), whereas divorce often has a longer run effect, especially if there is no remarriage.

An examination of the level and composition of income following divorce illustrates how the financial burden of divorce fell on the men, women, and children involved in it.[9] Table 2.8 presents calculations of the economic impact of divorce by showing average amounts of income, income-to-needs ratios,[10] and fractions poor in the year before, the year after, and five years after divorce or separation for the children, women, and men undergoing those events. Family incomes of the children and women include whatever alimony, child support, and welfare income was received by their families, whereas the family incomes of the men have had alimony and child support subtracted from them.

Income levels drop precipitously (by about 40%) between the years just before and just after divorce for children and women and more modestly (by 15%) for men. Because divorce or separation initially reduces the family size of both of the resulting households, it is not surprising that the income-to-needs measure shows less severe decreases. Living standards fall to about two-thirds of their former levels for children and women, and the average

9 The analysis presented here draws heavily from Duncan & Hoffman (1985) and is based on divorces or separations that occurred in the PSID between 1969 and 1975. The calendar year of divorce is treated as t, and information on income and employment is compiled in years $t - 1$ through $t + 5$ for the children, women, and men involved in a divorce. For both men and women, the sample was restricted to persons who were between the ages of 25 and 54 in the year prior to the divorce. Since their interest was in economic consequences, Duncan & Hoffman use a functional rather than a legal definition of marriage and do not distinguish between divorces and separations. A divorce or separation is defined as the transition from living with a spouse or long-term partner to living without that person for reasons other than death. Remarriages are defined analogously.

10 Income-to-needs ratios are obtained by dividing total family income by a poverty-line threshold based on family size. A family of four with a $6,000 income would have a ratio of 0.5, since its poverty-line threshold in 1988 dollars is roughly $12,000. A family with identical composition and a $24,000 income would have an income-to-needs ratio of 2.0.

Table 2.8. *Family income, income-to-needs ratios, and poverty rates before and after divorce for children, women, and men*

	Children			Women			Men		
	Family income	Family income/needs	Percentage poor	Family income	Income/ needs	Percentage poor	Family income	Income/ needs	Percentage poor
(1) One year *before* divorce	$23,213	2.7	12%	$26,168	3.6	7%	$25,403	3.6	6%
(2) One year *after* divorce	$13,822	1.8	27	$14,781	2.6	13	$21,488	3.7	4
(3) Five years *after* divorce – no remarriage	$14,511	1.9	20	$15,178	2.8	11	—	—	—
(4) Five years *after* divorce – all	$22,380	2.6	17	$22,781	3.4	10	$25,874	4.2	3
(2)/(1): One year after/one year before	.60	.67		.56	.72		.85	1.03	
(3)/(1): Five years after for women not remarried/one year before	.63	.70		.58	.78		—	—	
(4)/(1): Five years after – all/one year before	.96	.96		.87	.94		1.02	1.17	

Source: Calculated from Duncan and Hoffman (1985), based on data from the Panel Study of Income Dynamics.

divorced man is actually slightly better off in the year following divorce than he was in the year before.[11] For women and children not involved in remarriage, average living standards change little over the five years following the divorce.

The inclusion of women and children involved in remarriage in the calculation of the economic consequences of divorce improves substantially the average income -to-needs ratios. About half of the women will have remarried by the fifth year following the divorce or separation, and their economic status usually exceeds their predivorce status. Combining the remarried and still divorced into a single group leads to the result that the "average" divorcing woman and her children are about as well off after five years as in the year before divorce. But the average is formed by two very disparate groups – those who did remarry (the majority of whom are better off) and those who did not remarry (the majority of whom are in a worse position). Thus divorce generates a great deal of inequality in the subsequent distribution of income among women and children.

When the income-to-needs figures used in Table 2.8 are used to compute poverty rates, the dramatic impact of divorce is clear. In the year prior to divorce or separation, about 12% of the children and 7% of all of the women lived in families classified as poor. In the year following a divorce or separation, these figures double to about 27% for children and 13% for women. After five years, poverty rates decline only slightly for women who are still unmarried. Poverty rates for men actually fall from 6% to 4% in the year after divorce and remain at very low levels.

The relative stability of the family incomes of women who remain unmarried masks various changes in the composition of their postdivorce income packages. The women's own labor force income was clearly the dominant component of postdivorce family income. Labor force participation rates jumped from predivorce levels by 15 percentage points – from 67% to 82%. The women's labor income accounted for only 22% of family income before the divorce, for 60% of total family income in the year just after the divorce, and for nearly 70% in the fifth year after the divorce if there was no remarriage by that time.

Noncoverage and noncompliance with court awards of child support and alimony are widespread. The U.S. Bureau of the Census (1986) estimated that only about half of mother-only households containing minor children had child support awards or agreements in 1984, and only half of those due

---

11 These changes differ substantially from the well-publicized results of Weitzman (1985), who finds with California data that income-to-needs ratios of divorced women fell by 73% and rose by 42% for divorced men. Her figures, based on a needs standard similar to that used in this chapter, are grossly inconsistent with other figures she presents, based on the same data, in which needs are calculated on a per capita basis; they appear to be in error (Hoffman & Duncan, 1988).

payments received the full amount; one-quarter received no payments at all. The majority of PSID women reported receiving no alimony or child support, and both the incidence and the amount of such transfers decline as time passes following the divorce. Even in the year just after the divorce, when alimony and child support payments are highest, they account for only about one-tenth of the total average family income, and their average amount falls by nearly two-thirds by the fifth year following the divorce. The decline in support from the former husbands with time is much steeper for women coming from previously high-income marriages. Amounts of annual support from high-income former husbands were nearly twice as large as from low-income husbands in the year following divorce ($2,425 versus $940) but fell below the amounts paid by low-income husbands ($746 versus $764) by the fifth year.

In sum, the burden of financial losses following divorce is shared very unequally among the men, women, and children involved in it, with the economic status of the typical divorced man changing little and the living standards of the typical woman and child falling sharply. Less well-known is the income dynamic following divorce for women and children in which re-marriage is the key event, distinguishing those who restore their predivorce standard of living from those who do not.

Does parental income matter?

This chapter began with the premise that the economic environment in which children are raised affects the quality of their lives as children and their chances of success as adults. With due regard for the imperfect connections between income and quality of life, there can be little doubt that the average child raised in a poor household has a less enjoyable childhood than the typical child raised in greater affluence. Poverty standards reflect society's judgments of minimally acceptable living standards. Because children are completely dependent upon others for their security and can in no way be held responsible for their economic situation, there is a sense in which allowing any of them to live in a household with living standards below the poverty line, especially persistently, is socially unjustified.

Somewhat less clear-cut is the extent to which poverty, especially persistent poverty, reduces the opportunities for success during adulthood. This section reviews the evidence on this point, with an eye toward distinguishing the effects of poverty *as such* from other characteristics of poor families and the environments in which they live.

Most work on the effects of family background on child development lacks explicit poverty measures and effectively equates family background with "social class." Class is usually measured by some combination of the occupational and educational attainments of the parents. Implicitly, this view of family background is based on the notion that one's social class is fixed at birth and does not change throughout childhood.

However permanent social class may seem, our review of the evidence on the economic resources available throughout childhood shows resources to be quite volatile. Many more children experience temporary than experience persistent poverty, and events such as unemployment and divorce produce dramatic changes in living standards at all levels of the income distribution. Indeed, given the extent of some of the changes that take place, it is hard to imagine that the perception and reality of one's social class fails to change as well. Divorce often moves middle-class women and children into a working-class environment, or working-class women and children into poverty, if at times only temporarily.

Because family income is much more easily changed than almost any other aspect of family background through social policy, it is important to discover how changes in family income available during childhood might be expected to affect the life chances of children. One can imagine an experiment in which the incomes of randomly chosen families are either permanently augmented or "shocked" with sharp increases or decreases so that the long-run success of children raised in those families can be compared with that of children in otherwise similar families with lower or stable incomes. The negative income tax experiments approximated these conditions for income augmentation, and an examination of their effects on children often showed beneficial results (Salkind & Haskins, 1982). Certain subsets of children in families in the experimental, higher income group had greater increases in reading scores, lower dropout rates, and better diets than control-group children.[12]

Nonexperimental studies of the effects of parental income have been forced to use observations on the "natural" experiments of children raised in families with different income levels and trajectories. These studies rely on statistical controls to adjust for the many other ways in which life in a high-income family confers advantages.

Evidence from national samples on even the simple associations between the income of parents and children is rare since parental income levels and volatility cannot be recalled reliably by children when they reach adulthood. Longitudinal studies such as the PSID provide samples of children whose parents responded in the early years of the panel when the children were in their early teenage years, and who responded for themselves as young adults, up to their late 20s, in more recent years of the panel. Hill et al. (1985, Table D.1) used the PSID in this way to compare the relative success of children raised in the bottom and top quintiles of the income distribution. They found

---

12 Significant experimental control differences were usually confined to certain subgroups of children and varied by age, gender, and experimental site. See the Fall 1979 issue of the *Journal of Human Resources, 14*(4), 431–506, for a detailed summary of some of these findings.

that although only a minority (43.4%) of the children raised in families in the bottom fifth ended up in the bottom fifth as young adults, that fraction was still far greater than the comparable fraction (9.2%) of children raised in the most affluent fifth of parental families who ended up in the bottom fifth as adults. Only 1 child in 50 (2.2%) of the children raised in families in the lowest income quintile had reached the highest quintile as compared with more than 1 in 3 (35.9%) children raised in families in the highest fifth.

Although reduced, the effects of parental income on the success of children persist even after one controls for differences in the more conventional measures of parental background, such as the education and occupational prestige of the parents. One of the most widely known studies is that of Sewell and Hauser (1975), who analyzed a sample of Wisconsin high school graduates and found highly significant effects of the taxable income of parents on the completed schooling and particularly on the earnings of sons at about age 25. They concluded: "There can be little doubt that the association of socioeconomic background variables with son's earnings is due solely to the intergenerational effect of parents' income, while the latter cannot to any large extent be explained by differing abilities, educational attainments, or occupational achievements of the sons of rich and poor families" (Sewell & Hauser, 1975, p. 84). Studies based on national samples from the National Longitudinal Surveys (e.g., Shaw, 1982) and the PSID (e.g., McLanahan, 1985; Hill & Duncan, 1987) that include measures of both parental income and other social background factors also found a significant role for income in the attainments of children.

The few studies that focus on the effects of poverty experiences during childhood on adult attainments also find significant effects, especially if poverty has persisted for a number of years. Corcoran, Gordon, Laren, and Solon (1987) controlled for an elaborate set of social background and family structure measures and still found highly significant and substantively large, detrimental effects of the persistence of poverty during childhood on the later earnings and family incomes of sons. Kennedy, Jung, and Orland (1986) found highly significant links between the persistence of childhood poverty and a lagging behind their grade level by 16- to 18-year-old students. To our knowledge, no studies have systematically examined the links between income volatility during childhood and later attainments.

At this point, the highly suggestive links between the persistence of poverty during childhood and adult attainments only can be described as a black box. Subjecting a child to poverty during a substantial portion of his or her childhood lowers the odds that that child will have a successful career as an adult. Adjustments for measurable characteristics (e.g., living with a single parent, less educated parents, or parents with less prestigious jobs, or living in a "bad" neighborhood) associated with persistent poverty do not explain away its detrimental effect. Precious little is known about the *mechanisms* involved, however, and, as argued in the subsequent section, on important research issues, much more needs to be learned before we can point with confidence to a set of policies that will break the link we suspect exists between persistent poverty and later achievement.

Some important research issues

If nothing else, our review of the evidence on the economic environment of childhood demonstrates the inappropriateness of a life-cycle view in which children are presumed to grow up in fairly stable environments of either affluence, poverty, or middle-class incomes. Family incomes are quite volatile, producing a mixture of temporary and persistent poverty, as well as sudden changes in living standards at all points of the income distribution. Average level and change are distinct and important dimensions of economic status during childhood; each has the potential for adversely affecting the quality of life during childhood and later life chances.

Empirical work has established highly significant links between persistent poverty and later success, but it has not gone much further in laying out the process involved. The possible intervening links, involving the mental and physical health of the children and their emotional and cognitive development, are numerous indeed. There is, of course, a huge body of literature relating socioeconomic status to many of these intervening factors, but few of the studies measure income directly and virtually none measure it over periods longer than a single year. Furthermore, many of the studies that do contain income measures merely lump it into a broader index of socioeconomic status (SES).

A crucial item on the research agenda is thus increased study of the links between a variety of child-developmental outcomes and the duration of childhood poverty. These studies need multiyear measurement of family incomes and need to incorporate explicit measures of the duration of low income. Merely including a measure of average parental income is not sufficient, given the evidence from Corcoran et al. (1987) that shows substantial effects of poverty persistence even after controlling for average parental income level. The effects of persistent poverty need to be assessed in the context of a model that controls for other aspects of the families and neighborhoods in which poor children live. Ideally, developmental outcomes should be measured at many points during childhood and early adulthood and should be accompanied by measures of the process by which the economic, demographic, and other aspects of family background might be linked to the outcomes.

Even less is known about the consequences of family income instability on the health, career attainments, and psychological well-being of the children involved. There is literature on the consequences, usually for the adults involved, of events such as unemployment or divorce that are often associated with income variability, but it is impossible to disentangle the effects of income changes per se from other aspects of the events without measures of both. Such knowledge is crucial for the design of policies to mitigate the adverse effects of income loss. Do the adverse effects of divorce or job loss on children's mental health stem from the more easily remedied *financial* consequences or from the *psychological* effects on the parents? What mediating factors, including, perhaps most importantly, the family (Moen, Kain, & Elder, 1983) cause some losses to be less damaging (or even be beneficial) than others?

If modified to focus on children, the methodology of Perlin et al. (1981) might serve as a model for the needed research. Their attention was focused on the links between disruptive job events and changes in adult mental health for a representative sample of households in the Chicago area. Their design was longitudinal, and both undesirable job events and income change were measured directly. Furthermore, they attempted to measure a number of intervening factors, such as economic strain, coping behavior, and social support. With these various measures they were able to develop an empirical model of the ways in which job loss and its attendant income change affected the mental health of the individuals involved.

One can imagine a parallel longitudinal design, focused on the paths leading from the level and stability of the economic environment of childhood, with controls for the conditions and events associated with that environment and the measurement of a host of intervening developmental outcomes throughout childhood. The work of Elder and his colleagues (Elder, 1974; Elder, Liker, & Cross, 1984) is closest to what is needed, although with larger and more representative samples and covering more recent historical periods.

Some policy issues

In 1985 some 13 million children lived in families with incomes below the poverty line. It would have taken about $27 billion in that year to eliminate poverty among children, that is, to give all poor families with children an income equal to the poverty line (Committee on Ways and Means, 1987, Table 19). The $27 billion "poverty gap" for children is about twice as large as benefits paid by the Aid to Families with Dependent Children cash-assistance program but only about one-sixth as large as the total cost of Social Security retirement cash benefits. Would the problems of poverty among children be eliminated if the country were able to summon the political will necessary to eliminate the poverty gap?

The answer to this question obviously depends on the research issues discussed in the preceding section: To what extent is income itself, as opposed to other factors correlated with families with persistently low income, responsible for affecting the life chances of children? If income does matter, what are the mechanisms involved? Are the adverse effects of income loss the result of the changed living standard or of other aspects of the event that produced the loss?

Presuming that income itself matters, there are a set of complementary ways in which policies can be directed at children at risk. A first is through income transfers to the families involved. Transfer programs such as food stamps or Aid to Families with Dependent Children condition their benefits on low income itself, regardless of the reason why that income came to be as low as it is. Other transfers (e.g., unemployment compensation or child support) are directed at income losses associated with the events that caused the losses. Still other programs focus more directly on the children involved and attempt to augment skills (e.g., Head Start), improve health (e.g., Special Supplemental Food Program for Women, Infants and Children [WIC]), or upgrade schools or other services. A general discussion of the various programs that might be directed at poor or otherwise at-risk children (e.g., Danziger & Weinberg, 1986; Congressional Budget Office, 1986) would take us far afield. We can, however, highlight policy implications of some of the less well-known aspects of the economic environment of childhood discussed thus far.

Persistent childhood poverty

Patterns of poverty throughout childhood show that single-year estimates of the poverty rate of children substantially understate the fraction of children who ever come into contact with poverty and overstate the extent of quite persistent childhood poverty. Without further research we cannot discount completely the possibly detrimental effect of temporary poverty. We can be more confident in pointing out the severe disadvantages associated with persistent childhood poverty.

Persistent childhood poverty afflicts virtually no whites but nearly one-third of all black children. It is found as often in rural as urban areas, and thus it does not fit easily within the stereotype of an urban "underclass." It is more heavily concentrated in single-parent families and yet is found often enough in intact families that raising the living standards or reducing the numbers of single-parent families alone will not solve the problem. Most persistently poor children live in situations in which parents have at best weak links to the labor market, and yet there is enough work effort among the persistently poor to justify working toward further tax reform that would augment the incomes of low-income working families (Danziger, 1989a).

Income transfer programs such as AFDC and food stamps take on a new light in the context of the economic volatility we observe. Sharp declines in income are relatively widespread, but periods of need are often short. Correspondingly, longitudinal data show that spells of actual receipt of welfare program transfers are equally short. Only about one-sixth of all AFDC spells last more than eight years and fewer than one-third of first-time recipients will have total welfare "careers" lasting that long (Ellwood, 1986). Even Charles Murray, whose 1984 book *Losing Ground* led the conservative attack on Great Society welfare programs, now admits that current programs appear to function as benign income-loss insurance programs for many, and perhaps most, recipients (Murray, 1986).

Persistently poor children are more likely to live in the minority of long-term recipient households. Whether the programs themselves are responsible for inducing dependence in long-term recipients is an unresolved and obviously important question. Concern over the possible dependence of the parents, however, at some point, must be balanced against concern for the detrimental effects of persistent poverty on their children. Recent pushes for welfare reforms are encouraging but should not be viewed as a necessary precondition to channeling more resources to the children in greatest need of them.

The transitory nature of much childhood poverty raises concerns about the difficulty of identifying persistently poor children. Targeting programs at children who are poor in a given year might seem to be inefficient if many of those children are poor only temporarily. This concern turns out to be ill-founded. Although many of the children who ever experience poverty do so only temporarily, the majority of children poor at a given point are quite likely to experience extensive poverty during childhood. The apparent paradox is explained by the fact that the probability of being poor at a given time is necessarily greater for persistently poor children than for temporarily poor children (Bane & Ellwood, 1986).

Income volatility

In addition to examining the level of resources available during childhood, especially the levels associated with persistent poverty, we have also focused on the incidence of large income losses at other points of the income distribution. The majority of such losses left the families involved with modest incomes, and most of the losses happened to families who neither predicted them in advance nor had savings to help cushion their effects. As with persistent poverty, black children shouldered the brunt of these income losses.

A different set of policy issues arises if the goal is to minimize the incidence and effects of preventable losses that reduce income to points above the poverty line. Here the focus is on policies tied to events producing the losses, as with unemployment compensation tied to job loss and child support tied to divorce. Political strategies differ from those directed exclusively at poor children because events producing income losses occur in working- and middle-class families as well as poor families and thus have a larger potential constituency.

One reading of social policy over the last half century concludes that the Great Depression convinced the voting majority that private insurance did not offer sufficient protection against dramatic drops in their economic well-being (Burkhauser & Duncan, 1988). The pillars of social insurance stabilized then – Social Security and unemployment insurance – since have been supplemented with disability and health insurance. Taken together, they produced a set of insurance programs that provide some degree of protection against the potentially catastrophic events of disability, unemployment, retirement, and illness in old age. Although one can point to gaps in coverage or problems in implementation, by and large these programs have offered substantial protection to a worker, his nonworking spouse, and their children.

Today, however, the prevalence of out-of-wedlock births and divorce and separation have increased dramatically the proportion of children living in female-headed families. The social insurance programs, principally Aid to Families with Dependent Children, have been woefully inadequate to deal with the economic problems of single-parent families. As we have seen, private "insurance" in the form of court-ordered child support and alimony payments is even less adequate. Tougher enforcement of court orders, coupled with a government-provided minimum child support payment (Garfinkel & McLanahan, 1986), would go a long way in treating certain types of marital dissolutions as a "socially insurable" risk where insurance could be financed in a manner similar to socially insurable labor market risks.

Summary

Our description of the economic environment of childhood begins with an examination of trends in the incidence of childhood poverty. About one-fifth of America's children were poor in the mid-1980s, a rate higher than in the 1970s and much higher than in other advanced Western countries. Increasing numbers of single-parent families, a sluggish labor market, and declining benefit levels in transfer programs all played a role in the increased prevalence of childhood poverty.

Survey snapshots of children in poverty tell nothing about the duration of their material deprivation. A longitudinal examination of the prevalence of poverty across the entire period of childhood shows that it is often short-lived, although long-term poverty, especially among black children, is by no means unimportant. A small but growing body of research suggests that income poverty has a substantial effect on the life chances of children, even after controlling for more traditional measures of socioeconomic background such as parental schooling and occupational attainments.

The economic environment of working- and even middle-class families is often characterized by substantial income instability. This is disturbing given research evidence indicating that sharp income losses can produce long-lasting, adverse effects on the mental and physical health of the children and adults involved.

There are many unanswered research questions about the economic environment. Most importantly, what is the mechanism by which poverty and income instability disadvantage children? If lack of income is the problem then policies directed at providing a minimum income and equalizing the economic burdens of events such as divorce might be successful at offsetting the disadvantages. If, on the other hand, the disadvantages stem from psychological or social factors associated with low or unstable incomes then policies need to address these problems as well.

References

Bane, M. J. (1986). Household composition and poverty. In S. H. Danziger & D. H. Weinberg (Eds.), *Fighting poverty: What works and what doesn't* (pp. 209–231). Cambridge, MA: Harvard University Press.

Bane, M. J., & Ellwood, D. T. (1986, Winter). Slipping into and out of poverty: The dynamics of spells. *Journal of Human Resources, 21*, 1–23.

Burkhauser, R. V., & Duncan, G. J. (1988). Life events, public policy and economic vulnerability of children and the elderly (pp. 55–119) In J. Palmer & T. Smeeding (Eds.), *The vulnerable*. Washington, DC: Urban Institute Press.

Committee on Ways and Means. (1987). *Background material and data on progress within the jurisdiction of the Committee on Ways and Means*. Washington, DC: U.S. Government Printing Office.

Congressional Budget Office. (1988a). *Trends in family income: 1970–1986*. Washington, DC: Author.

Congressional Budget Office. (1988b). *Reducing poverty among children*. Washington, DC: Author.

Corcoran, M., Gordon, R., Laren, D., & Solon, G. (1987). *Intergenerational transmission of education, income, and earnings: Final report to the Ford Foundation*. Ann Arbor, MI: University of Michigan, Institute for Public Policy Studies.

Corcoran, M., & Hill, M. S. (1979). The incidence and consequences of short- and long-run unemployment. In G. J. Duncan & J. N. Morgan (Eds.), *Five thousand American families* (Vol. 7, pp. 1–64). Ann Arbor, MI: University of Michigan, Institute for Social Research.

Danziger, S. (1989a). Fighting poverty and reducing welfare dependency. In P. Cottingham & D. Ellwood (Eds.), *Welfare policy for the 1990s* (pp. 41–69). Cambridge, MA: Harvard University Press.

Danziger, S. (1989b). *Antipoverty policies and child poverty*. Discussion paper, Institute for Research on Poverty, University of Wisconsin, Madison, WI.

Danziger, S., & Gottschalk, P. (1985). *How have families with children been faring?* Discussion paper, Institute for Research on Poverty, University of Wisconsin, Madison, WI.

Danziger, S. H., & Weinberg, D. H. (Eds.). (1986). *Fighting poverty: What works and what doesn't*. Cambridge, MA: Harvard University Press.

Duncan, G. J. (1988). Volatility of the family over the life course. In P. Baltes, D. Featherman, & R. M. Lerner (Eds.), *Life-span development and behavior* (Vol. 9, pp. 317–358). Hillsdale, NJ: Erlbaum.

Duncan, G. J., & Hoffman, S. D. (1985). Economic consequences of marital instability. In M. David & T. Smeeding (Eds.), *Horizontal equity, uncertainty and well-being* (pp. 427–470).

National Bureau of Economic Research Income and Wealth Conference. Chicago: University of Chicago Press.

Duncan, G. J., & Rodgers, W. (1988). Longitudinal aspects of childhood poverty. *Journal of Marriage and Family, 50*, 1007–1021.

Elder, G. H. (1974). *Children of the Great Depression.* Chicago: University of Chicago Press.

Elder, G. H. (1979). Historical change in life patterns and personality. In P. B. Baltes & O. G. Brim, Jr. (Eds.), *Life-span development and behavior* (Vol. 2, pp. 117–159). New York: Academic Press.

Elder, G. H., & Liker, J. K. (1982). Hard times in women's lives: Historical influences across fifty years. *American Journal of Sociology, 88*, 241–269.

Elder, G. H., Liker, J. K., & Cross, C. E. (1984). Parent–child behavior in the Great Depression: Life course and intergenerational influences. In P. B. Baltes & O. G. Brim (Eds.), *Life-span development and behavior* (Vol. 6, pp. 109–158). New York: Academic Press.

Elder, G. H., Liker, J. K., & Jaworski, B. J. (1984). Hardship in lives: Depression influences in the 1930s to old age in postwar America. In K. A. McCluskey & H. W. Reese (Eds.), *Life-span developmental psychology: Historical and generational effects* (pp. 161–201). New York: Academic Press.

Ellwood, D. T. (1986, January). *Targeting the would-be long term recipients of AFDC: Who should be served?* Princeton, NJ: Mathamatica Policy Research.

Ellwood, D. T. (1988). *Poor support: Poverty in the American family.* New York: Basic Books.

Garfinkel, I., & McLanahan, S. (1986). *Single mothers and their children: A new American dilemma.* Washington, DC: Urban Institute Press.

Gottschalk, P., & Danziger, S. (1985). A framework for evaluating the effects of economic growth and transfers on poverty. *American Economic Review, 75*(1), 153–161.

Hill, M. S. (1983). Trends in the economic situation of U.S. families and children: 1970–1980. In R. Nelson & F. Skidmore (Eds.), *American families and the economy: The high cost of living.* Washington, DC: National Academy Press.

Hill, M. S., & Duncan, G. J. (1987). Parental family income and the socioeconomic attainment of children. *Social Science Research, 16*, 39–73.

Hill, M. S., Augustyniak, S., Duncan, G., Gurin, P., Liker, J., Morgan, J., & Ponza, M. (1985). *Motivation and economic mobility.* Research Report Series. Ann Arbor, MI: University of Michigan, Institute for Social Research.

Hoffman, S. D., & Duncan, G. J. (1988). What *are* the economic consequences of divorce? *Demography, 25*(4), 641–645.

Jargowsky, P. A., & Bane, M. J. (1991). Ghetto poverty in the United States, 1970–1980. In. C. Jencks & P. E. Peterson (Eds.), *The urban underclass* (pp. 235–273). Washington, DC: Brookings Institution.

Kennedy, M. M., Jung, R. K., & Orland, M. E. (1986, January). *Poverty, achievement and the distribution of compensatory educational services.* Washington DC: U.S. Department of Education, Office of Education Research and Improvement.

Levy, F. (1988). *Dollars and dreams: The changing American income distribution.* New York: Russell Sage Foundation.

Liker, J. K., & Elder, G. H. (1983). Economic hardship and marital relations in the 1930's. *American Sociological Review, 48*, 343–359.

McLanahan, S. (1985). Family structure and the reproduction of poverty. *American Journal of Sociology, 90*, 873–901.

Moen, P., Kain, E. L., & Elder, G. H. (1983). Economic conditions and family life: Contemporary and historical perspectives. In R. Nelson & F. Skidmore (Eds.), *American families and the economy: The high cost of living.* Washington, DC: National Academy Press.

Murray, C. (1986, September). *According to age: Longitudinal profiles of AFDC recipients and the poor by age group.* Paper prepared for the Working Seminar on the Family and American Welfare Policy, Washington, DC.

Perlin, L. I., Liberman, M. A., Menaghan, E. F., & Mullan, J. (1981). The stress process. *Journal of Health and Social Behavior, 22*, 337–356.

Salkind, N. J., & Haskins, R. (1982). Negative income tax: The impact on low-income families. *Journal of Family Issues, 34*(2), 165–180.

Sewell, W. H., & Hauser, R. M. (1975). *Education, occupation, and earnings: Achievement in the early career.* New York: Academic Press.

Shaw, L. B. (1982). High school completion for young women. *Journal of Family Issues, 34*(2), 147–163.

Sider, H. (1985). Unemployment duration and incidence, 1968–1982. *American Economic Review, 75,* 461–472.

Smeeding, T. M. (1988, February 25). The children of poverty: The evidence on poverty and comparative income support policies in eight countries. Testimony before the Select Committee on Children, Youth, and Families, U.S. House of Representatives, Washington, DC.

U.S. Bureau of the Census. (1986). *Child support and alimony, 1983 (Supplemental Report).* Current Population Reports, Series P–23, No. 148. Washington, DC: U.S. Government Printing Office.

Weitzman, L. (1985). *The divorce revolution.* New York: Free Press.

Wilson, W. J. (1987). *The truly disadvantaged.* Chicago: University of Chicago Press.

3   The role of mother-only families in reproducing poverty

*Sara S. McLanahan, Nan Marie Astone, and
Nadine F. Marks*

Introduction

Families headed by nonmarried women have increased dramatically during
the last three decades. Whereas in 1960 fewer than 7% of all children in the
United States were living in a female-headed family, by 1985 the proportion
was over 21% (U.S. Bureau of the Census, 1960, 1961, 1988). Indeed, if
present trends continue, half of all children born in the last decade will live
in a single-parent family at some point before reaching age 18 (Bumpass,
1984). Given the importance of the family as a social institution, and given
the high rates of poverty in families headed by single mothers, it is not
surprising that researchers as well as policy makers have responded to the
change in family structure with interest and concern.

What happens to children who live in mother-only families? Do they perform less well in school or exhibit more symptoms of psychological distress
than children who live with two parents? Most important, what happens to
these children when they become adults? Are they more likely to be poor?
Are they more likely to create mother-only families themselves? The answers
to these questions are not simple, and social scientific literature reflects several
changes of opinion during the last three decades.

During the 1950s and 1960s, the prevailing view was that divorce and
nonmarital births indicated individual pathology and that the children of such
unions (or nonunions) were likely to exhibit similar psychological problems.
Most of the research at this time was based on highly selective samples, such
as children who were in treatment for mental disorders or were wards of the
criminal justice system. Thus, it is not surprising that the dominant view
emphasized individual pathology rather than environmental constraints.

Support for this chapter was provided by the National Institute on Aging under grant A600129-
02 and by the National Institute for Child Health and Development under grant HD 19375-03.
Computer facilities were provided by the Wisconsin Center for Demography and Ecology under
grant HD 05876.

51

This view was seriously challenged in the early 1970s by Herzog and Sudia (1973). In their lengthy review of the research on children in fatherless families, these authors noted that most of the existing studies contained serious methodological flaws, including a failure to control for differences in race and socioeconomic status. They concluded that, given these omissions, most of the problems attributed to father absence were probably due to income and social class rather than to family structure. Herzog and Sudia ushered in a new perspective on single parenthood, which was accompanied by studies focusing on the strengths, as opposed to the weaknesses and problems, of mother-only families. In time, the warning that earlier studies were plagued by methodological problems was taken as evidence that single parenthood had no negative consequences for children. This period – in which single mothers and their children were observed through rose-colored glasses – lasted until the late seventies and is evident today in some reviews.

The shift in attitudes toward mother-only families was closely related to a change in attitudes toward black families. And both reflected the social scientific response to a changing political climate. Wilson has noted that in the early 1970s liberal researchers, and black liberals in particular, vigorously rejected the notion that some aspects of ghetto life were pathological and attempted to substitute a more positive view of the black family and ghetto culture (Wilson, 1986; Wilson & Aponte, 1985; Wilson & Neckerman, 1986). In doing so, these researchers used selective evidence to deny the existence of social dislocation and to highlight the adaptability and achievements of poor families. Wilson's comments apply equally well to research on single parenthood.

More recently, the pendulum has swung back toward a more critical view. Although not making attributions about individual pathology, researchers have become less optimistic about the consequences of family disruption and less certain that income is the only source of disadvantage in mother-only families. Evidence of a new perspective first appeared in the late 1970s with the publication of a major review article by Shinn (1978) on family structure and cognitive development. A second review, by Hetherington, Camara, and Featherman (1983) soon followed, covering a broader range of outcomes and reaching essentially the same conclusions. Although some analysts continue to emphasize the positive aspects of single parenthood, and although there is little doubt that in some cases divorce or nonmarriage is preferable to marriage, a new consensus is emerging in which it is acknowledged that, on average, even controlling for income and social class, family dissolution is associated with lower attainment among offspring.

In part, this new consensus indicates the willingness of researchers to look more critically at changing family patterns. In part, however, it is also a response to the availability of new longitudinal surveys that are better suited to answering many of the questions that have interested researchers for the last 20 years. Among these surveys are the Panel Study of Income Dynamics, the National Longitudinal Surveys, and the High School and Beyond Study, all of which provide information on family income as well as on children's early socioeconomic achievement.

The new research shows that, on average, offspring from disrupted or never-married families are less likely to complete high school and are more likely to have low earnings as adults than are offspring of intact families (Astone & McLanahan, 1991; Corcoran, Gordon, Laren, & Solon, 1987; Krein & Beller, 1986; McLanahan, 1985). There is also evidence that living with a single mother is related to the reproduction of female-headed families through teen marriage, teen fertility, premarital fertility, and marital disruption (Abrahamse, Morrison, & Waite, 1988; Hogan & Kitagawa, 1985; McLanahan, 1988; McLanahan & Bumpass, 1988). Finally, the research shows that adolescents in female-headed families have higher rates of delinquency and are more likely to use alcohol and drugs than those in two-parent families (Matsueda & Heimer, 1987; Mott & Haurin, 1987; Sampson, 1987). In most of these studies, the association between family structure and offspring's behavior remains significant even after controlling for race and family socioeconomic status.

This chapter focuses on why children raised in mother-only families have lower attainment than children raised in two-parent families and on what can be done to improve their life chances. We begin by discussing income differences in one- and two-parent families and by estimating the extent to which income accounts for differences in the attainment of children. Next, we look at how parental socialization practices vary across family forms. Children in mother-only families receive less parental time than children receive in two-parent families because the father is not living in the household and the mother is more likely to work outside the home. An important question, therefore, is whether the single mother is able to compensate for the loss of the father's time in terms of helping her offspring with schoolwork and maintaining an effective level of communication. In addition to their lacking income and parental time, children in mother-only families may be at a disadvantage with respect to community resources; they may be more likely to live in poor neighborhoods where there are high levels of crime and unemployment and to attend schools of poor quality. If this is true, we need to know whether single mothers cope as well as married parents in such environments and, again, whether they are able to control their adolescent children effectively. We conclude by discussing the effects of social policy on single mothers and by examining the current debate over welfare reform. Domestic programs, such as those related to child support and child care, are analyzed in terms of their potential to reduce economic insecurity and stress in mother-only families and, thereby, to improve the life chances of children.

Economic insecurity in mother-only families

Numerous researchers have argued that the lower socioeconomic attainment of children in mother-only families is due to their families having less income. According to this view, single mothers have less money and invest less of it in their children, which, in turn, affects the characteristics of the offspring as well as the quality of the parental household (Becker, 1981; Michael & Tuma, 1985). We know that family income has a strong influence on children's participation in extracurricular activities, in travel experiences, and in summer camps, all of which are related positively to school achievement (Heyns, 1985). Economic necessity also may promote the premature assumption of adult responsibilities (Elder, 1974; Weiss, 1979). Offspring from low-income families are more likely to leave school early in order to earn money for their families and to care for younger siblings than are offspring from middle-income families. They also may see marriage and parenthood as a means of escaping hardship and establishing an independent adult identity (Rubin, 1976).

How substantial is the economic difference between one- and two-parent families? Is it large enough to account for differences in school achievement and family behavior? The answer to this last question is yes. In 1983 approximately 50% of all mother-only families were poor, according to the official government definition of poverty, as compared with only 12% of married-couple families (Garfinkel & McLanahan, 1986). Trends in the poverty rates of mother-only families, married-couple families, and the aged are reported in Figure 3.1 for the years 1967 through 1985. These numbers are based on the official definition of poverty and include income from cash-transfer programs such as Aid to Families with Dependent Children (AFDC), Social Security, and disability insurance.

Mother-only families have substantially higher poverty rates than other groups, and the difference has increased since the early 1970s. The change in the relative status of mother-only families – often referred to as the "feminization of poverty" – was due to the increase in the proportion of such families and the decline in the poverty rates of other poor groups, primarily the aged. In addition to these compositional changes, per-family income in single-mother families declined during the 1980s (Bane & Ellwood, 1989).

Mother-only families not only are more likely than other groups to be poor but the dynamics of their poverty are also different. Specifically, mother-only families are more likely to experience *persistent* poverty. Duncan (1984; this volume) found that nearly a quarter of the population was poor for at least one year during the decade from 1967 to 1978. He also found considerable turnover in the poverty population, with most of the people who became poor remaining poor for less than two years. Among mother-only families,

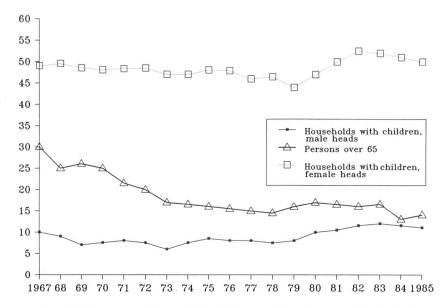

Figure 3.1. Percentage of households with incomes below the poverty line by family type. From *Single Mothers and Their Children* by I. Garfinkel and S. S. McLanahan, 1986, Washington, DC: Urban Institute Press.

however, poverty lasts longer and is more severe. Bane and Ellwood (1983) have shown that during the late 1970s the average length of time that children who ever have been poor spend in poverty was 7 years in families headed by single mothers. This compares with 4.6 years for children in two-parent families. For black children the difference was even greater: 12 years for those in families headed by single women compared with 6 years for those in two-parent families.

Poverty is not the only economic problem of mother-only families. Even families living above the poverty line are subject to income insecurity, and a large portion have experienced a substantial decline in their standard of living as a result of divorce. Duncan and Hoffman (1985) estimate that the income of single mothers and their children one year after a divorce is only 67% of their predivorce income. We would expect both partners to experience some drop in living standard after a divorce because two separate households are more expensive to maintain than one. However, the drop for mothers is much greater than the drop for fathers. According to Duncan and Hoffman, the income of nonresidential fathers one year after divorce is about 90% of their predivorce income.

It is important to remember that poverty and income insecurity in mother-only families are not entirely due to marital disruption or nonmarriage. A nontrivial proportion of single mothers were poor before their marriages ended or before they gave birth to children out of wedlock. Bane (1986) used the terms *event caused* and *reshuffled* to distinguish between poverty that is a consequence of marital disruption or premarital pregnancy and poverty that exists prior to such events. She estimates that about 25% of poor white single mothers and about 75% of poor black single mothers were poor prior to forming mother-only families. Although these figures show that becoming a single mother does not *cause* all spells of poverty among mother-only families, they beg the question of whether such families would have escaped poverty sooner if the parents had remained married or married in the first place.

In sum, children in mother-only families are much more likely to be poor than children in two-parent families in terms of both absolute income levels and income stability. Given these conditions, we would be surprised if they did not have lower socioeconomic attainment than children who grew up with both natural parents.

Two sets of questions are important: (1) How great are the differences in socioeconomic attainment between children in mother-only families and children in two-parent families; and (2) What part of these differences can be accounted for by differences in family income and what part by other factors, for example, by differences in parental socialization or neighborhood conditions?

During the last several years McLanahan and her colleagues have been using longitudinal data to examine the relationships among family structure, income, and a series of young adult transitions, including high school completion, teen birth, and premarital birth (Astone & McLanahan, 1990; McLanahan, 1985; McLanahan, 1988; McLanahan & Bumpass, 1988; Sandefur, McLanahan, & Wojtkiewicz, 1989). Their analyses are based on three surveys: the Panel Study of Income Dynamics (PSID), the National Longitudinal Survey, Youth-Cohort (NLSY), and the High School and Beyond Study (HSB). Table 3.1 presents estimates of the effects of family structure based on these data. The numbers report the percentage increase in the risk of experiencing a particular event for children in mother-only and step families as compared to children in intact families. The family effects are reported both before and after income is taken into account,[1] which allows us to evaluate the importance of socioeconomic factors in accounting for differences between one- and two-parent families.

Table 3.1 illustrates several important points. First, children from nonintact families clearly have a greater risk of experiencing each of the events examined

---

1 When using the PSID and NLSY data, we measured family income directly. The measure of family income in the HSB data is flawed; over 30% of the cases have missing data. In all results from the HSB data, we used a composite measure of socioeconomic status based on reports of family income, parental education, father's occupation, and possessions in the home.

Table 3.1. *Effects of family structure on high school graduation, teen birth, and premarital birth*

Family type	PSID		NLSY		HSB	
	Unadj.	Adj.	Unadj.	Adj.	Unadj.	Adj.
	High school dropout (males and females combined)					
Whites						
Mom only	79*	55	133*	99*	159*	62*
Stepparent			249*	215*	131*	103*
Blacks						
Mom only	73*	30	57*	43*	93*	43*
Stepparent			49	49	40	16
Hispanics						
Mom only			65*	57*	82*	42*
Stepparent			73	64	68	54
	Premarital birth and single motherhood (females only)					
Whites						
Mom only		84*	159*	138*	99*	42
Stepparent			209*	17*	103	82*
Blacks						
Mom only		108*	62*	54*	166*	131*
Stepparent			9	8	143*	120*
Hispanics						
Mom only			158*	148*	111*	109*
Stepparent			18	18	46	46
	Teen birth (females only)					
Whites						
Mom only			52*	35	8	−24
Stepparent			171*	141*	90*	72*
Blacks						
Mom only			60*	46*	122*	90*
Stepparent			24	24	103*	82*
Hispanics						
Mom only			65*	58*	52	33
Stepparent			99*	100*	155*	150*

Note: Effects are based on logit models and are expressed as the percentage increase in the risk of an event associated with each family type. The unadjusted percentages include the effects of income; the adjusted percentages indicate the increased risk due to factors other than income.

Estimates for premarital birth and teen birth are presented for daughters only. The effect of family structure on high school dropout is significant for Hispanic daughters but not for sons.

*p < .05.

here. The increase in risk (unadjusted) ranges from 50% to 150% with a few exceptions, and almost all of the effects are statistically significant. Second, living in a step family appears to be just as risky as living with a single mother, and in some cases, the risk is even greater. The latter is especially true of whites in the case of high school dropouts and premarital births. Third, income accounts for a substantial portion of the difference between children in mother-only and children in intact families. A comparison of the unadjusted and adjusted percentages indicates that in some cases income explains more than half of the family difference. And finally, income does not explain all of the variation across family types. Although the risk associated with living in a nonintact family is substantially smaller once income is taken into account, in most cases it remains statistically significant.

Parental socialization in mother-only families

If family income and socioeconomic status do not account for all of the differences in socioeconomic attainment between offspring from one- and two-parent families, what else might explain the remaining differences? One possibility is that unmarried parents adhere to a different set of values and expectations than married parents do and therefore train their children to behave in different ways and to aspire to different goals. For example, divorced or never-married parents may have lower educational aspirations for their offspring, or they may be more liberal with respect to nonmarital sexual behavior. The former could account for the higher incidence of dropping out of high school, whereas the latter might explain differences in family formation behavior. On this last point, Thornton and Camburn (1987) found that divorced mothers, especially those who had remarried, held less restrictive attitudes about premarital sex than did mothers who had been married continuously. In turn, mothers' attitudes were associated with offspring's attitudes and behavior.

Alternatively, single parents may hold the same values as married parents but be less successful in transmitting these values to their children. Such a failure could be due to differences in the amount of time devoted to children or to less effective parenting styles. Successful socialization requires the development and maintenance of a stable parent–child relationship, and marital disruption may undermine such a relationship. Clearly, nonresident fathers spend less time with their children, which should undermine their ability to influence their offspring's behavior. Furstenberg and his colleagues found that fewer than half of the children with divorced parents in their sample (ages 11 to 16) had seen their fathers during the past year (Furstenberg, Morgan, & Allison, 1987; Furstenberg, Nord, Peterson, & Zill, 1983). Not surprisingly, these children felt less close to their fathers than did children living with both parents. Not everyone agrees about the value of a good relationship with the nonresidential father. Although developmental theory suggests that fathers are an important influence in child development (Lamb, 1981), Furstenberg's research suggests that contact with the nonresidential father has no effect on children's well-being.

The mother–child relationship also may be altered by divorce. Whereas most studies report no difference in mother attachment among children from one- and two-parent families, some studies have found that the relationship between the mother and child becomes closer and less hierarchical after a divorce (Devall, Stoneman, & Brody, 1986; Weiss, 1979; White, Brinkerhoff, & Booth, 1985). Both Devall and Weiss report that the older daughters of divorced parents are likely to become confidantes of their mothers. Whether such a role builds responsibility or merely pushes the daughter into a premature adulthood is not clear. Because these studies are based on small convenience samples, their results cannot be generalized to the population of all disrupted families. Other studies suggest that there may be gender differences in how marital disruption and remarriage affect children, with sons showing poorer relationships with their mothers after their parents' divorce and improved relationships after their mothers' remarriage and the opposite pattern for girls (Hetherington & Arasteh, 1988). The arguments that parent–child relationships are affected by divorce are compelling, despite the lack of conclusive evidence to support them, and merit further investigation.

A final way in which socialization practices may differ is in the degree of social control that single mothers exercise over their children. Hetherington, Cox, and Cox (1978) found that divorced mothers were less consistent in their household schedules and their discipline patterns than married mothers, at least during the first year after a divorce. Other researchers have found that adolescents in mother-only families are more susceptible to peer influence than those living with both natural parents (Dornbrush et al., 1985; Kellam, Ensminger, & Turner, 1977; Steinberg, 1987). It is of interest that the latter studies also show that grandmothers strengthen parental influence and control, whereas stepfathers have no positive effect in this regard.

As was the case for low income, it is possible that parental values and socialization practices are not consequences of divorce but rather are preexisting conditions in families that break up or in couples who never marry. If this is true, the relationships observed between single mothers and their children would have existed whether or not a marriage or divorce occurred. Further, some people argue that divorce is actually a solution to rather than a cause of family problems. The most impressive evidence in support of this hypothesis comes from studies that distinguish between happily married and unhappily married couples, or low- and high-conflict couples. These studies, which focus on children still living at home, indicate that offspring in unhappy or high-conflict families are no better off than those in single-parent house-holds (Emery, 1982).

Not all of the data are consistent with the predivorce conflict interpretation, however. Some studies show, for example, that children of widowed mothers have lower attainment and are more likely to become single mothers than offspring from two-parent families (Levy-Shiff, 1982). Because there is no reason to believe that widowed families experience more conflict prior to disruption, or prior to the event or illness that caused the death of a parent, this suggests that it is loss rather than conflict that affects the child's behavior. Moreover, divorce itself may increase parental conflict as opposed to resolving it, as in cases where parents fight about the child-support obligations and visitation rights of the nonresidential parent.

Effects of family structure on parental socialization

We used the High School and Beyond data to investigate further how family structure is related to socialization practices. The data reported here are from boys and girls who were enrolled as sophomores in 1980 and who replied to follow-up surveys conducted in 1982 and 1984. Table 3.2 reports the rela-tionships between family type and four dimensions of parental involvement and aspirations: (1) involvement with schoolwork, (2) direct communication, (3) supervision of the child's activities, and (4) educational aspirations. The parental involvement variable indicates whether parents monitor homework and whether they help plan the school program. Communication is measured by a variable indicating whether or not the child talks with his or her parent at least weekly. The supervision measure indicates whether or not the parent always knows where the child is. The measure of educational aspirations is based on whether the mother expects the child to graduate from college and whether the parents agree about college attendance. All of the variables use the child's report of socialization practices. We make no claim that these indicators form an ideal or comprehensive set of measures of parental so-cialization. They are, however, the best measures currently available in a large, nationally representative dataset.

Table 3.2 contains several interesting findings. First, parents in nonintact families are less likely to be involved on a day-to-day basis with their children's schoolwork than the parents of children in intact families. On average, parents in nonintact families are only half as likely as parents in intact families to monitor homework and to help plan the academic program. These results are consistent across whites, blacks, and Hispanics.

Second, parents and children in mother-only families communicate more often than parents and children in intact families. On the one hand, this finding may come as a surprise to those who believe that single mothers have less time to spend with their children. On the other, it is consistent with

Table 3.2. *Effects of family structure on parental socialization patterns with income controlled*

Family Type	Whites	Blacks	Hispanics
Involvement day to day			
Monitors homework			
Mom only	−41*	−37*	−26*
Stepparent	−53*	−62*	−51*
Plans HS program			
Mom only	−50*	−58*	−49*
Stepparent	−35*	−50*	72*
Communication			
Talks weekly			
Mom only	46*	28*	54*
Stepparent	1	−9	−2
Supervision			
Knows where child is			
Mom only	−32*	−17	−7
Stepparent	7	−31	−39*
Educational aspirations			
Mom wants college			
Mom only	32*	−4	20
Stepparent	−16	−8	75*
Agree on college			
Mom only	−24*	5	−27*
Stepparent	−41*	−23	−41

Note: Effects are based on logit models and are expressed as the percentage increase in the score on the socialization measures associated with each family type.

Weiss's argument that single mothers rely more on their children for conversation, recreation, and advice than do mothers in intact families (Weiss, 1979). Of course, there is no information on the nature or quality of this communication; it could be that some students are reporting that their parents scold them often.

There is some indication that parents in disrupted families exercise less supervision over their children than parents exercise in intact families, although the evidence here is not entirely consistent. White adolescents in mother-only families and Hispanic adolescents in step families report less supervision, but black adolescents do not. The lack of a significant effect for blacks is somewhat surprising and contradicts the results of previous studies. Another surprise is that mothers in some nonintact families hold higher college aspirations for their children than are held by mothers in intact families. Again, this is true among whites and Hispanics but not among blacks.

Table 3.3. *Effects of family structure on school dropout, premarital birth, and teenage birth*

Family Type	Dropout		Premarital Birth		Teenage Birth	
	Unadj.[a]	Adj.[b]	Unadj.[a]	Adj.[b]	Unadj.[a]	Adj.[b]
Whites						
Mom only	57*	62*	34	27	−18	−16
Stepparent	103*	97*	125*	105*	95*	86*
Blacks						
Mom only	43*	43*	110*	110*	78*	80*
Stepparent	15	9	82*	82*	52	51
Hispanics						
Mom only	42*	40	51	52	25	20
Stepparent	54	51	65	75	118*	116*

Note: The effects are based on logit models and are expressed as the percentage increase in the risk of an event associated with each family type.
[a]Net of socioeconomic status.
[b]Net of socioeconomic status and parental socialization.
*$p < .05$.

Mediating effects of socialization

Having discovered that certain dimensions of parental socialization vary in important and interpretable ways by family type, the next step was to see if socialization is a significant mediator for the effects of family type on school completion or early parenthood. Table 3.3 reports the effect of family structure on each of the outcome variables for the three racial groups. The unadjusted column contains estimates for family structure, controlling for income, and the adjusted column contains estimates for family structure, controlling for income and socialization practices. A more detailed set of estimates showing the effects of each of the socialization variables on school graduation and fertility is reported later (see Tables 3.7, 3.8, and 3.9). Here we focus only on the change in the effect of family structure that results from taking the socialization variables into account.

A comparison of the two columns for each set of outcomes in Table 3.3 indicates that parental socialization does not "explain" the differences associated with family structure. Although the socialization variables are related to family type, as shown in Table 3.2, and although they are also related to the outcome variables, as reported in Tables 3.7, 3.8, and 3.9, they do not diminish the effects of family structure on high school graduation, teen birth, or premarital birth. Thus we conclude that socialization practices, at least those examined here, do not account for any additional differences in the outcomes associated with family structure, above and beyond the effects of income.

Characteristics of the neighborhood of children in mother-only families

A final explanation for why children in mother-only families might have lower socioeconomic attainment than children who live with both parents has to do with the characteristics of their neighborhoods. Wilson has argued that families living in poor inner-city neighborhoods with high rates of unemployment and high rates of welfare dependence are isolated from mainstream social institutions and have less chance of economic mobility (Wilson, 1986). If Wilson is correct and single mothers are more likely to live in such neighborhoods, then this might account for part of the lower attainment of offspring.

The neighborhood argument is a hybrid of the economic and socialization perspectives, incorporating elements of both approaches and raising them to a more macrolevel of analysis. Whereas the economic perspective generally emphasizes family income and parental investment, the neighborhood perspective stresses the demand side of the equation and the extent to which residential location is related to the availability of jobs. According to this view, children from mother-only families have fewer opportunities and therefore less incentive to invest in their own education or in other human capital. Similarly, whereas socialization theory focuses primarily on parent–child relations and communication and control within the family, the neighborhood theory stresses the importance of community attitudes, local networks, and peer-group activities. According to this line of argument, living in a neighborhood with high levels of poverty and disorganization undermines parental control and increases the likelihood that children will be exposed to antisocial youth cultures.

At least four studies have found evidence of neighborhood effects. Hogan and Kitagawa (1985), in their study of nonmarried black teens in Chicago, found that neighborhood quality was strongly related to parental supervision and, ultimately, to early pregnancy. Mothers who lived in poor neighborhoods were much less likely to supervise their daughters, and supervision is a significant predictor of early pregnancy. Corcoran and her colleagues at the University of Michigan (1987) also found that neighborhood characteristics were a good predictor of economic well-being and earnings capacity. Finally, two studies of delinquency have suggested that neighborhood conditions interact with family structure in determining offspring behavior (Matsueda & Heimer, 1987; Sampson, 1987).

Table 3.4. *Proportion of U.S. families living in urban poverty areas in 1980*

	20% poverty areas	40% poverty areas
Mother-only families	16.5	5.6
Other families	4.7	1.0
White mother-only families	4.5	1.0
Black mother-only families	34.2	10.5
Black persons	26.0	8.0

Note: Information is not available on the proportion of white and black mother-only families living in areas that are 40% poor. Therefore, these percentages were estimated by extrapolating from the proportions observed in 40% areas for other families and black persons. The estimate for white mother-only families was obtained by extrapolating from the ratio of white mother-only families to other families in 20% areas. The estimate for black mother-only families was obtained by extrapolating from the ratio of black mother-only families to black persons in 20% areas.
Source: U.S. Bureau of the Census (1985).

Effects of family structure on neighborhoods

Are children from mother-only families more likely than children from two-parent households to live in poor neighborhoods, and do poor neighborhoods create additional resource constraints that influence their behaviors? Table 3.4 describes the living arrangements of different family types in 1980 broken down by family structure and race. Poverty neighborhoods are defined as urban census tracts in which 20%, 30%, or 40% of the inhabitants are poor. Persons living in poverty areas outside the 100 largest central cities are not counted as living in poverty areas. Racial differences of families in the residential location are available only for 20% poverty areas, and, therefore, we must rely on extrapolation to estimate the proportions of black single mothers and white single mothers living in 40% areas. To assist in the extrapolation, we report percentages for black persons as well as for black families.

Overall, just a small proportion of mother-only families in the United States were living in poverty areas in 1980. Only 16.5% lived in 20% poverty areas, and only 5.6% lived in 40% areas. Although the absolute proportion is small, the risk of living in a poverty area was much greater for mother-only families than for other families. Mother-only families were about 3½ times more likely to reside in 20% poverty areas than other families were; in 40% areas, the ratio was nearly 6 to 1.

The residential isolation of black single mothers was much higher than that of whites in 1980. Over 34% of the former lived in urban poverty areas as compared to only 4.5% of the latter. Assuming that the ratio of white mother-only families to all families remains the same across areas with different levels

Table 3.5. *Effects of family structure on neighborhood characteristics net of family status*

Family type	Whites	Blacks	Hispanics
School characteristics			
School dropout rate			
Mom only	−0.43	−1.51*	−2.18*
Stepparent	−1.59*	−0.99	−0.09
School quality			
Mom only	0.01	0.12	−0.06
Stepparent	−0.20	−0.79*	0.93
School problems			
Mom only	−0.19[+]	−0.22	−0.01
Stepparent	−0.29*	−0.31	−0.18
Peer characteristics			
Academic orientation of closest friend			
Mom only	−0.06	−0.02	0.04
Stepparent	−0.14*	−0.23*	−0.10
Community norm			
Attitude toward having a nonmarital birth			
Mom only	13	25	10
Stepparent	22	24	39

Note: For school and peer characteristics, the effects given are the OLS regression coefficients associated with each family type. For the community norm, the effects are based on logit models and are expressed as the percentage increase in the likelihood of being willing to consider an out-of-wedlock birth associated with each family type.
*$p < .05$.
[+]$p < .10$.

of concentration, we estimate that less than 1% of white single mothers were living in 40% poverty areas. Assuming that the proportion of black mother-only families to black persons remains the same, we estimate that slightly over 10% of black single mothers were living in highly concentrated poverty areas in 1980.

Poverty concentration is not the only way of measuring neighborhood resources. Alternatively, we might ask whether children from mother-only families are disadvantaged with respect to the quality of the schools they attend, with respect to the characteristics of their peers, and with respect to community norms. The High School and Beyond sophomore cohort data again was used to explore the relationships between family structure and such neighborhood characteristics.

Table 3.5 reports the relationships between family structure and five measures of community resources and influence. Three measures of school characteristics are used: (1) a measure indicating the dropout rate in the respondent's high school (obtained from the principal's report); (2) a measure of school quality based on the student's rating of such school characteristics as condition of buildings, library facilities, discipline, teacher interest, school spirit, reputation, and academic instruction; and (3) a measure of school problems summarizing the student's perception of the extent of nonattendance, cutting classes, talking back to teachers, not obeying teachers, fighting, and attacking teachers. The peer quality measure indicates whether the student's closest friend in school is highly motivated toward educational achievement.

Another measure included in the category of neighborhood effects was the student's attitude toward nonmarital birth. We assumed that individual attitudes about out-of-wedlock births reflect community and peer-group norms and could tell us something about these effects. Thus acceptance of out-of-wedlock birth is interpreted as a community effect. The attitude variable indicates whether or not the student would be at all willing to consider having a nonmarital birth.

The most significant finding reported in Table 3.5 is the difference in graduation rates by family type. Whites from step families and blacks and Hispanics from mother-only families attend schools with a significantly lower percentage of high school graduates than are attended by their counterparts in intact families. For whites the graduating rate is 1.59 points lower, for blacks it is 1.51 points lower, and for Hispanics it is 2.18 points lower. Although these absolute numbers may seem small, their significance is clear in light of the small range of values the dropout rates take on. For example, the mean graduation rate for the schools attended by white sophomores is about 92%; for black sophomores it is 88%; and for Hispanic sophomores it is 87%. Significant differences between family types support the argument that blacks and Hispanics in mother-only families, as well as whites in step families, tend to live in neighborhoods with fewer resources, with, for example, fewer educational opportunities.

Other findings from Table 3.5 are that blacks in step families report a lower level of school quality and that whites from nonintact families report significantly more problems in their schools. Both whites and blacks from step families indicate that their closest friends are less academically oriented than the closest friends of students in intact families.

Students from nonintact families of all races are more likely to consider becoming a parent out of wedlock. Whites from step families and blacks from mother-only families are about 25% more likely to consider a nonmarital birth. Hispanic students from step families are 39% more likely to do so. If such attitudes derive, to some extent at least, from living in a neighborhood where such events are common and acceptable, these findings constitute additional evidence that children from nonintact families are exposed to different neighborhood conditions. However, the possibility that such differences in

Table 3.6. *Effects of family structure on school dropout, premarital birth, and teenage birth*

Family type	Dropout		Premarital birth		Teen birth	
	Unadj.[a]	Adj.[b]	Unadj.[a]	Adj.[b]	Unadj.[a]	Adj.[b]
Whites						
Mom only	57*	55*	34	26	−18	−24
Stepparent	103*	88*	125*	105*	95*	80*
Blacks						
Mom only	43*	36	110*	99*	79*	70*
Stepparent	16	2	82*	80*	52	45
Hispanics						
Mom only	42*	40	51	46	25	25
Stepparent	54	49	65	48	118*	105*

Note: Effects are based on logit models and are expressed as the percentage increase in the risk of an event associated with each family type.
[a]Net of socioeconomic status.
[b]Net of socioeconomic status and neighborhood characteristics.
*$p < .05$.

attitudes may be related primarily to factors other than neighborhood norms cannot be ruled out on the basis of these results.

Mediating effects of neighborhood

Do differences in neighborhood characteristics explain differences in the risk of children from nonintact families of dropping out of school and/or of having a nonmarital or teen birth? Table 3.6 compares the effects of family structure on school dropout and early birth, before and after the neighborhood variables are controlled. Again, more detailed information on the separate effects of each of the neighborhood variables on the outcome variables is reported in the last three tables.

Overall, the findings of Table 3.6 show that neighborhood influences do not significantly reduce the impact of family type on these outcomes. Neighborhood variables appear to have a very weak mediating effect on step families and virtually no effect on mother-only families. Despite their limited role as mediators of the effect of family structure, the neighborhood variables exhibit significant associations with the outcome variables net of family structure, socioeconomic status, and socialization measures already discussed. The neighborhood variables do appear to mediate the effect of socioeconomic status to some extent; see Tables 3.7, 3.8, and 3.9.

Table 3.7. *Effects of family structure, socioeconomic status, parental socialization, and neighborhood characteristics on school dropout*

	Whites	Blacks	Hispanics
Family type			
Mom only	62*	42⁺	38
Stepparent	84*	3	51
Socioeconomic status	−55*	−43*	−35*
Parental socialization			
Monitors homework	−27*	35	−21
Plans HS program	0	7	6
Talks weekly	−5	13	13
Knows where child is	−25*	−30⁺	−42*
College aspiration	−69*	−41*	−56*
Agree on college	12	3	−22
Neighborhood			
School dropout rate	−4*	−4*	−1
School quality	−4*	−3	−1
School problems	−7*	1	−2
Peer's academic orientation	−26*	−17*	−19*
Attitude toward nonmarital birth	45*	47*	36*
Log-likelihood	3793.8	1220.7	1225.3
DF	7888	1793	1646

Note: Effects are based on logit models and are expressed as the percentage increase in the risk of an event associated with each variable.
*$p < .05$.
⁺$p < .10$.

Policy recommendations

The results reported in the previous section indicate that income is the single most important factor, among those identified thus far, in accounting for differences in the socioeconomic attainment of children from intact and non-intact families. Not only does low income limit the amount of money available for college, travel, and other education-related goods but it also is associated with less effective parenting practices and with residence in neighborhoods with poorer quality schools. Given the importance of income and given the fact that income can be manipulated by policy makers, the last section of this chapter focuses on policies that have the potential to reduce poverty and economic insecurity in mother-only families.

Single mothers have three potential sources of income: individual earnings, private transfers (primarily child support from the nonresident parent), and public transfers (primarily welfare or survivors' insurance). Social policy can

Table 3.8. *Effects of family structure, socioeconomic status, parental socialization, and neighborhood characteristics on premarital birth*

	Whites	Blacks	Hispanics
Family type			
Mom only	22	101*	48
Stepparent	93*	82*	57
Socioeconomic status	−45*	−40*	12
Parental socialization			
Monitors homework	−33*	−28+	39
Plans HS program	13	35	−11
Talks weekly	−1	7	30
Knows where child is	−24	−21	−15
College aspiration	−33+	−21	−27
Agree on college	−31	22	5
Neighborhood			
School dropout rate	−2*	−1	−2*
School quality	2	3	0
School problems	−6*	0	−3
Peer's academic orientation	−24*	−6	−1
Attitude toward nonmarital birth	48*	41*	64*
Log-likelihood	1420.3	1127.2	551.5
DF	7700	1686	1556

Note: Effects are based on logit models and are expressed as the percentage increase in the risk of an event associated with each variable.
*$p < .05$.
+$p < .10$.

and does affect each of these income sources, not only for single mothers but for all families with children.

Increasing earnings

The most important source of income in mother-only families is earned income. Earnings account for about 60% of the total family income in mother-only families as compared with 90% of total family income in two-parent families (Garfinkel & McLanahan, 1986). The same authors report that even in families headed by never-married mothers, which are more likely than other families to rely on public assistance, the earnings of the household head is the major source of income during any given year.

Despite the importance of earnings, however, single mothers earn only 35% as much as the major breadwinner (usually the father) in two-parent families (Garfinkel & McLanahan, 1986). The lower earnings of single moth-

Table 3.9. *Effects of family structure, socioeconomic status, parental socialization, and neighborhood characteristics on teen birth*

	Whites	Blacks	Hispanics
Family type			
Mom only	−21	72*	19
Stepparent	73*	46	106*
Socioeconomic status	−46*	−46*	−17
Parental socialization			
Monitors homework	−22*	−25	−1
Plans HS program	9	40	2
Talks weekly	1	14	25
Knows where child is	12	−21	−35[+]
College aspiration	−39*	−9	−16
Agree on college	−8*	−2	−24
Neighborhood			
School dropout rate	−3	−1	−1
School quality	0	4*	−2
School problems	−8	−1	−3
Peer's academic orientation	−19*	−13*	−11
Attitude toward nonmarital birth	40*	42*	36*
Log-likelihood	3552.5	1221.8	974.4
DF	7710	1688	1564

Note: Effects are based on logit models and are expressed as the percentage increase in the risk of an event associated with each variable.
*$p < .05$.
[+]$p < .10$.

ers are due to their gender as well as to their parental/family status. Women who work full time, year-round, earn only about 60% as much as men, a ratio that has remained relatively constant for the last thirty years (Reskin, 1984). Whereas some of the gender gap in wages is due to differences in human capital (education, training, and work experience), a substantial portion (60%) is due to the fact that women are excluded from certain high-paying jobs and are concentrated in low-paying occupations (Corcoran & Duncan, 1979).

Although a detailed review of the considerable research about gender discrimination and job segregation is beyond the scope of this chapter, findings suggest that segregation across occupations and within firms is extensive and is closely associated with women's lower wages (Reskin, 1984). This evidence indicates that irrespective of the causes of segregation, policies such as affirmative action and pay equity, which are designed to increase the number of women in high-paying jobs and raise wages in low-paying sex-segregated jobs, can go a long way toward increasing the earnings and reducing poverty in mother-only families.

Another factor in accounting for the low earnings in mother-only families is labor supply. Not only do single mothers have lower wage rates but they also work fewer hours in the paid labor force than male breadwinners in two-parent households work. Between 30% and 40% of single mothers report no earnings at all during any given year, and among those who do report earnings, many work less than full time (Garfinkel & McLanahan, 1986). The importance of not working outside the home is profound. Ellwood has shown that only about 6% of single mothers who work full time, year-round, are poor as compared to more than 70% of nonemployed mothers (Ellwood, 1985). These findings should not be interpreted to mean that if all single mothers worked full time only 6% of them would be poor. Rather, the apparent advantage of employed mothers reflects the selection process that channels women with higher wage rates into the labor force and those with lower wage rates into homemaker status. The findings do serve, however, to show that single mothers who can "afford" to work full time year-round are much better off than their counterparts who either are not employed or work less than full time.

A major barrier to working is the cost of child care. For mothers with the lowest wage rates, net earnings after paying for child care are less than the income available through public assistance (Sawhill, 1976). In effect, these women cannot afford to work outside the home. For others, wages are low enough so that the mother must limit her hours of paid work to the times when she can arrange for free child care from a friend or relative. Thus, a second way that policy makers can increase the earnings of single mothers is to subsidize child care so that mothers can work more hours and take home more income.

At present, the government has two different mechanisms for providing child care. For families in the lower half of the income distribution, there are income-tested child care subsidies, which cost less than 2 billion dollars per year. For middle and upper middle-income families, there is the child care tax credit in the federal income tax, which costs over 3.5 billion dollars (Garfinkel, 1988). The current tax credit is of greater benefit to middle-income families than to low-income families because the former have a higher tax rate than the latter. One solution is to combine the two mechanisms into a single program that provides a refundable tax credit for those with very low earnings and a declining tax credit for those with higher earnings. An alternative would be to provide child care for all families and to charge a sliding-scale fee based upon income. These options are discussed in more detail by Phillips (this volume).

Increasing private transfers

A second source of income for single mothers is child support and alimony paid by the nonresidential parent. In theory, both parents are responsible for the economic support of their children. When parents divorce, or do not marry, the nonresidential parent bears an obligation to provide material support for his or her children. Unfortunately, our child support system has been a dismal failure, at least until recently. In 1983 only 60% of children with a living absent parent had a child support award, and only half of those with an award received full payment. In addition, awards are rarely indexed to the cost of living, and therefore their value declines over time. In 1983, child support and alimony payments accounted for less than 13% of total income in white mother-only families and for less than 3% of the total income in black mother-only families (Garfinkel & McLanahan, 1986).

Some people have argued that the nonresident parents cannot afford to pay child support and that requiring them to pay would push these parents and their new families into poverty. Although this prediction is undoubtedly true for some cases, the evidence suggests that it would not hold for the majority of nonresidential parents. First, as noted earlier, studies of the economic consequences of divorce show that the income loss experienced by the single mother is much greater than the loss experienced by the nonresident father (Duncan & Hoffman, 1985). Moreover, estimates of the absent father's ability to pay indicate that on average the income of nonresident fathers is about $19,000 per year, only $3,000 less than the average for all prime-age males (Garfinkel & Ollereich, 1989).

In response to this information, strong bipartisan support has developed for reforming the present child support system and for increasing the income available to single mothers through private transfers. The new Child Support Assurance System (CSAS) is an example of such a policy (Garfinkel, 1985). The philosophy underlying CSAS is that parents are responsible for sharing income with their children, and government is responsible for assuring that children receive the child support to which they are legally entitled. The financial obligation of the nonresident parent is expressed as a percentage of income and is withheld from earnings in the same way as income and payroll taxes are withheld. In cases where the father is unemployed or has low earnings, the government makes up the difference just as it does with the social security pension. Note that the third component of the CSAS proposal involves a public transfer in addition to governmental enforcement of private obligation. Garfinkel and his colleagues estimate that if implemented at the national level, the CSAS would reduce the poverty gap of mother-only families by about 40% (Garfinkel & McLanahan, 1986).

Increasing public transfers

A third potential source of income for mother-only females is public transfers. The two major programs in this domain are Aid to Families with Dependent Children (AFDC) and Survivors Insurance (SI). In 1983, these two programs accounted for 15% and 25% of the income of white mother-only and black mother-only families, respectively (Garfinkel & McLanahan, 1986).

The United States has always provided economic support to the most disadvantaged persons in society. During the colonial period, single mothers were protected by policies patterned after the British poor law system. Later, these policies were extended into programs such as the widows' pensions and mothers' pensions in the late 1800s and early 1900s and Aid to Dependent Children (ADC) and Survivors Insurance in the late 1930s. Although the latter two programs both provide support to single mothers, they differ in one very important respect. Aid to Families with Dependent Children (AFDC), or welfare as it is commonly called, is a means-tested program available only to poor single mothers, whereas SI is a universal program available to all widowed mothers.

Although ADC and SI benefits were not high enough to support a family, at least when the policies were first implemented, both programs were designed to allow single mothers to behave as much like married mothers as possible, that is, to stay at home and raise their children. Beginning in the mid-1950s, benefits began to rise and continued to increase throughout the 1960s and up to the mid-1970s. Ironically, just as benefits were becoming large enough to allow single mothers to stay home, married mothers began entering the labor force in ever-greater numbers. Since the mid-1970s, the real values of AFDC and other income-tested programs for single mothers have declined by about 30%. Initially, the decline was caused by inflation and the failure of benefits to keep up with the cost of living. More recently, it resulted from direct budget cuts legislated in early 1982. Survivor Insurance has done much better than welfare since the late seventies because it is part of the Social Security system, whose benefits are indexed to the rate of inflation and less vulnerable to budget cutbacks. Although widows have always been treated more generously than other single mothers, they represent a decreasing proportion of all mother-only families.

Welfare has come under considerable attack in recent years, and some analysts and policy makers feel that the program does more harm than good. A major criticism is that it discourages single mothers from entering the labor force by imposing a high tax rate on earnings. Welfare recipients lose nearly a dollar in benefits for each dollar earned. They also lose health care and other income-tested benefits. Given the high tax rate, the mothers' low earning capacity, and the cost of child care, many single mothers would be worse off working full time than they would be depending on welfare. The high tax rate implicit in welfare programs is especially problematic given the trends in the labor force participation of married women and given the importance of earned income in all mother-only families (Garfinkel & McLanahan, 1986).

In response to these concerns, many critics have called for replacing welfare with work. Although such concerns date back at least to the early 1960s, there is a greater sense of urgency and greater bipartisan support today than in the past. Many states have been experimenting with different versions of work and training programs since the early 1980s, and the Family Support Act of 1988 mandates such programs for all states. Included under the "work-welfare" rubric are a broad range of programs that differ greatly in their intent and implementation. Whereas some programs simply impose a work requirement on the mother in exchange for her welfare check, many are aimed at providing resources that facilitate work, for example, child care, transportation, training, and education (Gueron, 1986). To date, the evidence suggests that some states are spending a good deal of money on training and education, money that probably would not have been spent in the absence of a change in expectations regarding work.

Other critics are less optimistic about work-welfare programs. Some argue that work and training programs are simply strategies for reducing welfare costs and that single mothers and their children will be worse off than they were under the previous system (Handler, 1988). In fact, if welfare benefits are only replaced by work dollars, with no increase in total family income, the family would appear to be worse off in the sense that children have less time with their mother and no more income. Others note that although single mothers appear to have benefited from previous employment-training programs, such benefits may not extend to all welfare mothers; the earlier evaluations were based on voluntary participation and were restricted to mothers with children over the age of 6 (Garfinkel & McLanahan, 1986). Finally, critics note that whatever short-term benefits might arise from welfare reform, income-tested programs are inherently unstable and doomed to cutbacks because their political constituency is small and lacking in resources (Weir, Orloff, & Skocpol, 1988).

For these reasons, developing and expanding universal programs outside of welfare as opposed to reforming the system from within may be the best long-term strategy for reducing poverty and income insecurity in mother-only families. Universal programs, such as Survivors Insurance, treat all income groups in a similar fashion, and evidence suggests that they are more successful in reducing long-term economic insecurity than are programs aimed only at the poor. A recent comparison of six industrialized countries shows that poverty rates of single mothers are substantially lower in countries that rely on universal and employment-related income-transfer programs, for example, Sweden, West Germany, and England, than in countries that rely on means-tested programs, for example, Australia and the United States (Duncan, this volume; Torrey & Smeeding, 1988).

Two policies that fit the description of a universal program are the child care tax credit and the guaranteed minimum benefit in the Child Support Assurance System. Both of these proposals benefit all mother-only families as opposed to only those who are poor or who fall below a given income level. Moreover, both programs reinforce employment inasmuch as they make working in the paid labor force a more attractive alternative than staying at home and receiving welfare. This is because, unlike welfare, benefits are not reduced dollar for dollar as earnings increase. In the case of the child care credit, the subsidy decreases gradually as total income goes up; and in the case of the minimum child support benefit, the subsidy is taxed at the mother's normal tax rate.

Two final examples of universal social policies are a children's allowance and universal health insurance. As is the case with our child care policy, our current system has two mechanisms for helping families cover the cost of health care and child rearing. For families at the bottom end of the income distribution, we have welfare and Medicaid. For those in the middle and upper middle-income brackets, we have an income tax exemption for dependent children. In addition, health insurance provided through employers is not taxable, which represents a substantial public transfer to middle and upper income families. Replacing the child deduction with a smaller refundable tax credit that is more generous for those at the bottom of the income distribution and requiring employers to provide health insurance to all employees would greatly improve the living conditions of single mothers and their children without increasing the cost to society (McLanahan & Garfinkel, 1989).

Together, the policies just described would go a long way toward increasing economic stability and reducing poverty in mother-only families. Moreover, they complement one another and therefore have important interaction effects. Employment-related policies such as affirmative action and pay equity increase the wages of single mothers as well as of all women. Policies such as child care, child support, and children's allowances supplement the earnings of single mothers and make working in the paid labor force a more viable alternative to welfare. Given that the well-being of children is essential to our nation's future, and given that over half of all children today will spend some time in a mother-only family, such policies deserve careful consideration.

References

Abrahamse, A., Morrison, D., & Waite, L. (1988). *Beyond stereotypes: Who becomes a single teenage mother*. Santa Monica, CA: RAND Corporation.

Astone, N. M., & McLanahan, S. S. (1991). Family structure, parental practices and high school completion. *American Sociological Review, 56*, 1–12.

Bane, M. J. (1986). Household composition and poverty. In S. H. Danziger & D. H. Weinberg (Eds.), *Fighting poverty: What works and what doesn't* (pp. 209–231). Cambridge, MA: Harvard University Press.

Bane, M. J., & Ellwood, D. (1983). *The dynamics of dependence: The routes to self-sufficiency.* Report prepared for the Assistant Secretary for Planning and Evaluation, Department of Health and Human Services. Cambridge, MA: Harvard University.

Bane, M. J., & Ellwood, D. (1989). One fifth of the nation's children: Why are they poor? *Science, 245*, 1047–1053.

Becker, G. B. (1981). *A treatise on the family.* Cambridge, MA: Harvard University Press.

Bumpass, L. (1984). Children and marital disruption: A replication and update. *Demography, 21*, 71–82.

Corcoran, M., & Duncan, G. (1979). Work history, labor force attachment and earnings differences between the races and sexes. *Journal of Human Resources, 14*, 3–20.

Corcoran, M., Gordon, R., Laren, D., & Solon, G. (1987). *Intergenerational transmission of education, income, and earnings: Final report to the Ford Foundation.* Ann Arbor, MI: University of Michigan, Institute for Public Policy Studies.

Devall, E., Stoneman, Z., & Brody, G. (1986). The impact of divorce and maternal employment on preadolescent children. *Family Relations, 35*, 153–159.

Dornbush, S. M., Carlsmith, J. M., Bushwall, S. J., Litter, P. L., Leiderman, H., Hastorf, A. H., & Gross, R. T. (1985). Single parents, extended households and the control of adolescents. *Child Development, 56*, 326–341.

Duncan, G. (1984). *Years of poverty, years of plenty.* Ann Arbor, MI: Institute for Social Research.

Duncan, G., & Hoffman, S. (1985). A reconsideration of the economic consequences of marital disruption. *Demography, 22*, 485–497.

Elder, G. (1974). *Children of the Great Depression.* Chicago: University of Chicago Press.

Ellwood, D. (1985). *Working off welfare, prospects and policies for self-sufficiency of female family heads.* Unpublished manuscript, Harvard University.

Emery, R. E. (1982). Interparental conflict and the children of discord and divorce. *Psychological Bulletin, 92*, 310–330.

Furstenberg, F., Morgan, S. P., & Allison, P. (1987). Parental participation and children's well-being after marital disruption. *American Sociological Review, 52*, 695–701.

Furstenberg, F., Nord, C. W., Peterson, J. L., & Zill, N. (1983). The life course of children of divorce: Marital disruption and parental contact. *American Sociological Review, 48*, 656–667.

Garfinkel, I. (1985). The role of child support insurance in antipoverty policy. *The Annals of the American Academy of Political and Social Science, 479*, 119–131.

Garfinkel, I., & McLanahan, S. S. (1986). *Single mothers and their children.* Washington, DC: Urban Institute Press.

Garfinkel, I., & Ollereich, D. (1989). Noncustodial fathers' ability to pay child support. *Demography, 26*, 219–235.

Garfinkel, I., Meyer, D., & Wong, P. (1990). The potential of child care tax credits to reduce poverty and welfare recipiency. *Population Research and Policy Review, 9*, 45–65.

Gueron, J. M. (1986). *Work initiatives for welfare recipients: Lessons from a multi-state experiment.* New York: Manpower Demonstration Research Corporation.

Handler, J. H. (1988). Consequences on redirection – which direction? *Focus, 11*, 29–34.

Herzog, E., & Sudia, C. (1973). Children in fatherless families. In B. Caldwell & H. Ricciuti (Eds.), *Review of child development research* (Vol. 3, pp. 141–231). Chicago: University of Chicago Press.

Hetherington, E. M., & Arasteh, J. D. (1988). *Impact of divorce, single-parenting and step-parenting on children.* Hillsdale, NJ: Erlbaum.

Hetherington, E. M., Camara, K. A., & Featherman, D. L. (1983). Achievement and intellectual functioning of children in one-parent households. In J. Spence (Ed.), *Achievement and achievement motives* (pp. 205–284). San Francisco: Freeman.

Hetherington, E. M., Cox, M., & Cox, R. (1978). The aftermath of divorce. In J. H. Stevens (Ed.), *Mother–child, father–child relations*. Washington, DC: National Association for the Education of Young Children.

Heyns, B. (1985). The influence of parental work on children's school achievement. In S. B. Kamerman & C. D. Hayes (Eds.), *Families that work: Children in a changing world* (pp. 229–267). Washington, DC: National Academy Press.

Hogan, D. P., & Kitagawa, E. M. (1985). The impact of social status, family structure and neighborhood on the fertility of black adolescents. *American Journal of Sociology, 90,* 825–855.

Kellam, S. G., Ensminger, M. E., & Turner, R. J. (1977). Family structure and the mental health of children. *Archives of General Psychiatry, 34,* 1012–1022.

Krein, S. F., & Beller, A. H. (1986). *Family structure and the educational attainment of children: Differences by duration, age and gender.* Paper presented to the annual meetings of the Population Association of America, San Francisco.

Lamb, M. (1981). *The role of the father in child development.* New York: Wiley.

Levy-Shiff, R. (1982). The effects of father absence on young children in mother-headed families. *Child Development, 53,* 1400–1405.

Matsueda, R. L., & Heimer, K. (1987). Race, family structure and delinquency: A test of differential association and social control theories. *American Sociological Review, 52,* 826–840.

McLanahan, S. S. (1985). Family structure and the reproduction of poverty. *American Journal of Sociology, 90,* 873–901.

McLanahan, S. S. (1988). Family structure and dependency: Early transitions to female household headship. *Demography, 25,* 1–16.

McLanahan, S. S., & Bumpass, L. (1988). Intergenerational consequences of family disruption. *American Journal of Sociology, 94,* 130–152.

McLanahan, S. S., & Garfinkel, I. (1989). Single mothers, the underclass and social policy. *The Annals of the American Academy of Political and Social Science, 501,* 92–104.

Michael, R. T., & Tuma, N. B. (1985). Entry into marriage and parenthood by young men and women: The influence of family background. *Demography, 22,* 515–544.

Mott, F. L., & Haurin, R. J. (1987). *The interrelatedness of age at first intercourse, early childbearing, alcohol and drug-use among young American women.* Paper presented to the annual meetings of the Population Association of America, Chicago.

Reskin, B. (1984). Introduction. In B. Reskin (Ed.), *Sex segregation in the workplace* (pp. 1–8). Washington, DC: National Academy Press.

Rubin, L. B. (1976). *Worlds of pain: Life in the working class family.* New York: Basic Books.

Sampson, R. J. (1987). Urban black violence: The effect of male joblessness and family disruption. *American Journal of Sociology, 93,* 348–405.

Sandefur, G. D., McLanahan, S. S., & Wojtkiewicz, R. A. (1989). *Race, family structure, and high school graduation.* Paper presented to the annual meetings of the Population Association of America, Baltimore.

Sawhill, I. (1976). Discrimination and poverty among women who head families. *Signs, 2,* 201–211.

Shinn, M. B. (1978). Father absence and children's cognitive development. *Psychological Bulletin, 85,* 295–324.

Steinberg, L. (1987). Single parents, stepparents and the susceptibility of adolescents to antisocial peer pressure. *Child Development, 58,* 269–275.

Thornton, A., & Camburn, D. (1987). The influence of the family on premarital sexual attitudes and behavior. *Demography, 24,* 323–340.

Torrey, B. B., & Smeeding, T. (1988). *Poor children in rich countries.* Paper presented to the annual meeting of the Population Association of America, New Orleans.

U.S. Bureau of the Census. (1960). *Marital status and family status, March 1960*. Current Population Reports, P-20, No. 105. Washington, DC: U.S. Government Printing Office.

U.S. Bureau of the Census. (1988). *Marital status and living arrangements, March 1987*. Current Population Reports, Series P-20, No. 423. Washington, DC: U.S. Government Printing Office.

U.S. Bureau of the Census. (1961). *Household and family characteristics, March 1960*. Current Population Reports, Series P-20, No. 106. Washington, DC: U.S. Government Printing Office.

Weir, M., Orloff, A. S., & Skocpol, T. (1988). The future of social policy in the United States: Political constraints and possibilities. In M. Weir, A. S. Orloff, & T. Skocpol (Eds.), *The politics of social policies in the United States* (pp. 421–446). Princeton, NJ: Princeton University Press.

Weiss, R. (1979). Growing up a little faster: The experience of growing up in a single parent household. *Journal of Social Issues, 35*, 97–111.

White, L. K., Brinkerhoff, D. B., & Booth, A. (1985). The effect of marital disruption on child's attachment to parents. *Journal of Family Issues, 6*, 5–22.

Wilson, W. J. (1986). *The truly disadvantaged*. Chicago: University of Chicago Press.

Wilson, W. J., & Aponte, R. (1985). Urban poverty. *Annual Review of Sociology, 11*, 231–258.

Wilson, W. J., & Neckerman, K. M. (1986). Poverty and family structure: The widening gap between evidence and public policy issues. In S. H. Danziger & D. H. Weinberg (Eds.), *Fighting poverty: What works and what doesn't* (pp. 232–259). Cambridge, MA: Harvard University Press.

4 The association between adolescent parenting and childhood poverty

Lorraine V. Klerman

Adolescent parenting has not always been associated with poverty. Pregnancy in a teenager, as long as she was married, was considered quite normal through the middle of the current century. Among working-class families it was not at all unusual for a young girl to graduate from high school, marry her high school sweetheart, and bear a child before her 20th birthday. Even in middle and upper income families, marriage and childbearing in the teen years were accepted, until college graduation became expected for women in these social classes. Health and social problems were believed to be related to *illegitimacy* at any age, not to adolescent child rearing regardless of marital status. In fact, a review of the medical and social welfare literature prior to 1960 reveals few references to adolescent, teenage, or school-age pregnancy or parenting. It is only in the mid-1960s that these subjects, rather than births outside of marriage, began to attract the attention of health, education, and social service professionals.

One triggering factor appears to have been the research associated with the War on Poverty initiated by President Lyndon Johnson in 1964. As the soldiers in that war began studying the problems associated with poverty, they found teenage mothers overrepresented in three areas: infant mortality, noncompletion of high school, and welfare dependency. Infant mortality was higher among children born to women under 20 than among those born to women in their 20s, although not as high as among children born to women over 35 (Hogue, Buehler, Strauss, & Smith, 1987). The most frequent reason given by women for dropping out of school was pregnancy. And the recipients of Aid to Families with Dependent Children (AFDC) were disproportionately women who had borne their first child before reaching age 20. These findings generated an interest in the problem of pregnancy in a group of women defined by age rather than by marital status, and scholars began to study the phenomenon.

Early studies, reviewed in the 1975 Conference on Consequences of Adolescent Pregnancy and Childbearing (Chilman, 1980), documented the relationship between teenage child rearing and poor pregnancy outcomes, academic underachievement, and welfare dependency. In 1971 Kantner and

79

Zelnik (1972) conducted the first of three studies of never-married women 15 to 19 years of age, and it became possible to compare the characteristics of young unmarried women who were or were not sexually active, using contraceptives, or pregnant. Two subsequent studies by this team (Zelnik & Kantner, 1977, 1980), as well as the 1982 National Survey of Family Growth (NSFG), Cycle III (Pratt, Mosher, Bachrach, & Horn, 1984), helped expand the picture of the sexual life of teenagers. Demographic studies clarified the relative importance of the baby boom and of the increased rates of sexual activity as reasons for the rising rate of teenage pregnancy; later they showed the effect of abortions and family planning in lowering these rates; and, most recently, they focused on the change in marital status among adolescent parents.

Meanwhile, studies using other large national data bases, such as the on-going Current Population Survey, the Panel Study of Income Dynamics, and the National Longitudinal Surveys, as well as studies of small areas, such as the Young Chicagoans Survey, and studies of programs designed to assist pregnant teenagers and their male partners, provided additional information about the characteristics of sexually active adolescents and young parents and about the relationship between poverty and adolescent parenting.

This chapter will synthesize recent research in an attempt to address three questions. First, does adolescent parenting contribute to childhood poverty, and, if so, why? Second, what is the effect of adolescent parenting on children's health, intellectual development, and behavior? Finally, what social policies and programs are currently addressing the problem of adolescent parenting?

How many pregnant adolescents and adolescent parents are there and who are they?

Before examining the research for answers to these questions, it is essential to consider the dimensions of the problem, including rates of sexual activity, pregnancy, childbearing, and child rearing among women under 20 and the patterns of sexuality and parenting among young fathers.

Female sexual activity, pregnancy, and parenting

In 1982, 19.2% of all women had experienced intercourse by age 15; 43.0% by age 17; and 70.7% by age 19 (Pratt, Mosher, Bachrach, & Horn, 1984).[1] By 1988, the percentages for those having *premarital* sexual intercourse at the same ages were 25.6%, 51.0%, and 75.3% (Centers for Disease Control,

---

1 For a comparison of the data on adolescent sexuality in the NSFG, Cycle III, and in the earlier studies by Kantner and Zelnik, see Hofferth, Kahn, & Baldwin, 1987.

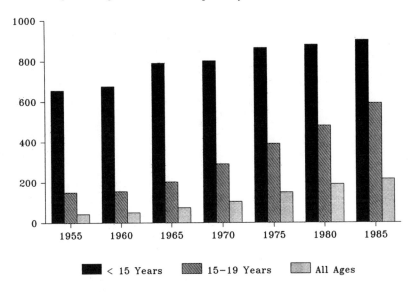

Figure 4.1. Number of births to unmarried women per 1,000 live births in specified group, 1955–1988.

1991). Despite this high level of sexual activity, not all sexually active adolescent females become pregnant nor do all pregnancies lead to live births or active child rearing. An oft-quoted figure is that 4 in 10 females become pregnant before their 20th birthday (Alan Guttmacher Institute, 1981). Hayes (1987) estimated that in 1984 over one million women under the age of 20 become pregnant, 46.7% gave birth, 40.0% had induced abortions, and 13.3% had miscarriages. The ratio of abortions to births was about 1.5 among adolescents under 15, but this figure declined to about 0.66 by ages 18 and 19.

Almost all adolescents who give birth, including those who are unmarried, choose to keep their infants at least in the immediate postpartum period. Experts estimate that less than 10% of infants are given up formally for adoption after birth. Follow-up studies, however, show many infants and children living separately from their biological mothers, with sisters, aunts, grandmothers, or other relatives, usually in informal relationships but occasionally as a result of a formal adoption (Hayes, 1987).

Demographic differences. In 1988, there were 489,941 births to women under the age of 20, representing 12.5% of all births in that year. Over a quarter (25.7%) of all births were to unmarried women. Among those women under 15 years of age, 93.6% were unmarried, and among those 15 to 19, 65.3% (see Figure 4.1). The percentage of births to married women increases with age to age 35 (National Center for Health Statistics, 1990).

Blacks generally initiate sexual activity earlier than whites and are more

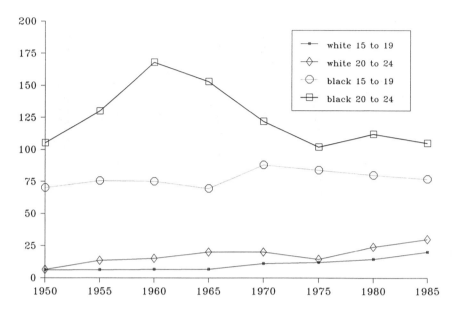

Figure 4.2. Number of births per 1,000 unmarried women, 15 to 24 years old, by race: 1950 to 1985. *Source*: U.S. Department of Commerce, Bureau of the Census, *Historical Statistics of the United States to 1975*. U.S. Department of Health and Human Services, National Center for Health Statistics, *Monthly Vital Statistics Report*, various years.

likely to be sexually active in any teen year. Although the *number* of pregnancies is much higher among white than black adolescents, the *rates* are higher among blacks, particularly at the younger ages. The gap between white rates and black rates is diminishing, however, with the white rates increasing as the black ones decrease. The rate of abortions is higher among blacks than among whites. Rates of premarital conceptions and births outside of marriage are higher among blacks than whites, but again the gap is diminishing (see Figure 4.2). Adoptions are more frequent among whites than blacks (Hayes, 1987).

Hispanic teenagers have levels of sexual activity closer to that of whites than blacks. In 1984 Hispanic adolescents gave birth to an estimated 59,000 infants. Hispanic adolescent fertility, however, is higher than non-Hispanic, and a higher percentage of Hispanic as compared to non-Hispanic births are to women under 20 (17% vs. 12.5%) (Hayes, 1987).

Time trends. The rates of female sexual activity increased at all ages and among all races during the 1970s but appear to have leveled off in the 1980s.

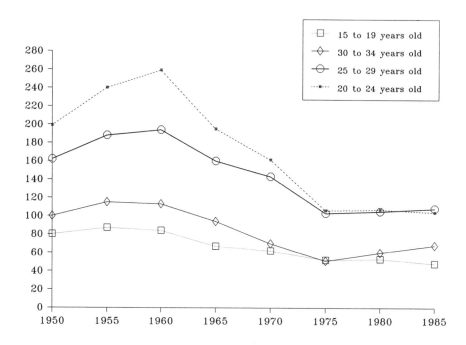

Figure 4.3. Number of births per 1,000 women, by age of mother: 1950 to 1985. *Source*: U.S. Department of Commerce, Bureau of the Census, *Historical Statistics of the United States to 1975*, U.S. Department of Health and Human Services, National Center for Health Statistics, *Monthly Vital Statistics Report*, various years.

Rates of pregnancy also increased until the early 1980s, when they began to decline (see Figure 4.3).

The fertility rate for 15- to 19-year-olds reached a postwar peak in the mid-1950s. It declined through the 1960s and early 1970s, and has been relatively stable since 1976 (1988: 15–17 = 33.8; 18–19 = 81.7). This trend parallels the fertility rate for all women, which also declined between the 1950s and 1987. It increased in 1988 and 1989 (National Center for Health Statistics, 1990.) The birth rate for 10- to 14-year-olds has fluctuated between 0.8 and 1.3 (1988) in the same period, but there are less than 15,000 births per year in this age group (National Center for Health Statistics, 1990). Most of the decline in adolescent births seems to be related to an increase in abortions, but some proportion may be attributable to improved contraception.

The rate of adoption is believed to have declined. However, the Reagan administration's efforts to reduce the federal government's data collection activities have made accurate figures particularly difficult to obtain in this area.

Given a general decline in the rate of teenage births since 1960, the strong societal concern about this problem starting in the late 1970s is puzzling. Several reasons for the attention have been suggested. One was the large *number* of births to teenage women in the 1960s and 1970s, close to or just over 600,000 from 1960 through 1975. The decrease in *rates* had not compensated for the increase in the *number* of teenage women who could become pregnant as the baby boom generation reached sexual maturity. Another reason was the large percentage of all births that were to teenagers, between 18 and 20% between 1971 and 1976. The percentage peaked at 19.7 in 1973. Concern was also expressed about the high rate of abortions among teenagers. In addition, expectations for women were increasing. Women were expected to prepare for a career and enter the labor market, goals that teenage parenthood usually precluded.

Perhaps of greatest importance in generating societal concern was the increasing rate of teenage births outside of marriage. In 1970, the birth rate for unmarried women ages 15 to 19 was 22.4; in 1980, 27.6; and in 1988, 36.8. The comparative rates for all women between ages 15 and 44 were 26.4, 29.4, and 38.6. Thus the birth rate for unmarried teens rose 64% from 1970 to 1988 whereas that for all unmarried women rose only 46%. In 1955, among women under 15, there were 663 births to unmarried women for every 1,000 live births; by 1988 this number had risen to 936. Among women 15 to 19, the ratio rose from 142 to 653; and among all women it rose from 45 to 257 (see Figure 4.1) (National Center for Health Statistics, 1990).

Male sexual activity and parenthood

Males initiate sexual activity earlier than females and black males do so before white males. Over 16% of all males are sexually active by age 15 and 83% by age 20. For blacks the percentages are 42.4% and 93.9% (Hayes, 1987).

An analysis of 1984 data from the National Longitudinal Survey of Labor Market Experience of Youth revealed that 6.8% of 20- to 27-year-old males had a child as a teenager, 5.5% outside of marriage (Marsiglio, 1987). At age 18, 2.2% were fathers and 1.4% were absent fathers; at 19, 5.8% were fathers and 2.4% were absent; and at 20, 9.6% were fathers and 3.9% were absent. The percentage of males with children was higher among blacks and Hispanics, and the percentage of absent fathers was higher among blacks at all three ages and among Hispanics at age 20 only (Lerman, 1986).

Does adolescent parenting contribute to childhood poverty?

The first major popular report on adolescent pregnancy, *11 Million Teenagers: What Can Be Done about the Epidemic of Adolescent Pregnancies in the United*

States, was published by the Alan Guttmacher Institute (AGI) in 1976. The report stated that "Teen Mothers Face Greater Risk of Unemployment, Welfare Dependency" (p. 26); "The Younger the Woman at First Birth, the Poorer the Family" (p. 27); and "Twice as Many Young as Older Families are Poor" (p. 27). Although these three statements are still generally true, current analyses of these problems associated with adolescent pregnancy are more sophisticated than those cited in the AGI document.

Poverty at the birth of a child

Actually, it is more difficult than might be expected to obtain information about the poverty status of children born to adolescent mothers. Data on economic status are not included on birth certificates, so poverty status at birth is not usually known for nationwide samples. Data on poverty status of families, such as that collected by the Current Population Survey, group the youngest head of household as 15- to 24-year-olds and do not routinely give the age of the mother at first birth in poverty households. For policy development and program planning purposes, it is also essential to decide whether child poverty status is to be determined at birth, years 1 to 5, or later. Despite the data limitations, it seems clear that women who bear their first child before age 20 are likely to be in poverty following the birth of that child and for several years thereafter. In 1988, 29.7% of families with a householder below 25 years of age were below the poverty level, as compared to 10.1% of those 25 to 64 years of age (U.S. Bureau of the Census, 1989).

Many studies of the economic status of adolescent mothers and their children use as indicators the receipt of AFDC or other welfare benefits such as food stamps or Medicaid. Eligibility for AFDC and Medicaid are established by the states and are highly variable across the states, so such data do not accurately reflect the percentage of young families in poverty. Nevertheless, Moore (1978) showed that approximately half of AFDC payments in 1975 went to households containing at least one woman who had borne her first child before age 20. More recent studies confirm the fact that teenage mothers are overrepresented among welfare families. Few studies, however, compare the percentage of younger and older mothers who receive AFDC.

The permanence of poverty

Given that adolescent mothers frequently are in poverty when they bear their children, how permanent is that poverty? Infants and young children born to teenage mothers often live in households with incomes below the federal poverty line; but as the children grow older, many of these families achieve incomes above the poverty level and are able to leave the welfare roles.

The various sources of support for adolescent mothers and their children were studied in two samples of largely black and poor women in the late 1960s and early 1970s. In New Haven, Connecticut, 80% of the study group was receiving some type of welfare assistance at the time that they registered for prenatal care. This percentage declined to 77% at 3 months, 69% at 15 months, and 61% at 26 months postpartum. In Baltimore, Maryland, almost two-thirds of the study group were on welfare between their pregnancies and the five-year follow-up. At five years postpartum, two-fifths were receiving benefits. Both samples were reinterviewed approximately 20 years after the birth of their first child. By then only 18% of the New Haven and 29% of the Baltimore samples had received welfare payments in the last year and almost half of both samples had incomes over $15,000 (Furstenberg, Brooks-Gunn, & Morgan, 1987; Horwitz, Klerman, Kuo, & Jekel, 1991). Hence, many of those women pregnant as adolescents eventually escaped from poverty and welfare dependence, particularly if they completed their education and had few children. Welfare dependence during pregnancy and for several years after is almost inevitable for women who are either unmarried or from poverty families. For teenage mothers this occurs early in their lives, and they may enter the labor market in their mid- or late 20s. Women who bear children while in their 20s may have long periods of welfare dependency at a later age.

On the basis of its review of many studies of the economic status of families formed by adolescent mothers, the Panel on Adolescent Pregnancy and Childbearing of the National Research Council (NRC) concluded:

> While the popular image of severe and life-long social and economic disadvantage for adolescent mothers is exaggerated, women who begin childbearing as teenagers are nevertheless at greater disadvantage than those who delay childbearing. Because they are likely to complete less schooling and to have more children, their ability to obtain positions with higher wages is reduced, and their earnings usually must support a larger family. In addition, because those who begin childbearing at a younger age have fewer prospects of achieving a stable marital relationship, many more of these women are the only or the major source of economic support for their families. . . . Despite the fact that differences in work status and income between early and later childbearers diminish somewhat over time, women who enter parenthood as teenagers are at greater risk of living in poverty both in the short and long term (Hayes, 1987, p. 132).

Although some women who give birth as teenagers eventually become self-sufficient and achieve satisfying lives, questions remain about the short- and long-term consequences of poverty for their children. In both the New Haven and the Baltimore follow-up studies, a large proportion of the children, now in their late teens, were experiencing educational and social problems (Furstenberg et al., 1987; Furstenberg, Levine, & Brooks-Gunn, 1990). But whether these problems differed in type or in magnitude from those experienced by children of older mothers who spent similar lengths of time in poverty is unknown.

Why does adolescent pregnancy contribute to childhood poverty?

An understanding of the mechanisms by which adolescent pregnancy contributes to temporary or permanent childhood poverty is essential to the development of programs to correct the situation. This analysis will be divided into three major sections. The first section will describe the immediate causes of poverty among children of adolescent mothers: inadequate earnings by the mother, father, or other older household members; the absence of support from the father; or insufficient welfare benefits. The second section will explore some reasons for these phenomena: inadequate education, unstable marriages, large family size, and inadequate work experiences. Given the fact that adolescent childbearing is associated with negative economic consequences, the third section will suggest some reasons why some adolescents initiate sexual activity early, have unprotected intercourse, and decide to bear and rear children.

Immediate causes

Traditionally, the major sources of support for children are the earnings of the mother, father, or other family members; families without such income usually depend on welfare benefits. If a family's earnings and/or welfare benefits are absent or inadequate, the child or children are likely to live in poverty (Bane & Ellwood, 1989).

Maternal earnings. The rate of employment among adolescent mothers with young children is relatively low. Unless a family member is willing to baby-sit or low-cost child care is available, the new mother must stay home to care for her infant. Even if child care is available, adolescent mothers may chose to complete high school rather than find employment. Those who seek employment may have trouble obtaining jobs at a wage that lifts them and their child or children out of poverty. Women who begin childbearing early earn less money than those who defer childbearing.

Paternal support. As the majority of adolescent mothers are unmarried, a *husband's* earnings are often not available. Even if an adolescent mother marries, the presence of a husband does not assure that the family will be economically secure. Particularly if the husband is himself a teenager or is in his early 20s, he may be unemployed or working at a job that does not pay enough to support a family. Because in some states the presence of a male wage earner, regardless of his income, makes the family ineligible for AFDC and for Medicaid, marriage to the child's father if he is un- or underemployed will not enable the mother to avoid poverty.

Courts may determine that a father is legally responsible for his children, regardless of marital status or AFDC support. The federal and state governments are increasingly active in the pursuit of fathers who do not meet their obligations, particularly if the mother is receiving AFDC. States are less likely to attempt to secure child support if the father is a teenager, however, because many teenage fathers are poor and undereducated and have few economic resources. Not all fathers of children borne by teenage mothers, however, are themselves teenagers.

A 1980 Wisconsin study showed that among single mothers whose first birth occurred when they were under age 20, 25.4% received child support within the year as compared to 35.7% of single mothers who had their first birth at 20 or older. Among those who received child support, the mean annual amount for teenage mothers was $1,690 and for older mothers, $2,245 (Danziger & Nichols-Casebolt, 1987/1988).

Even when child support is ordered and payments are made, if the mother is receiving AFDC only $50 per month goes to the family. The rest of the aid is returned to the state and federal governments. Absent fathers may provide some cash to adolescent mothers "under the table"; the amounts, however, are usually meager and tend to decline with time.

Family support. For economic and social support reasons, many adolescents remain in their parents' homes in the years immediately following the birth of their first child. If the family income was sufficiently high prior to the infant's birth, the additional family member may not reduce the family to poverty levels. But often the family was in poverty prior to the birth or the birth caused their income to become inadequate, so many children of adolescent mothers are in poverty even though they do not live in independent households. Those who live in independent households, however, are even more likely to be in poverty.

Welfare support. Finally, one of the major reasons why children of adolescent mothers are in poverty is that welfare payments rather than household earnings are the major source of support – and welfare payments are very low. In 1989, according to the Children's Defense Fund, the combined value of AFDC and food stamps was less than the federal poverty level for a family of three in 48 states and the District of Columbia. It was less than three- quarters of the poverty level in 30 states and less than half of the poverty level in 2 states (Children's Defense Fund, 1990).

Pathways to poverty

Education, marital status, and family size appear to affect the ability of adolescent mothers to earn sufficient income to support themselves and their children adequately. Similar factors influence the economic status of the children's fathers.

Education. A large prospective nationwide study of high school boys and girls, Project Talent, found that approximately one-fifth of young women who gave birth before age 18 graduated from high school at age 18 as compared to nearly three-quarters of those who waited to have a child until age 18 or 19 and to almost nine-tenths of those who waited until age 20 or later. By age 29, one-half of the earliest childbearers had high school diplomas or the equivalent as compared to over four-fifths of those who waited until 18 or 19 and to almost all of those who waited until 20 or older. The findings were similar in relation to college with 1.6% of the earliest mothers receiving degrees, 7.9% of the intermediate group, and 22.4% of the oldest group. These findings held when possible confounding variables were controlled (Card & Wise, 1978).

A comparable study was conducted more recently using data from the National Longitudinal Survey of Work Experience of Youth (NLSY). Among women who were 27 years of age in 1983, 95% of those without children had completed high school as compared to 79% of those who conceived and gave birth after leaving school, 64% of those who gave birth before leaving school, and 53% of those who conceived before leaving school and gave birth within seven months after leaving. Rates of high school completion in each category were similar for blacks and whites but much lower for Hispanics. The General Educational Development (GED) program, which grants high school credit through the testing of competency in mathematics, social studies, science, and reading and writing skills, was particularly important for young mothers. Among those who completed high school, 87% had received high school diplomas and 13%, GED certificates (Mott & Marsiglio, 1985).

The rate of high school completion among young mothers increased between the mid-1960s and the present, perhaps as a result of Title IX legislation or of special programs for pregnant students. Childless women and those who give birth at later ages, however, also have experienced gains in educational attainment. Thus teenage mothers are still at the same relative disadvantage as compared to other women (McCarthy & Radish, 1982).

Analyses of the National Longitudinal Surveys of Work Experience of Young Women and of Youth demonstrate the relationship between education, receiving welfare, and employment. Among those mothers who were 14 to 22 years old when they were surveyed in 1979, the percentage receiving AFDC was 9.1% among white high school graduates, 16.9% among white high school dropouts, 21.2% among black high school graduates, and 42.6% among black high school dropouts. Their labor force participation rate (percentage of population group working or looking for work) also varied by education: 38.2% of black high school dropouts were in the labor force as compared to 47.2% of white high school dropouts, 55.3% of white high school graduates, and 66.5% of black high school graduates. The unemployment rate (percentage of labor force without a job but looking for work) was lowest among white high school graduates (19.2%) and highest among black high school dropouts (81.6%) (Mott & Maxwell, 1981).

Marital status. Increasingly, lower and middle class households require two incomes to support a family. Thus the high rate of childbearing outside of marriage makes it more likely that the children of adolescent mothers will be in poverty. Although many adolescent mothers marry eventually, many of the marriages are unstable. Whereas early marriage may lead to dropping out of school and to large family size, marriage to employed men is one important way of avoiding poverty or of leaving poverty. The increasing delay in age at first marriage and the low rate of remarriage among black women is one cause of persistent poverty for black children. Several researchers have suggested that single motherhood among blacks is related to the relatively small pool of marriageable males. High rates of male mortality and incarceration, combined with increasing rates of joblessness, are hypothesized to result in female-headed households and low incomes (Wilson, 1987).

Family size. Large completed family size also contributes to poverty. A large number of children makes it more difficult for mothers to enter the labor force and to hold a job once it is found. Also, a low-paying job may be sufficient for a small family, but the same wages may leave a large family below the federal poverty level. Traditionally, the earlier a woman began to have children, the larger the number of children she eventually had. Fortunately, the disparity in family size between younger and older mothers has begun to decline, as adolescents and young mothers appear to use effective methods of family planning, to abort unwanted or mistimed fetuses, and, somewhat surprisingly, to be sterilized.

Drawing conclusions from these studies is made difficult by two factors. The first is that few studies are available on teenagers who gave birth in the 1980s. Most of the studies are of earlier cohorts, and the economic situation, particularly for poor families, may have changed sufficiently to make early study findings almost irrelevant. The second is the problem of causal direction, separating the effects of teenage childbearing from the poverty of the mothers' parent(s), the mothers' low academic achievement, and other associated problems. In many studies of early childbearing, differences between younger and older mothers diminish, if not disappear, once economic status and related variables are controlled. If the young women who are now giving birth before they reach age 20 delayed their births but otherwise did not change – that is, their education, educational aspirations, marital status, and other characteristics remained the same – would the economic status of their children be improved? Only if the delay led to changes in education, marital status, and employment might it lead to better economic circumstances.

Factors leading to early childbearing

Although not all adolescent parents are from poor families, a large percentage of them are. In general, adolescents from poor and minority families are more likely to initiate sexual activity early, to use contraceptives irregularly or ineffectively, and, if the female becomes pregnant, to choose to carry to term and rear the child rather than to abort or to place the baby for adoption.

The effect of social and environmental factors on the fertility of black adolescents was analyzed in the Young Chicagoans Survey, based on a random sample of over 1,000 unmarried black females 13 to 19 years of age in 1979. The investigators reported that the risk of becoming pregnant was strongly associated with the social environment. Those women from high-risk environments, characterized by lower class status, residence in a ghetto neighborhood, a nonintact family, five or more siblings, a sister who became a teenage mother, and lax parental control of dating, had pregnancy rates over 8 times higher than those women who did not experience such an environment (Hogan & Kitagawa, 1985). Use and nonuse of contraceptives was one mediator for this association. Among females and males, social class and career aspirations were significantly related to use of contraceptives at first intercourse. In addition, for females only, neighborhood quality and parents' marital status affected use (Hogan, Astone, & Kitagawa, 1985).

The reasons why adolescents allow themselves to bear and raise children are unclear. Earlier studies indicating that a high percentage of adolescent pregnancies were unwanted are now being questioned. Some but not all adolescent pregnancies are truly mistakes. Most occur because the adolescent did not try hard enough to prevent them. Some are actually planned because the young woman wants the attention of pregnancy or motherhood, hopes to "keep" her male partner by having a child, wants to escape from home, or believes that the child will make her feel loved. Adolescent pregnancy and parenting provide an entry into adulthood for both adolescent females and males and may even enhance self-esteem.

The effect of adolescent parenting on children

Adolescent childbearing has negative effects on children as well as on their parents. But again, it is difficult to separate the effects of poverty and maternal education from that of maternal age per se.

Health

Rates of infant mortality and low birth weight are higher among the children of adolescent mothers than among the children of older mothers. Early studies suggested that anatomical or physiological immaturity accounted for less than optimal outcomes of pregnancy. More recent analyses, however, have indicated that the problem is largely one of poverty, nutritional inadequacy, and insufficient prenatal care rather than age per se (Hofferth, 1987a). When socioeconomic status is controlled, the maternal age differences diminish. Moreover, when adolescents receive prenatal care adequate in quality, content, and quantity, their birth outcomes are usually as good as those of older mothers.

Intellectual development

The children of adolescent mothers score lower on standardized tests of language and intellectual functioning beginning in the preschool years and continuing into the elementary grades. Again, some studies have found that the difference between the children of older and of younger mothers is largely a function of other social factors, such as family socioeconomic class, parental education, and household composition. Although there are fewer long-term studies, children of adolescent mothers appear still to be at a disadvantage on test scores, academic achievement, retention in grade, and teacher evaluations (Brooks-Gunn & Furstenberg, 1986; Hofferth, 1987a).

Behavior problems

Children of adolescent mothers appear more likely than children of older mothers to have behavior problems ranging from hyperactivity to poor impulse control. High rates of school misbehavior and suspension have been reported with high frequency in some studies. In high school, delinquency, substance abuse, and early sexual activity are often problems. Most research has found that differences between the children of older and of younger mothers diminish but do not disappear when other social factors are controlled (Brooks-Gunn & Furstenberg, 1986; Hofferth, 1987a).

Mechanisms of effect

Many theories have been proposed to account for the less than optimum intellectual achievement and social behavior of the children of adolescent mothers. The inadequate education of the mother herself certainly is an important factor. The pressures of poverty leave the mother with little time for meeting a child's needs, and they create an environment that is not conducive to intellectual development or appropriate behavior. The psychological immaturity of the mother, particularly in the child's youngest years, is receiving increasing attention. Adolescence is a period of striving for independence. Pregnancy-related needs, as well as the demands of an infant or a toddler, may increase the adolescent mother's dependence on other family members and interfere with her attaining her own independence.

One intervening variable may be parenting behavior, particularly during infancy. Children of adolescent mothers are more often reported as victims of child abuse and neglect than are the children of older mothers. Whether this disparity is an artifact of reporting or a real difference is uncertain. Again, when social class is controlled the differences between younger and older mothers diminish (Kinard & Klerman, 1980; Leventhal, Egerter, & Murphy, 1984). Observations of maternal–child interaction often show that adolescent mothers are less supportive of their children's emotional and intellectual development than older mothers. Older studies of this type were criticized for finding very small differences, for not using low-income mothers as controls, and for possible rater bias (Hofferth, 1987a), but more recent studies have shown maternal age differences even when education and social class are comparable.

Another factor affecting the development of the children of adolescent mothers may be the lack of a father or father figure (National Commission on Children, 1990). As noted earlier, these children often spend much of their lives in single-mother families, an environment associated with more behavior problems and poorer school achievement than two-parent families even when income is controlled (cf. McLanahan, Astone, & Marks, this volume).

Social policies and programs

The evidence presented in the preceding sections indicates that, in most instances, adolescent childbearing has negative consequences for children. Children of adolescent parents are more likely than those of older mothers to be raised in poverty with all its attendant difficulties and to have intellectual and behavioral problems. This is a result not only of the poverty but also of their parents' inability to raise them appropriately. Thus, there is an urgent need for policies and programs directed at (1) preventing early childbearing whenever possible; and (2) ameliorating its consequences, when prevention has failed. Several recent publications have addressed these issues, most notably the report of the NRC's Panel on Adolescent Pregnancy and Childbearing, *Risking the Future: Adolescent Sexuality, Pregnancy, and Childbearing* (Hayes, 1987); a series of brochures from the Children's Defense Fund's Adolescent Pregnancy Prevention Clearinghouse, and a Family Impact

Seminar (1989) report, *Teenage pregnancy prevention programs: What have we learned?*

Some adolescents are convinced that bringing up a child would interfere with their life plans, and this group will either delay sexual activity or find a source of contraceptives or of abortion almost regardless of the difficulty. Another group of adolescents actively seek pregnancy or see so few disadvantages to early child rearing that they do little or nothing to prevent it. A third group is "on the fence." They may have some questions about the advisability of starting a family, but they may not take the actions necessary to delay childbearing because of inadequate information, the absence of family and peer support, or the difficulty in obtaining needed services. This third group is probably the one most likely to benefit from prevention-oriented programs.

To address all of these issues, the NRC panel suggested that three types of preventive interventions were needed to avoid pregnancy and childbearing: those that impart knowledge or influence attitudes, those that provide access to contraception, and those that enhance life options.[2]

Knowledge and attitudes. Programs that impart knowledge or influence attitudes include sex and family life education, assertiveness and decision-making training, family communication training, teenage theater, and media approaches. Sex and family life education programs vary widely in effectiveness. Well-conducted programs increase student knowledge and may even make students more tolerant of others' attitudes and behavior; but such programs have not been demonstrated to change attitudes and behavior about nonmarital sexual activity or family planning. Assertiveness and decision-making training programs are usually integrated into sex and family life education courses. They teach problem solving and interpersonal communication through role playing and other techniques.

Several demonstrations of programs to improve parent–child communication are currently underway, including a major effort by the Girls Clubs of America. This approach is promising, given research findings showing that mother–daughter communication may encourage contraceptive use. Preliminary results suggest that planned programs can increase communication about sexual matters.

Teenage theater, in which adolescents prepare and act out skits and often handle audience questions after the performance, are an attractive and relatively inexpensive method of increasing awareness of the problems of adolescent sexuality and parenting among adolescents. They can also be used to increase community knowledge of and support for local programs.

2 For publications describing the programs mentioned in the following sections, see the NRC monograph, *Risking the Future.*

Efforts are being made to use the mass media in several ways that might influence adolescent behavior. The Children's Defense Fund has prepared and distributed nationwide posters for use in school and on buses and billboards. Several national and local television and radio stations have presented documentaries on the subject. Newspapers and magazines periodically feature the problem of adolescent childbearing. Public service announcements have been prepared for television and radio, but there is some resistance to the use of material that is very specific about sexual activity or contraception. Several organizations have tried to influence television writers to provide more positive views about abstinence and contraceptive use and more realistic portrayals of the consequences of early or unprotected sexual activity. Contraceptive advertising is another media approach to pregnancy prevention, but one that has met with considerable resistance.

Few programs targeted at knowledge and attitudes are able to document effects on behavior. A recent report from the School/Community Program for Sexual Risk Reduction among Teens in the western portion of a South Carolina county, however, suggests that a communitywide program had positive effects. This educational intervention was targeted at parents, teachers, community leaders, and ministers and representatives of churches, as well as at children enrolled in the public schools. Designed for never-married teens and preteens, the program attempted primarily to postpone initial voluntary sexual intercourse and secondarily to promote the consistent use of contraception among those individuals who chose to become sexually active and who did not desire a pregnancy. The project used various techniques to increase decision-making skills, improve interpersonal communications, enhance self-esteem, align personal values with those of the family, church, and community, and increase knowledge of human reproductive anatomy, physiology, and contraception. The research team reported a reduction in the estimated pregnancy rate in the intervention area as compared to the other section of the county and three other counties with similar sociodemographic characteristics (Vincent, Clearie, & Schluchter, 1987).

Access to contraception. Programs that increase access to contraception and abortion include those that provide contraceptive services in private physicians' offices and in various types of clinics, make nonprescription contraceptives available in stores, and distribute condoms. They also include programs that conduct pregnancy testing and provide counseling services, maintain hot lines, and run school-based clinics.

Contraceptive services have become more available to adolescents in the last 20 years. Access is still difficult for some adolescents, however, because of financial barriers, distance and time problems, absence of public facilities in some areas coupled with reluctance to use private physicians, and, again in some areas and some facilities, issues of consent and confidentiality. Programs to attract adolescents to family planning services and to maintain them in care have been developed in many communities, and a great deal is known about what makes such programs more or less effective. For example, an AGI study showed that clinics that attract teenagers are more likely to have special outreach and follow-up programs, programs for males, areawide hot lines, and specific recruitment activities. These clinics combine family planning with other health services, such as prenatal care or abortion, are more likely to provide free services to adolescents and to see them without appointments, and are less likely to require parental consent (Chamie, Eisman, Forrest, Orr, & Torres, 1982). Another study noted that the main factors influencing an adolescent's choice of a family planning clinic were confidentiality, a caring staff, and proximity (Zabin & Clark, 1983).

Adolescents who use effective contraceptive methods are less likely to become pregnant, and national data suggest that some of the overall decline in adolescent pregnancies is due to better use of contraceptives. Nevertheless, it is difficult to prove that family planning programs per se, particularly those publicly financed and operated by health departments, community health centers, Planned Parenthood organizations, hospitals, and other agencies, are effective in reducing adolescent pregnancy. Some area studies suggest that they are, although others show less positive results.

Community attitudes, as well as the attitudes of the individual store owners or store managers, determine whether nonprescription conctraceptives such as condoms and spermicides will be easily available to adolescents. Condoms also are being distributed free of charge by clinics, youth organizations, and public employment programs. Other groups make them available in places where young males congregate and through male outreach workers and give them to female adolescents to pass on to their male partners.

Pregnancy testing services provide an opportunity for family planning counseling, if the test is negative and a pregnancy was not planned. Unfortunately, some pregnancy testing is done at home, and some facilities provide the results of the test by phone or in a hurried manner. Thus, this excellent moment for teaching is often wasted because of insufficient or insensitive staff.

Hot lines have been organized in many communities to provide adolescents with confidential information about sexuality, contraception, abortion, and other sexually related matters. Program operators report high rates of utilization, if the line is adequately publicized.

School-based clinics are probably the fastest growing and most controversial approach to the prevention of adolescent childbearing. The original school-based clinic in St. Paul, Minnesota, demonstrated an ability to reduce fertility rates within the school; but there was no control group, and pregnancies ending in abortions were not included in the data analysis (Edwards, Steinman, Arnold, & Hakanson, 1980; Schorr, 1988). Nevertheless, because it was one of the few programs to show positive results on fertility, the school-based clinic model has been actively promoted by many groups, and the number of such clinics is increasing rapidly.

The clinics are usually primary-care centers within or near the grounds of a high school. They offer students a range of preventive services, such as physical examinations for athletics or work and immunizations, and they treat minor health problems such as acne, dysmenorrhea, and minor injuries. Nearly all of these clinics provide counseling on sexually related matters, although facilities and even individual practitioners within a facility vary on whether they raise the issue with all who visit the clinic, regardless of cause, or whether they wait for the adolescent to mention it. Most clinics also refer for family planning services, but very few actually dispense contraceptives, with the possible exception of condoms.

Evaluations of the impact of school-based clinics on pregnancies and births show mixed results, perhaps because of variations among the programs (Center for Population Options, 1989). One program, the Self Center in Baltimore, was located in a storefront adjacent to, but separate from a senior and a junior high school. The center provided sex education, counseling, and free contraceptive services. Its evaluation showed positive results in knowledge, postponement of first intercourse, clinic attendance for both sexes, contraceptive use, and reduction in pregnancies (Schorr, 1988; Zabin, Hirsch, Smith, Street, & Hardy, 1986).

As noted earlier, abortions make it possible for a large number of adolescents to avoid childbearing. The percentage of pregnancies ending in abortions appears to have stabilized after many years of increase. Public attitudes and the active opposition of the federal administration as well as of many members of Congress have made it difficult to advocate abortion as one solution to the problem of adolescent childbearing. Moreover, substantial barriers exist to the use of abortions, including cost, which cannot be covered by federal Medicaid and is not covered by many state programs; absence in many areas of any providers or of providers who will accept patients covered by state Medicaid or patients who need free or reduced-cost service; distance and time problems even when providers are available; and laws requiring parental permission. Nevertheless, the NRC panel supported retaining the availability of abortion, without which many adolescents would be forced to continue unwanted pregnancies. Easier availability of services might increase the percentage of pregnant teenagers who chose this option.

Adoption continues as an alternative to abortion and to adolescent child rearing. It has been actively promoted by the federal Office of Adolescent Pregnancy Programs, despite the decline in the number of adolescents relinquishing their children.

Enhance life options. Unless adolescent males and females truly believe that having a child will interfere with the way in which they would like to live their lives, many of them are going to have children because it is easy to do and because they believe it is satisfying and fulfilling. Changing these attitudes and the resulting behaviors is very difficult, but these are the objectives of the so-called life options approach. Such programs are designed to improve life planning, to provide role models and mentoring, to improve school performance, and to enhance employability by teaching job skills, finding employment, and providing incentives for firms to hire adolescents.

Life planning programs are usually directed at female adolescents and operate on several levels. They try to improve self-esteem and to explore life choices other than motherhood and also try to link these goals with advice about sexual activity and contraception. Several demonstration programs, including the Teen Outreach Program (TOP) in St. Louis, Missouri, have shown encouraging initial results (Allen, Philliber, & Hoggson, 1990). Role modeling and mentoring programs are directed at both males and females and often involve peers as well as adults.

Programs designed to keep adolescents in school and to provide them with marketable skills or to assist them in obtaining full- or part-time employment may be able to prevent adolescent childbearing by convincing youth that alternative approaches to adulthood are within their reach. Most such programs, however, are evaluated in terms of school completion and employment, not delay of childbearing. An exception is the Summer Training and Employment Program (STEP), which has shown more responsible use of birth control among participants (Family Impact Seminar, 1989).

Amelioration of effects of adolescent child rearing

No society has been able to prevent all childbearing among adolescents. International comparisons, however, indicate that this country lags behind many other industrialized nations in the prevention of early childbearing (Jones et al., 1986). And this society, with its ambivalent attitudes toward contraception, abortion, and female/male sexuality, its blatant exploitation of sexual themes, its inadequate educational system, and its high rates of poverty, is unlikely to make major progress in the near future. Thus, it is urgent that programs that would ameliorate the effect on children of being reared by adolescent parents be expanded.

Reducing poverty. One reason why children of adolescent parents are likely to be in poverty is insufficient earned family income. Therefore, programs are needed to help adolescent mothers and fathers obtain employment that would raise them out of poverty. These would include many of the life options programs discussed in the previous section. Counseling, role modeling, and mentoring would make adolescents aware of what they can do with their lives, and programs designed to promote education, job training, and employment would help the adolescents to achieve their goals. Especially for the adolescent woman, child care is essential if the young mother is to complete her education, receive employment training, and obtain work. In addition, high-quality child care can be a positive intervention to counteract the effects of poverty on children's intellectual and social development (cf. Phillips; Ramey & Campbell, this volume).

Poverty and its negative effect on children also can be reduced by increasing welfare benefits. Children should not be punished for the "sins" of their parents. AFDC payments along with noncash programs such as Medicaid, the Special Supplemental Food Program for Women, Infants, and Children (WIC), food stamps, and housing, fuel, and other allowances should be sufficient to raise a household out of poverty. The fear that increasing benefits will encourage more women to have children or discourage mothers and fathers from seeking work appears unfounded. No research to date has shown such an effect, although there are indications that benefits may cause young mothers to leave their parents' household and, among older women, to dissolve a difficult marriage. Increasing welfare benefits, however, may improve the physical environment in which children are raised, thereby reducing their illnesses and injuries, and perhaps, by reducing the stresses caused by continuing financial pressures, may enhance children's self-esteem and the family's emotional climate (cf. McLoyd & Wilson, this volume).

The role of child support enforcement programs is debatable. They might serve as a deterrent to irresponsible male sexuality. If young men, or even older men, can be convinced that they will be required to support their children regardless of present or future marital status or present lack of financial resources, that they will be found regardless of their location, and that the requirement will be legally enforced, they might give more thought to engaging in unprotected intercourse. On the other hand, many fathers are currently without any or much income, and some have income from illegal sources. Moreover, the money that they pay does not significantly increase the mother's income if she receives AFDC. Also, pregnant adolescents may be reluctant to seek AFDC and the Medicaid necessary to finance prenatal care if they believe that they are going to be forced to reveal the name of their male partner. Pressure for child support on the male partner may cause him to be less attentive, to leave the area, or to engage in illegal activities. Thus, present disadvantages for mother and child must be balanced against the potential for payments in the future, and the income to the state balanced against both the state's expenses in obtaining child support and the small economic benefit to the mother.

Provision of services. Among the direct services needed by pregnant adolescents, young mothers and their children are those related to health, including prenatal care, care during labor and delivery, services for well, sick, and injured children, and nutritional supplementation. Programs across the country have shown that adolescents who receive comprehensive health services can have infants as healthy as those of older mothers (Hofferth, 1987b; Korenbrot, Showstack, Loomis, & Brindis, 1989).

Comprehensive service programs for pregnant and parenting adolescents also can incorporate objectives such as reducing subsequent pregnancies, completing parental education, decreasing welfare dependence, and developing parenting skills. Many such programs report delays in subsequent pregnancies, but within a year or two the family size of those served is usually the same as that of unserved controls. The programs are successful in maintaining many pregnant adolescents in school during pregnancy (or in returning dropouts to school) and in assisting them in staying in school after the birth of their child. Few programs follow the adolescents for a long enough time to determine the parents' welfare/employment status once their children are no longer infants (Hofferth, 1987b).

More research is needed about the most effective ways of improving the parenting skills of adolescent mothers and fathers in order to reduce the cognitive deficits and behavioral problems experienced by some of their children. Among the programs currently in operation are parenting education, family support, and home visiting – and these three forms are closely related (Schorr, 1988). Parenting education usually starts during the prenatal period and continues into the immediate postpartum period. It may take the form of classes in a clinic or a social agency, it may be done through home visiting, and it is certainly a part of family support programs. Often it is somewhat didactic and ends during infancy.

Family support programs are designed for families considered at high risk of child abuse and neglect, of dissolution, or of inadequate parenting. They are not directed exclusively at adolescents, although women who started child rearing as adolescents are frequently in the caseload. Services, including friendly support, counseling, referrals, and direct assistance with household tasks, may be offered in the home or in drop-in centers or family support centers. The objectives are both to relieve the stress of continual exposure to poor and otherwise disadvantaged environments and to assist families to find more effective ways to deal with their problems, including the care of their children.

Home visiting may be one component of a family support program or a separate service. Often it is more health oriented than the general family support services. The objectives of home visiting include reducing the number of low-birth weight infants, placing children in a medical care system, educating parents about how to help their children avoid illnesses and injuries, and preventing child abuse and neglect. Evaluations of these programs have shown positive effects (Chapman, Siegel, & Cross, 1990).

Programs directed at fathers. Increasing attention is being paid to the fathers of the children of adolescent mothers, especially if they are themselves teenagers or in their early 20s. Studies have suggested that some of these fathers, and perhaps many of them, are actually involved with the young mother and their infant or would be if encouraged. Much research is being conducted in this area, and several experimental programs have received support and are being implemented (Robinson, 1988; Sander & Rosen, 1987; Smollar & Ooms, 1987).

Conclusions

Programs that attempt to ameliorate the effects of the poverty and inadequate parenting skills characteristic of adolescent parents face a difficult, if not impossible, task. The effects of many years of poverty, low self-esteem, and inadequate schooling are hard to overcome in a few months during pregnancy, in the immediate postpartum period, or later in the life of a child. Nevertheless, several such programs have shown positive impacts, at least in regard to their short-term goals. Thus programs directed at already pregnant teenagers and their male partners, particularly if they are also young, should be continued, and the programs' activities expanded to include more attention to males, more support in the home, and assistance to young mothers for a longer time after the birth of the child. These programs, directed at the already pregnant, generate little conflict and usually are able to obtain support at federal, state, and local levels.

It remains likely, however, that programs that delay childbearing, indirectly through preventing poverty and improving education and aspirations or directly through provision of family life education and family planning and abortion services, will positively affect the lives of more children. (A study by Moore & Wertheimer [1984] actually modeled the greater effects of preventive as compared to ameliorative approaches on reducing AFDC payments to women aged 20 to 24.) The evaluative evidence in regard to the life options approaches, provision of contraceptives and abortion, and school-based or affiliated clinics suggests that such programs work, if pursued vigorously. Unfortunately, these programs are more controversial and have more difficulty obtaining the support they deserve.

Some final thoughts

We lack sufficient knowledge of how to improve the climate in which some children develop; and even when some answers are known, we seem to lack the will to implement them on the scale necessary to bring about significant change (Schorr, 1988). Of one thing we are certain, poverty is bad for most children, although a few strong individuals and families appear able to shield their children from its worst effects. Thus this country should expend major energies and funds on ways to reduce its rates of poverty through education, employment, and transfer payments. But although we continue to strive for such megalevel changes, we must also aggressively explore the potential of smaller and more discrete programs to reduce poverty and its effects on children. Programs designed to prevent child rearing among adolescent men and women should be given high priority; but because not all adolescent pregnancies can be prevented, programs to ameliorate their short- and long-term consequences also should be strengthened.

References

Alan Guttmacher Institute. (1976). *11 million teenagers: What can be done about the epidemic of adolescent pregnancies in the United States.* New York: Author.

Alan Guttmacher Institute. (1981). *Teenage pregnancy: The problem that hasn't gone away.* New York: Author.

Allen, J. P., Philliber, S., & Hoggson, N. (1990). School-based prevention of teenage pregnancy and school dropout: Process evaluation of the national replication of the Teen Outreach Program. *American Journal of Community Psychology, 18,* 505–524.

Bane, M. J., & Ellwood, D. T. (1989). One fifth of the nation's children: Why are they poor? *Science, 245,* 1047–1053.

Brooks-Gunn, J., & Furstenberg, F. F. Jr., (1986). The children of adolescent mothers: Physical, academic, and psychological outcomes. *Developmental Review, 6,* 224–251.

Card, J. J., & Wise, L. L. (1978). Teenage mothers and teenage fathers: The impact of early childbearing on the parents' personal and professional lives. *Family Planning Perspectives, 10,* 199–205.

Center for Population Options. (1989). *School-based clinics enter the '90s: Update, evaluation and future challenges.* Washington, DC: Author.

Centers for Disease Control.(1991). Premarital sexual intercourse among adolescent women – United States, 1970–1988. *Morbidity and Mortality Weekly Report, 39,* 929–932.

Chamie, M., Eisman, S., Forrest, J. D., Orr, M. T., & Torres, A. (1982). Factors affecting adolescents' use of family planning clinics. *Family Planning Perspectives, 14,* 126–139.

Chapman, J., Siegel, E., & Cross, A. (1990). Home visitors and child health: Analysis of selected programs. *Pediatrics, 85,* 1059–1068.

Children's Defense Fund. (1990). *S.O.S. America! A children's defense budget.* Washington, DC: Author.

Children's Defense Fund. *Adolescent Pregnancy Prevention Clearinghouse* (multiple publications).

Chilman, C. S. (1980). *Adolescent pregnancy and childbearing. Findings from research* (NIH Pub. No. 81-2077). Washington, DC: U.S. Government Printing Office.

Danziger, S. K., & Nichols-Casebolt, A. (1987/1988). Teen parents and child support: Eligibility, participation, and payment. *Journal of Social Service Research, 11,* 1–20.

Edwards, L. E., Steinman, M. E., Arnold, K. A., & Hakanson, E. Y. (1980). Adolescent pregnancy prevention services in high school clinics. *Family Planning Perspectives, 12,* 6–14.

Family Impact Seminar. (1989). *Teenage pregnancy prevention programs: What have we learned?* Washington, DC: Author.

Furstenberg, F. F., Jr., Brooks-Gunn, J., & Morgan, S. P. (1987). *Adolescent mothers in later life.* New York: Cambridge University Press.

Furstenberg, F. F., Jr., Levine, J. A., & Brooks-Gunn, J. (1990). The children of teenage mothers: Patterns of early childbearing in two generations. *Family Planning Perspectives,* 22, 54–61.

Hayes, C. D. (1987). *Risking the future: Adolescent sexuality, pregnancy, and childbearing.* Washington, DC: National Academy Press.

Hofferth, S. L. (1987a). The children of teenage childbearers. In S. L. Hofferth & C. D. Hayes (Eds.), *Risking the future: Adolescent sexuality, pregnancy, and childbearing: Vol. 2. Working papers and statistical appendices* (pp. 174–206). Washington, DC: National Academy Press.

Hofferth, S. L. (1987b). The effects of programs and policies on adolescent pregnancy and childbearing. In S. L. Hofferth & C. D. Hayes (Eds.), *Risking the future: Adolescent sexuality, pregnancy, and childbearing: Vol. 2. Working papers and statistical appendices* (pp. 207–263). Washington, DC: National Academy Press.

Hofferth, S. L., Kahn, J. R., & Baldwin, W. (1987). Premarital sexual activity among U.S. teenage women over the past decade. *Family Planning Perspectives, 19,* 46–53.

Hogan, D. P., Astone, N. M., Kitagawa, E. M. (1985). Social and environmental factors influencing contraceptive use among black adolescents. *Family Planning Perspectives, 17,* 165–169.

Hogan, D. P., & Kitagawa, E. M. (1985). The impact of social status, family structure, and neighborhood on the fertility of black adolescents. *American Journal of Sociology, 90,* 825–855.

Hogue, C. J. R., Buehler, J. W., Strauss, L. T., & Smith, J. C. (1987). Overview of the National Infant Mortality Surveillance (NIMS) project – design methods, and results. *Public Health Reports, 102,* 126–138.

Horwitz, S. M., Klerman, L. V., Kuo, H. S., & Jeckel, J. F. (1991). School-age mothers: Predictors of long-term educational and economic outcome. *Pediatrics, 87,* 862–868.

Jones, E. F., Forrest, J. D., Goldman, N., Henshaw, S., Lincoln, P., Rosoff, J. F., Westoff, C. F., & Wulf, D. (1986). *Teenage pregnancy in industrialized countries.* New Haven, CT: Yale University Press.

Kantner, J. F., & Zelnik, M. (1972). Sexual experiences of young unmarried women in the United States. *Family Planning Perspective, 4,* 9–18.

Kinard, E. M., & Klerman, L. V. (1980). Teenage parenting and child abuse: Are they related? *American Journal of Orthopsychiatry, 50,* 481–488.

Korenbrot, C. C., Showstack, J., Loomis, A., & Brindis, C. (1989). Birth weight outcomes in a teenage pregnancy case management project. *Journal of Adolescent Health Care, 10,* 97–104.

Lerman, R. I. (1986). Who are the young absent fathers? *Youth and Society, 18,* 3–27.

Leventhal, J. M., Egerter, S. A., & Murphy, J. M. (1984). Reassessment of the relationship of perinatal risk factors and child abuse. *American Journal of Diseases of Children, 139,* 1034–1039.

Marsiglio, W. (1987). Adolescent fathers in the United States: Their initial living arrangements, marital experiences and educational outcomes. *Family Planning Perspectives, 19,* 240–251.

McCarthy, J., & Radish, E. S. (1982). Education and childbearing among teenagers. *Family Planning Perspectives, 14,* 154–155.

Moore, K. A. (1978). Teenage childbirth and welfare dependency. *Family Planning Perspectives, 10,* 233–235.

Moore, K. A., & Wertheimer, R. E. (1984). Teenage childbearing and welfare: Preventive and ameliorative strategies. *Family Planning Perspectives, 16,* 285–289.

Mott, F. L., & Marsiglio, W. (1985). Early childbearing and completion of high school. *Family Planning Perspectives, 17,* 234–237.

Mott, F. L., & Maxwell, N. L. (1981). School-age mothers: 1968–1979. *Family Planning Perspectives, 13,* 287–292.

National Center for Health Statistics. (1990). Advance report of final natality statistics. *Monthly vital statistics report*, Vol. 39, No. 4, Suppl. (DHHS Pub. No. [PHS] 90–1120). Hyattsville, MD: Public Health Service, 1990.

National Commission on Children. (1990). *Opening doors for America's children.* Washington, DC: Author.

Pratt, W. F., Mosher, W. D., Bachrach, C. A., & Horn, M. C. (1984). Understanding U.S. fertility: Findings from the National Survey of Family Growth, Cycle III. *Population Bulletin* (entire issue).

Robinson, B. (1988). *Teenage fathers.* Lexington, MA: Heath.

Sander, J. H., & Rosen, J. L. (1987). Teenage fathers: Working with the neglected partner in adolescent childbearing. *Family Planning Perspectives, 19*, 107–110.

Schorr, L. B. (1988). *Within our reach: Breaking the cycle of disadvantage.* New York: Doubleday.

Smoller, J., & Ooms, T. (1987). *Young unwed fathers: Research review, policy dilemmas and options. Summary report.* Washington, DC: Family Impact Seminar.

U.S. Bureau of the Census. (1989). Money, income and poverty status of family and persons in the United States, 1988. Advance data from the March 1989 current population survey. Current Population Reports, Series P–60, No. 166. Washington, DC: U.S. Government Printing Office.

Vincent, M. L., Clearie, A. F., & Schluchter, M. D. (1987). Reducing adolescent pregnancy through school and community-based education. *Journal of the American Medical Association, 257*, 3382–3386.

Wilson, W. J. (1987). *The truly disadvantaged: The inner city, the underclass and public policy.* Chicago: University of Chicago Press.

Zabin, L. S., & Clark, S. D., Jr. (1983). Institutional factors affecting teenagers' choice and reasons for delay in attending a family planning clinic. *Family Planning Perspectives, 15*, 25–29.

Zabin, L. S., Hirsch, M. B., Smith, E. A., Street, R. & Hardy, J. B. (1986). Evaluation of a pregnancy prevention program for urban teenagers. *Family Planning Perspectives, 18*, 119–126.

Zelnik, M., & Kantner, J. F. (1977). Sexual and contraceptive experience of young unmarried women in the United States, 1976 and 1971. *Family Planning Perspectives, 9*, 55–71.

Zelnik, M., & Kantner, J. F. (1980). Sexual activity, contraceptive use and pregnancy among metropolitan-area teenagers: 1971–1979. *Family Planning Perspectives, 12*, 230–237.

5   The strain of living poor: Parenting, social support, and child mental health

Vonnie C. McLoyd and Leon Wilson

Chronic stressors, in combination with an unremitting, rapid succession of negative life events, militate against positive mental health in poor children (Belle, 1984). Poverty, especially if it is long standing, is a pervasive rather than bounded crisis distinguished by a high contagion of stressors that grind away and deplete emotional reserves (Makosky, 1982; Ray & McLoyd, 1986). The most glaring ongoing stressors derive from the ecological context – inadequate housing, environmental instability, and, in urban settings, dangerous neighborhoods. Tragic and riveting stories published in the media during the late 1980s chronicled poor, inner-city children's steady exposure to violence, death, and criminal activity, the effects of which have been likened to the post-traumatic stress symptoms that plague Vietnam combat veterans. These experiences induce palpable fear and insecurity in children, which are often manifested in nightmares, depression, and personality disorders. The psychological suffering of others is evidenced by apathy, withdrawal, or aggression (Churchville, 1987; Kotlowitz, 1987, 1991).

One of the most extensive journalistic accounts of the physical and psychological threats posed by urban poverty is based on three months in the lives of Lafeyette, a 12-year-old African-American boy, and his family and friends, all of whom lived in one of Chicago's public housing projects (Kotlowitz, 1987, 1991). Lafeyette's story is all too familiar to children in inner-city ghettos. He has maneuvered quickly to avoid being hit by the cross fire of bullets, has seen friends shot and adults severely beaten, and has stood over a dying teenager who had been gunned down outside his apartment

The research reported in this chapter was supported in part by a Faculty Scholar Award in Child Mental Health from the William T. Grant Foundation and a postdoctoral fellowship from the Rockefeller Foundation, both awarded to Vonnie C. McLoyd. Leon Wilson was supported by a Rodney-DuBois-Mandela postdoctoral fellowship from the Center for Afro-American and African Studies at the University of Michigan. We thank the families who participated in this study as well as the staffs of the Michigan Department of Social Services and the Ypsilanti, Michigan, public schools for their cooperation. We gratefully acknowledge the assistance of Liese Hull, Reshall James, Natasha Lifton, Shannon Nelson, Patty Rich, and Eve Trager in data collection and coding.

105

door. Lafeyette and his 9-year-old brother, Pharoah, experience headaches when they hear gunfire. Pharoah sometimes shakes uncontrollably when surprised by a loud noise; at one point he fainted after pleading with his mother to stop the shooting outside. The brothers have been counseled by their mother, "when you hear the shooting, first to walk because you don't know where the bullets are coming from." Lafeyette attends funerals routinely. When a resident of the project is killed, mimeographed sheets go up in the halls giving details of the funeral. He is suspicious of certain peers, refusing to play basketball with them because "they might try to make me join a gang." He can distinguish a .45-caliber revolver from a .357-caliber Magnum and identify the neighborhood buildings "where they have rapes." He and his friend, James, talk incessantly about leaving the projects and moving to a condominium in a Chicago suburb. They agree that "It's nice out there. You could sit outside all night and nothing would happen." James recommends that if children want to make it out of the projects, they should "try to make as little friends as possible." Lafeyette's mother, who permanently lost the use of two fingers when she was attacked by muggers, worries that Lafeyette has become unusually withdrawn. Of Lafeyette she says, "He says talking isn't going to help him . . . that everything that goes wrong keeps going on and everything that's right doesn't stay right so why should I talk. He's got a lot of hate built up inside him." She has taken out burial insurance on all six of her children.

Journalists also have assembled arresting case studies testifying to the demoralizing and hazardous housing conditions of the poor. Residents in public housing projects routinely contend with lack of heat, inadequate plumbing, peeling lead-based paint, insect infestation, rodents that attack sleeping children, overcrowding, inoperable elevators, and lack of laundry facilities. In addition to their threats to tenants' physical health, these pernicious conditions chip away at the individual's self-esteem, dignity, and sense of hope. In the words of one resident of a federally subsidized apartment building, "A rotten place to live leads to a rotten life. You feel less of a human being. You feel nobody cares. Eventually, you don't care" (Jordan, 1987a). Poverty often is marked by high residential mobility, partly because rent increases make housing unaffordable, because financial instability makes it impossible for poor tenants to pay the rent, resulting in their eviction, or because landlords refuse to make even minimal repairs, leaving residents no resort but to look for better housing (Jordan, 1987b). But as one researcher noted on the basis of his intensive study of poor families living in a public housing project:

> the moves do not mean increasing status and a better way of life. At best their style of life remains essentially the same. At worst the tyranny of slumlords and the exploitation of newly found neighbors increase their burden of deprivation and expose them more completely to the violence of ghetto

streets. Further, the constant moving creates an almost insurmountable problem for their school-age children, many of whom attend five or six schools before they get out of grade school. School progress is thus retarded and another generation locked more securely inside ghetto walls. Everywhere the accumulation of disadvantages works against ghetto dwellers to reduce their chances of escape (Shultz, 1969, p. 15).

In addition to its interference with the child's academic routines and progress, relocation disrupts peer relations and may put the child at risk for rejection by peers. In recent years, increasing numbers of the poor have lost access to even the worst government-assisted and privately owned housing. Homelessness, especially among children, increased precipitously during the 1980s, due in part to deep cuts in federal housing assistance, the elimination of federal housing construction operations, rampant conversions of apartments to condominiums, and local government policies and zoning laws that, in effect, keep low-cost housing out of their jurisdiction (Jordan, 1987b).

Research consistently reports that economically deprived children are at high risk of mental health problems. Social maladaptation and psychological problems such as depression, low self-confidence, peer conflict, and conduct disorders are more prevalent among poor children than among economically advantaged children (Gibbs, 1986; Kellam, Ensminger, & Turner, 1977; Langner, Greene, Herson, Jameson, Goff, Rostkowski, & Zykorie, 1969; Langner, Herson, Greene, Jameson, & Goff, 1970; Levinson, 1969; Myers & King, 1983). Children in families receiving Aid to Families with Dependent Children (AFDC) have significantly more emotional and behavioral problems (e.g., acting out, delinquency) than children in families that have never received nor applied for AFDC (Levinson, 1969). Compared to children living in nonpoor, two-parent households, children in poor female-headed households have an admission rate to psychiatric outpatient services that is two to four times higher (Belle, 1980). There is also evidence that poor children in both AFDC and non-AFDC families suffer greater impairment of self-confidence, school functioning, and relationships with their peers than children from higher income families although, in general, impairment tends to be greatest among poor children in AFDC families (Levinson, 1969). Undoubtedly, poor children's encounters with random violence and their struggle with ongoing, negative, physical conditions and with circumstances such as those described earlier contribute to the psychological problems they experience.

Although psychological problems are more prevalent among children experiencing economic hardship, as compared to their economically advantaged counterparts, there is considerable variation in psychological functioning among economically deprived children. A major goal of the research reported in this chapter is to identify some of the factors that account for variation in the psychological well-being of poor children whose families receive AFDC. We do not directly measure the ecology of the physical environment in which these children live. We do, however, assess the contribution to psychological distress of a set of factors related to the ecological context, namely, negative life events. In addition, we give considerable attention to mothers' psychological functioning and child rearing behavior as predictors of children's mental health. There is reason to believe that at least some of the psychological and behavioral problems of poor children are mediated by punitive, inconsistent, and unresponsive parenting brought on by economic hardship (Elder, 1974; Elder, Nguyen, & Caspi, 1985; McLoyd, 1990). In the present study, we consider the effects on children's psychological functioning of: (1) maternal psychological functioning, (2) maternal nurturance, (3) mothers' discussion of financial matters and personal problems with their children, and (4) mothers' use of income generation and curtailment of family consumption as strategies to cope with economic hardship.

Poverty, parenting, and maternal mental health

Because of its implications for child rearing behavior, the mental health of parents is important to consider in any discussion of children's psychological well-being. Economically disadvantaged parents, like their children, are vulnerable to the assaults on mental health exacted by the exigencies of day-to-day existence in the context of poverty. A plethora of research indicates that adults who are poor or who have sustained major economic loss experience more mental health problems than their economically advantaged counterparts (McLoyd, 1989; 1990). An inverse relation between socioeconomic status and various forms of psychological distress in adults (e.g., depression, anxiety, somatic complaints) has been reported by several researchers (Liem & Liem, 1978; McAdoo, 1986; Neff & Husaini, 1980). Data suggest that poverty, in addition to exposing the individual to more acute and chronic stressors, weakens the individual's ability to cope with new problems and difficulties, which, consequently, have more debilitating effects. That is, adults who are poor are more likely than higher-status persons to suffer mental health problems following negative life events, a conclusion based on the fact that the positive relation between life-change scores and impairment is strongest in the lower class. This relation is even stronger when events outside the control of the individual are analyzed separately (Kessler & Cleary, 1980; Liem & Liem, 1978).

Single motherhood, common among the poor, is a salient risk factor for psychological distress. Anxiety, depression, and health problems are more prevalent among single mothers than they are among other marital status groups, and single mothers' risk of physical and psychological problems is intensified if they are poor and live alone with their children. Some of this distress is rooted in the burdens and responsibilities of solo parenting – the younger the child and the greater the number of children in the households, the greater is the association between marital status and mental health problems (Pearlin & Johnson, 1977). Adding to the plight of poor single mothers is their social isolation and their oftentimes demeaning and dehumanizing interaction with the public welfare system (Goodban, 1985; Marshall, 1982; Pearlin & Johnson, 1977). As Pearlin and Johnson (1977) put it, "The combination most productive of psychological distress is to be simultaneously single, isolated, exposed to burdensome parental obligations and – most serious of all – poor" (p. 714).

What is the impact of psychological distress on parenting behavior? The last decade witnessed a burgeoning of research documenting a close link between mental health and child rearing behavior among both poor and more affluent parents. In general, these studies indicate that negative emotional states in the parent are highly predictive of parental punitiveness, inconsistency, and unresponsiveness. Mothers who report higher levels of emotional distress exhibit less positive behavior (e.g., hugs, praise, supportive statements) and more negative behavior (e.g., threats, derogatory statements, slaps) toward the child. Similarly, maternal emotional distress has been found to be associated with diminished maternal sensitivity and satisfaction with parenting and increased use of aversive, coercive discipline (Crnic & Greenberg, 1987; Daniel, Hampton, & Newberger, 1983; Patterson, 1986).

These findings based on self-report measures of emotional distress are consistent with findings from studies of depressed (or manic-depressive) mothers identified on the basis of clinical diagnosis. In general, the parenting behavior of clinically diagnosed depressed mothers is marked by unresponsiveness, nonsupportiveness, and hostile coerciveness toward the child. When interacting with their preschool children, depressed mothers are more critical, less positive in affective expression, less responsive to the child's overtures, and less active and spontaneous (Davenport, Zahn-Waxler, Adland, & Mayfield, 1984; Downey & Coyne, 1990; Radke-Yarrow, Richters, & Wilson, 1988). They are more likely to choose conflict resolution strategies that require little effort, such as dropping initial demands when the child is resistant or enforcing obedience unilaterally rather than negotiating with the child (Kochanska, Kuczynski, Radke-Yarrow, & Walsh, 1987). The more severe the mother's depression, the more likely she is to slap and shout at the child to signal disapproval and the more negative is her perception of the child (Panaccione & Wahler, 1986).

A relation between psychological distress and child rearing behavior also has been found among economically deprived parents. Poor parents whose total stress burden is high are less happy and less involved in the activities of their preschool and adolescent children than poor parents who experience fewer stressors (Wilson, 1974). High levels of psychological distress also dispose poor adolescent mothers toward custodial and unstimulating contact with their infants (Crockenberg, 1987). Investigations by Longfellow, Zelkowitz, and Saunders (1982) and Zelkowitz (1982) of poor mothers of 5- to 7-year-olds provide additional evidence concerning the relation between child rearing behavior and parental mental health. Longfellow et al. reported that the more highly stressed and depressed the mothers were, the less responsive they were to the child's dependency needs and the more likely they were to be hostile and dominating when initiating behavior toward the child and responding to the child's requests. Highly depressed mothers scolded and hit the child more frequently and relied less on reasoning and loss of privileges in disciplining the child. They also demanded more extensive involvement in household maintenance from the child and placed greater responsibility on the child. In a similar vein, Zelkowitz (1982) reported that poor mothers who were anxious and depressed were more likely to expect immediate compliance from the child, although they were less consistent in following through on their requests if the child did not comply. They were more likely to see their maternal role as teaching socially appropriate behavior and valued obedience and "good" behavior more highly.

It is reasonable to conclude on the basis of studies directly linking negative emotional states and punitive, nonsupportive parenting that environmental and psychological distress partially account for well-established social class differences in parenting behavior. Numerous studies employing interview and observational methods report that mothers who are poor are more likely than their advantaged counterparts to use power assertive techniques in disciplinary encounters and generally are less supportive and affectionate toward their children. They value obedience more, are less likely to use reasoning, and are more likely to use physical punishment as a means of disciplining and controlling the child. Lower class parents also are more likely to issue commands without explanation, less likely to consult the child about his or her wishes, and less likely to verbally reward the child for behaving in desirable ways (Conger, McCarty, Yang, Lahey, & Kropp, 1984; Gecas, 1979; Hess, 1970; Kamii & Radin, 1967; Kriesberg, 1970; Langner et al., 1970; Peterson & Peters, 1985; Portes, Dunham, & Williams, 1986; Wilson, 1974). Child abuse is reported to be more prevalent among the poor as well (e.g., Daniel et al., 1983; Garbarino, 1976). Several life conditions and circumstances that are associated with poverty and that are known to cause psychological distress appear to explain these differences. In their study of African-American families, for instance, Daniel et al. (1983) found that abusive mothers not only were more likely than nonabusive mothers to be very poor but also suffered more losses due to recent deaths in their families, more recent changes in their life situations, and generally more negative family stress. Even within poor abusive families, degree of material deprivation is associated with severity of maltreatment (Horowitz & Wolock, 1985). Furthermore, there is evidence that even ephemeral, relatively minor hassles produce detectable and negative changes in maternal behavior. Patterson's (1988) observations of mother–child dyads over the course of several days indicated that day-to-day fluctuations in the mother's tendency to initiate and continue aversive exchanges with their children were systematically related to the *daily* frequency of hassles or crises that the mothers experienced. Hence, as suggested earlier, there is good reason to believe that the higher levels of psychological distress deriving from the dangers, hassles, and inconveniences that mark day-to-day existence in the context of poverty is a major factor that explains why poor mothers are less nurturant, less supportive, and less inductive in their parenting than middle-class mothers.

The observations of one newspaper reporter who lived for a year in one of Washington, DC's poorest neighborhoods make plain the oftentimes debilitating effects of poverty on parenting:

> I saw a young looking mother holding an infant in her arms and trying to keep track of two boys walking behind her. The younger boy, who looked about 3, clutched an umbrella but seemed to be having trouble with it. He was dragging its curved handle along the ground, and that seemed to irritate the woman. "Carry that umbrella right or I'll slap the (expletive) out of you," she screamed at him. "Carry it right, I said . . . " and then she slapped him in the face, knocking him off balance. This incident was extreme, but I often saw teenaged parents cursing and cuffing, and I occasionally saw them striking their children. Early in their lives, these children learn that violence is one way to relate to people. . . . Often the violence is triggered by a perceived affront to someone's dignity (Dash, 1986).

Poor mothers often are not unaware of how negative psychological states affect their parenting behavior. In one study, they reported that among the hardest things to do when they were feeling depressed was be nurturant, patient, and involved with their children (Longfellow et al., 1982). They also seemed to be aware that the parenting strategies that they were most prone to use when they were depressed were, in the main, ineffective and changeworthy. Such findings challenge the view of some (Piuck, 1975) that poor parents' ignorance of the principles of effective parenting is the major reason for differences between poor and nonpoor parents' styles of interaction with their children. On the basis of prior research, we expected that mothers experiencing more severe economic hardship would report higher levels of psychological distress and that increased psychological distress would be associated with decreased maternal nurturance.

Parenting and child mental health

A vast literature exists concerning the consequences for children's socioemotional functioning of nonsupportive behavior by parents, where nonsupfjportive behavior is defined as low levels of behavior that make the child feel comfortable in the presence of the parent and communicate to the child that he or she is basically accepted and approved (Rollins & Thomas, 1979).

Research consistently shows that children whose parents are nonsupportive have lower self-esteem (Coopersmith, 1967; Gecas, 1979; Rollins & Thomas, 1979) and more psychological disorders, exhibit more antisocial aggression and behavioral problems (Rollins & Thomas, 1979), and are more likely to show arrested ego development (Powers, Hauser, & Kilner, 1989). Consistent with these findings is evidence that children of parents who are physically and verbally abusive and use harsh, punitive, and inconsistent discipline are prone to behavioral and psychological problems (Aber & Cicchetti, 1984; Egeland & Sroufe, 1981; Elder, 1979). Furthermore, young children of depressed parents are at increased risk of maladjustment, and a harsh disciplinary parenting style is one of the key mediators of this relation (Downey & Coyne, 1990).

The fact that child rearing practices more prevalent among impoverished parents (e.g., harsh discipline, nonsupportiveness) predict a range of socioemotional problems strongly suggests that at least some of the psychological and behavioral problems of poor children are mediated by negative parenting precipitated by economic hardship. This causal pathway has been demonstrated with samples of children whose parents have suffered job loss or severe income loss. Elder's pioneering studies of families of the Great Depression indicated that fathers who sustained heavy financial loss became more irritable, tense, and explosive, which, in turn, increased their tendency to be punitive and inconsistent in the discipline of their children. These fathering behaviors in turn predicted temper tantrums, irritability, and negativism in young children especially boys, and moodiness and hypersensitivity, feelings of inadequacy, and lowered aspirations in adolescent girls (Elder, 1979; Elder, Liker, & Cross, 1984; Elder et al., 1985). More recent studies of contemporary children in families experiencing economic loss report findings consistent with Elder's mediational model (Galambos & Silbereisen, 1987; Lempers, Clark-Lempers, & Simon, 1989; Silbereisen, Walper, & Albrecht, 1990). These findings lead us to expect that low maternal nurturance would predict impaired psychological functioning among children in our study.

A growing body of research underscores the sensitivity of children of varying ages to their parents' emotional states. For example, when nondepressed mothers simulate depression, their infants become distressed and make efforts to restore the mother's normal mood (Cohn & Tronick, 1983). Elder (1974) found that adolescent children whose fathers suffered major economic loss were more likely than children of nondeprived fathers to wish that "father were happier." In Longfellow et al.'s (1982) study of low-income families, children of stressed or depressed mothers were less likely to view their family life as a happy one, when compared to children whose mothers were less stressed or depressed. Infants and young children of depressed mothers behave in ways similar to their mothers. These children smile and express happiness less often and are more irritable and fussy than children of nondepressed mothers, perhaps reflecting a tendency of children to imitate negative affect modeled by their mothers (Downey & Coyne, 1990). These findings suggest that in addition to negative parenting, economically disadvantaged parents may influence the socioemotional functioning of their children through a more passive mode. Specifically, the despondency and despair these parents model and the gloomy climate it establishes in the home may foster melancholy in the child. Parents communicate the meaning of events and circumstances to their children by their affect and behavior and, in turn, instruct children about how to respond to particular situations (Bandura, 1977). Hence, deterioration in the parent's psychological functioning in the context of economic loss or poverty may become a communicable social phenomenon to the extent that the child imitates the symptomatic affect and behavior of the parent (Kelley, Sheldon, & Fox, 1985). Indeed, unemployed parents generally recognize that their reaction to being without a job may serve as a model for the response of their children and worry that their children will sense their depression and anxiety about finances and the future (Cunningham, 1983; Elder, 1974). Children in single-parent families may be especially prone to model depressive affect because they lack the advantage of an additional parent or other resident adult who may temper a depressive outlook with a more optimistic and affectively positive style of coping (Brenner, 1984). In view of these considerations, we hypothesized that anxiety and depressive symptoms among single mothers would predict psychological distress among children. We also expected that psychological distress would be greater among children whose mothers frequently discussed their personal worries and financial matters with their children.

Another dimension of maternal functioning examined in our study is the strategies mothers adopted to ease economic hardship. We were particularly interested in whether the mother coped with economic hardship by making specific attempts to generate income or reduce family spending and the relation of these coping efforts to her psychological functioning and that of the child. A number of studies have examined whether particular styles of coping in the context of economic hardship are associated with more positive psychological functioning among adults. For example, Rosen (1983) found that working-class, unemployed women who made more curtailments in family spending following their loss of employment suffered significantly higher psychological distress and demoralization, as compared to women who made fewer cutbacks. Similarly, the findings of a recent study of rural, middle-class families experiencing economic loss indicated that fathers in families that made more substantial economic adjustments to make ends meet experienced greater psychological distress (Elder, Conger, & Foster, 1989).

Although links between coping strategies and adults' psychological well-being have been established, little is known about how children are affected by adaptations to economic hardship. Greater adaptations in the form of income generation and reduction of expenditures may undermine the child's psychological well-being directly or through its impact on the parent's affect and behavior toward the child. Alternatively, adaptation marked by specific problem-solving behaviors intended to ease economic hardship, compared to more palliative forms of coping, may foster family unity and a sense of efficacy in the child that may, in turn, contribute to positive psychological functioning. In a study reported by Elder et al. (1989), family economic adjustments had no direct effect on the child's emotional state or the father's affect toward the child. Rather, adaptations to hardship fueled men's irritability and hostility toward their wives, and this led to hostility toward the child. In short, fathers displaced their anger toward the mother to the child. Our investigation examines the links between coping behavior and psychological functioning among children and in so doing, provides additional data on this understudied issue.

Socioemotional functioning and children's support networks

Conflicting findings have been reported regarding the effects of social support on children's competence and socioemotional well-being. On the one hand, there is compelling evidence from numerous studies that social support fosters psychological adjustment and protects children from the negative effects of stressful experiences (Sandler, Miller, Short, & Wolchik, 1989). Social support discriminates between resilient youth and youth with serious coping problems (Werner & Smith, 1982), moderates the relationship between stress and maladjustment in poor inner-city children (Sandler, 1980), and buffers the negative impact of parental divorce (Sandler et al., 1989) and of school transitions (Berndt, 1989; Felner, Ginter, & Primavera, 1982).

Support from both peers and adults can benefit children under stress. For example, perceived emotional support from friends and the number of reciprocated best friends contributed independently to school competence, peer competence, and perceived self-competence in Cauce's (1986) sample of lower class, African-American adolescents. In Williams and Kornblum's (1985) ethnographic study of poor, urban, African-American children, positive adult role models who demonstrated interest in the children and shielded them from the more pernicious aspects of economically depressed neighborhoods figured prominently in the lives of the "superkids," that is, those children who were functioning well socioemotionally and educationally. Similarly, all of the high-risk but resilient individuals in Werner and Smith's (1982) well-known study of children of Kauai, Hawaii, at various points in their development, recruited a mentor to help them meet life's challenges. Many of these children had very early memories of a special adult who fostered confidence in their ability to succeed in spite of obstacles (William T. Grant Foundation Commission on Work, Family and Citizenship, 1988).

The buffering effect of support is enhanced when it is provided in the context of an enduring social bond. Riley and Cochran (1987) found evidence that both the kinship status and the gender of the supporter influenced the effect of support on young children. The school performance of sons of single mothers increased with an increase in the number of adult male relatives who took the child on outings away from home but was unrelated to the frequency of outings with female relatives or nonkin.

Contrary to evidence of a buffering effect, social support also has been found to be negatively related to psychological functioning. Higher levels of informal support (i.e., friends, nonfamilial adults) have been linked with lower academic adjustment among lower class, nonwhite adolescents attending inner-city schools (Cauce, Felner, & Primavera, 1982; Felner, Aber, Primavera, & Cauce, 1985). Furthermore, family support was negatively related to the academic self-concept, general self-concept, and total self-concept of these adolescents (Cauce et al., 1982). In a similar vein, Hirsch and Reischl (1985), in a study of children of depressed parents, found that those children who had stronger friendships and received more social support in relation to their most difficult family and school problem were more poorly adjusted than those who had weaker friendships and received less social support. Treadwell and Johnson's (1980) study of adolescents from diverse racial and socioeconomic backgrounds found no evidence that social support buffered the effects of negative life changes. Irrespective of the level of support received by the adolescents, negative life change related positively to various indicators of psychological and physical distress.

Discrepancies in research findings have fostered an appreciation for the multidimensionality of social support and led some researchers to posit that the salience of social support as a mediator of positive adjustment depends on both the dimension of social support examined and the area of adjustment considered (Felner et al., 1985). In the study reported here, we assess the contribution to children's psychological functioning of three dimensions of their support networks, as reported by the children: (1) number of peer and adult relatives and non-relatives in the network, (2) diversity of support (that is, the number of different kinds of support provided by each individual in the network), and (3) perceived quality of interaction between the child and network members. We expected that fewer adult relatives and non-relatives in the child support network, lower diversity in the kinds of support provided by individual members of the network, and lower perceived quality of support would predict higher levels of psychological distress. Also assessed in this study is the relation of psychological functioning to children's worries about the future, to various demographic variables (i.e., child's age, sex, and race), and to quality of life indicators (e.g., number of negative life events).

Description of research

The participants of the study were 92 children and their mothers. Mothers ranged in age from 25 to 58 with a mean age of 35. They had a mean of 3.1 children (range = 1–6). All families were receiving public welfare assistance in the form of Aid to Families with Dependent Children (AFDC) (mean income = $6,482 per year). Seventeen (18.5%) of the mothers worked part time, 7 (7.6%) worked full time, and 68 (73.9%) were not working for pay. All of the mothers were single; 39 (42.4%) were separated or divorced, 43 (46.7%) had never been married, 8 (8.7%) were living with a partner, and 2 (2.2%) were widowed. The children, all of whom resided with their mothers, ranged in age from 10 to 17 with a mean age of 14. Fifty-three (58%) were female and 38 (42%) were male. Fifty-four (59%) of the children were African-American, 33 (36%) were Anglo-American, 3 (3%) were Asian-American, and 2 (2%) were Hispanic-American. The Department of Social Services sent letters written by the principal investigator to mothers who received AFDC, lived in a targeted county of the state of Michigan, and had at least one child between 10 and 17 years of age. This letter described the study and requested mothers interested in participating to complete and return a 1-page questionnaire concerning their employment status, work history, and household membership. Attempts were made to contact each single mother who responded to the letter for the purpose of scheduling an interview with her and the target child. Two research assistants went to the participant's home; one interviewed the mother and the other interviewed the child. The interviews were conducted in *separate* rooms.

Children's psychological functioning

(1) Birleson's Self-Rating Scale of Depression, an 18-item scale, assessed the presence of several symptoms of *depression*, including appetite disturbance, feelings of loneliness, and reduction in activity level. The child indicated whether or not each item applied to him or her most of the time (score of 2), sometimes (1), or never (0). (2) *Anxiety* was assessed with the "What I Think and Feel" Scale, a revision of the Children's Manifest Anxiety Scale. It is a 37-item yes/no questionnaire with three factors: physiological manifestations of anxiety (e.g., sweaty hands), worry and hypersensitivity, and fear and difficulty concentrating. (3) Selected items from the Hopkins Symptom Checklist were used to assess *somatization*. The child indicated on a 5-point scale how often he or she had each of 17 problems or complaints (e.g., headaches, nervousness) during the past 30 days (1 = not at all; 5 = a great deal). The scores on these three measures were highly correlated. Therefore, the scales were combined to constitute a single indicator of the child's psy-

chological distress. The internal consistency of this composite measure was acceptable (alpha = .76).

Children's worries about the future

A scale developed for the present study consisting of six items assessed the child's degree of worry or concern about the future and his or her life as an adult. For example, children were asked how worried they were that they might not be able to find a job when they became an adult, to make enough money on their job, or to get the money necessary to go to college. They were asked how worried they were about the possibility of having to go on welfare as adults. For each item, the child was asked to indicate on a 5-point scale the degree of worry she or he experienced (1 = not worried at all; 5 = very worried) (alpha = .82).

Mothers' psychological functioning

(1) *Depression* was measured with the Center for Epidemiological Studies Depression Scale (CES-D), which consists of 20 items representing the major components of the depressive syndrome: depressed mood, feelings of guilt and worthlessness, helplessness, and changes in eating and sleeping patterns. The mother indicated on a 4-point scale how frequently she experienced these symptoms during the past week (1 = rarely or none of the time; 4 = most of the time). (2) *Anxiety/somatization* was assessed with the anxiety and somatization scales of the Hopkins Symptom Checklist. Each mother indicated on a 5-point scale how often she had each of 21 problems and complaints (e.g., headaches, nervousness, mind going blank) during the past 30 days (1 = not at all; 5 = a great deal). Because scores on the two measures were highly correlated, the scales were combined to constitute a single indicator of the mother's mental health (alpha = .76).

Maternal child rearing behavior

(1) To assess the salience of *nurturant versus punitive* parenting behavior, mothers were asked to indicate on a 5-point scale how often they used nine different methods to reward or punish their children (e.g., verbal compliment, show of affection, scolding, taking away privileges). Based on a factor analysis, scores for these items were combined into two additive scales of nurturance and punitiveness. The final measure was the difference of the total scores for the two scales (nurturance minus punitiveness). Higher scores, therefore, indicate a greater tendency toward nurturant behavior. (2) Mothers indicated on a frequency scale how often they shared their worries with the child, discussed personal problems, and discussed the family's financial situation

with the child. This 3-item scale was used as an indicator of *maternal communication about problems* (alpha = .77). (3) *Maternal adaptation to economic stress* was based on the mother's response (1 = yes; 0 = no) to a 17-item scale about things she did in the past three months to reduce family expenditures (e.g., moved in with another adult to share rent, ate out at restaurants or fast food places less often) or generate income (e.g., pawned household or personal items). Scores were computed by adding the number of coping behaviors reported by each mother. (4) Finally, each mother indicated on a 4-point scale the *degree of difficulty* she experienced in her role as a parent.

Dimensions of children's support networks

Using the Children's Inventory of Social Support developed by Wolchik, Sandler, and Braver, five kinds of support were identified: recreation/play; advice/information; services/goods (e.g., help with homework, taking the child someplace); emotional support (e.g., listening to the child when he or she is sad or afraid); and positive feedback (e.g., telling the child something good about himself or herself). (1) *Network size* was assessed by having children list all of the people inside (relatives) and outside (non-relatives) their families who provided each kind of support during the previous two months. For each supporter, the child indicated whether the person was an adult or a child. (2) As an indicator of *perceived quality of support*, the child rated how he or she felt about the time spent with each supporter (7 = "terrific"; 1 = "OK, not really good or bad"). (3) A measure of the *diversity of support* was derived by assessing the number of different kinds of support each person in the network provided to the child.

Negative life events

Information about the occurrence of negative life changes experienced by the child within the past 12 months was gathered in a 55-item inventory (yes/no format) administered to the mother. The core of this inventory consists of Coddington's Stressful Life Events Inventory for Children. In the analyses that follow, we include only those events that are negative or undesirable (e.g., child being a victim of violence, death of a family member or friend of the child). Our analytic variable, therefore, is the total number of negative life changes experienced by the child (maximum score = 53).

Demographic variables

We considered the following demographic indicators in our analyses: (1) *ethnicity* of the child (0 = non-African-American; 1 = African-American);

(2) *sex* of the child (0 = male; 1 = female); (3) *age* of the child, which was collapsed into five categories (12 years or less; 12.1 to 13 years; 13.1 to 14 years; 14.1 to 15 years; over 15 years); and (4) *degree of economic hardship*, based on the mother's response to three questions: "How difficult is it for you to meet the monthly payments on your family's bills?," "In general, how do your family's finances usually work out at the end of the month? Do you find that you usually end up with some money left over, just enough to make ends meet, or not enough money to make ends meet?", and "In the past three months, how often have you decided not to buy something you had been planning to purchase for yourself or for your children?" (alpha = .61). Higher scores indicate greater economic hardship.

Results

We present the results for three sets of analyses. First, the factors we consider as important antecedents and outcomes of maternal psychological functioning are discussed. These results provide a context for our later analysis of the impact of maternal functioning on children's psychological well-being. In the second set of analyses, the bivariate relationships between psychological distress in children and various maternal, social network, and demographic variables are examined. Finally, we use ordinary least squares regression (OLS) to model the multivariate relationship of several predictors of children's distress.

Antecedents and outcomes of maternal psychological functioning

Economic hardship, adaptation, and maternal functioning

Our data confirmed a significant link between degree of economic hardship and mothers' psychological distress. The positive coefficient (r = .29, p < .006) indicates, as predicted, that mothers experiencing greater economic hardship reported significantly higher levels of psychological distress than mothers who had fewer economic difficulties. Those under more economic strain also tended to make more efforts to generate income or to reduce family expenditures (r = .57, p < .001). The most frequent ways in which mothers attempted to make ends meet was by cutting back on their social or recreation activities (69.6%), buying cheaper clothes for themselves (68.5%), eating out at restaurants or fast food establishments less often (62.6%), purchasing cheaper food (62%), postponing a trip or vacation (53.3%), buying cheaper clothes for their children (51%), and reducing the use of household utilities (47.8%). Sixty-five percent of the women did not have savings from which they could draw; of those women who did have savings, 45% indicated that they had used between 25% and 100% of their savings in the past three months to make ends meet. The more efforts the mothers made to balance family needs and family income, the more distressed they were ($r = .33$, $p < .002$). Mothers experiencing greater economic hardship were more likely to discuss personal and financial problems with their children than mothers whose economic situation was more favorable, but this relation was only marginally significant ($r = .19$, $p < .06$).

Maternal functioning and parenting

The mental health status of the mothers in our study was also related to their parenting behaviors. Consistent with our prediction, mothers experiencing more psychological distress were less nurturant of their children ($r = -.28$, $p < .01$) and perceived their parenting roles as more difficult, compared to mothers experiencing less psychological distress. Not surprisingly, mothers who found their maternal roles more difficult were less nurturant ($r = -.27$, $p < .01$) and discussed money matters and personal problems somewhat more frequently with their children ($r = .19$, $p < .07$).

Correlates of psychological distress in children

In the next level of analyses, we assessed the links of various aspects of maternal functioning, social support, and demographic factors to psychological distress in children.

Maternal functioning

First, as we expected, our data indicated a significant association between the psychological status of mothers and the level of psychological distress experienced by their pre-adolescent and adolescent children. The positive coefficient ($r = .22$, $p < .04$) indicates higher levels of distress in the child with increases in the level of psychological distress reported by the mother. Increased psychological distress in the child also was associated with decreased maternal nurturance ($r = -.21$, $p < .05$). Also of interest was that mothers who more frequently discussed with their children financial matters and personal problems had children with elevated levels of psychological distress compared to children whose mothers discussed these matters less often ($r = .22$, $p < .04$).

The strategies adopted by mothers for coping with economic hardship were unrelated to children's mental health. Additionally, our data indicated no statistically significant *direct* link between levels of economic hardship, as reported by the mother, and psychological distress in the child.

Social support

Of the dimensions of social support considered, both the number of non-relative adults in the network and the diversity of support provided by individual members of the child's network were positively related to psychological distress in the child ($r = .22, p < .03, r = .27, p < .02$, respectively.). These results are contrary to our expectations. Perceived quality of support from family members was unrelated to the child's level of psychological distress, but the negative coefficient ($r = -.10$) indicating that children who were more satisfied with the quality of contact with family members reported less psychological distress is consistent with our prediction.

Worries about the future and negative life events

A significant positive relation was found between worries about the future and children's level of psychological distress ($r = .31, p < .004$). However, negative life events and psychological distress in the child were unrelated ($r = .13$).

Demographic factors

None of the demographic variables used in the bivariate analyses was a statistically significant predictor of psychological distress. The directions of the coefficients indicate that psychological distress was somewhat higher among girls compared to boys ($r = .19$), among non-African-American children compared to African-American children ($r = -.06$), and among younger children compared to older children ($r = -.05$). Despite the very marginal relationships observed for these demographic variables, they are considered necessary for the specification of the multivariate models that follow.

Multivariate models of children's psychological distress

In this final set of analyses, we develop three multivariate models of children's psychological distress using linear regression analyses. The first is an incremental model examining the extent to which maternal psychological functioning and behavior account for variation in children's mental health. In the second, also an incremental model, we assess the contribution of demographic and economic factors and aspects of children's social networks to explaining variation in children's mental health. Finally, we present a parsimonious model that integrates variables from these two sets of predictors into a single equation. This analysis strategy is dictated by multicollinearity problems in the data and by the fact that we are interested in a variety of variables but have a limited number of cases with which to work.

Table 5.1. *Incremental regression models: Maternal mental health and behavior as predictors of psychological distress in children*

Predictors	Step 0		Step 1		Step 2		Step 3		Step 4	
	Marg. R^2	Beta	Marg. R^2	Beta	Marg. R^2	Beta	Marg. R^2	Beta	Marg. R^2	Beta
Maternal mental health	.048		.048	.220**	.041	.202**	.021	.153	.029	.185*
Share problems	.050		.042		.042	.206**	.046	.217**	.050	.225**
Maternal nurturance	.043		.024		.028		.028	−.174*	.031	−.184*
Coping behavior	.000		.001		.007		.010		.010	−.108
R^2	.048		.048	.038 (adj.)	.090	.070 (adj.)	.118	.088 (adj.)	.128	.088 (adj.)

*$p < .05$.
**$p < .01$.

Table 5.1 presents an incremental model of maternal mental health, maternal nurturance, and maternal coping style as predictors of the level of psychological distress reported by the children. In this and the second incremental model, we are concerned with the unique (marginal) variance explained by each predictor and the changes in the beta coefficients at each step. At Step 0, the unique variance explained by each predictor is presented. These figures represent the variation in the dependent variable that would be explained entering the predictors one at a time, that is, without considering their intercorrelations. The figures indicate that except for the coping strategies of mothers, each variable accounts for some variation in children's psychological distress. In each case, except for the model with coping strategies as the dependent variable, the F test for the model was significant. This was to be expected given the magnitude of the correlations noted earlier.

Step 1 is essentially a bivariate regression in which mothers' psychological functioning is a "forced" predictor. The unique variances for the other variables are recomputed considering the intercorrelation of the variable with the other (potential) predictors. Although there is some effect on the marginal contribution of each of the other predictors, the greatest effect is on maternal nurturance for which the marginal contribution is reduced approximately 50%.

At Step 2 the variable describing the degree to which mothers share problems with their children was entered. With the introduction of this variable, the unique variance explained by mothers' mental health is only slightly reduced and thus the coefficient remains significant. The unique variances for the other two variables are recomputed. Considering the intercorrelations with the two variables in the model, the changes in the two predictors yet to be entered are negligible.

At Step 3, maternal nurturance is entered, and the marginal contribution of mothers' mental health is substantially reduced, such that the effect of the latter is no longer significant. Our examination of the available regression diagnostics led us to conclude that the effect on the coefficient for mothers' mental health is not due to multicollinearity problems. Rather, we suggest that diminished nurturance is a significant way through which poor maternal psychological health is manifested. However, the predictive power of mothers' mental health improves when the mothers' coping strategies are taken into account at Step 4.

The variance explained by shared problems with children is relatively constant at each step of the analysis. This suggests that the contribution of this predictor to explaining variation in children's mental health is independent of maternal well-being, nurturance, and coping behavior. Finally, the improved specification of the relationship between mothers' and children's psychological well-being by considering the former's coping strategies is demonstrated in the table. Overall, then, the maternal variables considered here explain approximately 9% of the variation (adjusted) in children's psychological distress, with the strongest predictor in the final model being the degree to which financial and personal problems of the mother are shared with the child.

Table 5.2 presents an incremental model with variables pertaining to the child as predictors of the level of psychological distress reported by the child. At Step 0, we present the unique variance explained by each predictor without regard for their intercorrelations. As noted in earlier analyses, the most important predictors, in the bivariate case, are the child's sex, the diversity of support provided by members of the child's support network, and the child's worry about the future.

At Step 1 we fitted a model with demographic predictors and a variable assessing the economic condition of the household only. The results indicate little change in the information we obtained in Step 0. Of the demographic and economic variables considered, only the sex of the child significantly predicts psychological distress. The contribution to explained variance net of the effects of the other predictors is 5%. Approximately 2% of the variance is accounted for by the economic condition of the household, but the beta coefficient is nonsignificant. Age and ethnicity have virtually no effect on psychological distress. The variables considered at Step 1 explain only about 2% of the variance (adjusted).

The scale assessing the degree to which children worry about the future was added to the equation at Step 2. As in the bivariate analyses, this variable is significantly associated with psychological distress in children and increments the adjusted variance explained to almost 10%. Although the effect of the sex variable is somewhat reduced with the addition of children's worries, the beta coefficient is still significant.

With the addition of the two network variables, both of which are significant, the sex effect is reduced while the predictability of children's worries is improved considerably. Thus, it would seem that the diversity of support and the size of children's non-relative networks augment the effect of children's worry about the future, thus incrementing the effects of children's worries on psychological distress. This model accounts for 19% of the variation (adjusted) in children's psychological distress. The addition of negative life events experienced by the children had little effect on the coefficients and, therefore, was not reported as an extra step in the analyses.

The final model we present combines maternal and "child" factors as predictors of psychological distress in children. For reasons suggested earlier, we report a fairly reduced model, but one that best combines the two sets of predictors into a single equation. The beta coefficients and their related standard errors are reported in Table 5.3. Overall, this model accounts for 26% (adjusted) of the variation in the dependent variable.

The coefficients in the integrative model indicate that children's worry about

Table 5.2. *Incremental regression models: Demographic and child variables as predictors of psychological distress in children*

Predictors	Step 0	Step 1		Step 2		Step 3	
	Marg. R^2	Marg. R^2	Beta	Marg. R^2	Beta	Marg. R^2	Beta
Sex of child	.035	.045	.218*	.037	.197*	.012	.117
Age	.003	.002	.039	.001	.031	.000	−.010
Ethnicity	.003	.001	−.003	.001	.026	.011	.112
Economic stress	.012	.020	.147	.020	.144	.007	.086
Worry about future	.095	.083		.083	.295**	.109	.341**
Diversity of support	.075	.038		.044		.065	.291**
Non-relative network	.026	.029		.043		.063	.262**
R^2	.061	.018 (adj.)		.144	.094 (adj.)	.252	.189

* $p < .05$.
** $p < .01$.

Table 5.3. *Regression coefficients for combined model: Child and maternal variables as predictors of psychological distress in children*

Predictors	Beta coefficients	Standard errors
Personal variables		
Sex of child	.144	.093
Age	−.161	.010
Ethnicity	.110	.096
Worry about future	.344**	.092
Non-relative network	.339**	.092
Diversity of support	.256*	.099
Maternal variables		
Share problems	.306*	.099
Maternal nurturance	−.163+	.090
R^2	.37 (unadj.)	.31 (adj.)

$+ p < .07.$
$* p < .01.$
$** p < .001.$

the future, social networks distinguished by a large number of adult non-relatives, and diversity of support are associated with increased psychological distress in children. As shown in Table 5.3, all three of these variables had significant effects on the dependent variable. However, neither the age nor sex of the child had any effect on psychological distress once other factors are considered.

We considered only two characteristics of maternal behavior as important in the combined model. The marginally significant ($p < .07$) effect of maternal nurturance and the significant effect of sharing problems should be noted. Thus, whereas higher levels of nurturant behavior by mothers tended to result in less psychological distress in children, a significant increase in psychological distress is observed for children whose mothers share problems with them. We omitted mothers' psychological distress as a predictor in the final model because the residual unique variance explained by this variable, after considering maternal nurturance and children's worries, was reduced to zero.

Discussion

Although all of the mothers in this study were living in poverty, some were experiencing more economic stress than others. Increased economic hardship as evidenced by greater difficulty paying family bills, chronic shortfalls of money, and more frequent postponements of purchases was associated with significantly greater psychological distress in mothers. Several other researchers have documented a link between economic hardship and mental health problems. In their study of 43 poor women and their children, Belle, Long-fellow, and Makosky (1982) found that of 11 different ongoing circumstances that might engender stress (e.g., living conditions, parenting, extended family), money (e.g., insufficient amounts of money, not knowing in advance how much money is available for the household, not being able to get $100 on short notice if necessary) was the single stressor area most strongly associated with maternal depression. Similarly, chronic economic stress (e.g., difficulty paying bills, worrying about money, not having enough money for health care) was the strongest predictor of depression in Dressler's (1985) study of African-Americans living in randomly selected households.

Studies employing more distal measures of economic hardship (e.g., social class, income level) report findings consistent with those that assess more directly the relation between family needs and family income. An inverse relation between socioeconomic status and psychological distress among adults is well-documented (Liem & Liem, 1978; Neff & Husaini, 1980). For example, in her study of a sample of single, African-American women, McAdoo (1986) found perceived psychological distress to be significantly higher among those women who had lower incomes. It is also important to note that stressful conditions associated with poverty, such as chronic shortfalls of money and inadequate housing, are more debilitating than acute crises and negative events (Belle, 1984; Brown, Bhrolchain, & Harris, 1975; Makosky, 1982). Although the link between economic hardship and mental health is well-established, more research is required to specify the processes that underlie this link. For example, Belle (1990) observes that we still do not know whether poverty hastens or precipitates the onset of psychological disorders, prolongs their duration, and/or increases the like-lihood of relapse following recovery.

We found a significant positive relation between the levels of psychological distress reported by mothers and their children. However, as indicated in the incremental regression models and the combined model, this relation was largely accounted for by reduced maternal nurturance. Our interpretation of these data is that when a mother is in poor mental health – a state that increases as her economic situation worsens – she is less satisfied with the parenting role and less likely to behave positively and supportively toward her child. This behavior, in turn, appears to contribute to feelings of depression and anxiety in the child. Collectively, these findings are consistent with those reported by Belle et al. (1982), Crnic and Greenberg (1987), Longfellow et al. (1982), and Patterson (1986).

Several theoretical formulations postulate similar causal relations to explain child rearing patterns among the poor and negative child outcomes. However, unlike our analytic framework, the centerpiece of many of these theories, especially those growing out of the "culture of poverty" framework, is the personality characteristics of parents. These characteristics are seen as stable, deficient, and maintained by intergenerational transmission of lifeways independent of poverty, even though they are thought to have developed initially as adaptations to the life conditions of poverty. Moreover, many of these theories assign primary responsibility for negative child outcomes to parents and their socialization practices.

The analytic framework guiding the research reported in this chapter departs from these assumptions in two significant ways. First, it conceptualizes psychological distress and mental health problems among mothers not as stable "cultural" traits but rather as normative and situational responses to economic hardship. Second, although the analytic framework emphasizes the role of mothers as a mediator of the impact of poverty on children's mental health, it does not blame mothers for the mental health problems of their children. Rather, both mothers and their children are seen as victims of economic and social inequality. Ultimately, it is poverty itself that creates suboptimal conditions for maternal psychological functioning, child rearing, and child development. It also should be noted here that the notion that certain psychological or motivational characteristics predispose individuals to fall into or remain in poverty has received very little empirical support. The Panel Study of Income Dynamics, a longitudinal study that has charted the economic well-being of a nationally representative sample of American families each year since 1968, found that differences between individuals in various personality and motivational characteristics were, in the main, the result of past changes in economic status, not the cause of subsequent improvement or deterioration in economic status (Corcoran, Duncan, Gurin, & Gurin, 1985).

Mothers in the present study tended to have more problem-focused discussions with their children the more pressing their economic situation. This behavior was independent of maternal distress, nurturance, and coping behavior. Perhaps it reflects a relatively stable child rearing philosophy or belief that children should be aware of, rather than shielded from, family problems so that they can develop good coping and survival skills. Unfortunately, however, our data suggest that maternal discussion of problems predicts psychological distress in the child. The link between these two variables is reminiscent of Weiss's (1979) discussion of how single parenthood modifies the family's echelon structure and the impact of this structure on children's mental health. He noted that in order to reduce role strain, single parents often encourage children to assume the role of partner rather than that of a subordinate member of the household. Children in such households generally do more household tasks and are more involved in household management and decision making than children in two-parent households. In addition, children in these single-parent households often assume the role of confidant to parents, listening to and even counseling their parents. In Weiss's study, adolescents who assumed the role of friend and confidant to their single mothers came to have the same worries as their mothers. Many of the adolescents were acutely aware that their mothers were hard pressed for money, and this awareness caused anxiety and insecurity in some of them. Weiss suggested that although the demands of single-parent households may foster maturity and feelings of competence and self-worth in children, they also may overwhelm children psychologically and undermine their mental health, especially if their dependency needs are high (e.g., preadolescents and younger adolescents).

Mental health professionals need to deepen their appreciation for the strong link between the psychological functioning of poor mothers and the ongoing struggle of these women to survive and raise their children in the midst of daunting environmental realities. This level of understanding cannot be achieved without concerted efforts on the part of therapists and mental health workers to bridge the chasms between them and the poor created by cultural, class, and gender differences. The typical middle-class therapist or mental health worker has never experienced the stressors that poor women routinely confront. The tendency of mental health professionals to blame the economic and psychological plight of poor women on the women themselves appears to be widespread, even though this tendency serves only to exacerbate mothers' psychological problems and undercut the professionals' role as facilitator of intrapsychic and maternal functioning (Belle, 1984). There is evidence that the ineffectiveness of mental health professionals working with adolescent mothers is rooted in the professionals' contemptuous attitudes toward economically strapped clients – a finding that is likely to generalize to older mothers living in poverty. Regrettably, several investigations have found the use of community or neighborhood health services to have no enhancing effect on the maternal behavior and psychological well-being of adolescent mothers (Colletta, 1981; Colletta & Lee, 1983; Crockenberg, 1987). In fact, in one study, adolescent mothers were more dissatisfied with professionals than with any other group of helpers. The professionals were often seen as unsympathetic, impatient, disapproving, and uninformative (Crockenberg, 1987). It is not surprising, then, that these professionals had no positive impact on the mental health status and parenting behavior of these mothers.

Treatment that focuses on intrapsychic processes and parent education but ignores the environmental difficulties that undermine psychological and maternal functioning is likely to be of limited usefulness. Treatment for the individual woman needs to be complemented with advocacy activities that help women resolve concrete, environmental problems and pressure bureaucracies and societal agents to be more responsive to their needs and the needs of their children. The provision of adequate, low-cost housing; job-training programs that help women enter nontraditional occupations rather than traditionally "female" jobs, which pay low wages; affordable, high-quality child care; and competent legal aid are high priority needs requiring sustained attention from advocates and social reformers (Belle, 1984). Our findings, along with those reported in investigations of individuals who have suffered job or severe income loss, led us to the sobering conclusion that individual or family coping efforts directed toward cutting back on consumption and generating cash (e.g., pawning), at least in the context of economic hardship, are more likely to undermine rather than to enhance parents' psychological functioning. Such efforts, however heroic, do little to change fundamentally a negative existence. The ultimate goal of intervention and treatment should be alleviation and prevention of psychological distress by eradicating its sources. This goal requires that we challenge those policy decisions that result in poverty, joblessness, low wages, inadequate housing, and the dismal quality of life suffered by America's poor (Myers, 1989).

The most significant and prominent policy initiative directed primarily toward welfare recipients in the decade of the 1980s was the Family Support Act. Enacted by Congress in 1988, this law is designed in part to move welfare recipients into the labor market through participation in education and training programs and to provide them with support services (e.g., child care, transportation) that ease that transition (Blum, 1990). Among other requirements, the law mandates that all welfare recipients participate in the Jobs Opportunities and Basic Skills program (JOBS), with the exception of parents who have children under age 3 (or at state option, age 1) and parents who are ill, incapacitated, needed in the home because another member of the household is ill or disabled, employed 30 hours or more per week, under the age of 16 and attending school full time, or residing in an area in which the program is not available. Women in the second trimester or later of pregnancy are also exempt (Blank, 1989).

For several reasons, movement from welfare to work, whatever its impetus, should be viewed as a family transition rather than an individual transition made by the mother. The transition will affect the daily activities of not only mothers but their children as well. Among other things, it will require that preschool-age children adjust to caretakers other than their mothers. Precisely because it is a shared transition, many adaptations are likely to occur at the family level rather than at the individual level (e.g., modification of household rules and domestic responsibilities). Moreover, the findings of our study, as well as those reported by numerous other researchers, suggest that this transition is likely to have indirect effects on the child through its effects on the mother's psychological well-being. If the physical and psychological demands, role strain, and other pressures generated by the transition are not counterbalanced by psychological and material rewards such as a meaningful increase in the family's standard of living or in the mother's self-esteem, feelings of efficacy or control over her life, and expectancies for the future, the transition may actually have deleterious effects on the mother's psychological functioning. This outcome may adversely affect the quality of child rearing and family life and, in turn, children's mental health. It is also worth noting that a mother's mental health is likely to be influenced by whether her children cope well or poorly with new experiences precipitated by the transition (e.g., daycare).

Predictions are that the economic condition of the families of mothers who move off welfare and into the work force is not likely to improve dramatically given that families will experience reductions in a number of subsidies following the transition and that the jobs of many mothers will pay low wages (Brooks-Gunn, 1989). Based on the link between economic hardship and psychological functioning, it is unlikely, then, that mothers' psychological functioning is likely to improve dramatically following the transition, although there is reason to believe that the effects of the transition will vary for different groups of individuals. The strong, positive relation between children's worries about the future and level of psychological distress found in the present study suggests that mothers' participation in the JOBS program could have a positive effect on children's mental health if it gives children cause to view their future more optimistically. However, it is likely that such an effect would be dependent on how participation influences mothers' perception of their future and the future of their children. Research is currently underway to understand the impact of the welfare-to-work transition on the economic well-being, family life, and psychological functioning of mothers and their children.

We were surprised to find that supportive relations with an increased number of adult nonrelatives and greater variety in the type of support each network member provided were associated with higher psychological distress in the child. These two findings may reflect a tendency of children experiencing more mental health problems to seek more support from adults outside the family (e.g., teachers). This tendency also may explain the negative relation between psychological support and adjustment reported by other researchers (Cauce et al., 1982; Hirsch & Reischl, 1985). Another possibility is that the support provided by adult non-relatives to the children in our study actually threatened, rather than enhanced, their self-esteem and in turn, produced more rather than less psychological distress. There is evidence that supportive acts perceived by the recipients to enhance their self-esteem are positively linked to self-esteem, whereas supportive acts that elicit negative self-cognitions are positively linked to self-deprecation, anxiety, and depression (Sandler et al., 1989). These findings, along with those of the present study, emphasize the need for research that specifies the conditions under which supportive relationships either facilitate or undermine children's psychological functioning.

References

Aber, J. L., & Cicchetti, D. (1984). The socio-emotional development of maltreated children: An empirical and theoretical analysis. In H. Fitzgerald, B. Lester, & M. Yogman, (Eds.), *Theory and research in behavioral pediatrics* (Vol. 2, pp. 147–205). New York: Plenum.

Bandura, A. (1977). *Social learning theory*, Englewood Cliffs, NJ: Prentice-Hall.

Belle, D. (1980). Who uses mental health facilities? In M. Guttentag, S. Salasin, & D. Belle (Eds.), *The mental health of women*. New York: Wiley.

Belle, D. (1982). Social ties and social support. In D. Belle (Ed.), *Lives in stress: Women and depression* (pp. 133–144). Beverly Hills, CA: Sage.

Belle, D. (1984). Inequality and mental health: Low income and minority women. In L. Walker (Ed.), *Women and mental health policy* (pp. 135–150). Beverly Hills, CA: Sage.

Belle, D. (1990). Poverty and women's mental health. *American Psychologist, 45*, 385–389.

Belle, D., Longfellow, C., & Makosky, V. P. (1982). Stress, depression and the mother–child relationship: Report of a field study. *International Journal of Sociology of the Family, 12*, 251–263.

Berndt, T. (1989). Obtaining support from friends during childhood and adolescence. In D. Belle (Ed.), *Children's social networks and social supports* (pp. 308–331). New York: Wiley.

Blank, S. (1989). *Children and the Family Support Act*. Unpublished manuscript, Foundation for Child Development, New York.

Blum, B. (1990). Preface to *One program, two generations: A report of the Forum on Children and the Family Support Act*. New York: Foundation for Child Development and Columbia University, National Center for Children in Poverty.

Brenner, A. (1984). *Helping children cope with stress*. Lexington, MA: Heath.

Brooks-Gunn, J. (1989, November). *Opportunites for change: Effects of intervention programs on mothers*. Paper presented at the National Forum on Children and the Family Support Act, Foundation for Child Development, Washington, DC.

Brown, G., Bhrolchain, M., & Harris, T. (1975). Social class and psychiatric disturbance among women in an urban population. *Sociology, 9*, 225–254.

Cauce, A. M. (1986). Social networks and social competence: Exploring the effects of early adolescent friendships. *American Journal of Community Psychology, 14*, 609–628.

Cauce, A. M., Felner, R. D., & Primavera, J. (1982). Social support in high-risk adolescents: Structural components and adaptive impact. *American Journal of Community Psychology, 10*, 417–428.

Churchville, V. (1987, August 2). NE tenants hope to outlast siege of drug violence. *The Washington Post*, pp. A1, A16.

Cohn, J., & Tronick, E. (1983). Three-month old infants' reaction to simulated maternal depression. *Child Development, 54*, 185–190.

Colletta, N. (1981). Social support and the risk of maternal rejection by adolescent mothers. *Journal of Psychology, 109*, 191–197.

Colletta, N., & Lee, D. (1983). The impact of support for black adolescent mothers. *Journal of Family Issues, 4*, 127–143.

Conger, R., McCarty, J., Yang, R., Lahey, B., & Kropp, J. (1984). Perception of child, child-rearing values, and emotional distress as mediating links between environmental stressors and observed maternal behavior. *Child Development, 54*, 2234–2247.

Coopersmith, S. (1967). *The antecedents of self-esteem*. San Francisco: Freeman.

Corcoran, M., Duncan, G., Gurin, G., & Gurin, P. (1985). Myth and reality: The causes and persistence of poverty. *Journal of Policy Analysis and Management, 4*, 516–536.

Crnic, K., & Greenberg, M. (1987). Maternal stress, social support, and coping: Influences on early mother–child relationship. In C. Boukydis (Ed.), *Research on support for parents and infants in the postnatal period* (pp. 25–40). Norwood, NJ: Ablex.

Crockenberg, S. (1987). Support for adolescent mothers during the postnatal period: Theory and research. In C. Boukydis (Ed.), *Research on support for parents and infants in the postnatal period* (pp. 3–24). Norwood, NJ: Ablex.

Cunningham, S. (1983). Shock of layoff felt deep inside family circle. *American Psychological Association Monitor, 14*, 10–14.

Daniel, J., Hampton, R., & Newberger, E. (1983). Child abuse and accidents in black families: A controlled comparative study. *American Journal of Orthopsychiatry, 53*, 645–653.

Dash, L. (1986, January 26). Children's children: The crisis up close. *The Washington Post*, pp. A1, A12.

Davenport, Y. B., Zahn-Waxler, C., Adland, M. L., & Mayfield, A. (1984). Early child rearing practices in families with a manic-depressive parent. *American Journal of Psychiatry, 142*, 230–235.

Downey, G., & Coyne, J. (1990). Children of depressed parents: An integrative review. *Psychological Bulletin, 108*, 50–76.

Dressler, W. (1985). Extended family relationships, social support, and mental health in a southern black community. *Journal of Health and Social Behavior, 26*, 39–48.

Egeland, B., & Sroufe, A. (1981). Developmental sequelae of maltreatment in infancy. In R. Rizley & D. Cicchetti (Eds.), *New directions for child development: Vol. 11. Developmental perspectives on child maltreatment.* San Francisco: Jossey-Bass (pp. 77–92).

Elder, G. (1974). *Children of the Great Depression.* Chicago: University of Chicago Press.

Elder, G. (1979). Historical change in life patterns and personality. In P. Baltes & O. Brim (Eds.), *Life span development and behavior* (Vol. 2, pp. 117–159). New York: Academic Press.

Elder, G., Conger, R., & Foster, E. (1989). *Families under economic pressure.* Unpublished manuscript, University of North Carolina, Chapel Hill.

Elder, G., Liker, J., & Cross, C. (1984). Parent–child behavior in the Great Depression: Life course and intergenerational influences. In P. Baltes & O. Brim (Eds.), *Life-span development and behavior* (Vol. 6, pp. 109–158). Orlando, FL: Academic Press.

Elder, G., Nguyen, T., & Caspi, A. (1985). Linking family hardship to children's lives. *Child Development, 56*, 361–375.

Felner, R. D., Aber, M. S., Primavera, J., & Cauce, A. M. (1985). Adaptation and vulnerability in high-risk adolescents. *American Journal of Community Psychology, 13*, 365–379.

Felner, R. D., Ginter, M., & Primavera, J. (1982). Primary prevention during school transitions: Social support and environmental structure. *American Journal of Community Psychology, 10*, 277–290.

Galambos, N., & Silbereisen, R. (1987). Influences of income change and parental acceptance on adolescent transgression proneness and peer relations. *European Journal of Psychology of Education, 1*, 17–28.

Garbarino, J. (1976). A preliminary study of some ecological correlates of child abuse: The impact of socioeconomic stress on mothers. *Child Development, 47*, 178–185.

Gecas, V. (1979). The influence of social class on socialization. In W. Burr, R. Hill, F. Nye, & I. Reiss (Eds.), *Contemporary theories about the family: Research-based theories* (Vol. 1, pp. 365–404). New York: Free Press.

Gibbs, J. (1986). Assessment of depression in urban adolescent females: Implications for early intervention strategies. *American Journal of Social Psychiatry, 6*, 50–56.

Goodban, N. (1985). The psychological impact of being on welfare. *Social Service Review, 59*, 403–422.

Hess, R. (1970). Social class and ethnic influences upon socialization. In P. Mussen (Ed.), *Carmichael's manual of child psychology* (Vol. 2, pp. 457–557). New York: Wiley.

Hirsch, B. J., & Reischl, T. (1985). Social networks and developmental psychopathology: A comparison of adolescent children of a depressed, arthritic, or normal parent. *Journal of Abnormal Psychology, 94*, 272–281.

Horowitz, B., & Wolock, I. (1985). Material deprivation, child maltreatment, and agency interventions among poor families. In L. Pelton (Ed.), *The social context of child abuse and neglect* (pp. 137–184). New York: Human Sciences Press.

Jordan, M. (1987a, March 29). Lack of housing changes the course of people's lives. *The Washington Post*, p. A16.

Jordan, M. (1987b, March 29). Renovations come and residents go: Poor left with few options. *The Washington Post*, p. A1, A16, A17.

Kamii, C., & Radin, N. (1967). Class differences in the socialization practices of Negro mothers. *Journal of Marriage and the Family, 29*, 302–310.

Kellam, S., Ensminger, M. E., Turner, R. (1977). Family structure and the mental health of children. *Archives of General Psychiatry, 34*, 1012–1022.

Kelley, T., Sheldon, S., & Fox, G. (1985). The impact of economic dislocation on the health of children. In J. Boulet, A. M. DeBritto, & S. A. Ray (Eds.), *The impact of poverty and unemployment on children* (pp. 94–108). Ann Arbor, MI: University of Michigan, Bush Program in Child Development and Social Policy.

Kessler, R., & Cleary, P. (1980). Social class and psychological distress. *American Sociological Review, 45,* 463–478.

Kochanska, G., Kuczynski, L., Radke-Yarrow, M., & Walsh, J. D. (1987). Resolutions of control episodes between well and affectively ill mothers and their young child. *Journal of Abnormal Child Psychology, 15,* 441–456.

Kotlowitz, A. (1987, October 27). Urban trauma: Day-to-day violence takes a terrible toll on inner-city youth. *The Wall Street Journal,* pp. 1, 26.

Kotlowitz, A. (1991). *There are no children here.* New York: Doubleday.

Kriesberg, L. (1970). *Mothers in poverty: A study of fatherless families.* Chicago: Aldine.

Langner, R., Greene, E., Herson, J., Jameson, J., Goff, J., Rostkowski, J., & Zykorie, D. (1969). Psychiatric impairment in welfare and nonwelfare children. *Welfare in Review, 7,* 10–21.

Langner, T., Herson, J., Greene, E., Jameson, J., & Goff, J. (1970). Children of the city: Affluence, poverty, and mental health. In V. Allen (Ed.), *Psychological factors in poverty* (pp. 185–209). Chicago: Markham.

Lempers, J., Clark-Lempers, D., & Simon, R. (1989). Economic hardship, parenting, and distress in adolescence. *Child Development, 60,* 25–49.

Levinson, P. (1969). The next generation: A study of children in AFDC families. *Welfare in Review, 7,* 1–9.

Liem, R., & Liem, J. (1978). Social class and mental illness reconsidered: The role of economic stress and social support. *Journal of Health and Social Behavior, 19,* 139–156.

Longfellow, C., Zelkowitz, P., & Saunders, E. (1982). The quality of mother–child relationships. In D. Belle (Ed.), *Lives in stress: Women and depression* (pp. 163–176). Beverly Hills, CA: Sage.

Makosky, V. P. (1982). Sources of stress: Events or conditions? In D. Belle (Ed.), *Lives in stress: Women and depression* (pp. 35–53). Beverly Hills, CA: Sage.

Marshall, N. (1982). The public welfare system: Regulation and dehumanization. In D. Belle (Ed.), *Lives in stress: Women and depression* (pp. 96–108). Beverly Hills, CA: Sage.

McAdoo, H. P. (1986). Strategies used by black single mothers against stress. In M. Simms & J. Malveaux (Eds.), *Slipping through the cracks: The status of black women* (pp. 153–166). New Brunswick, NJ: Transaction Books.

McLoyd, V. C. (1989). Socialization and development in a changing economy: The effects of paternal job and income loss on children. *American Psychologist, 44,* 293–302.

McLoyd, V. C. (1990). The impact of economic hardship on black families and children: Psychological distress, parenting, and socioemotional development. *Child Development, 61,* 311–346.

McLoyd, V. C., & Wilson, L. (1990). Maternal behavior, social support, and economic conditions as predictors of psychological distress in children. In V. C. McLoyd & C. Flanagan (Eds.), *New directions for child development: Vol. 46. Economic stress: Effects on family life and child development* (pp. 49–69). San Francisco: Jossey-Bass.

Myers, H. F. (1989). Urban stress and mental health in black youth: An epidemiologic and conceptual update. In R. L. Jones (Ed.), *Black adolescents* (pp. 123–152). Berkeley, CA: Cobb & Henry.

Myers, H. F., & King, L. (1983). Mental health issues in the development of the black American children. In G. Powell, J. Yamamoto, A. Romero, & A. Morales (Eds.), *The psychosocial development of minority group children* (pp. 275–306). New York: Brunner/Mazel.

Neff, J., & Husaini, B. (1980). Race, socioeconomic status, and psychiatric impairment: A research note. *Journal of Community Psychology, 8,* 16–19.

Panaccione, V., & Wahler, R. (1986). Child behavior, maternal depression, and social coercion as factors in the quality of child care. *Journal of Abnormal Child Psychology, 14,* 273–284.

Patterson, G. (1986). Performance models for antisocial boys. *American Psychologist, 41,* 434–444.

Patterson, G. (1988). Stress: A change agent for family process. In N. Garmezy & M. Rutter (Eds.), *Stress, coping and development in children* (pp. 235–264). Baltimore: Johns Hopkins University Press.

Pearlin, L., & Johnson, J. (1977). Marital status, life-strains and depression. *American Sociological Review, 42,* 704–715.

Peterson, G., & Peters, D. (1985). The socialization values of low-income Appalachian white and rural black mothers: A comparative study. *Journal of Comparative Family Studies, 16,* 75–91.

Piuck, C. (1975). Child-rearing patterns of poverty. *American Journal of Psychotherapy, 29,* 485–502.

Portes, P., Dunham, R., & Williams, S. (1986). Assessing child-rearing style in ecological settings: Its relation to culture, social class, early age intervention and scholastic achievement. *Adolescence, 21,* 723–735.

Powers, S., Hauser, S., & Kilner, L. (1989). Adolescent mental health. *American Psychologist, 44,* 200–208.

Radke-Yarrow, M., Richters, J., & Wilson, W. (1988). Child development in a network of relationships. In R. Hinde & J. Stevenson-Hinde (Eds.), *Relationships within families: Mutual influences* (pp. 48–67). New York: Oxford University Press.

Ray, S. A., & McLoyd, V. C. (1986). Fathers in hard times: The impact of unemployment and poverty on paternal and marital relations. In M. Lamb (Ed.), *The father's role* (pp. 339–383). New York: Wiley.

Riley, D., & Cochran, M. (1987). Children's relationships with nonparental adults: Sex-specific connections to early school success. *Sex Roles, 17,* 637–655.

Rollins, B., & Thomas, D. (1979). Parental support, power, and control techniques in the socialization of children. In W. Burr, R. Hill, F. Nye, & I. Reiss (Eds.), *Contemporary theories about the family: Research-based theories* (Vol. 1, pp. 317–364). New York: Free Press.

Rosen, E. (1983, September). *Laid off: Displaced blue collar women in New England.* Paper presented at annual meeting of the Society for the Study of Social Problems, Detroit.

Sandler, I. (1980). Social support resources, stress, and maladjustment of poor children. *American Journal of Community Psychology, 8,* 41–52.

Sandler, I., Miller, P., Short, J., & Wolchik, S. (1989). Social support as a protective factor for children in stress. In D. Belle (Ed.), *Children's social networks and social supports* (pp. 277–307). New York: Wiley.

Shultz, D. A. (1969). *Coming up black: Patterns of ghetto socialization.* Englewood Cliffs, NJ: Prentice Hall.

Silbereisen, R., Walper, S., & Albrecht, H. (1990). Family income loss and economic hardship: Antecedents of adolescents' problem behavior. In V. C. McLoyd & C. Flanagan (Eds.), *New directions for child development: Vol. 46. Economic stress: Effects on family life and child development* (pp. 27–47). San Francisco: Jossey-Bass.

Treadwell, M., & Johnson, J. (1980). Correlates of adolescent life stress as related to race, SES, and levels of perceived social support. *Journal of Clinical Child Psychology, 9,* 13–16.

Weiss, R. (1979). Growing up a little faster: The experience of growing up in a single-parent household. *Journal of Social Issues, 35,* 97–111.

Werner, E., & Smith, R. (1982). *Vulnerable but invincible: A study of resilient children.* New York: McGraw-Hill.

Williams, T., & Kornblum, W. (1985). *Growing up poor.* Lexington, MA: Lexington Books.

William, T. Grant Foundation Commission on Work, Family and Citizenship. (1988). *The forgotten half: Pathways to success for America's youth and young families.* Washington, DC: Author.

Wilson, H. (1974). Parenting in poverty. *British Journal of Social Work, 4,* 241–254.

Zelkowitz, P. (1982). Parenting philosophies and practices. In D. Belle (Ed.), *Lives in stress: Women and depression* (pp. 154–162). Beverly Hills, CA: Sage.

6   The health of poor children: Problems and programs

Lorraine V. Klerman

The images of children emanating from the media are of plump, smiling infants, of toddlers and small children riding bicycles or playing ball, and of adolescents studying or socializing. All appear healthy, well nourished, and able to cope at the level appropriate to their age.

Fortunately, these pictures are correct for most of America's children, but not for all; and poor children are disproportionately represented among those whose health status is less than optimum. Illness, disability, and death may strike any child, regardless of economic circumstance. For example, congenital malformations appear to be independent of economic status. And a few health-related problems are found more often among the affluent because of their access to potentially dangerous equipment: drowning among toddlers is more frequent in families who own or use private pools and automobile accidents occur more often among adolescents who own or can borrow a car. But these are exceptions. In general, illness, disability, and premature death are more frequent among infants, children, and adolescents who either live in poor families or live in poverty without family support.

The first section of this chapter will examine the health status of poor children. It will suggest some reasons why poor children have more health problems than affluent children and will examine the possible differential impacts of persistent versus transient poverty. The potential effects of poor health on physical, cognitive, social, and emotional development will be noted. The second section will review the approaches that have been taken to prevent and treat childhood health problems. Finally, recommendations will be offered for programs that could relieve these health problems.

Health Status

Although much has been written about the health of poor children, analyses of their problems are limited because of the paucity of studies that relate

This chapter is based on *Alive and Well? A Research and Policy Review of Health Programs for Poor Young Children* (New York: National Center for Children in Poverty, 1991).

health to the *economic* circumstances of children and families. The most valid and reliable health data are obtained from birth and death certificates. Neither of these documents has any direct measure of economic status. Most state birth certificates, however, provide several proxy measures, such as parental educational level, occupation, age, marital status, and race. Race and marital status especially may not be adequate substitutes for economic data. Some researchers classify birth or death certificates by census tract or other residential groups and then divide the groups by socioeconomic status (SES), using one or more indicators usually obtained from census data. This method suffers from the ecological fallacy and is particularly subject to errors as the intercensal period increases. Although death certificates do not include parental education, occupation, marital status, or age, most states now link birth and death certificates for infants (children under 1 year of age), thus providing proxy data for analyses of infant mortality by SES.

Several of the periodic and ongoing surveys of the National Center for Health Statistics (NCHS) analyze data by family income and percentage of federal poverty level (149% or less, 150% or more, 300% or more). NCHS's publications, however, do not always include analyses by age groups within childhood. Fortunately, NCHS survey data tapes are available, and many investigators publish studies of infants, children, or adolescents.

In addition, household surveys by other governmental and private groups, as well as studies of such provider facilities as physicians' offices, health maintenance organizations, hospitals, and clinics, sometimes contain economic indicators, such as payment source. Nevertheless, data on childhood health by economic status are relatively meager, although analyses by race are common.

Indicators of health status

Poor children are more likely than nonpoor children to die young, and to suffer from illnesses and handicapping conditions. The parents of poor children are less likely to report that their children are in excellent or very good health.

Infant mortality. In 1990, the infant mortality rate (deaths under 1 year of life per 1,000 live births) for the United States was 9.1 (provisional), the lowest figure ever recorded (NCHS, 1991). Nevertheless, the United States has a significantly higher rate of infant mortality than Japan and many European countries, some of which have rates under 6.

The major causes of death in the 1st year of life are conditions originating in the perinatal period, including congenital anomalies, disorders related to short gestation and unspecified low birth weight, Respiratory Distress Syndrome, and Sudden Infant Death Syndrome (SIDS) (NCHS, 1990). All except congenital anomalies are found more often among infants born to poor families. The higher rate of infant mortality holds true whether one calculates it based on parental education, maternal age less than 20 (Hogue, Buehler, Strauss, & Smith, 1987), or economic status of the census tract (Wise, Kotelchuck, Wilson, & Mills, 1985).

Rates are higher among the poor not only for overall infant mortality but also for neonatal mortality (deaths before the 28th day of life) and postneonatal mortality (deaths from the 28th day through the end of the 1st year). Approximately two-thirds of infant deaths are neonatal, and these deaths are generally related to maternal health problems prior to or during pregnancy or in the labor and delivery period. Some of these problems, such as preterm labor or inadequate maternal weight gain, may be due to the stress of poverty or to insufficient income to obtain necessities, including food and medical care. The remaining one-third of infant deaths (postneonatal) are generally believed to be related to the environments that infants experience after returning home, and thus, these deaths are even more strongly associated with socioeconomic conditions. An important cause of postneonatal death, SIDS is associated with low maternal education, first pregnancy before age 20 (Hoffman et al., 1987), and economic status of the census track (Stockwell, Swanson, & Wicks, 1988).

Childhood and adolescent mortality. The major causes of death for children 1 to 14 years of age are accidents/adverse effects, malignant neoplasms, and congenital anomalies. Accidents remain the first cause of death for adolescents and young adults (ages 15 to 24), but homicide and suicide become second and third (NCHS, 1990).

In the 1983 through 1985 period, the death rate for children aged 1 to 4 was 53.1 per 100,000 population; for those 5 to 9, 25.5; for those 10 to 14, 27.7; and for those 15 to 19, 81.3. In the three younger groups, rates for blacks were higher than those for whites. The black–white ratios were 1.7, 1.5, and 1.3. Almost all of the differential was due to "external causes," including motor vehicle injuries, homicide, fire and flames, and drowning. Only malignant neoplasms and congenital anomalies were important "natural causes" of death, and the racial differences for these two were relatively small.

In each age group – 1 to 4, 5 to 9, 10 to 14, and 15 to 19 – death rates in the United States were almost always higher than those in Australia, Canada, England and Wales, Federal Republic of Germany, France, Japan, Netherlands, and Sweden. The differences were particularly striking for injuries, where only Australia and Canada had rates similar to the United States, and for homicide, where no country even approached this country's rate (Fingerhut, 1989).

Deaths from some illnesses are also higher among the poor. These illnesses include infectious diseases (Jason & Jarvis, 1987; Spurlock, Hinds, Skaggs, & Hernandez, 1987; Stockwell et al., 1988; Wise et al., 1985) and asthma (Evans et al., 1987). In 1988, Acquired Immunodeficiency Disease Syndrome (AIDS) was the sixth leading cause of death among children between the ages of 1 and 14, as well as of adolescents and young adults, 15 to 24 (NCHS, 1990). Because most cases of childhood AIDS are now diagnosed in children whose mothers either were intravenous drug users or had sexual relations with such individuals, infant and childhood AIDS is a disease of the poor.

Low birth weight, preterm birth, and intrauterine growth retardation. Infants who are born weighing less than 2,500 g (low birth weight infants) are at increased risk for a variety of health problems. They are likely to spend days, weeks, or months in neonatal intensive care units, be rehospitalized in the 1st year of life, and experience neurodevelopmental handicaps and lower respiratory tract conditions (McCormick, 1985). In 1985, an Institute of Medicine (IOM) committee conducted a thorough review of recent studies of the relationship between socioeconomic factors and low birth weight. The committee concluded:

> Low socioeconomic status (SES) measured in several different ways (social class, income, education, or census tract) is clearly associated with an increased risk of low birthweight and preterm delivery. The literature suggests that at least some of the excess risk is due to other variables that are also associated with both low social class and low birthweight. These include low maternal weight gain and short stature; certain obstetrical complications such as hypertension and preeclampsia; possible infection; smoking; and access, source, and utilization of prenatal care. The effect of socioeconomic status is probably the sum of multiple factors, many of which may be affected by specific interventions (p. 57).

Low birth weight is caused by preterm births (prior to 37 completed weeks of gestation) and/or intrauterine growth retardation (IUGR), each of which is independently associated with births among poor women. Kramer (1987), in his review of the literature on gestational duration, found that SES and maternal age affected gestational duration indirectly, through their influence on direct causes such as cigarette smoking and low prepregnancy weight. SES and maternal age also were indirect causes of IUGR through cigarette smoking, low caloric intake or weight gain, and low prepregnancy weight.

A California hospital survey (Binsacca, Ellis, Martin, & Petitti, 1987) found that women who experienced financial problems during their pregnancies were at greater risk of bearing a low birth weight infant than were other women, even after possibly confounding variables were controlled. A Boston Hospital study (Lieberman, Ryan, Monson, & Schoenbaum, 1987) reported that the presence of one or more measures of low maternal economic status (welfare support, not having graduated from high school, single martial status, and less than 20 years old) was strongly associated with a preterm birth.

Childhood health problems. The National Health Interview Survey (NHIS) asks parents to report whether they consider their children's health to be excellent, very good, good, fair, or poor. In 1989, families with annual incomes less than $10,000 reported a smaller percentage of children in excellent health than families with annual incomes of $35,000 or more: for children under age 5, 38.9% versus 63.8%, and for children aged 5 to 17, 35.4% versus 64.1% (Adams & Benson, 1990).

Several infectious diseases usually are associated with poverty. These diseases include rheumatic fever, hemophilus influenza, meningitis, gastroenteritis, and parasitic diseases (Egbuonu & Starfield, 1982). Occurrences of measles and other childhood diseases for which vaccines are now available are more frequent among the poor because their immunization status is less adequate (Wood, Hayward, Corey, Freeman, & Shapiro, 1990). As previously noted, pediatric AIDS is found more often among poor children because of its association with maternal drug use.

Chronic conditions are also more prevalent among the poor, probably because of the higher incidence of low birth weight, injuries, and illnesses that often are their precursors. Asthma appears associated with socioeconomic factors (Weitzman, Gortmaker, Walker, & Sobol, 1989; Wissow, Gittelsohn, Szklo, Starfield, & Mussman, 1988). Activity limitation due to chronic conditions, as reported in the NHIS, is higher among poor than nonpoor children (Office of Maternal and Child Health, 1990).

Anemia is associated with less maternal education, unmarried status, and young maternal age (Yip, Binkin, Fleshood, & Trowbridge, 1987). Several recent studies of low-income areas have found children with chronic hunger problems or at high risk of developing them (Connecticut Association for Human Services, 1987).

Vision and hearing problems are found more often among poor children (Egbuonu & Starfield, 1982). Although few national data are available on dental health by economic indicators, the patterns of dental visits, use of fluoride supplements, and data in state studies suggest that dental health problems are higher among poor children. Psychosocial and psychosomatic problems are more frequent and more severe in poor children (Egbuonu & Starfield, 1982). A 1988 study found that learning disabilities were strongly related to family income. In families with incomes under $10,000 per year, 8.4% of children between the ages of 3 and 17 were reported to ever have had a learning disability; the percentage decreased steadily to 5.8% among families with incomes of $40,000 or more. Emotional and behavioral problems that lasted three months or more or required psychological help also decreased as income increased, from 15.8% in the lowest income group to 12.8% in the highest. Delays in growth or development from birth to 17 years were reported for 5.4% of the children in the lowest income bracket and for 3.9% in the highest (Zill & Schoenborn, 1990).

Lead poisoning is a particular problem for poor children. In its 1988 report *The Nature and Extent of Lead Poisoning in Children in the United States*, the Agency for Toxic Substances and Disease Registry stated:

> no economic or racial subgrouping of children is exempt from the risk of having Pb-B [blood lead] levels sufficiently high to cause averse health effects. Indeed, sizable numbers of children from families with incomes above the poverty level have been reported with Pb-B levels above 15 ug/dl. Nevertheless, the prevalence of elevated Pb-B levels in inner city, underprivileged children remains the highest among the various strata (p. 5).

The agency estimated that 10.6% of urban black and 3.0% of urban white children (6 months to 5 years of age) with annual family incomes less than $6,000 had high blood lead levels (25 ug/dl) as compared to 5.9% and 1.5% for those with incomes between $6,000 and $14,999, and 2.2% and 0.5% for those with incomes of $15,000 or more.

Given the data on deaths from childhood injuries, it is not surprising that the rates of nonfatal injuries are also higher among the poor (Rivara & Barber, 1985). In a recent Canadian study, childhood pedestrian and bicyclist injuries were found more often among children living in low socioeconomic areas. When age, gender, and socioeconomic area were controlled, injuries occurred more frequently where the environment was judged unsafe and in families where parents had fewer years of education, supervised their children poorly, and engaged in few preventive behaviors. The authors urged that rather than "blame the victim," that is, rather than blame the child and its parents, programs should be targeted at changing the behavior of the driver or improving urban environments through traffic engineering (Pless, Verreault, & Tenina, 1989).

Of perhaps even greater concern are the rates of intentional injuries. In the *Study of National Incidence and Prevalence of Child Abuse and Neglect: 1988*, the National Center on Child Abuse and Neglect found that children from families with incomes of less than $15,000 experienced more physical, sexual, and emotional abuse and more physical, educational, and emotional neglect than children in families with higher incomes. The injuries in low-income families were also more likely to be serious or fatal (National Center on Child Abuse and Neglect, 1988). Although few analysts challenge this or other studies showing that families with low incomes and other indicators of low SES are more often *reported* to child welfare agencies for child abuse and neglect, some assume that this is due largely to biased reporting. They believe that both clinicians and the general public are more likely to suspect child abuse and neglect if the injured child or its family looks or sounds poor and to infer accidental injury if the child or its family looks or sounds affluent. The truth may be somewhere between – the real differences by SES are less than the reported ones, but they probably do exist.

Reasons for poor health

There is a tendency to believe that personal health services are the major influence on the health of children. Previous sections, which reviewed the most important reasons for childhood health problems, suggest that traditional medical care might be limited in its ability to prevent these problems, although it can limit their sequelae. The lower health status of poor children is related not only to the lack of access to personal health services but also to demographic and psychological factors, to lack of funds to purchase goods and services, to time constraints, and unhealthy life-styles and nonparticipation in health-promoting activities. Medical care can contribute to the health of children, particularly before and during pregnancy and through childhood preventive services, to the alleviation of pain, and to the reduction of handicaps. Unfortunately, the poor tend to underuse personal health services for a variety of reasons. Also, the content of the health care provided to the poor may be inadequate to their needs.

Demographic and psychological factors. Families in persistent poverty often have several other characteristics associated with poor health. These include birth of some or all of the children before the mother completes high school and/or marries and a household headed by a female. Not surprisingly, families in enduring poverty often also have low self-esteem and a feeling of lack of control over their lives, which may lead them to inappropriate health-related behaviors. It is unclear to what extent these factors directly contribute to poor health among children and to what extent they are just aspects of poverty.

Lack of funds to purchase goods and services. Many commodities are essential for optimal health, such as adequate housing, food, and medical supplies. Families in poor housing may be exposed to lead paint, particularly if the housing is old. They may be overcrowded leading to high levels of disease transmission and of stress. There may be safety hazards, rodent and insect infestation, and incidents of deviant or violent behavior in the neighborhood. Homeless families, usually housed in shelters, welfare motels, or other temporary quarters, not only often suffer from crowding and dislocation but also may have inadequate cooking or refrigeration equipment and may be located in neighborhoods that are unsafe or provide inadequate opportunities for children to play.

Food may be in short supply not only because of inadequate funds but also because of the high prices charged by small food stores in poor neighborhoods. Lack of private automobiles and inadequate public transportation may make it tiring and time consuming for the poor to shop or to seek medical care. Poor families may find it difficult to purchase prescribed medications or medical devices. They may not buy smoke detectors, stairway guards, and other items that would reduce safety hazards.

Time constraints. Members of poor families may have little free time because they are holding more than one job, because it is difficult for them to get time off, or, if the family is on welfare, because of the many procedures they must follow to maintain their status. Nor can poor families purchase assistance with child care. As a result they may be heavily stressed and have less time to seek medical care or engage in health-promoting activities, such as recreation.

Unhealthy life-styles and nonparticipation in health-promoting activities. Although the reasons are unclear, poor families often have life-styles that are not conducive to the health of children, and they engage in fewer health-promoting activities. Poor women are less likely to use contraceptives so they have more unwanted or inadequately spaced children. The diets of poor families are less nutritious; poor families use seat belts less often, install and check smoke detectors less frequently, and are less likely to maintain a program of physical fitness. Possible reasons for these lapses have been mentioned already: lack of education, insufficient funds, inadequate time, life stresses, feelings of powerlessness and lack of control, and preoccupation with the crises of daily living.

Cigarette smoking and the use of illegal drugs are more prevalent among low-income than among high-income families. Cigarette smoking may cause preterm birth or IUGR. Children whose parents smoke have more respiratory conditions, including asthma, bed days, and hospitalizations (Fielding & Phenow, 1988; Weitzman, Gortmaker, Walker, & Sobol, 1990). Maternal use of heroin, crack or cocaine, or other mind-altering drugs may have a range of negative effects on the infant and child. These substances can cause perinatal mortality, preterm births, growth retardation, congenital anomalies, withdrawal symptoms, developmental neurobehavioral disabilities, and other problems. In addition, the use of illegal drugs can have negative effects on the mother's ability to care for her child (Jones & Lopez, 1990).

The data relating family income to health-promoting activities are striking. As the income of NHIS respondents rises from less than $10,000 to $50,000 or more, the percentage who report that they brought their infant home in a car seat following its birth in a hospital rises from 43.1% to 78.0%; that children under 4 are buckled in a car safety seat or wear seat belts all or most of the time, 67.6% to 91.8%; that ipecac syrup is in the household (child under 9), 11.4% to 45.8%; and that the telephone number of a poison control center is available (child under 9), 43.8% to 75.6% (Schoenborn, 1988).

Underuse of personal health services. If, as the American Academy of Pediatrics urges, all children should be born wanted and born well, personal health services need to begin prior to pregnancy with family planning and preconception care. Unwanted and mistimed pregnancies are reported more often by poor women, suggesting underuse of family planning services (Forrest & Singh, 1990).

Analyses of birth certificates, which include information on prenatal care, and NCHS surveys indicate that women living below the poverty level, as well as women from minority groups, who have fewer years of education, are unmarried, are under age 20 and over 35, and have high parity receive less prenatal care measured in terms of the month care was initiated, the number of visits, and visits adjusted for weeks of gestation (Brown, 1988).

Although the differences in the use of ambulatory health services between poor and nonpoor children have decreased since the advent of Medicaid, they have not disappeared, particularly when use is adjusted for health status. Number of physician and dentist visits, interval since last medical visit, and immunization status are affected by income level and other SES indicators (Newacheck & Halfon, 1986; Wood et al., 1990).

The lower use of personal health services among poorer families is due primarily to their inability to secure appropriate personal health services. Several studies have shown that poor children are less likely to have a regular source of care or a recent physician visit. They have fewer physician visits and do not receive routine preventive care on a timely basis. Medicaid reduces the disparities in medical care utilization between the poor and the nonpoor, but it seems to promote the use of community clinics, hospital out-patient departments and emergency rooms rather than of private providers (Newacheck & Halfon, 1988; Newacheck, 1989; Wood, Hayward, Corey, Freeman, & Shapiro, 1990). Although the general public seems to believe that all working families have health insurance through employment and that all nonworking families receive medical care through Medicaid or some other public insurance program, neither of these assumptions is true. Many of the working poor are self-employed, work for companies that do not provide health insurance, or have company-based health insurance that is severely limited in coverage. And many of the nonworking poor are not eligible for Medicaid. In 1988, 71.8% of children 17 years of age and under in families with incomes below $10,000 were covered by a health insurance plan or Medicaid, as compared to 92.4% in families with incomes of $40,000 or more (Bloom, 1990).

Even when private or public funds are available to pay for care, the poor often find it difficult to locate a provider; and when they must seek free or reduced-cost care, the problem is worse. Few private physicians practice where many poor families live – inner-city ghettos and isolated pockets of rural poverty – and those who do may be reluctant to accept Medicaid payments, which are usually lower than those received from other sources. Delay in receiving payments, complex billing procedures, and a belief that Medicaid patients are more likely to sue also contribute to the reluctance of physicians to care for Medicaid patients.

Free or low-cost care is available in health department clinics, community and migrant health centers, and some hospitals, particularly those operated by city or county governments. Unfortunately, the number and scope of these facilities, always limited, were further curtailed in the federal cutbacks of the early 1980s.

Most but not all underuse of health services by poor families is due to financial barriers to care and to the shortage of providers willing to treat them. Problems with transportation, child care, and time also contribute. In addition, providers and facilities may be inaccessible or unacceptable because of language barriers, attitudes, and hours of operation. A small percentage of families, however, may underuse because of ignorance, fear, apathy, or previous negative experiences with the health care system. For these families, major outreach efforts are needed.

Content of care. The care that poor families receive may not be appropriate to their needs. Many of their problems have a psychosocial component that the average physician may be unable to manage. Some families may need interpreters, nutritional education, or financial assistance, which are often not available.

Persistent versus transient poverty

Families temporarily in poverty may have fewer reasons for poor health than those in persistent poverty. Families in transient poverty usually do not have the same demographic or psychological characteristics, such as low education or births outside of marriage. Problems due to inadequate funds probably have more impact on families in persistent poverty than on those families whose poverty is of shorter duration. Children tend to be very resilient, and unless the deprivation occurs at a particularly vulnerable time, such as during pregnancy, they may not be permanently damaged by temporary lack of goods and services. Also, providers may be willing to continue to serve previous patients who have temporarily "fallen on hard times," even allowing them to postpone payments. Life-styles are unlikely to change, and health-promoting behaviors may be reduced but probably not eliminated by families in temporary poverty. And families that were adequate users of medical care previously will usually find ways to continue to obtain care despite temporary financial problems.

Effect of poor health on development

One of the ways by which poverty affects the physical, cognitive, social, and emotional development of children is through its impact on health. Infants who are born too small or too soon, with the Fetal Alcohol Syndrome, or of drug-abusing mothers often suffer long-term physical, and sometimes cognitive, impairment. Moreover, Werner, Bierman, and French (1971), in their study of a cohort of Hawaiian births, found that the children born to mothers rated low in intelligence or with little education, and/or growing up in homes that did not provide adequately for their physical and emotional needs were less able to overcome the health problems with which they were born than were children raised in more favorable environments. Anemia and lead poisoning can also negatively influence physical and cognitive development. Hearing loss, often due to untreated ear infections, and poor, uncorrected vision may affect children's ability to learn and, over time, their self-esteem.

Disease and physical handicaps can also have a negative impact on the social development of children. Children with serious illnesses may be isolated from other children, and children with cosmetic handicaps are often shunned by other children. To the extent that poor children experience these conditions more often, their social development may suffer.

Major or chronic illness may cause serious psychological and social stress. Consequently, some categories of chronically ill children are at risk of developing behavioral or emotional problems (Dougherty, Saxe, Cross, & Silverman, 1987). The experience of child abuse or neglect, and particularly of sexual abuse, may have a negative effect on a child's emotional development. Again, if these problems are more prevalent among the poor, emotional development will be disproportionately affected in this group.

Approaches to improving health

Ever since 1892 when Nathan Straus opened his first milk station in a successful attempt to reduce mortality among New York's infants by providing a clean milk supply, citizens and legislators have sought ways to improve the health of children. In examining approaches to preventing the excessive health burden carried by poor children or to reducing its magnitude, several types of distinctions need to be made.

One distinction is that between public health interventions addressed at entire populations and often not requiring their participation (e.g., fluoridation of water supplies) and personal health services directed toward individuals, usually those who have sought care voluntarily or because it is required, (e.g., immunization prior to school entrance). Another distinction is between approaches, particularly in areas of public health, whose benefits should be approximately equal for all children and those that are particularly targeted at poor children or will benefit them disproportionately, such as programs of lead abatement.

Finally, some services are provided through programs that are clearly health related, whereas others are a component, sometimes relatively small, of programs with other educational or social services goals. The health portion of the Head Start program is an example of the latter.

For the purposes of this chapter, a program will be defined as an attempt by a federal, state, or local governmental agency, a foundation, or some other group to use legislation/regulation, education/enforcement, financing mechanisms, development or expansion of facilities, increases in personnel, or a combination of these, in order to improve health status.

Public health programs

Many public health programs have improved the health of both the poor and the nonpoor. Others have primarily benefited the poor.

Benefiting all children. Injuries are the most important cause of mortality and disability among children. There is probably no area that needs more attention, particularly because several injury prevention programs have had positive impacts, as shown in the decline in death rates from injuries (Guyer et al., 1989). Legislation requiring children to be restrained in passenger vehicles, reducing the speed limit, and modifying motor vehicle design have caused decreases in automotive fatalities and injuries. Burns have been reduced through legislation mandating fire retardant clothing and smoke detectors. Other legislative measures have resulted in childproof caps on bottles with dangerous contents, warnings on plastic bags, fences and gates around swimming pools, window barriers, and back-up signals on trucks. In these cases and others that could be cited, the legislation was effective because it was accompanied by public education and by enforcement efforts. Most of these measures had a positive impact on both nonpoor and poor children.

Fluoridation of water supplies has markedly improved the dental health of all children. It may have had a more significant effect on poor children because their level of dental hygiene and use of dental services is lower than that of nonpoor children.

State-mandated programs of newborn screening for such congenital defects as phenylketonuria also have been an effective health intervention. These programs have benefited both poor and nonpoor children (Office of Technology Assessment, 1988).

Targeting poor children. Levels of blood lead in children have been reduced primarily through restrictions in the level of lead in gasoline, and the prohibition of lead in interior paint, with housing modifications also contributing. Programs of lead screening and treatment of children may also have been effective (Annest et al., 1983).

The nutritional status of children also has improved, at least partially as a result of programs of food supplementation targeted at poor families (Yip et al., 1987). The federal Special Supplemental Food Program for Women, Infants and Children (WIC) assists pregnant and lactating women, infants, and children up to age 6 who are below 185% of poverty and at nutritional risk. This program, however, is not available to all who qualify because of the limited size of the federal appropriation and state reluctance or inability to supplement federal funds. Food stamps, school breakfasts and lunches, and other federally funded food programs also have improved the nutritional status of poor children.

Personal health services

During the last three decades, a variety of services have been developed or improved that have benefited the health of poor children. Family planning has reduced unwanted and mistimed pregnancies and prevented pregnancies among adolescents. Prenatal care has enabled more infants to be born healthy. Immunizations have reduced illness and mortality from several childhood diseases. More effective treatments have become available for many conditions, and the burden of handicapping conditions has been reduced by new methods of rehabilitation.

The nonpoor usually benefit quickly from these medical advances because of their ability to pay for services and to locate practitioners willing to serve them. Governmental, and to a lesser extent charitable, activity has been necessary, however, to provide access for the poor. Two basic mechanisms have been used to increase the availability of personal health services to the poor: public financing and the creation and/or expansion of public and quasi-public facilities.

Public financing. The major vehicle by which personal health services have been made available to the poor is Medicaid, a public medical care insurance program. Although the federal and state governments had financed a limited amount of medical care for the welfare poor prior to the passage of Title XIX of the Social Security Act in 1965, Medicaid represented a bold step forward. States that wished to participate (and all but Arizona joined the program relatively quickly) were required to provide a specified set of benefits to certain categories of welfare recipients (including all women and children on AFDC), who received care from specified providers. In addition, other benefits could be provided, other groups covered, and other providers reimbursed at the discretion of the state. Today, the federal government reimburses the states for half or more of their Medicaid expenses. Reimbursement rates are higher in poorer states and for certain services. Although it is impossible to disentangle the effect of Medicaid from other health influences in the intervening years, it is generally believed that this financing program is responsible for the increased utilization of medical care by the poor since the mid-1960s (Gortmaker, 1981). The Health Care Financing Administration reported that in 1988 there were 15.5 million recipients of Medicaid in AFDC families (children and adults) and that almost $12 billion in benefits were paid to these families (Health Insurance Association of America, 1990).

In 1967, the Medicaid legislation was amended to require that all states offer Early and Periodic Screening, Diagnosis, and Treatment (EPSDT) to all Medicaid-eligible children. In 1989, over ten million children were eligible for EPSDT, but only one million were enrolled in continuing care arrangements and an additional 3.2 million had initial or periodic screening examinations (Health Care Financing Administration, 1989). Several studies have provided evidence of the effectiveness of the EPSDT program (Irwin & Conroy-Hughes, 1982; Keller, 1983).

Facility development. Although the framers of the Medicaid legislation hoped that it would create a one-track medical care system, enabling all citizens to obtain medical care from the same providers, this has not occurred. The clinics in existence prior to the passage of Medicaid continue to be needed and now receive a large share of their financing from Medicaid. These facilities include both local and state health department clinics and outpatient clinics in public and voluntary hospitals. In addition, new types of facilities were created as the country became increasingly aware of the health problems of the poor. Neighborhood health centers were first established by the Office of Economic Opportunity in 1965. Shortly thereafter the Public Health Service began funding community health centers and, later, migrant health centers. The two groups of centers were integrated in 1973.

Medical care programs

Family planning programs are among the most effective approaches to improving the health of poor children because of the ability of these programs to prevent the unwanted and mistimed pregnancies that are frequent among the poor. Family planning clinics in health departments, Planned Parenthood facilities, hospitals, women's centers, and other sites are supported by Medicaid, by federal family planning grants, by the federal Social Services and Maternal and Child Health Services Block Grants, and, often, by state funds. They are generally believed to have lowered the rates of unintended pregnancies, particularly among adolescents (Anderson & Cope, 1987). Abortion services have also contributed, but these services cannot be supported by federal funds.

Programs to increase the availability of prenatal care have a long history. Some were funded by states with assistance from the federal Sheppard-Towner Act (1921–1929) and later from Title V, the Maternal and Child Health section of the Social Security Act passed in 1935. The Emergency Maternity and Infant Care program provided prenatal care to wives of servicemen during World War II. In 1963, Congress authorized Maternity and Infant Care (MIC) projects, demonstration programs that reduced rates of infant mortality in many high-risk areas. More recently, many states, counties, and cities have undertaken prenatal care initiatives designed to lower rates of infant mortality and low birth weight. The Ob Access program in California, Healthy Start in Massachusetts, and several county-level programs have been evaluated and found effective (Brown, 1988).

Programs of perinatal regionalization, usually developed by state health departments, have assured that high-risk pregnant women and newborns receive the level of care that they require. These programs combine designation of certain hospitals as referral centers, provision of transportation services for women in labor or newborns, education of practitioners regarding the use of the regionalization network, and other components (Gortmaker, Clark, Graven, Sobol, & Geronimus, 1987; Shapiro, McCormick, Starfield, & Gawley, 1983).

Programs of primary care for infants and children usually include the care of those with illnesses and injuries not requiring specialists and periodic examinations of apparently well infants and young children. These visits provide opportunities to immunize, to detect health problems (often while they can be easily corrected), and to offer anticipatory guidance (e.g., advice regarding child safety). The Children and Youth projects, demonstration projects authorized by Congress in 1965 and modeled after the MIC projects, as well as other primary care programs operated by health departments, community/ migrant health centers, and hospitals, however, have experienced difficulty in proving their effectiveness. In its 1988 report, *Healthy Children*, the Congress's Office of Technology Assessment (OTA) found prenatal care, newborn screening for congenital disorders, and immunizations cost-effective but indicated that existing research does not support the value of other components of well-child care. Several OTA staff members, however, have recently recommended "innovative, intensive, multidisciplinary approaches to well-child care" as a substitute for a rigid schedule of traditional services (Wagner, Herdman, & Alberts, 1989).

The WIC program, which combines provision of nourishing food with nutrition education and close links with prenatal and well-child care, has been proven effective with poor families in many studies. WIC has been found to reduce the incidence of anemia among pregnant women, to improve pregnancy outcomes, and to be cost-effective (Mathematica Policy Research, 1990; Rush et al., 1988; Stockbauer, 1987).

Programs in which public health nurses or specially trained indigenous workers regularly visit poor or young women in the women's homes during pregnancy and continue these visits during the first few years of the infant's life have been developed and studied in several communities. The Prenatal /Early Infancy Project in Elmira, New York, used public health nurses in a randomized experiment. The researchers reported that during pregnancy, the visited mothers, as compared to control mothers, were more aware of community services, attended childbirth classes more frequently, had fewer kidney infections, made greater improvements in their diets, and reduced smoking. After giving birth, visited mothers had fewer verified cases of child abuse and neglect, restricted and punished their children less frequently, provided more appropriate play materials, and made less use of the emergency room. They also had fewer subsequent pregnancies and postponed the birth of a second child longer (Olds, Henderson, Tatelbaum, & Chamberlain, 1986a; Olds, Henderson, Chamberlain, & Tatelbaum, 1986b; Olds, Henderson, Tatelbaum, & Chamberlain, 1988). The Resource Mothers Program directed at pregnant and parenting teenagers in three South Carolina counties reported that visited mothers, as compared to matched controls, had more adequate prenatal care and fewer low birth weight and small-for-gestational-age infants (Heins, Nance, & Ferguson, 1987).

Several categories of programs are directed largely at *adolescents* from poor families. School-based or school-affiliated clinics provide primary care, with an emphasis on reproductive health services, in over 150 schools across the country. Several evaluations have suggested that these clinics can reduce the number of teenage births and, if prenatal care is provided on site, the number of low birth weight infants (Edwards, Steinman, & Hakanson, 1977; Hayes, 1987).

Programs providing comprehensive services for pregnant and parenting adolescents have been developed in hundreds of communities, some with assistance from the federal Office of Adolescent Pregnancy Programs as well as with other federal, state, local, and foundation funds. These programs assist young women, and sometimes their partners and families, by providing directly or by referral and often with case management, health, educational, casework, and other services. Evaluations of many of these programs have shown that they are effective in reducing the incidence of poor birth outcomes, keeping the young women in school, and delaying subsequent pregnancies (Brown, 1988; Hayes, 1987; Korenbrot, Showstock, Loomis, & Brindis, 1989; see also chapter 4 by Klerman in this volume).

The Head Start program has a health component (North, 1979). All children in Head Start must be immunized and examined. An evaluation of the Head

Start health program found that Head Start children received more preventive and remedial services than other low-income children. Head Start children were also more likely to show improvement in motor development and speech and language performance, and Head Start families were more likely to serve nutritious meals at home (Abt Associates, Inc., 1984).

Other examples of programs with a health component are those developed by state and local educational agencies in response to Public Laws 94–142 and 99–457. These amendments to the federal education statutes require states to provide free and appropriate education to all children of school age regardless of handicap, broadly defined, and to prepare infants and toddlers with health problems for entry into the educational system. As a result of this legislation, children with handicaps actually are being sought out (and they are often poor children whose needs had been ignored) and the schools, although not usually responsible for providing health care, have become involved in assisting families to obtain treatment.

Although this description of programs is not all-inclusive, it provides an overview of the variety of mechanisms being used to bring health services to children in poor families. Although most of the programs described have been shown to have favorable effects, rates of mortality and disability remain higher among the poor than among the nonpoor. Many experts believe that the health care system needs major modifications if the situation is to be improved.

Recommendations

Four types of recommendations will be offered: improvements in overall living conditions; increases in public health programs; incremental improvements in access to personal health services; and reorientation of the system of personal health services.

Improvements in living conditions

Some experts believe that most of the improvement in child health over the last century is due to improvements in sanitation, housing, and nutrition. It is possible that further efforts in these areas would be very effective. One approach would be to increase the income of poor families through AFDC or another welfare program and allow the families to purchase improved housing, more and better food, and other essentials. Alternatively, governments could build housing and provide food and other necessities directly or through grant programs. This country lags behind other industrialized nations in the provision of essential services to families with insufficient income to purchase them.

Increases in public health programs

The review of the causes of mortality and morbidity makes it clear that greater attention to public health programs is essential. Experts in the safety field have lists of legislation whose passage and enforcement would further reduce motor vehicle accidents, drownings, fires, falls, and other injuries (Robertson, 1987). Radical restriction of the right to own hand guns would undoubtedly lower the number of accidental firearm injuries and deaths as well as homicides. Lead poisoning could be reduced further by eliminating the use of leaded gasolines, deleading houses, removing lead-contaminated soils, and other measures (Agency for Toxic Substances and Disease Registry, 1988). Education also plays an important role in preventing illness and injury. Programs emphasizing childhood safety measures, the importance of family planning and prenatal care, and many types of health promotion are clearly needed.

Incremental improvements in access to personal health services

Growth in many of the federal- and state-funded health programs would undoubtedly improve access to services. Congress gradually has expanded Medicaid so that more pregnant women and children must be included and has given the states the option to include additional groups. Continued expansion to encompass all families under 200% of poverty and all children through age 20, and perhaps a buy-in provision for the working poor, are among the proposals being considered. In addition, states need further encouragement and assistance with their EPSDT programs so that more children are reached and health conditions improved. Additional funding for primary care through the community/migrant health centers and health department clinics also would make services more available and increase their use.

The WIC program should be made an entitlement so that all pregnant and lactating women, infants, and children under 6 who meet income and nutritional risk criteria can be enrolled. At present, enrollment depends on whether funds are available. Similarly, Head Start should be made an entitlement instead of a grant program so that all eligible children can benefit from the program, including its health component.

Reorientation of the personal health services system

Although incremental changes would benefit poor families, a reorientation of the system would have greater impact and make the system less demeaning. The most radical proposal is for a national health service, similar to the British system. Proposals for national health insurance, similar to that in Canada and many European countries, have been introduced into the Congress and many state legislatures. Some proposals would require all employers to offer approved health insurance plans to all employees with the government providing similar coverage for the unemployed.

Such plans would remove most financial barriers to health care. Nevertheless, shortages of providers, provider unwillingness to accept certain patients, the special health problems of the poor, and a variety of other factors probably would require the continuation and possibly the expansion of some public and quasi-public facilities, educational and outreach efforts, and other services targeted to poor families.

Conclusions

Children in poor families in this country suffer disproportionately from the consequences of poor health. Although many public health measures and programs of medical care have reduced this burden, it is still a significant one. The experience both in other industrialized nations and with the more affluent in this country proves that health status can be improved. The technology is available – what is needed is a sincere public concern and the will to carry out the changes necessary in the life circumstances of poor families, in the environment, and in public health and medical care programs.

References

Abt Associates, Inc. (1984, March). *The effects of Head Start health services. Report of the Head Start evaluation.* Cambridge, MA: Author.

Adams, P. F., & Benson, V. (1990). Current estimates from the National Health Interview Survey, 1989. *Vital and health statistics*, Series 10, No. 176. (DHHS Pub. No. [PHS] 90–1504). Hyattsville, MD: National Center for Health Statistics.

Agency for Toxic Substances and Disease Registry. (1988, July). *The nature and extent of lead poisoning in children in the United States. A report to Congress.* Atlanta, GA: Public Health Service.

Anderson, J. E., & Cope, L. G. (1987). The impact of family planning program activity on fertility. *Family Planning Perspectives, 19*, 152–157.

Annest, J. L., Pirkle, J. L., Makuc, D., Nesse, J. W., Bayse, D. D., & Kovar, M. G. (1983). Chronological trend in blood lead levels between 1976 and 1980. *New England Journal of Medicine, 308*, 1373–1377.

Binsacca, D. B., Ellis, J., Martin, D. G., & Petitti, D. B. (1987). Factors associated with low birthweight in an inner-city population: The role of financial problems. *American Journal of Public Health, 77*, 505–506.

Bloom, B. (1990). Health insurance and medical care. Health of our nation's children, United States, 1988. *Advance data from vital and health statistics.* No. 188. Hyattsville, MD: National Center for Health Statistics.

Brown, S. S. (Ed.). (1988). *Prenatal care: Reaching mothers, reaching infants.* Washington, DC: National Academy Press.

Connecticut Association for Human Services. (1987). *Community childhood hunger identification project: New Haven risk factor study.* Hartford, CT: Author.

Dougherty, D. H., Saxe, L. M., Cross, T., & Silverman, N. (1987). *Children's mental health: Problems and services.* Durham, NC: Duke University Press.

Edwards, L. E., Steinman, M. E., & Hakanson, E. Y. (1977). An experimental high school clinic. *American Journal of Public Health, 67*, 765–766.

Egbuonu, L., & Starfield, B. (1982). Child health and social status. *Pediatrics, 69*, 550–557.

Evans, R., Mullally, D. I., Wilson, R. W., Gergen, P. J., Rosenberg, H. M., Grauman, J. S., Chevarley, F. M., & Feinleib, M. (1987). National trends in the morbidity and mortality of asthma in the U.S. *Chest, 91*, 65–74.

Fielding J. E., & Phenow, K. J. (1988). Health effects of involuntary smoking. *New England Journal of Medicine, 319*, 1452–1459.

Fingerhut, L: (1989). Trends and current status in childhood mortality, United States, 1900–85. *Vital and health statistics*, Series 3, No. 26. (DHHS Pub. No. [PHS] 89–1410) Washington, DC: U.S. Government Printing Office.

Forrest, J. D., & Singh, S. (1990). The sexual and reproductive behavior of American women, 1982–1988. *Family Planning Perspectives, 22*, 206–214.

Gortmaker, S. L. (1981). Medicaid and the health care of children in poverty and near poverty: Some successes and failures. *Medical Care, 18*, 567–582.

Gortmaker, S. L., Clark, C. J. G., Graven, S. N., Sobol, A. M., & Geronimus, A. (1987). Reducing infant mortality in rural America: Evaluation of the Rural Infant Care Program. *Health Services Research, 22*, 91–116.

Guyer, B., Gallagher, S. S., Chang, B. H. Azzara, C. V., Cupples, L. A., & Colton, T. (1989). Prevention of childhood injuries: Evaluation of the statewide childhood injury prevention program (SCIPP). *American Journal of Public Health, 79*, 1521–1527.

Hayes, C. D. (1987). *Risking the future: Adolescent sexuality, pregnancy, and childbearing.* Washington, DC: National Academy Press.

Health Care Financing Administration. (1989). EPSDT program performance indicators. State Medicaid Agency Regional Bulletin, No. 89–61.

Health Insurance Association of America. (1990). *Source book of health insurance data.* Washington, DC: Author.

Heins, H. C., Nance, N. W., & Ferguson, J. E. (1987). Social support in improving perinatal outcome: The Resource Mothers Program. *Obstetrics and Gynecology, 70*, 263–266.

Hoffman, H. J., Hunter, J. C., Damus, K., Pakter, J., Peterson, D. R., Van Belle, G., & Hasselmeyer, E. G. (1987). Diphtheria-tetanus-pertussis immunization and sudden infant death. Results of the National Institute of Child Health and Human Development cooperative epidemiological study of sudden infant death syndrome risk factors. *Pediatrics, 79*, 598–611.

Hogue, C. J. R., Buehler, J. W., Strauss, L. T., & Smith, J. C. (1987). Overview of the National Infant Mortality Surveillance (NIMS) project – design, methods, results. *Public Health Reports, 102*, 126–138.

Institute of Medicine, Committee to Study the Prevention of Low Birthweight. (1985). *Preventing low birthweight.* Washington, DC: National Academy Press.

Irwin, P. H., & Conroy-Hughes, R. (1982). EPSDT impact on health status: Estimates based on secondary analysis of administratively generated data. *Medical Care, 20*, 216–234.

Jason, J. M., & Jarvis, W. R. (1987). Infectious diseases: Preventable causes of infant mortality. *Pediatrics, 80*, 335–341.

Jones, C. L., & Lopez, R. E. (1990). Drug abuse and pregnancy. In I. R. Merkatz & J. E. Thompson (Eds.), *New perspectives on prenatal care* (pp. 273–318). New York: Elsevier.

Keller, W. J. (1983). Study of selected outcomes of the Early and Periodic Screening, Diagnosis, and Treatment program in Michigan. *Public Health Reports, 98*, 111–119.

Korenbrot, C. C., Showstock, J., Loomis, A., & Brindis, C. (1989). Birth weight outcomes in a teenage pregnancy case management project. *Journal of Adolescent Health Care, 10*, 97–104.

Kramer, M. S. (1987). Intrauterine growth and gestational duration determinants. *Pediatrics, 80*, 502–511.

Lieberman, E., Ryan, K. J., Monson, R. R., & Schoenbaum, S. C. (1987). Risk factors accounting for racial differences in the rate of premature birth. *New England Journal of Medicine, 317,* 743–748.

Mathematica Policy Research, Inc. (1990). The savings in Medicaid costs for newborns and their mothers from prenatal participation in the WIC program. Washington, DC: U.S. Department of Agriculture.

McCormick, M. C. (1985). The contribution of low birth weight to infant mortality and childhood morbidity. *New England Journal of Medicine, 312,* 82–90.

National Center for Health Statistics. (1990). Advance report of final mortality statistics, 1988. *Monthly Vital Statistics report,* Vol. 39, No. 7, Suppl. (DHHS Pub. No. [PHS] 90–1120). Hyattsville, MD: Public Health Service.

National Center for Health Statistics. (1991). Births, marriages, divorces, and deaths for 1990. *Monthly Vital Statistics Report,* Vol. 39, No. 12 (DHHS Pub. No. [PHS] 91–1120). Hyattsville, MD: Public Health Service.

National Center on Child Abuse and Neglect. (1988). *Study Findings. Study of national incidence and prevalence of child abuse and neglect: 1988.* Washington, DC: Author.

Newacheck, P. W. (1989). Improving access to health services for adolescents from economically disadvantaged families. *Pediatrics, 84,* 1056–1063.

Newacheck, P. W., & Halfon, N. (1986). Access to ambulatory care services for economically disadvantaged children. *Pediatrics, 78,* 813–819.

Newacheck, P. W., & Halfon N. (1988). Preventive care use by school-aged children: Differences by socioeconomic status. *Pediatrics, 82,* 462–468.

North, A. F. (1979). Health services in Head Start. In E. Zigler & J. Valentine (Eds.), *Project Head Start: A legacy of the war on poverty.* New York: Free Press.

Office of Maternal and Child Health. (1990). *Child health USA '90.* (HRS-M-CH 90–1). Public Health Service.

Office of Technology Assessment, U.S. Congress. (1988, February). *Healthy children: Investing in the future.* (OTA-H–35). Washington, DC: U.S. Government Printing Office.

Olds, D. L., Henderson, C. R., Tatelbaum, R., & Chamberlain, R. (1986a). Improving the delivery of prenatal care and outcomes of pregnancy: A randomized trial of nurse home visitation. *Pediatrics, 77,* 16–28.

Olds, D. L., Henderson, C. R., Chamberlain, R., & Tatelbaum, R. (1986b). Preventing child abuse and neglect: A randomized trial of nurse home visitation. *Pediatrics, 78,* 65–78.

Olds, D. L., Henderson, C. R., Tatelbaum, R., & Chamberlain, R. (1988). Improving the life-course development of socially disadvantaged mothers: A randomized trial of nurse home visitation. *American Journal of Public Health, 78,* 1436–1445.

Pless, I. B., Verreault, R., & Tenina, S. (1989). A case-control study of pedestrian and bicyclist injuries in childhood. *American Journal of Public Health, 79,* 995–998.

Rivara, F. P., & Barber, M. (1985). Demographic analysis of childhood pedestrian injuries. *Pediatrics, 76,* 375–381.

Robertson, L. S. (1987, February). *Childhood injuries: Knowledge and strategies for prevention.* Paper prepared for the Office of Technology Assessment, U.S. Congress. Branford, CT.

Rush, D., Sloan, N. L., Leighton, J., Alvir, J. M., Horvitz, D. G., Seaver, W. B., Garbowski, G. C., Johnson, S. S., Kulka, D., Holt, M., Devore, J. W., Lynch, J. T., Woodside, B., & Shanklin, D. S. (1988). Longitudinal study of pregnant women. *American Journal of Clinical Nutrition, 48,* 439–483.

Schoenborn, C. A. (1988). *Health promotion and disease prevention: United States 1985.* Vital and health statistics, Series 10, No. 163. National Center for Health Statistics (DHHS Pub. No. [PHS] 88–1591). Washington, DC: U. S. Government Printing Office.

Shapiro, S., McCormick, M. C., Starfield, B. H., & Gawley, B. (1983). Changes in infant morbidity associated with decreases in neonatal mortality. *Pediatrics, 72,* 408–415.

Spurlock, C. W., Hinds, M. W., Skaggs, J. W., & Hernandez, C. E. (1987). Infant death rates among the poor and nonpoor in Kentucky, 1982 to 1983. *Pediatrics, 80,* 262–269.

Starfield, B. (1985). Postneonatal mortality. *American Review of Public Health, 6,* 21–38.

Stockbauer, J. W. (1987). WIC prenatal participation and its relation to pregnancy outcomes in Missouri: A second look. *American Journal of Public Health, 77,* 813–818.

Stockwell, E. G., Swanson, D. A., & Wicks, J. W. (1988). Economic status differences in infant mortality by cause of death. *Public Health Reports, 103,* 135–142.

Wagner, J. L., Herdman, R. G., & Alberts, D. W. (1989). Well-child care: How much is enough? *Health Affairs, 8,* 147–157.

Weitzman, M., Gortmaker, S., Walker, D. K., & Sobol, A. (1989). Social and environmental risks for childhood asthma. *American Journal of Diseases of Children, 143,* 436.

Werner, E. E., Bierman, J. M., & French, F. E. (1971). *The children of Kauai: A longitudinal study from the prenatal period to age ten.* Honolulu: University of Hawaii Press.

Weitzman, M., Gortmaker, S., Walker, D. K., & Sobol, A. (1990). Maternal smoking and childhood asthma. *Pediatrics, 85,* 505–511.

Wise, P. H., Kotelchuck, M., Wilson, M. L., & Mills, M. (1985). Racial and socioeconomic disparities in childhood mortality in Boston. *New England Journal of Medicine, 313,* 360–366.

Wissow, L. S., Gittlelsohn, A. M., Szklo, M., Starfield, B., & Mussman, M. (1988). Poverty, race, and hospitalization for childhood asthma. *American Journal of Public Health, 78,* 777–782.

Wood, D. L., Hayward, R. A., Corey, C. R., Freeman, H. E., & Shapiro, M. F. (1990). Access to medical care for children and adolescents in the United States. *Pediatrics, 86,* 666–673.

Yip, R., Binkin, N. J., Fleshood, L., & Trowbridge, F. L. (1987). Declining prevalence of anemia among low-income children in the United States. *Journal of the American Medical Association, 258,* 1619–1623.

Zill, N., & Schoenborn, C. A. (1990). *Health of our nation's children: Developmental, learning, and emotional problems, United States, 1988. Advance Data.* Number 190. Hyattsville, MD: National Center for Health Statistics.

7   With a little help: Children in poverty and child care

Deborah A. Phillips

Child care has figured prominently in policies aimed at reducing poverty over the last 30 years. Tax provisions were created in the mid-1950s to defray the work-related child care expenses of low-income parents. Head Start was enacted in 1965 to "break the cycle of poverty," and child care subsidies have been appended repeatedly to welfare policies mandating parental employment.

The net result is a haphazard array of child care programs and benefits, funded from a host of different sources, that serve a fragment of the eligible families. The popular Head Start program, for example, serves an estimated 16% of the eligible children (Select Committee on Children, Youth, and Families, 1987). The ad hoc nature of federal child care programs is well reflected in the estimate that child care support is provided under 28 to 38 federal programs (Stephan, 1989). As a group, these programs have proven woefully inadequate to the task of promoting self-sufficiency among U.S. families. Between 1970 and 1987, the childhood poverty rate rose by 36% (U.S. Bureau of the Census, 1971, 1988), female-headed families doubled from 10% to 20% of all families with children (U.S. Department of Labor, 1971, 1988), and inflation-adjusted expenditures on Aid to Families with Dependent Children (AFDC) tripled (Gordon, 1987) despite a loss of about one-third in the average benefit received by an AFDC family during this 16-year period. Just between 1979 and 1986, the number of poor families with children climbed from 4.1 million to 5.5 million, an increase of 35% (Greenstein, 1987).

Today, these conditions are converging with a renewed national discussion about child care. The contemporary debate is driven largely by escalating rates of employment among nonpoor, married mothers. Need for child care

The author is indebted to her colleagues Greg Duncan, Aletha Huston, Lorraine Klerman, Henry Levin, Sara McLanahan, Vonnie McLoyd, Craig Ramey, and Lisbeth Schorr, who provided valuable comments on an earlier presentation and draft of this chapter. Thanks are also owed to Fern Marx, who provided access to her recent writings on child care for adolescent parents. Martin O'Connell at the U.S. Bureau of the Census generously shared unpublished tabulations on recent child care data.

is no longer restricted to poor and low-income families but has become pervasive among families at all socioeconomic levels (Hofferth & Phillips, 1987; Phillips, 1989). In the process, federal child care policies have come under intense scrutiny, and numerous proposals for restructuring the federal role have surfaced.

This chapter examines the role of child care in national efforts to reduce childhood poverty. The dual purposes of child care as an economic support for parents and as a developmental program for children are first compared. Existing child care programs targeted on poor children are then described, and available data concerning the effectiveness of the various approaches are summarized. The federal role in child care provides the major focus for this portion of the chapter. Contemporary pressures affecting child care policies are then discussed, with special attention to their implications for poverty-linked child care policy. Responses to these pressures exemplified by state-level preschool education and welfare reform efforts, and by new federal efforts to improve the delivery of child care services to poor children, are also reviewed. The chapter concludes with a summary of major issues for research.

Poverty-related purposes of child care

Reduction of poverty has provided the most long-standing rationale for child care policies. Although the bulk of federal support for child care is now channeled through the tax system, and thus no longer serves to reduce poverty (Clifford & Russell, 1988; Phillips, 1989; Robins, 1989), public perception links government child care subsidies to poverty, and policy debates emphasize the role of child care in promoting self-sufficiency among welfare clients. This political fact of life derives from two salient themes.

First, unlike child-related policies that are justified as child protection measures (e.g., policies covering child abuse, prenatal care and child health, and child labor), child care policy typically has been justified as an instrument of social change (Fein & Clarke-Stewart, 1973; Phillips & Zigler, 1987). Promotion of broad national goals, rather than the prevention of harm to children, has guided the development of federal child care policy. These goals have encompassed providing jobs for unemployed adults (Marver & Larson, 1978), enabling women to work in wartime factories (Steinfels, 1973), and socializing children into mainstream American culture (Grubb & Lazerson, 1988; Rothman, 1973). But the central goal to be served by child care has been to move families from poverty to economic self-sufficiency and, thereby, to reduce public expenditures on welfare.

Second, in the United States, government involvement in child care consistently has provoked controversy given prevailing beliefs that the family is the proper and natural institution for providing care, nurturance, and supervision of children. As a consequence, child care policy is played out in the context of value-laden debates about state intervention in family life (McCartney & Phillips, 1989; Phillips & Zigler, 1987; Rothman, 1973; Steiner, 1981; Steinfels, 1973). The effect has been to restrict government involvement in child care – particularly federal involvement – to extraordinary times and to families beset with problems. The brief heydays of direct federal support for child care during the Great Depression and World War II represent instances of the first condition. The second condition has focused child care policies on poor and disorganized families who do not exemplify the middle-class standard of "good parenting."

Strategies for subsidizing child care

Both the instrumental purposes of child care and the socially accepted link between publicly supported child care and poor families have directed federal policies to poverty reduction efforts. Within this context, two markedly different strategies have evolved, each with important implications for the nature of the subsidized child care.

One strategy has involved supporting child care as a necessary adjunct to mandated training and employment for welfare clients. This role for child care emerged during the mid-1960s in conjunction with a growing consensus that the AFDC program should promote maternal employment as a bridge to self-sufficiency rather than simply support mothers at home. In 1963, $800,000 was appropriated for child care as part of President John F. Kennedy's efforts to encourage employment among mothers who previously had been supported to stay at home with their young children. Thirteen states implemented community work and training programs under the Kennedy plan (Carson, Merck, Richardson, & Solomon, 1987).

By 1967 mounting welfare costs and the increasing acceptability of maternal employment led to the establishment of a work incentive (WIN) program, which was designed to provide skills assessment, job training, and employment placement to AFDC recipients. A portion of WIN funds also could be spent on support services such as child care. But an exemption for mothers with children under age 6, enacted in 1971, minimized the need for child care support and has kept WIN child care expenditures very low. Also in 1967, amendments to the AFDC program provided matching grants to states for the purpose of expanding and subsidizing child care for AFDC recipients who were in training or employed. By 1970 child care had been placed squarely in the service of promoting employment among welfare recipients.

The alternative strategy for subsidizing child care provides developmental child care to children living in poverty with the intent of short-circuiting intergenerational cycles of welfare dependence. The Head Start program is the federal representative of this strategy (Phillips & Zigler, 1987; Zigler &

Valentine, 1979). Although rising welfare costs were not incidental to the creation of Head Start, of equal influence were contemporary theories of development that identified the preschool years as a critical period for intellectual development and thus as a time when cognitive enrichment could launch poor children on the path toward school success and economic independence (Bloom, 1964; Hunt, 1961).

By the end of the 1960s, these two child care strategies – as an adjunct to welfare reform and as compensatory education – were firmly entrenched in federal policy. They remain the centerpieces of child care policy for low-income families. Despite their common clientele and broad intent, however, the welfare and education approaches have strikingly different implications for the quality of care supported by federal monies.

Services that are linked to welfare reform are necessarily tied to cost reduction. In this context, child care removes one impediment to women's participation in the education and training programs that are central to welfare reform proposals. Child care, in effect, is placed on a par with transportation and work uniforms. The incentives are to provide as much care as possible at the lowest feasible cost. The increased costs associated with high-quality care run directly counter to the goals of welfare reform. Low-cost, "custodial" care that is principally designed to enable welfare clients to work is all that is required in this equation. Senator Russell Long was one of the most articulate proponents of this position:

> "It was my hope that we might be able to drastically reduce welfare costs by finding a way to get some children in day care centers so that the mothers would be free to take a job. If you are going to run the cost of day care up to $3,000, then you can just forget about trying to get the mothers off of welfare by using the day care centers. It would be a lot cheaper to leave the children home with mama and pay them to stay there rather than try to do the day care bit (*Congressional Record*, June 30, 1980, p. S8932).

Child care that is linked to compensatory education, in contrast, is necessarily tied to concerns about quality. Head Start was designed to "compensate for" disadvantaged environments; high-quality, "developmental" care was critical to that goal. Prevailing theories of intellectual development, moreover, implied that the stakes involved in providing child care to poor children were greater than previously imagined. Rather than merely being a convenience for employed welfare mothers, or a mechanism for short-term reductions in welfare costs, child care centers constituted investments in human development that could serve to prevent poverty (Steiner, 1976). In this equation, supply is traded off against quality, with the effect that fewer children are provided with better services than in welfare-linked child care.

In sum, child care policies toward children in poverty are characterized by one of two basic strategies: one remedial and targeted on promoting adult employment – the welfare reform approach; the other more preventive in spirit and targeted on children – the Head Start approach. The former trades off quality of care for low costs and ample supply; the latter, premised on developmental research, trades off cost and supply for high-quality, comprehensive care. What is noticeably similar across the two approaches, however, is that they serve children from identically poor families. The children and their mothers, whether they receive child care through welfare or through Head Start subsidies, need both work-related and developmental child care. For example, recent estimates suggest that between 39% and 47% of the parents whose children are enrolled in part-day Head Start are in the labor force, placing pressure on Head Start programs to provide supplementary child care (W. Prosser, personal communication, April 1988).

The contemporary landscape: Child care, public policy, and children in poverty

Are low-income families characterized by a distinct pattern of reliance on child care? What are their average expenditures on child care? What federal programs are presently available to these families? This section provides an overview of the current status of child care use, costs, and support for children in poverty.

Patterns of child care use by family income and marital status

Table 7.1 presents the distribution of primary child care arrangements used by mothers for children under 5 years of age by family income and marital status (O'Connell, 1989; U.S. Bureau of the Census, 1983). Families relying on unsupervised care or on care by mothers, fathers, and siblings are excluded from the baselines from which the percentages were calculated.

Both similarities and differences are evident. Reliance on in-home care by non-relatives is uncommon across all family types. Similar patterns of moderate reliance (23% to 31% of mothers across income and marital groups) on group care arrangements are also revealed. The major income-based differential appears for the balance of reliance on relatives and family day-care homes. Within the lower two income groups, 36% to 42% of mothers rely on relatives as child care providers, whereas only 22% of mothers with monthly family incomes at or above $3,750 rely on relatives. Conversely, about 35% of mothers with family incomes above $3,750 use family day-care homes, whereas only 21% to 26% of mothers with incomes below $2,500 use family day-care homes. Similarly, married women living with their husbands are more likely to rely on family day-care home providers and less likely to rely on relatives for child care than are women without husbands in the household.

These patterns of use correspond closely to the costs of different forms of

Table 7.1. *Distribution of child care arrangements used by mothers 18 to 44 years old for their youngest child under 5 years, by family income and marital status*

Monthly family income	Relative	Non-relative in home	Family day-care home	Group care
Under $1,250	35.6	8.3	20.7	30.7
$1,250–$2,499	42.0	3.8	25.8	26.0
$2,500–$3,749	32.5	6.4	36.4	23.1
$3,750 and over	22.0	12.7	35.2	28.6
Marital status				
Married, husband present	39.7	7.1	33.5	19.8
All other statuses	45.3	9.9	21.8	23.0

Note: Baseline consists of all mothers using supervised child care not provided by the mother, father, or sibling. All numbers are percentages.
Source: Income distribution is from O'Connell, 1989 (analyses of the Survey of Income and Program Participation); marital status distribution is from U.S. Bureau of the Census (November 1983). *Child care arrangements of working mothers: June 1982.* Current Population Reports, Series P-23, No. 129. Washington, DC: U.S. Department of Commerce.

child care. For example, in 1986, half of all care provided by a relative was arranged with no cash payment, compared to 10% of all care provided in a family day-care home and 17% of group care arrangements (Hofferth, 1989). When these types of care are puchased, care by a relative is substantially less expensive (about $30 weekly in 1985) than any other type of arrangement. Average weekly costs of both family day-care and group care were about $38 in 1985 (Hofferth, 1987). Thus, women not living with husbands, and those with monthly family incomes below $2,500 (1986 dollars), rely to a much greater extent on forms of child care that are often provided without payment or at low cost. It is impossible to decipher, however, if these patterns result from the relation between the mothers' purchasing power and the cost of care or if they reflect preferences for care by relatives among lower-income families.

Expenditures on child care by poor and nonpoor families

Child care can be a considerable expense. In 1986 estimates of the average weekly dollar cost of child care for families with an employed mother and a child under 5 years was $63 (Hofferth, Brayfield, Deich, & Holcomb, 1991).[1]

---

1 It should be noted that these average costs include care by relatives as well as more formal family day-care home and center arrangements. Also, these costs include all parents who pay something for child care, regardless of the hours of care used per week. The costs of care to families can vary considerably depending on the type and amount of care used.

If these costs were incurred for 52 weeks per year, the average annual cost of child care would be $3,276. This estimate represents over 30% of the poverty threshold of $10,419 for a family of three (single mother and two children) in 1990. It is not surprising, therefore, that family income and race are significant determinants of families' total expenditures on child care (Hofferth, 1987; Hofferth et al., 1991). Nonpoor families pay more than poor families, and, after controlling for income differences and other factors, white families and Hispanic families pay more per week for child care than black families pay. Yet poor families spend a larger proportion of their total income on child care than do nonpoor families (Hofferth, 1989; Hofferth & Brayfield, 1991). Families living in poverty spend 22% to 25% of their income on child care compared to 6% for nonpoor families with a youngest child under age 5. Similarly, AFDC recipients spend 20% of their income on child care compared to 10% for non-AFDC recipients, and single mothers pay 20% of their family income versus 7% paid by married mothers.

In sum, among those who pay for care, child care expenditures constitute a substantial family expense – approximately 11% of family income on average, but as high as 20% to 25% among poor, AFDC-eligible families. This may explain family structure differentials in patterns of reliance on donated or self-provided child care.

Federal child care programs serving low-income children:
1981 to 1988

An array of federal benefits and programs provide child care support to children in poverty. Table 7.2 summarizes the major programs for which current data on child care expenditures are available. Approximately $2.31 billion in federal funds was channeled to these sources of low-income child care support in 1987 (Haskins, 1988a).

Head Start. Head Start consists of part-day programs that offer a comprehensive range of education, health, and social services to low-income children and their families. At least 10% of Head Start recipients must be handicapped children. Almost half of the $2.31 billion – $1.13 billion in 1987 – is attributable to Head Start. This represents a substantial increase over the 1981 appropriation of $819 million. Most other child care benefits channeled to poor children at best have failed to keep pace with inflation.

Social Services Block Grant. Total federal funding for the Social Services Block Grant (SSBG), of which 18% was spent on child care in 1980, now constitutes approximately 50% of its fiscal year (FY) 1977 level and 75% of its FY 1981 level in inflation-adjusted dollars. It has been estimated that federal expenditures on child care channeled through the SSBG fell from

Table 7.2. *Current federal programs and expenditures on child care for children in poverty*

Program	Target population	Expenditures (in millions)
Head Start	90% are to be low-income children; 10% of enrollment required to be handicapped	$1,130
Social Services Block Grant (SSBG)	States target low-income families although eligibility no longer stipulated in federal law	$ 540
Child Care Food Program	Children in child care centers serving low-income children and in family day-care homes unrestricted by income	$ 537
Work Incentive (WIN) program	AFDC recipients with jobs or in training	$ 37
AFDC child care disregard	AFDC recipients with jobs or in training	$ 40
AFDC work programs (CWEP, job search, work supplementation)	AFDC recipients with jobs, in training, or in job search	Not available

Note: Excludes Chapter I funds used to provide prekindergarten programs for children from low-income families, the Job Training and Partnership Act, and several other smaller child care programs, either because no data are available to identify expenditures for child care or because the program is not specifically targeted on low-income families. See Haskins (1988c) for a more complete listing of federal child care programs.

$600 million in 1980 to about $400 million in 1986 (Bloom & Steen, 1988). As a consequence, 26 states spent less on child care through the SSBG in 1988 than in 1981, and 23 states now serve fewer children than in 1981 (Blank, Savage, & Wilkins, 1988). These child care funds are often targeted on certain priority groups determined by the state, such as children at risk of abuse or neglect or children of working AFDC mothers (Nightingale & Burbridge, 1987).

Child Care Food Program. The Child Care Food Program, which provides subsidized meals to children in child care centers and in family day-care and group homes, received $317.5 million in federal funds in FY 1981 and $537 million in FY 1987. In center-based programs, these subsidies are provided to low-income children, and in family day-care homes they are provided without regard to the family income of the children served. All programs receiving food program benefits are required to meet state child care regulations. Accordingly, this program has been heralded as a major incentive for family day-care providers to shift from unregulated (and, in many cases, illegal) to regulated operation (Martinez, 1989).

AFDC child care disregard. Employed parents on AFDC are eligible for a child care disregard. Between 1981 and 1986, federal expenditures for the disregard fell from an estimated $70 million to $40 million. Under the disregard, families pay child care providers directly for their own child care costs and then deduct the amount paid – up to a statutory maximum of $160 per month per child – from their income when computing their AFDC benefit level. Some states enable parents to choose between the disregard and the Social Services Block Grant as their source of child care subsidy.

The $160 monthly maximum, which may be reduced for part-time workers, was set in 1981 and was modestly adjusted for the first time in conjunction with the Family Support Act of 1988 (see later discussion of federal welfare reform initiatives). It is unknown whether this amount unduly limits the child care choices available to AFDC clients. It is likely, however, that the $160 monthly rate is not sufficient to purchase good quality options in the formal child care market. For example, in 1988 costs for center-based care in Boston ranged from $180 to $364 per month for preschoolers ($488 to $604 for infants); in Atlanta the costs were $216 to $232 ($248 to $264 for infants); and in Seattle, center-based care for preschoolers ranged from $300 to $308 ($408 to $416 for infants) (Whitebook, Howes, & Phillips, 1989).

Work Incentive program. Federal subsidies for child care for low-income families are also available through the Work Incentive (WIN) program. The WIN program, enacted in 1967, provides the closest approximation to a federal employment and workfare program for AFDC recipients presently in existence. It requires "employable" AFDC recipients to register for work, education, or training programs. In late 1986, more than two-thirds of the states operated at least one WIN-related work program for AFDC recipients.

Historically, the two most important sources of child care subsidy for AFDC clients in training or employment have been WIN funds and Social Service Block Grant funds. Within the WIN program, however, child care does not figure prominently, primarily as a result of the provision that women with children under age 6 are exempted from participation and because school-age programs have not been a priority for WIN funds. In a recent state survey of AFDC-work programs (Nightingale & Burbridge, 1987), discussed in more detail later, 12 states did not use any WIN funds for child care, and 11 states did not use SSBG funds for work-related child care. Among states that use these sources of support, respondents noted that not many clients are provided with subsidized child care. Moreover, WIN expenditures on child care – never very large – fell from an estimated $50 million in 1981 to $37 million in 1986.

Education versus welfare revisited. It is not coincidental that Head Start, which exemplifies the child-focused, developmental model of child care provision, is the single source of low-income child care support that has been protected in recent years. Head Start has clearly defined goals, an outspoken constituency of Head Start parents (and now graduates), and some evidence of effectiveness (Peters, 1980). These features do not characterize any of the other child care programs targeted on low-income children. The Social Services Block Grant and WIN program merge child care with other services for which support is available, making it difficult to tag child care as a focus for enhanced funding. The AFDC disregard shares the disparagement that accompanies welfare dependence in our society. In general, child care for children generates greater public sympathy, particularly when framed in investment language, than does child care that is portrayed as a work-related benefit for low-income adults.

On a grander scale, the $2.3 billion in federal child care support for low-income families stands in stark contrast to the $3.7 billion that is presently provided to nonpoor families who incur work-related child care expenses through the Dependent Care Tax Credit (Haskins, 1988a). Whereas funding for the vast majority of low-income child care programs has been cut or eroded by inflation since 1981, the tax credit has grown steadily and rapidly from its 1981 expenditure level of $1.2 billion. By 1990 the tax credit is expected to cost $4.4 billion (Haskins, 1988b).

The differing priorities placed on quality versus costs that accompany the education versus welfare reform strategies are also abundantly evident in the existing array of federal regulations (Phillips & Zigler, 1987). Head Start programs are required to comply with federally imposed performance standards that are designed to assure a baseline level of comprehensive, quality service delivery to children. None of the other subsidies are accompanied by federal standards, nor, with the exception of the Social Services Block Grant and the Child Care Food Program, do they require that funds be spent in state-regulated child care programs. Unregulated or exempted arrangements tend to be less expensive and thus more in line with the cost-reduction goals of workfare-type programs.

Associations between child care and employment

It has been assumed that parents' decisions to join the labor force and their decisions to use child care are closely intertwined (Blau & Robins, 1986; Presser & Baldwin, 1980; Robins, 1987, 1989). This is the basic assumption underlying the inclusion of child care support in welfare reform proposals, and it is also the premise that supports tax benefits designed to partially reimburse the child care expenses of nonpoor (tax-paying) families. Two strands of evidence suggest that this assumption is warranted.

Child care as a constraint on employment

One strand of evidence related to child care and employment examines whether lack of child care constrains labor force participation. In 1982 the U.S. Bureau of the Census (1983) included responses to two pertinent questions in the June Current Population Survey. First, 26% of a sample of nonworking mothers of preschoolers said that they would seek employment if child care were available to them at a "reasonable cost." But markedly different response rates characterized women of different marital statuses and family income (U.S. Bureau of the Census, 1983). The Census found that 35% of unmarried women, compared to 26% of married women, indicated that lack of reasonably priced child care deterred their employment. Family income showed a negative association with child constraints: 33% of women with family incomes below $15,000, 25% of those with incomes ranging from $15,000 to $24,999, and 19% of those with family incomes at or above $25,000 indicated that lack of reasonably priced child care prevented them from working.

A more recent study conducted in Detroit (Mason, 1987) confirms these basic patterns. Among a socioeconomically heterogeneous sample of women with a youngest child under age 6, 12% of those not employed gave as their only or most important reason for not working, "Unable to find work that pays enough to cover the cost of child care and other expenses." Close to 40% of the nonemployed women in the sample said "yes" in response to the question, "If satisfactory child care were available at reasonable cost, would you look for work or return to work at this time?" The author speculates that this considerably higher rate of affirmative responses compared to the 1982 census data reflects the relative difficulty of finding employment in Detroit. Also paralleling the census data, Mason (1987) found that child care constraints were experienced to a greater degree by women from low- income, as compared to high-income, households and by women living without a male partner or spouse.

Both economic and social resources appear to affect the association between child care and employment, such that the employment decisions of single mothers living in poverty are particularly vulnerable to child care constraints. These self-report data, while consistent, provide no behavioral confirmation of the child care–employment link. Moreover, they do not distinguish between constraints that arise from the availability, cost, and/or quality of child care.

Child care provision and employment

The second strand of evidence focuses on the flip side of the constraint question. Specifically, Robins (1987) has examined whether the provision of child care actually removes a disincentive to employment. In a study for the Department of Housing and Urban Development (Robins, 1987; 1988), it was found that provision of low-cost child care services to public housing residents had a substantial effect on the likelihood that these families would achieve economic self-sufficiency.

Specifically, two matched groups of housing project residents were compared – one group lived in projects that contained a child care center, and the other group lived in projects without a child care center. The availability of a center was nonsignificantly associated with higher average hours of work, higher earnings, lower welfare benefits, and higher total family income. The associations became highly significant, however, when the size of the effect was allowed to vary with the relative size of the center. For example, a 50% increase in center size was found to increase hours of work by about 13.5%, earnings by 19.5%, and family income by about 5.5%. The effects were strongest for low-income families not presently receiving welfare benefits (Robins, 1988).

Evaluations of employment, training, and welfare reform efforts offer another source of evidence regarding the work-incentive effect of child care. Unfortunately, because these programs generally eliminate mothers with preschool children from mandatory coverage, little is known about the effectiveness of these child care subsidies. For example, in a recent evaluation of selected sites that implemented the new AFDC and WIN programs, the Manpower Demonstration and Research Corporation (Gueron, 1986) concluded that most projects did not require participation by parents with children under 6, thereby substantially restricting the portion of the AFDC caseload that benefited from these programs.

Similarly, the General Accounting Office (GAO) in a national survey of these new programs (General Accounting Office [GAO], 1987), concluded that only a minority of adult AFDC recipients with young children were served, largely as a result of the added costs and demands associated with providing support services such as child care. Of the 50 programs (out of 61 surveys) with registration or participation requirements, only 14 required women with children under 6 years of age to participate, thereby excluding about 60% of AFDC families from the pool of mandatory participants. Within the original WIN program, as of 1987 only 8 states had requested and received federal waivers from the requirement that women with children under age 6 be exempted from participation (Nightingale & Burbridge, 1987). Oklahoma was one of these states requesting a waiver. Women with children under age 6 grew from 37% to 70% of the participants in Oklahoma's federally funded Employment and Training Program between 1982 and 1985 and accounted for 67% of the participants who found employment (GAO, 1987). Child care support constituted two-thirds of Oklahoma's expenditures on this program.

These patterns of participation explain the finding that child care services accounted for a median of only 6.4% of total expenditures across the programs studied by the GAO. They also reflect the perception of 60% of program administrators that lack of child care hindered participation on the part of some AFDC families (GAO, 1987).

A related literature examines the effect of child care provision on school attendance and completion among adolescent mothers (see Marx, 1987, and Marx, Bailey, & Francis, 1988, for reviews). It suggests that quality child care services that are easily accessible can facilitate the educational progress of these young mothers (Campbell, Breitmayer, & Ramey, 1986; Project Redirection, 1985; Zellman, 1981). In Sarasota, Florida, for example, a longitudinal study of participants in a school-based child care program for pregnant and parenting teens revealed that 73% were still in school or had graduated at one year after delivery as compared with 37% in a comparison group (Marx, Bailey, & Francis, 1988).

Summary

Survey data and economic analyses suggest that the availability and cost of child care affect women's decisions about whether and how much to work. Whereas the self-report data collected by the U.S. Bureau of the Census (1983) and by Mason (1987) imply that child care unavailability is most likely to inhibit the labor force participation of low-income, unmarried mothers, Robins's (1987, 1988) work suggests that the effects of providing and subsidizing child care are greatest for families that already have achieved some degree of economic independence. Providing child care also may affect the school completion rates of adolescent mothers. Evaluations of welfare-to-work programs are singularly uninformative given that, until recently, only a minority of these programs have explicitly encouraged the participation of women with preschool-age children. The perceived unavailability of child care, and the added costs and effort associated with providing it, serve to constrain states' efforts to encourage economic self-sufficiency among welfare clients with young children.

Pressures for reform

Taken together, evidence of an economically stratified child care market, income-based differentials in family expenditures on child care, lost ground in federal child care support for low-income families, and a basic pattern of inattention to AFDC recipients with young children in state welfare-to-work programs provides a disheartening status report on children in poverty and child care. These conditions are not particularly new. Marginal public support, and hardship for families who either do not have access to low-cost options or cannot avail themselves of market forms of child care, have characterized the United States for decades (Fein & Clarke-Stewart, 1973; Steinfels, 1973).

Today, however, these conditions are being examined in a new context. The convergence of changing family demographics, macroeconomic trends, and renewed concerns about the social costs of failing to "invest" in children has created pressures for reform at both the state and federal levels. In the process, new laws and proposals for both developmental child care and improved policies in the context of welfare reform efforts have surfaced. In this section, several pressures for reform are reviewed, followed by a discussion of current state and federal efforts to respond to these pressures.

Demographic trends affecting families with children

The two trends with the most significant implications for low-income child care programs are the substantial increase in childhood poverty during the 1980s and the similarly dramatic increase in maternal employment (Duncan, Huston, this volume). Our apparent inability to stem poverty among children, with its attendant public costs in welfare and other subsidies, has led to a renewed resolve to target welfare reform efforts on the single women and children who constitute the major recipients of AFDC benefits. It also has refueled the compensatory education debate of the 1960s, with states taking the leadership role in implementing new preschool programs for low-income children.

The dramatic increase in maternal labor force participation has also shaped the contemporary welfare reform debate. Specifically, in the general population, the majority of women with children under age 6 are in the labor force, including 51% of those with children under 1 year of age (U.S. Department of Labor, 1987). Two-thirds of these mothers are employed in fulltime positions, although they do not necessarily work year-round. It is projected that by 1995 two-thirds of all children under age 6 will be reared by working mothers (Hofferth & Phillips, 1987).

These demographic facts have created an equity argument against exempting women with preschool-age children from participation in employment and training programs. The norm among middle-income, married women with infants and toddlers to work has challenged the mother-at-home model that has provided the rationale for these exemptions. Moreover, recent analyses of patterns of reliance on AFDC have pinpointed young, unmarried women who enter AFDC when their children are less than 3 years old as the group at greatest risk of becoming long-term recipients. Over time, more than 40% of this population will spend at least 10 years on AFDC (Ellwood, 1986). As a consequence, child care has moved center stage in welfare reform debates.

Macroeconomic trends

Immediately after World War II, the growth of the U.S. economy was accompanied by the expansion of employment opportunities, higher labor productivity, and increased real wages. Since the Vietnam War, however, different macroeconomic factors have shaped the labor force. As a consequence of the so-called deindustrialization of America (Bluestone & Harrison, 1982), new jobs have been created disproportionately in the service sector. Jobs in the service sector are generally poorly paid, offering limited fringe benefits and restricted career opportunities. Fully one-third of net new full-time, full-year jobs created since 1978 have paid an annual wage below the poverty level for a family of four (Bluestone & Harrison, 1986). Part-time employment by both men and women is also an important characteristic of the burgeoning service sector.

These economic shifts occurred as the large baby boom generation entered the labor force thus encouraging the two-career family. An additional wage makes a decisive contribution to total family income. It is estimated that working wives contribute one-fourth of total family income among whites and one-third of total income among blacks. For poor families with incomes below $10,000, women contributed 69% to total family income (Reskin & Hartmann, 1986).

This is the structural context that has contributed to mothers' rapid entry into the labor force. It also has contributed to the increase in poverty among female-headed families with only one available wage earner (Congressional Budget Office, 1988). Since 1970, as the median incomes of elderly individuals grew by 50% and the population as a whole experienced a 20% increase, the median income of single-mother families with children fell by 13% (Congressional Budget Office, 1988). Among the various factors that have aggravated childhood poverty in recent years – demographic trends, cutbacks in income support programs, and economic trends – the impact of the economy is the single most important factor (Gordon, 1987).

Children as an investment

Facts about childhood poverty, working mothers, and child care become increasingly compelling when they are subsumed by a theme. During the late 1980s, "investment" or human capital rhetoric provided this theme. As stated by one economist, human capital is "invested in acquiring valued capacities with some expectation that future benefits will be derived from exercising those capacities" (Watts & Donovan, 1988, p. 2). The benefits that are cited as warranting an investment in young children range from savings on the public costs associated with educational failure and juvenile delinquency to regaining for the United States its competitive position in the world economy.

A recent report issued by the Committee for Economic Development represented this perspective: "This nation cannot continue to compete and prosper in the global arena when more than one-fifth of our children live in poverty and a third grow up in ignorance" (Committee for Economic Development, 1987, p. 1).

Investment arguments place child care in a longitudinal perspective, not unlike the original arguments for Head Start, and identify the future productivity of the U.S. work force as a relevant goal for child care policy. We in effect have resurrected "public good" arguments for supporting child care for children in poverty and raised the spectre of nonproductive citizens and an economy in crisis as possible outcomes of ineffective child care policies.

Budgetary pressures

A final pressure to reduce poverty among families with children derives from the federal deficit. This pressure cuts two ways. On the one hand, increasing concern that the persistent growth in AFDC expenditures is uncontrollable has alarmed budget-conscious members of Congress and served as a catalyst for efforts to restructure the work incentives in this program. On the other hand, the mandatory cap on federal spending established in 1986 by the Gramm-Rudman-Hollings budget reform legislation has seriously constrained the scope and nature of the federal welfare reform debate.

These dual pressures become particularly important in light of the trade-offs that have typically been made in welfare reform efforts between quick reductions in the welfare rolls and long-term enhancement of self-sufficiency (GAO, 1987). The former strategy places the focus of employment and training efforts on individuals for whom there are few barriers to employment, and who are only transitionally in poverty (see Duncan, this volume). The latter, more expensive, strategy directs welfare reform efforts to populations that are at-risk of persistent poverty and for whom more extensive efforts must be made to promote self-sufficiency. Women with young children fall into both groups. However, they require more intensive services and greater support and thus higher per-person expenditures on training and employment services. Nevertheless, in the long term serving this population may produce a greater payoff precisely because they otherwise are more likely to become persistent, and thus more costly, AFDC recipients (Ellwood, 1986; GAO, 1987).

Current policy efforts and proposals

Both compensatory education programs for 4-year-olds and welfare reform efforts have proliferated at the state level in recent years, replicating the two-track system of child care support for the poor at the federal level. National welfare reform recently has been enacted by the U.S. Congress, and, independently, several major child care bills are being considered. The late 1980s appear to have been a watershed period for poverty-related child care policies. In this section, a brief summary of these state and federal efforts, as of 1988,[2] is provided.

State-level policy initiatives

In 1979, 6 states and the District of Columbia had state early childhood education legislation; by 1987, 26 states and the District had such legislation (Marx & Seligson, 1988). Not since the mid-1960s has there been such a significant start-up of early childhood programs. Most of these programs are targeted on children considered to be at risk for school failure (Marx & Seligson, 1988), with income typically providing either the explicit or implicit standard of risk. During the same period, new welfare reform efforts that include significant child care provisions have been undertaken in several states. These efforts are, by definition, directed at poor families. Some differ from prior welfare reform efforts, however, in their specific targeting on families headed by single mothers.

Early education initiatives. In 1987, 6 new states, Connecticut, Michigan, New Jersey, Oregon, Rhode Island, and Vermont, joined the 21 states[3] that have been been providing some level of state funding for compensatory preschool programs. Programs created in the last four years range from $189,000 for three pilot programs in Delaware to more than $37.5 million to initiate a statewide program in Texas. Some states simply have added permissive language to their school codes, allowing schools to operate preschool programs; others have enacted separate laws to create new streams of early education funding (Gnezda & Robinson, 1986; Marx & Seligson, 1988).

The specific approaches taken by the states are also remarkably diverse. Minnesota and Missouri, for example, fund early childhood family education programs through local school districts. Among other services, these programs provide home visits to parents with children from birth to school age. New Jersey invested $1 million in 1987 to initiate a statewide comprehensive, developmental child care program modeled after Head Start. In similar fashion, New York City launched the Giant Step program in 1987, which provides comprehensive, part-day preschool programs to disadvantaged 3- and 4-year-olds. Maine has provided supplemental funds to Head Start for the last three

2 This discussion reflects state initiatives as of 1988. States' financing of these programs can vary tremendously from year to year.
3 New York, California, New Jersey, Pennsylvania, Maryland, Louisiana, Oklahoma, South Carolina, Florida, Maine, Minnesota, Missouri, Ohio, Illinois, Michigan, Massachusetts, Texas, Washington, Alaska, West Virginia, and Wisconsin.

years, and both Florida and Massachusetts include Head Start programs among those eligible to receive new state preschool funds (Blank, Wilkins, & Crawley, 1987; Gnezda & Robinson, 1986).

These programs have been enacted as part of broader education reform efforts, spurred by a spate of reports claiming that our nation's schools had failed. Several rationales have been put forth for the inclusion of compensatory preschool education programs in these efforts: (1) the need to compete with private schools that offer pre-kindergarten programs and hence contribute to the drain of children from public schools, (2) the need to respond to growing acceptance and use of preschool programs by all parents, and (3) the need to utilize empty classrooms and employ teachers who are out of work.

The most explicit state rationale for embarking on preschool education harkens back to the original hopes for Head Start. Successive evaluations of compensatory education programs, augmented recently by highly publicized reports of the long-term impact of the Perry Preschool Project (Berrueta-Clement, Schweinhart, Barnett, Epstein, & Weikart, 1984; Schweinhart, Weikart, & Larner, 1986), have led educators to view early education as a panacea for school failure among low-income, disadvantaged children. The robustness of these evaluations has been called into question recently (Haskins, 1989), given the small sample sizes, noncomparable treatment and comparison groups, and questionable outcome measurement. A recent review of longitudinal assessments of early intervention programs (Barnett & Escobar, 1988), focusing on issues of cost-effectiveness, concluded that the evidence for investing in these programs is "persuasive, but uncomfortably thin" (p. 408).

Even if the evaluation evidence on early intervention projects was flawless and consistently encouraging, the generalizability to contemporary state efforts is dubious. The Perry Preschool Project cost $6,300 per child annually, and the more intensive Yale Family Support Project cost $20,000 per family over three years (Seitz, Rosenbaum, & Apfel, 1985). No state has committed the funds to provide the intensity and quality of services that these costs suggest. Texas, for example, spent about $770 per child, and South Carolina spent $1,290 per child in 1986–1987 (Blank, Wilkins, & Crawley, 1987).

Welfare reform initiatives. Paralleling the preschool initiatives in many states are renewed efforts to revamp welfare programs to encourage job training, employment, and, ultimately, economic self-sufficiency. Spurred in part by the federal welfare-employment programs passed in the early 1980s, the majority of states have initiated new or revised employment and training programs (GAO, 1987). As historically has been the case, these programs are focused on adult goals and premised on expectations of financial savings.

As with the preschool initiatives, a diversity of approaches is being attempted. In every instance, child care provisions accompany the reform initiatives and are receiving funds from a variety of sources. As already noted, SSBG and WIN funds are the most commonly used sources, but it is notable that 31 states have allocated supplemental state funds for this purpose. Provision of child care is not new to welfare reform efforts. In 1971, for example, President Richard Nixon included substantial support for child care in his ill-fated Family Assistance Plan (Steiner, 1976). However, there appears to be a growing appreciation that the temporary, custodial care that typically has characterized federal welfare reform proposals is not adequate to assure reduced reliance on public assistance.

Three states – California, Massachusetts, and Michigan – provide examples of some of the more experimental child care provisions accompanying welfare reform efforts. Table 7.3 summarizes these provisions.

California enacted the Greater Avenues for Independence (GAIN) program in September 1985 with mandatory participation by AFDC families with children age 6 and older and voluntary participation permitted families with younger children. The program began operation in two counties in July 1986 and was in effect in 26 of California's 58 counties by 1988 (McKeever, 1988). Given the emphasis on families with older children, the GAIN legislation was attached to child care legislation that provided a one-time appropriation of $22.5 million for capital costs to enhance the supply of *school-age* child care in California.

Children in families enrolled in GAIN may receive child care benefits through the new school-age program (which is not restricted to GAIN participants but does place a priority on distributing funds to school districts with high numbers of GAIN participants) or through the GAIN-specific subsidies. The GAIN child care subsidies may be used to reimburse either licensed or unlicensed arrangements. Care by relatives is encouraged as a cost-saving measure. Transitional child care is provided for a maximum of three months after a participant finds unsubsidized employment, although the statutory language states that transitional child care support must be provided for "not less than" three months. Total expenditures on child care amounted to $8.6 million in 1986. As of 1988, fewer than half of the counties in California had implemented GAIN programs.

Despite these elaborate child care provisions, in the 16-month period from July 1986 to October 1987, only 19.8% of all GAIN participants were provided with child care assistance. Of the single-parent households, 30% were provided with child care under GAIN (McKeever, 1988). Although some participants are assigned work during school hours, thereby obviating the need for child care, concerns are now surfacing about the adequacy and implemention of the child care component of GAIN. For example, the practice of encouraging participants to rely on no-cost or low-cost relative care has led some analysts to speculate that families are unaware that child care subsidies are available.

Table 7.3. *Child care provisions of welfare reform efforts in three selected states*

Provision	GAIN (California)	ET Choices (Massachusetts)	MOST (Michigan)
Total state expenditures, 1987	$210 million	$57 million	$21 million
Total child care expenditures, 1987	Not available	$27 million (voucher program)	$3.9 million (1986 figure)
Eligibility criteria	Mandatory for parents with children > 6 years; voluntary for parents with children < 6 years	Voluntary for all groups	Mandatory for parents with children > 6 months
Percentage participants with children < 6 years old	Not available	41%	56%
Participants receiving child care assistance	19.8% of all participants; 30% of single-mother households	31%	Not available
Child care reimbursement rates	Not available	$267/month average	$160/month max.
Duration of child care support	3 months transitional support	12 months transitional support; can be extended	No transitional support; may enter state/SSBG system based on income
Eligible types of child care	No restriction; relative care encouraged	Regulated or registered centers and homes; independent providers must be 16 years	No restriction
Primary form of child care support	Contracts	ET vouchers	AFDC special needs payments (disregard)
Supply-building mechanism included?	Yes, school-age care	Yes, focus on infant and toddler care	No

Sources: California: Personal communication, Barbara Clayton, Child Care Law Center; Massachusetts: General Accounting Office (1987), *Work and Welfare: Employment Programs in Four States*, Glynn (1987), Sanders (1987); Michigan: General Accounting Office (1987), *Work and Welfare*.

Massachusetts enacted the Employment and Training (ET) Choices program in October 1983. Participation in ET Choices is voluntary for all AFDC recipients. As of 1986, women with children under age 6 comprised about 40% of ET Choices participants, up from 18% of the participants in 1984. In

1987, Massachusetts spent over half of its total ET Choices budget (approximately $27 million) on child care services. Child care is provided through a voucher system, which was established by the legislature specifically to support the ET Choices program. ET Choices participants select their own providers and receive vouchers that cover some proportion of the cost of care, based on a sliding-fee scale. At the same time, they are placed on the waiting list for slots in the state's contract care system.

All child care funded with ET Choices vouchers must be licensed or registered. The average reimbursement rate for child care in 1987 was $267 per month. The vouchers are available for up to one year after job placement, at which time it is hoped that the participant will be able to shift to the contracted child care system, although the voucher may be extended beyond one year as an alternative source of subsidized care.

The Michigan Opportunity and Skills Training (MOST) program, enacted in 1983, also includes an explicit child care component. Michigan requires parents with children over *6 months* of age to register for MOST. Actual participation in job training is not required unless child care is available. Over half of all MOST registrants between 1983 and March 1985 were women with preschool-age children, with actual participation rates varying from 34% to 46% of all MOST participants (GAO, 1987). Child care subsidies are provided through special needs payments in the welfare grants of MOST participants, although in a few cases local school districts provided child care to participants. The special needs payment functions by adjusting participants' AFDC grants to take into account their child care expenses, up to a maximum of $160 per month per child.

Summary. Propelled by hopes that large benefits will accrue in the form of reduced costs on a range of public assistance programs, in both the short and long term, preschool initiatives and welfare reform efforts are proliferating at the state level. With few exceptions, children and families in poverty provide the target population for these efforts.

Unlike similar efforts initiated in the 1960s, however, child care has moved center stage as a critical component of the welfare reform strategy for reducing poverty. States that have devoted substantial portions of their welfare-to-work budgets to child care have produced impressive results. In Massachusetts, for example, more than 25,000 welfare recipients had obtained jobs as of 1988. Over one-third of these individuals had children under 6 years of age. A 1986 evaluation revealed that, one year post-job placement, 85% of ET Choices graduates were still off welfare (Employment and Training Choices, 1986). Yet we know virtually nothing about whether these programs promote enhanced development for children (see Huston, this volume). At the federal level, these successful efforts have informed new welfare reform and child care legislation.

Federal initiatives

Policy makers at the federal level are also grappling with pressures to reform national child care and welfare policies (Haskins, 1988b). Some of the issues raised in contemporary child care debates are familiar: How much added benefit is gained by supporting regulated versus unregulated child care? Should profit-making child care operations be eligible to receive federal funds? Other issues are new: Should child care reimbursement rates be adjusted for infants versus older children? Should child care benefits be extended beyond the point at which welfare recipients enter nonsubsidized employment?

Welfare reform. Just as child care has become a central topic of state welfare reform initiatives, recent federal legislation in this area clearly acknowledged the contribution of child care to the success of welfare-to-work efforts. The Family Support Act of 1988 (P.L. 100–485) represents the first major overhaul of the nation's welfare system in 53 years. The act requires all states to establish a "Job Opportunities and Basic Skills Training Program" (JOBS) for recipients of AFDC whose youngest child is at least 3 years of age. This is a significant change from prior federal legislation mandating participation only for parents with children older than 6 years of age. Moreover, under the new provisons, states can opt to require participation by parents with infants and toddlers over 1 year of age. Parents younger than age 20 without high school diplomas must participate in an educational activity regardless of the age of their children. In recognition of the support needs of parents with preschool-age children, the Family Support Act provides a major new source of child care assistance for AFDC recipients and for families that leave the AFDC rolls due to earned income. Unlike other welfare-based child care programs, the Family Support Act explicitly guarantees child care support to a JOBS participant if such care is deemed necessary for participation.

The child care provisions of the Family Support Act represent an interesting compromise between advocates of comprehensive, developmental child care and those who felt that the child care provisions in existing employment legislation, such as the WIN program, were adequate. On the side of developmental care, all AFDC-related child care must meet applicable state and local standards. Each state must develop basic health and safety provisions for center-based care that is otherwise exempt from state child care standards. Thus, all center-based care receiving support through the Family Support Act would be covered by state standards. To assure adequate funding for families who seek licensed child care, the Family Support Act gives states the option to pay up to the market rate for child care and receive federal matching funds of between 50% and 80% of state costs. Moreover, a new monthly limit on child care reimbursements was set at $175 per child for children age 2 and older and $200 per month for children younger than 2, a substantial increase over the previous $160 per month limit on AFDC subsidies. To assure continuity of care for children, the act guarantees child care support on a sliding-fee basis for one year after parents leave welfare for paid employment. Finally, there is a specific requirement that child care be coordinated with Head Start and other existing early childhood education programs.

On the side of low-cost, nondevelopmental child care, the Family Support Act allows states considerable flexibility to implement nonoptimal child care services. For example, parents are not required to use licensed care and may be reimbursed for forms of care that are not covered by state standards. This not only enhances parental choice but also allows states the opportunity to encourage parents to seek "free" and low-cost child care options before offering them licensed, center-based care.

In sum, the Family Support Act of 1988 incorporates child care provisions that have not previously appeared in this type of legislation. For example, both the guarantee of child care as an *explicit* requirement for mandated participation and recognition of the need to provide transitional child care are improvements over prior legislations. It remains to be seen whether the quality and reimbursement provisions of the law will prevail as states begin to implement their JOBS and child care programs.

Child care. Independent of the welfare reform debate, child care is among the most actively debated topics on the federal agenda. Approximately 100 bills with child care provisions were introduced during the 101st Congress (Stephan, 1989). These bills reflect a range of approaches to perceived child care problems, including supply shortages, cost constraints on parental choice, inadequate quality, and lack of government leadership. In this section, the major points of controversy in the contemporary child care debate are summarized. Most relevant to the theme of this chapter, however, is the persistent distinction between child care as compensatory education and child care as a benefit for low-income children with working parents.

The federal child care debate is no longer about whether there will be federal support for child care, or whether families will continue to rely on child care. Instead, it has focused on relatively pragmatic questions about delivery systems, financing, and the role of quality standards. Among these questions, the most controversial are what policy approach should be adopted? For whom should child care support be provided? What delivery system, if any, should be encouraged? And what are the respective federal and state roles in assuring quality care?

Two basic policy approaches are being considered. The first, "demand-side" approach, would provide child care subsidies through the tax system. The second, "supply-side" approach, would authorize direct grant programs to provide subsidies to parents and child care programs. Among the tax proposals, several would expand the existing Dependent Care Tax Credit and

target it more explicitly on lower income families by making the credit refundable (perhaps with advance payment provisions) and increasing the
amount of credit available to families earning, for example, under $20,000.
A contrasting tax approach would expand and adjust the Earned Income Tax
Credit (EITC) for family size or create a new "child tax credit" that would
provide tax relief to low-income working families with children. These latter
two approaches would provide benefits to families whether or not they use
child care. Among the direct grant proposals, such as the well-publicized Act
for Better Child Care Services (ABC), a basic allocation issue concerns the
proportion of funds that is dedicated toward subsidizing families' child care
costs through direct mechanisms (e.g., vouchers and subsidized "slots" in
eligible child care programs) and the proportion that is allocated toward
improving the child care system by implementing child care standards, supporting provider training and salary enhancements, and encouraging the recruitment of new providers. As the active child care proposals are narrowed
to a few that are receiving serious consideration, it has become apparent that
a combined tax-grant approach is likely to be adopted.

A second controversy focuses on the question of *who* should receive federal
child care benefits. Accordingly, the proposed bills differ on whether to target
federal subsidies on low-income and poor families or to institute a nonmeans-
tested child care program. Virtually all of the non-tax proposals adopt a
means-tested approach in which families at any income level could be served,
but only those with incomes below a specified level (e.g., 115% of poverty)
would be served without charge; those families at or above this level would
be charged on a sliding-fee scale up to the full cost of services. The tax
approaches vary on this question. Those that utilize the Dependent Care Tax
Credit leave intact the existing provisions that place no upper income limit
on eligibility. Alternatively, the EITC and the child tax credit proposals are
restricted to very low-income families. For example, under the child tax credit,
taxpayers with incomes over $13,000 in 1990 would receive no benefits.

Delivery system questions, affecting the direct grants proposals, have
sparked the most contentious debates. Two issues have been particularly
problematic. The first concerns the role of the public schools in child care.
Some proposals, such as Zigler's (1988) proposal to place public schools at
the hub of a federally funded network of demonstration child care programs,
are explicit in their support of school-based child care. Other proposals, such
as the ABC bill, balance efforts to sustain the existing array of community-
based delivery mechanisms and support the entry of new types of providers,
such as the public schools, into the child care market.

The second delivery system issue concerns the legality of federal assistance
for church-sponsored child care. Churches and synagogues are the single
largest providers of center-based child care in the United States. The controversy has revolved around whether religious organizations should as a

policy matter, and can as a constitutional matter, receive federal child care subsidies.

The third point of controversy concerns the role envisioned for state and federal regulation of child care. Provisions vary from those that reassert a federal role in child care regulation by, for example, requiring all funded programs to comply with a mandated set of federal standards to those that maintain the current system of exclusively state-licensed child care. Under one proposal, federal advisory standards would be developed and adopted as a goal toward which all states must strive (Costin, 1980; Phillips, Lande, & Goldberg, in press). States that meet the federal standards over a specified period of time would be rewarded with a higher federal grant or some other financial incentive. States that fail to meet the federal standards could be eligible to receive incentive grants aimed at bringing their standards into compliance with the federal guidelines.

Alongside these child care proposals, which emphasize care for the children of working parents, are proposals that explicitly cast child care as a compensatory education program. These include legislative proposals to increase the Head Start authorization level and to authorize a new federal matching grant program, Smart Start: The Community Collaboration for Early Childhood Development Act of 1989, to states and localities for all-day, all-year early childhood development programs for 4-year-olds. The Head Start proposal would maintain the Head Start Performance Standards. The "Smart Start" legislation requires that each provider receiving funding meet minimum, federal standards that, for example, require child:staff ratios of 10:1 or lower, group sizes of 20 children or less, and that at least one staff member per group of children have early childhood education certification or credentials. These standards, in both their national scope and their specific provisions, far exceed any of the regulatory provisions that presently accompany proposed child care legislation.

In sum, the most prominent federal child care proposals exemplify distinct views of how the future federal role in child care should evolve. Some proposals utilize the tax system to expand subsidies for parents at all income levels, whereas others target new funds on low-income parents and simultaneously attempt to improve the availability and quality of child care. Some proposals are explicit in supporting greater public school involvement in child care, whereas others support the current, highly diversified delivery system. The role of church-housed child care is among the most divisive issues in this debate. The proposals' positions on the appropriateness of federal child care standards range from those that endorse an incentive approach to those that oppose any federal role. It is only when proposals are explicit in their definition of child care as early education and when they provide for services to low-income children regardless of the employment status of their parents that high-quality care through mandated federal standards is supported.

Summary. Perhaps the most striking feature of policy activity at the federal and state levels is its continued endorsement of the two-tiered, education versus welfare-reform, strategy of providing child care to children in poverty. Although the Family Support Act represents an attempt to weave these two strands together, the many loopholes in the legislation and the weak regulations that have been proposed to guide the act's implementation threaten to maintain the poorly funded, inadequate-quality child care that typically accompanies welfare reform efforts. Despite the clear impact of contemporary trends on the new proposals, seen, for example, in the mandatory extension of welfare-to-work policies to mothers with children age 3 years and older, the basic framework persists. Its influence is also seen in the current child care debate in which proposals for early childhood programs, emphasizing quality care, are considered apart from proposals that emphasize the care of children (generally, low-income) of working mothers.

Conclusions and directions for research

In the late 1980s, Sawhill (1987) asserted that a "new realism" is evident in debates about poverty and, specifically, in efforts to design a constructive role for government in alleviating poverty. Part of this new realism has involved reaching a consensus on the broad outlines of a reform strategy that includes three principles: (1) a belief that work has value, (2) a value that parents should support their children, and (3) a commitment to help those who help themselves (Sawhill, 1987).

Child care is the benefit that weaves these principles together. For mothers with young children, working and supporting their children entails reliance on child care. Their efforts to escape dependence on welfare, therefore, require a public commitment to supporting their child care needs. This seemingly logical equation is lent urgency by the growing recognition that young mothers with young children may benefit most from job training programs and reap the greatest cost savings from efforts to move families from welfare dependence to employment. Available evidence suggests that this is one of the groups most at risk of long-term welfare dependence (Ellwood, 1986) and thus most likely to be helped as a target of welfare reform efforts.

The short-term costs associated with accomplishing this goal will be high, largely as a result of these women's child care needs. These high short-term costs have led, historically, either to a relative neglect of mothers with young children in efforts to promote self-sufficiency or when these mothers' participation is sought, to a "bare minimum" approach to subsidizing child care. The contemporary welfare reform debate shows signs that this link is weakening. Exemptions from participation are being pared back to women with children under 3 years of age, several states are concentrating their welfare-to-work programs on women with young children, and, as an inevitable consequence, child care is increasingly being acknowledged as a substantial component of these programs.

What remains to be accomplished is to dovetail these promising developments within the welfare reform debate to parallel discussions of the value of compensatory education. Not only can mothers be encouraged to acquire and maintain jobs if child care is provided but the children can benefit as well if they are placed in programs that emphasize developmental care rather than in purely custodial care. This joining of the welfare reform and education strategies for providing child care to children in poverty has met with strong resistance, primarily as a result of the short-term conflict between reducing welfare costs and purchasing expensive child care. Accordingly, a truly intergenerational child care policy for low-income families remains a vision.

Directions for research

Although economists have begun to examine the association between parents' employment decisions and the availability and cost of child care, no attention has been paid to the effect of variation in child care quality. Cost is not necessarily a valid proxy for quality, and the meaning of "satisfactory" and "appropriate" care in surveys of employed and nonemployed mothers (see Mason, 1987; U.S. Bureau of the Census, 1987a) is ambiguous. These terms are as likely to be interpreted to mean "convenient" as they are to mean "good quality." If definitions of quality care are expanded beyond static measures of program characteristics (e.g., staff–child ratio, group size, age-appropriate curriculum) to encompass the stability of care, the capacity of the provider to care for sick children, and the availability of comprehensive services such as health screening, it is possible that stronger associations would be found between the availability of care and labor force participation.

Children have been neglected in research on the effects of work incentive programs. The literature on maternal employment (Hoffman, 1989; Kamerman & Hayes, 1982) suggests that children can benefit from the increased self-esteem of, and model of competence provided by, working mothers. We do not know whether these relations hold for children whose mothers are enabled by employment and training programs to move off welfare (Stipek & McCroskey, 1989). The effects on children of the improved standard of living that presumably accompanies stable employment also warrant study.

Research that examines directly the intergenerational effects of work incentive programs would be extremely valuable. If cast in a longitudinal framework, the questions just raised about developmental effects hold the potential to demonstrate the importance of integrating compensatory education and welfare reform policies in the area of child care. Intergenerational research designs are also particularly well suited for the study of child care programs for adolescent parents. These programs are proliferating (Marx, 1987) and are sorely in need of careful evaluation. Numerous issues could be examined: Do children placed in stable, good quality care while their mothers attend school or participate in employment and training programs fare differently than children placed in nonoptimal arrangements? Do short-term effects on children of having an employed versus a dependent parent extend to their longer term educational and career paths? What are the direct and indirect effects to adolescent mothers of near- or on-site (school) programs that combine developmental care and parenting education?

Some of the state welfare reform proposals include opportunities for welfare recipients to work as child care providers. This is a social experiment that warrants careful study. As a work force, child care providers receive among the lowest wages, the fewest benefits, and experience the highest turnover rates of any employment sector (Phillips & Whitebook, 1990). It is not clear that child care employment would serve to remove women from dependence on public assistance. Moreover, the role of job training in their performance as child care workers requires study. Evidence in the child care literature suggests that the caregivers' child-related education and training is among the strongest predictors of children's development in child care (Phillips & Howes, 1987; Ruopp, Travers, Glantz, & Coelen, 1979). The effects on children of being cared for in these arrangements is also an important topic for research.

These issues are among the numerous possibilities for research offered by contemporary efforts to provide child care to children in poverty. Weiss (1984) has found that timing in the political arena affects the utilization of research. When the broad outlines of policy are being developed, or when new policies are being designed to replace ineffective policies, research has a greater chance of being seriously considered than at other stages in the policy process. Child care policies for children in poverty are undergoing intense scrutiny and revision, suggesting that the time is ripe for the input of research-based knowledge.

The potential contribution is vast. As the majority of children from all walks of life spend substantial portions of their childhood in child care, the significance of assuring that their experiences are beneficial is magnified. This is particularly true for children who are reared in impoverished living conditions. Here, the possibility is not only to offer their parents an opportunity to gain skills and employment but also to offer the children opportunities to partake of the preschool experiences that the majority of mothers, working and not working, seek for their children's development.

Summary

The reduction of poverty has provided the most long-standing goal for child care policy in the United States. Two strategies have distinguished these policies: One casts child care as an adjunct to adult-focused welfare reform efforts, and the other offers child care as a form of early intervention for young children. Although contemporary budgetary pressures and social trends have fueled new child care policies at the federal and state levels, this dichotomy of approaches has persisted, with important ramifications for the level and quality of services provided to low-income families. Future research needs to address this dichotomy and to cast empirical questions about child care in a truly intergenerational framework that simultaneously considers outcomes for parents and for their children.

References

Ackerman, D. M. (1989, March). *Day care and the law of church and state: Constitutional mandates and policy options*. CRS Report for Congress. Washington, DC: Congressional Research Service.

Barnett, W. S., & Escobar, C. M. (1988). The economics of early educational intervention: A review. *Review of Educational Research, 57*, 387–414.

Berrueta-Clement, J. R., Schweinhart, L. J., Barnett, W. S., Epstein, A. S., & Weikart, D. P. (1984). *Changed lives: The effects of the Perry Preschool program on youths through age 19* (Monographs of the High/Scope Education Research Foundation, 8). Ypsilanti, MI: High/Scope Press.

Blank, H., Savage, J., & Wilkins, A. (1988). *State child care fact book, 1988*. Washington, DC: Children's Defense Fund.

Blank, H., Wilkins, A., & Crawley, M. (1987). *State child care fact book, 1987*. Washington, DC: Children's Defense Fund.

Blau, D. M., & Robins, P. K. (1986, October). *Fertility, employment, and child care*. Report submitted to the Department of Health and Human Services, National Institute of Child Health and Human Development, Bethesda, MD.

Bloom, B. S. (1964). *Stability and change in human characteristics*. New York: Wiley.

Bloom, D. E., & Steen, T. P. (1988, January). *The labor force implications of expanding the child care industry*. Paper presented at a conference on "the economic implications and benefits of child care, Wingspread, Racine, WI.

Bluestone, B., & Harrison, B. (1982). *The deindustrialization of America: Plant closing, community abandonment, and the dismantling of basic industry*. New York: Basic Books.

Bluestone, B., & Harrison, B. (1986, December). *The great American job machine: The proliferation of low wage employment in the U.S. economy*. Study prepared for the Joint Economic Committee. Washington, DC: U.S. Congress.

Campbell, F. A., Breitmayer, B., & Ramey, C. (1986). Disadvantaged single teen mothers and their children: Consequences of free educational day care. *Family Relations*, 63–68.

Carson, E., Merck, C., Richardson, J., & Solomon, C. (1987, July). *AFDC, food stamps, and work: History, rules, and research*. Washington, DC: Congressional Research Service.

Clifford, R., & Russell, S. D. (1988, April). *Financing programs for preschool-aged children*. Paper presented at the meetings of the American Educational Research Association, New Orleans.

Committee for Economic Development. (1987). *Children in need: Investment strategies for the educationally disadvantaged*. New York: Author.

Congressional Budget Office. (1988). *Trends in family income: 1970–1986*. Washington, DC: Author.

Costin, L. B. (1980). Federal–state relations and children's daytime care and development. In S. Kilmer (Ed.), *Advances in early education and day care* (Vol. 1, pp. 63–76). Greenwich, CT: JAI Press.

Ellwood, D. (1986). *Targeting "would-be" long-term recipients of AFDC*. Washington, DC: Mathematica Policy Research.

Fein, G., & Clarke-Stewart, A. (1973). *Child care in context.* New York: Wiley.

General Accounting Office.(1987, January). *Work and welfare: Current AFDC work programs and implications for federal policy* (Report No. HRD-87-34). Washington, DC: Author.

Gnezda, T., & Robinson, S. (1986, October). State approaches to early childhood education. *State Legislative Report, 11*(4).

Gordon, N. (1987, November 9). Testimony before the Income Security Task Force, Committee on the Budget, U.S. House of Representatives, Washington, DC.

Greenstein, R. (1987, November 9). Testimony before the Income Security Task Force, Committee on the Budget, U.S. House of Representatives, Washington, DC.

Grubb, N., & Lazerson, M. (1988). *Broken promises: How Americans fail their children.* New York: Basic Books.

Gueron, J. M. (1986). *Work initiatives for welfare recipients: Lessons from a multi-state experiment.* New York: Manpower Demonstration and Research Corporation.

Haskins, R. (1988a). *The day care crisis: Who said so?* Unpublished manuscript prepared for the Committee on Ways and Means, U.S. House of Representatives, Washington, DC.

Haskins, R. (1988b, January). *Summary of federal provisions for child care.* Paper prepared for the minority staff of the Committee on Ways and Means, U.S. House of Representatives, Washington, DC.

Haskins, R. (1989). Beyond metaphor: The efficacy of early childhood education. *American Psychologist, 44*, 274–282.

Hofferth, S. L. (1987, July 1). *Child care in the U.S.* Statement before the Select Committee on Children, Youth, and Families, U.S. House of Representatives, Washington, DC.

Hofferth, S. L. (1989). Unpublished tabulations from the National Longitudinal Survey of Youth, 1986.

Hofferth, S. L., Brayfield, A., Deich, S., & Holcomb, P. (1991). *The National Child Care Survey, 1990.* Washington, DC: Urban Institute.

Hofferth, S. L., & Phillips, D. A. (1987). Child care in the United States, 1970 to 1995. *Journal of Marriage and the Family, 49*(3), 559–71.

Hoffman, L. W. (1989). Effects of maternal employment in the two-parent family. *American Psychologist, 44*, 283–292.

Hunt, J. McV. (1961). *Intelligence and experience.* New York: Ronald Press.

It's your move . . . employment and training choices. (1987). Massachusetts Department of Public Welfare.

Kamerman, S., & Hayes, C. (1982). *Families that work: Children in a changing world.* Washington, DC: National Academy Press.

McCartney, K., & Phillips, D. (1989). Motherhood and child care. In B. Birns & D. Hay (Eds.), *Different faces of motherhood* (pp. 157–183). New York: Plenum Press.

McKeever, C. (1988, January). *Sixteen months of GAIN: Troubling trends.* Sacramento, CA: Western Center on Law and Poverty.

Martinez, S. (1989). Child care and federal policy. In J. Lande, S. Scarr, & N. Gunzenhauser (Eds.), *Caring for children: Challenge to America* (pp. 111–124). Hillsdale, NJ: Erlbaum.

Marver, J. D., & Larson, M. A. (1978). Public policy toward child care in America: A historical perspective. In P. K. Robins & S. Weinrer (Eds.), *Child care and public policy* (pp. 17–42). Lexington, MA: Heath.

Marx, F. (1987). *The role of day care in serving the needs of school-age parents and their children: A review of the literature* (Working Paper, No. 174). Boston: Wellesley College, Center for Research on Women.

Marx, F., Bailey, S., & Francis, J. (1988). *Child care for the children of adolescent parents: Findings from a national survey and case studies* (Working Paper, No. 184). Boston: Wellesley College, Center for Research on Women.

Marx, F., & Seligson, M. (1988). *The public school early childhood study: The state survey.* New York: Bank Street College of Education.

Mason, K. O. (June, 1987). *The perceived impact of child care costs on women's labor supply and fertility*. Research report to the National Institute of Child Health and Development, Washington, DC.

Nightingale, D. S., & Burbridge, L. C. (1987). *The status of state work-welfare programs in 1986: Implications for welfare reform*. Washington, DC: Urban Institute.

O'Connell, M. (1989, July). Child care costs estimated at $14 billion in 1986, Census Bureau survey shows. Press release. Washington, DC: U.S. Bureau of the Census.

Peters, D. L. (1980). Social science and social policy and the care of young children: Head Start and after. *Journal of Applied Developmental Psychology, 1*, 7–27.

Phillips, D. (1989). Future directions and need for child care in the United States. In J. Lande, S. Scarr, & N. Gunzenhauser (Eds.), *Caring for children: Challenge to America* (pp. 257–273). Hillsdale, NJ: Erlbaum.

Phillips, D., & Howes, C. (1987). Indicators of quality in child care: Review of research. In D. Phillips (Ed.), *Quality in child care: What does research tell us?* (pp. 1–19). Washington, DC: National Association for the Education of Young Children.

Phillips, D., Lande, J., & Goldberg, M. (in press). The state of child care regulation: A comparative analysis. *Early Childhood Research Quarterly*.

Phillips, D., & Whitebook, M. (1990). The child care provider: Pivotal player in the child's world. In S. S. Chehrazi (Ed.), *Psychosocial issues in day care* (pp. 129–146). Washington, DC: American Psychiatric Press.

Phillips, D., & Zigler, E. (1987). The checkered history of federal child care regulation. In E. Rothkopf (Ed.), *Review of research in education* (Vol. 14, pp. 3–42). Washington, DC: American Educational Research Association.

Presser, H. B., & Baldwin, W. (1980). Child care as a constraint on employment: Prevalence, correlates, and bearing on the work and fertility nexus. *American Journal of Sociology, 85*, 1202–1231.

Project Redirection (1985). *Final impacts of the Project Redirection program on pregnant and parenting teens*. New York: Manpower Demonstration Research Corporation.

Reskin, B. F., & Hartmann, H. I. (Eds.). (1986). *Women's work, men's work: Sex segregation on the job*. Washington, DC: National Academy Press.

Robins, P. (1987, March 10). *The role of child care in promoting economic self-sufficiency among low-income families*. Testimony before the House Select Committee on Children, Youth, and Families, Washington, DC.

Robins, P. (1988). Child care and convenience: The effects of labor market entry cost on economic self-sufficiency among public housing residents. *Social Science Quarterly, 69*, 122–136.

Robins, P. (1989, April). Paper presented at the annual meetings of the Population Association of America, Baltimore.

Rothman, S. (1973, Winter). Other people's children: The day care experience in America. *The Public Interest, 30*, 11–27.

Ruopp, R., Travers, J., Glantz, F., & Coelen, C. (1979). *Children at the center: Final results of the National Day Care Study*. Cambridge, MA: Abt Associates.

Sawhill, I. V. (1987). Anti-poverty strategies for the 1980s. In *Reducing poverty and dependency*. Washington, DC: Center for National Policy.

Schweinhart, L. J., Weikart, D. P., & Larner, M. B. (1986). Consequences of three preschool curriculum models through age 15. *Early Childhood Research Quarterly, 1*, 15–45.

Seitz, V., Rosenbaum, L. K., & Apfel, N. (1985). Effects of family support intervention: A tenyear follow-up. *Child Development, 56*, 376–391.

Select Committee on Children, Youth, and Families. (1987). *Programs that work*. Washington, DC: U.S. Congress.

Steiner, G. Y. (1976). *The children's cause*. Washington, DC: Brookings.

Steiner, G. Y. (1981). *The futility of family policy*. Washington, DC: Brookings.

Steinfels, M. O. (1973). *Who's minding the children? The history and politics of day care in America*. New York: Simon & Schuster.

Stephan, S. (1989, May). *Child day care*. CRS Issue Brief. Washington, DC: Congressional Research Service.

Stipek, D., & McCroskey, J. (1989). Investing in children: Government and workplace policies for parents. *American Psychologist, 44*, 416–423.

U.S. Bureau of the Census. (1971). *Money income and poverty status of families and persons in the United States: 1970*. Current Population Reports, No. 30. Washington, DC: U.S. Department of Commerce.

U.S. Bureau of the Census. (1983, November). *Child care arrangements of working mothers: June 1982*. Current Population Reports, Series P–23, No. 129. Washington, DC: U.S. Government Printing Office.

U.S. Bureau of the Census. (1987a). *Who's minding the kids? Child care arrangements: Winter 1984–85* (P–70). Washington, DC: U.S. Department of Commerce.

U.S. Bureau of the Census (1987b, October). *Poverty in the United States, 1985*. Current Population Reports, Consumer Income, Series P–60, No. 158. Washington, DC: U.S. Department of Commerce.

U.S. Bureau of the Census (1988). *Money income and poverty status of families and persons in the United States: 1987*. Current Population Reports, No. 30. Washington, DC: U.S. Department of Commerce.

U.S. Department of Labor (1971). *Household and family characteristics, March 1970*. Current Population Reports, Series P–20. No. 218. Washington, DC: U.S. Department of Labor.

U.S. Department of Labor (1987, August). Over half of mothers with children one year old or under in labor force in March, 1987. *News*. Washington, DC: U.S. Department of Labor.

U.S. Department of Labor (1988). *Household and family characteristics, March 1987*. Current Population Reports, Series P–20. No. 424, Washington, DC: U.S. Department of Labor.

Watts, H. W., & Donovan, S. (1988, January). *What can child care do for human capital and vice versa?* Paper presented at a conference on the economic implications and benefits of child care, Wingspread, Racine, WI.

Weiss, C. (1984). Increasing the likelihood of influencing decisions. In L. Rutman (Ed.), *Evaluation research methods: A basic guide* (pp. 159–190). Beverly Hills, CA: Sage.

Whitebook, M., Howes, C., & Phillips, D. (1989). *Who cares? Child care workers and the quality of care in America*. Executive summary of the National Child Care Staffing Study. Berkeley, CA: Child Care Employee Project.

Zellman, G. L. (1981). *The response of the schools to teenage pregnancy and parenthood*. Santa Monica, CA: RAND Corporation.

Zigler, E. (1988). A solution to the nation's child care crisis: The school of the twenty-first century. Unpublished manuscript.

Zigler, E., & Valentine, J. (1979). *Project Head Start: A legacy of the War on Poverty*. New York: Free Press.

8 Poverty, early childhood education, and academic competence: The Abecedarian experiment

Craig T. Ramey and Frances A. Campbell

Children from low-resource families are at high risk for academic underachievement as early in their school careers as first grade (Ramey, Stedman, Borders-Patterson, & Mengel, 1978). Low-resource children are at increased risk for retention in grade, for special education placement, (Lazar, Darlington, Murray, Royce, & Snipper, 1982), and for failure to complete high school (Brooks-Gunn & Furstenberg, 1986). Dropping out of school is linked, in turn, to increased rates of juvenile delinquency (Berrueta-Clement, Schweinhart, Barnett, Epstein, & Weikart, 1984), increased likelihood of teenage pregnancy, and intergenerational economic dependency (Furstenberg, 1976).

A crucial mediating factor in successful academic achievement is intellectual competence. Brighter individuals go further in school, have greater economic power (Jencks, 1972), and appear to lead healthier, more prestigious lives. Therefore, it is important to determine the extent to which intellectual competence can be enhanced through systematic interventions for high-risk children from low-resource families.

Early childhood education and family support are theoretically justified (e.g., Hunt, 1961; Ramey, Bryant, Campbell, Sparling, & Wasik, 1989), practical, and increasingly popular methods of intervention. A central theoretical and policy-relevant question is what are the relative effects of different methods of intervention? This chapter describes one long-term research effort

This research was supported by grants from the National Institutes of Child Health and Human Development, the Spencer Foundation, the Carnegie Foundation, and the Department of Human Resources of the state of North Carolina. The authors wish to acknowledge and thank the multidisciplinary team of researchers and assistants whose creative efforts and diligence undergirded the Carolina Abecedarian Project. For this chapter, we thank Margaret Burchinal and the Design and Statistical Computing Section of the Frank Porter Graham Child Development Center for help with data analysis. We also wish to thank the teachers and administrators of the school systems involved in this study for their enthusiastic and continued cooperation. School systems include those of Chapel Hill/Carrboro, Orange County, Durham County, Pittsboro, and Chatham County. Finally, we most especially thank the Abecedarian children and their families, without whose generous gift of time and wonderful spirit of cooperation this study could not have been accomplished. Our hope is that their participation in this research will result in better life opportunites for their families.

190

to address that question – the Carolina Abecedarian Project, a program designed to determine the relative efficacy of multiple interventions intended to enhance the intellectual competence and academic achievement of children from socioeconomically disadvantaged families.

Method

Rationale

In 1972 we began the Abecedarian[1] Project at the Frank Porter Graham Child Development Center of the University of North Carolina. The research program involved investigators from developmental psychology, pediatrics, and early childhood education. The initial phase of the intervention program combined early childhood education, pediatric care, and family support services into an integrated intervention system. The focus of our efforts was on the question of whether these coordinated high-quality services, delivered from early in the child's life, could be instrumental in promoting intellectual competence during the so-called preschool years. Accordingly, in the Abecedarian Project, preschool educational intervention, in a day-care setting, was begun in infancy and provided continuously for the first 5 years of the child's life. A second phase of the intervention, in which parents were systematically supported in assisting their child's educational progress, began when the children entered public school as kindergarteners and continued for three school years. An endpoint evaluation took place when the children had completed these three years; the children were then approximately 8 years old. The primary outcome measures at age 8 included assessments of the children's intellectual development and academic performance as well as parent and teacher judgments concerning social competence.

Design

The design of the preschool study required two initially equivalent groups of high-risk children who subsequently would be treated educationally differently to determine if the treatment produced increased intellectual competence. Therefore, one of the key features of the Abecedarian Project was the random assignment of children to treatment and control groups. This assignment procedure is especially important because studies of educational intervention that treat only volunteers and have no experimentally adequate comparison group cannot determine if intellectual changes are the result of the educational treatment or of some other influence on development. Random assignment

1 *Abecedarian* means one who learns the fundamentals of something, such as the alphabet.

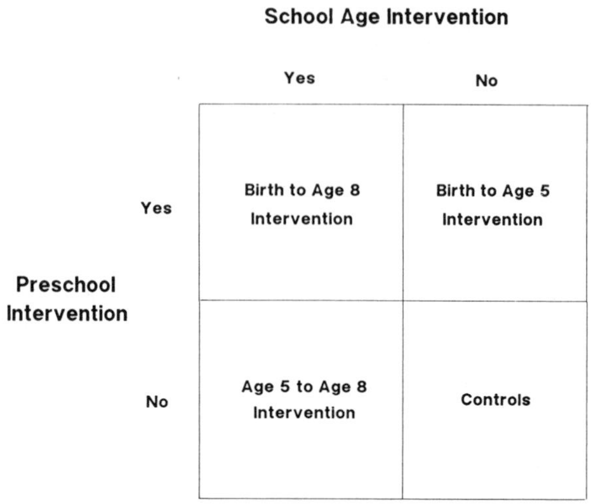

School Age Intervention

| | Yes | No |

Figure 8.1. Experimental design of the Carolina Abecedarian Project.

is, therefore, a powerful scientific tool to ensure initial group equivalence, which is an essential feature for strong causal inferences.

Because children were randomly assigned to treatment groups at birth, the basis for equating the groups was derived from a combination of family risk factors. These were summarized into a High-Risk Index (Ramey & Smith, 1977). Equated pairs of children were assigned either to the preschool intervention group or to the preschool control group. Four cohorts of approximately 28 children each were admitted to the project between 1972 and 1977.

Before their entry into public school kindergarten, the children within the preschool intervention and control groups were re-randomized by equating pairs of children, within groups, on the basis of their Stanford–Binet IQ scores at 48 months and then assigning one of each pair to a school-age intervention group and the other to a school-age control group. Thus, half of each preschool group received the school-age intervention program. The resulting four-cell design shown in Figure 8.1 permitted a comparison of intellectual and academic outcomes in children who had a total of eight years of intervention, five in preschool and three in early elementary school (preschool plus follow-through), five years of intervention in preschool only (preschool intervention only), three years of school-age intervention only (school-age only), and no educational intervention provided by the Abecedarian Project (control condition).

Recruitment

The High-Risk Index (Table 8.1) that was used to screen families for eligibility included factors previously reported in the literature to be associated with

Table 8.1. *High-risk index*

Factor	Weight
Mother's educational level (last grade completed)	
6	8
7	7
8	6
9	3
10	2
11	1
12	0
Father's educational level (last grade completed)	
6	8
7	7
8	6
9	3
10	2
11	1
12	0
Family income (per year)	
$1,000	8
1,001–2,000	7
2,001–3,000	6
3,001–4,000	5
4,001–5,000	4
5,001–6,000	0
Father absent for reasons other than health or death	3
Absence of maternal relatives in local area	3
Siblings of school age one or more grades behind age-appropriate level or with equivalently low scores on school-administered achievement tests	3
Payments received from welfare agencies within past three years	3
Record of father's work indicates unstable or unskilled and semiskilled labor	3
Records of mother's or father's IQ indicate scores of 90 or below	3
Records of sibling's IQ indicates scores of 90 or below	3
Relevant social agencies in the community indicate the family is in need of assistance	3
One or more members of the family has sought counseling or professional help in the past three years	1
Special circumstances not included in any of the above that are likely contributors to cultural or social disadvantage	1

mild mental retardation and academic failure, including low levels of parental education and family income and evidence of retardation or social maladjustment in family members. These factors were preassigned weights according to consensual professional estimates of their psychological importance. A family's total score was the sum of applicable weights earned. A family had to score 11 points or higher on the High-Risk Index to be included in the study.

Prenatal clinics and social service agencies were used to identify families

Table 8.2. *Entry level demographic data for preschool experimental and control families*

| | Group | | |
| | Experimental | Control | Total |
Variable	($N = 55$)	($N = 54$)	($N = 109$)
Mean maternal age (years)	19.56	20.28	19.92
	(3.88)	(5.77)	(4.90)
Mean maternal education (years)	10.45	9.98	10.22
	(1.75)	(1.91)	(1.84)
Mean maternal full-scale IQ	85.49	84.18	84.84
	(12.43)	(10.78)	(11.61)
Percentage intact family	23%	26%	24%
Percentage black	96%	100%	98%

who appeared likely to qualify for the experiment. These families were then visited by a member of the center's staff who explained the project and obtained informed consent for participation. A final determination of eligibility was made after the mother of a prospective project family visited the center. On this occasion, the mother was again interviewed and administered an intelligence test, either the Wechsler Adult Intelligence Scale (Wechsler, 1955) or the Wechsler Intelligence Scale for Children (Wechsler, 1949), depending on her age. Following this second contact, scoring of the High-Risk Index was completed, and enrollment offered or not. Random assignment to groups was completed prior to an infant's 6-week birthday.

Participants

All children in the sample were full-term infants free from conditions known to have genetic or infectious links to mental retardation, but all were from homes with low levels of parental income and education. A total of 122 families were invited to participate in the study; 109 families to whom 111 children were born agreed to participate, accepted their random group assignments, and actually took part. By the beginning of the elementary school phase, attrition due to a wide variety of reasons had reduced the number to 96 children. Of these, 90 had IQ data collected by "blinded" assessors at the end of three years in public school, and 88 had scholastic achievement test data. Using the figure of 90 as the final sample size gives an attrition rate of 18.9%, or 1.46% per year over the 13-year span from entry of the oldest subjects until the youngest reached the 8-year-old endpoint. No systematic effects of attrition have been detected (Martin, Ramey, & Ramey, 1990).

Table 8.2 shows selected demographic characteristics of the mothers in the study at the time of the child's birth. The mothers tended to be young, to have less than a high school education, and to be single parents. Maternal ages ranged between 13 and 43; approximately one-third of the mothers were 17 years old or younger when their children were born. Maternal IQs ranged from 49 to 124, with the mean falling at approximately 85 in both groups. Ninety-eight percent of all subjects were black, although race was not considered a risk factor on the High-Risk Index. The high proportion of blacks reflects the demographic characteristics of the university town where the study was conducted. Almost no qualified whites could be found within a distance that made daily participation feasible. (Participant families had to live within commuting distance of the center to allow the child potentially to attend the educational Child Development Center program.)

Preschool intervention

As just noted, preschool educational intervention was delivered in a child development center setting, where children were taught by the staff. Treated children attended the Child Development Center until they entered public school kindergarten at age 5. Families were offered and encouraged to participate in parent group sessions on a wide variety of topics related to parenting and family development. Parents also had access to the project's social workers, who provided instrumental, social, and emotional support. This support included direct assistance with such issues as housing and social services as well as personal counseling. Pediatric care was provided by a team of on-site research nurses and pediatricians.

Infants in the preschool intervention group began attending the center as young as 6 weeks of age; mean age at entry was 8.8 weeks. The project's goal for families was to have a warm and friendly, homelike atmosphere that families would find helpful and positive. For children the goal was to provide them with a safe and healthful environment staffed by sensitive and resourceful early childhood educators who would offer high-quality education and emotional support. The infant nursery accommodated 14 babies and was staffed by four caregivers. Curriculum materials to enhance cognitive, language, perceptual-motor, and social development were devised by Sparling and Lewis (1981) for use in this program. Educational experiences were chosen for infants based on the curriculum developers' and teachers' assessments of each child's needs, and the experiences were changed as the infant appeared to be ready for new challenges. These activities were fit into the child's daily schedule as natural events while infants paced themselves through the day. Toddlers likewise had flexible schedules for activities and nap times.

The preschool program became increasingly structured as children became developmentally more mature. The classrooms for 3- and 4-year-olds resembled other high-quality developmentally appropriate preschool programs, with centers for housekeeping, blocks, water play, books, and art and quiet corners for 1:1 teaching or solitude.

Because a number of theorists have hypothesized that deficits (Blank, 1982; Tough, 1976) or differences (Heath, 1983; Labov, 1970) in the early language environments of disadvantaged children leave them unprepared for success in mainstream public schools, language development was especially emphasized in the preschool program. The focus was on pragmatic features of adult–child language in the context of natural conversations about daily life. Teachers received specific training so that their verbal exchanges with the children would be developmentally appropriate and would elicit prolonged conversations (McGinness & Ramey, 1981; Ramey, McGinness, Cross, Collier, & Barrie-Blackley, 1981). In addition, preliteracy curricula were used with older preschool children (Greenberg & Epstein, 1973; Wallach & Wallach, 1976).

In summary, the preschool educational program was designed to appear playful and spontaneous from the child's viewpoint, yet planful and structured from the adults' perspective. A more detailed description of the preschool program and its biosocial systems theory rationale can be found elsewhere (Ramey, Bryant, Campbell, Sparling, & Wasik, 1988; Ramey, MacPhee, & Yeates, 1982).

To increase confidence that developmental outcomes might be causally attributed to participation in the educational intervention rather than to improved nutrition via meals at the Child Development Center or general family support, some services were provided to participants in the control group. Thus, nutritional supplements were provided to children in the control group and supportive social work services were provided to families in both groups. Because children who attended the center received their primary medical care on-site, control children either received similar care on-site or were enrolled in local clinics developed by the same group of pediatricians. Thus, the main difference between the preschool intervention and control groups was that the intervention group received systematic education at the Child Development Center and the control group did not.

A number of basic scientific questions regarding early development have been addressed as an integral part of the research design. Thus, studies of basic language development (e.g., Gordon, 1984), health (e.g., Henderson, Gilligan, Wait, & Goff, 1988), mother–child interactions (e.g., Ramey, Farran, & Campbell, 1979), children's attachment to parents and day-care teachers (e.g., Farran, Burchinal, Hutaff, & Ramey, 1984), biological vulnerability (Breitmayer & Ramey, 1986), and parental beliefs and values (Campbell, Goldstein, Schaefer, & Ramey, in press) were conducted, to name but a few. However, because the central question being addressed was that of the malleability of intellectual competence, the children's performance on standardized tests of intellectual development provided the primary outcome measure of the effectiveness of the intervention during the preschool years.

The intellectual outcomes from the preschool intervention have been reported in previous scientific publications (e.g., Ramey & Campbell, 1984; Ramey, Yeates, & Short, 1984). On standardized tests of intellectual development the treated children significantly outperformed the control children at every testing occasion after the infancy period through the preschool endpoint assessment. On the McCarthy Scales of Children's Abilities (McCarthy, 1972) administered to children at 54 months of age, which was the preschool endpoint evaluation occasion, the intervention group children's mean General Cognitive Index score was 101, 10 points higher than the control group's mean score of 91 points ($t = 4.00$, $p < .001$). Moreover, by the age of 4 years, children in the control group were 6 times more likely to score within the mildly retarded range (IQ < 70) than were children in the intervention group (Ramey & Campbell, 1984). We made extensive efforts to assure that the intervention group children were not "taught the tests" upon which these outcomes were based. Tests were administered by persons not involved in the planning or delivery of the intervention program. Young children were tested with their parents present, not their teachers. Teachers were not allowed to observe testing procedures and were never given specific feedback about test results. Thus, we are confident that the intellectual results are as free of systematic bias as we know how to make them.

School-age intervention

The Carolina Abecedarian Project is not alone in having demonstrated that children from socioeconomically disadvantaged families, if given high-quality early educational intervention, outperform control children on intelligence tests during the preschool years. However, many investigators have reported also that early group differences in intellectual test scores tend to diminish over time, leading to questions of their durability and control factors (e.g., Baroff, 1974; Lazar et al., 1982). Incidentally, the diminishing of group differences is frequently due to the rising performance of control groups rather than to a fade-out effect of performance by the experimental groups. Generally, positive effects on later academic outcomes have been found for high-quality programs with sound experimental designs (Lazar et al., 1982).

In order to investigate the form, duration, and mechanisms of preschool intellectual effects, we designed a second phase of intervention to be applied to half the preschool intervention group and half the preschool control group. This design permitted an examination of the questions of the extent to which early gains might be maintained in elementary school with and without a follow-through program and of what could be accomplished, relatively speaking, through early elementary school intervention in conjunction with regular education. Half the preschool control group, educationally untreated in either phase, provided a basis for estimating the expected outcome for local high-risk children under typical conditions in a highly resourceful and socially aware school system and a standard for comparison of the effectiveness of the three treatment conditions.

The rationale for the school-age intervention was that high-risk children might learn more slowly than average and thus would benefit from increased exposure to and tutoring in basic concepts in two key academic subjects: reading and mathematics. In addition, it was expected that the children would profit from having their parents become more directly involved in their educational program. The intervention program during the primary grades thus consisted of providing the children with extra exposure to academic concepts by having their parents engage in specific supplemental educational activities at home. Materials for this supplemental curriculum were developed by master-level home/school resource teachers. These resource teachers also provided emotional and social support to parents and consultation to classroom teachers.

To guarantee that the supplemental materials were of high quality and to enhance the program's credibility with classroom teachers, graduate-level teachers with backgrounds in primary education were recruited for the positions of Home/School Resource Teachers. The Home/School Teachers thus were qualified to act as consultants to classroom teachers when problems arose. Typically, a Home/School Resource Teacher worked each year with 12 children, their families, and their classroom teachers.

After meeting with the classroom teacher to learn which concepts were currently being taught in school, the Home/School Resource Teacher designed attractive, enjoyable and compatible home activities. The resource teacher then discussed these activities with the family, explained their purpose and their relationship to classroom activities, demonstrated their use, and encouraged parents to use them with their children on a regular basis. We hypothesized that regular visits by a professional educator who had specific knowledge about the child's classroom opportunities and performance, and who demonstrated *specific materials and procedures*, would lead high-risk parents to have a clearer idea of how to help their children. It was also expected that this process might lead the parent to take a more substantive interest in and to place greater value on the child's academic accomplishments. Another important goal of the Home/School Resource Program was to facilitate communication and establish trust between the high-risk family and the school system. In the Home/School Resource Teacher's dual role, working between home and school, the educator became an advocate for the family within the school system and for the school within the family.

A brief summary of the implementation data of the Home/School Resource Program is presented in Table 8.3. The Home/School Teacher met every other week with the parent, usually in the home but occasionally at the parent's workplace or some other location. The Home/School Teacher

Table 8.3. *Summary of Home/School Resource Program contacts by years*

	Year 1	Year 2	Year 3
1. Grade level	kindergarten	grade 1	grade 2
2. Number of children treated	46	46	45
3. Mean school visits	18.3	17.6	13.9
4. Mean home visits	15.4	14.2	12.5
5. Mean total contacts[a]	42.4	40.3	35.0
6. Ratings of parental acceptance of activities			
Positive	84%	82%	83%
Neutral	15%	16%	16%
Negatve	1%	1%	0%

[a]Includes all telephone calls, special visits to home, and "other" contacts for each family.

conveyed any special messages from the classroom teacher regarding the child's academic achievements or behavior in class and introduced the new activities. Family life and adult issues were also discussed. Mothers sometimes revealed personal problems and sought advice. Accordingly, Home/School Teachers helped families with situations that, unattended, might have made it difficult or impossible for parents to devote energy to their child's school progress. Parents were helped to find jobs and decent housing as well as to secure appropriate social services to which they were entitled. In one case, a Home/School Resource Teacher arranged for a custodial grandparent to take adult literacy classes so that the child and his guardian learned to read at the same time.

In a typical year, approximately 60 different learning activities were designed for each child. These activities were maintained in research notebooks to document the curriculum. Many of these activities were original games created by Home/School Resource Teachers. In addition, ready-made activities to give practice in handwriting, phonics, and math concepts and facts were provided. Parents always were asked for feedback on these activities, including how much time they had spent doing them during the previous two weeks. The average amount of time parents reported working with their children on the activities was about 15 minutes a day.

The activities were generally popular with parents and well received. Most parents reported high levels of success and satisfaction in using them. Overall the parents participated enthusiastically and frequently; at the project's end the parents reported that they had found it a very positive experience and would have liked to continue to participate if the program had lasted longer.

During summers the school-age intervention group children participated in special programs. These activities included day camps, special tutoring in reading and mathematics, and organized field trips that were planned by the Home/School Resource Teachers.

Throughout the program the opinions and ideas of parents were solicited, and the parents' contribution to their child's development was emphasized. Parents were encouraged and assisted in their role as advocates for their children's welfare and development.

Results

Intellectual competence

Because level of intellectual functioning is a central issue for this educational experiment, IQ scores constituted an outcome of major interest. Figure 8.2 depicts average longitudinal preschool scores on tests of intellectual development for the preschool intervention and control groups across the range of child ages from 6 to 96 months. The early intervention significantly enhanced IQ performance. Multivariate analysis of variance for repeated measures showed that the scores of the preschool intervention group were consistently higher than those of the control group, particularly after the first year of life. Children in both groups showed some decline from above-average performance in infancy to age 8, but the control group declined significantly more than the intervention group, which was at national average at age 8. The control group initially showed a steeper decline followed by an increase in mean IQ scores after the 36-month assessment occasion until age 8 years. In contrast, the intervention group had a more even profile of higher IQ scores over the time span after infancy.[2]

To determine whether there were detectable intellectual effects during the second phase of intervention, scores on the Wechsler Preschool and Primary Scale of Intelligence (WPPSI) (Wechsler, 1967) at 60 months, and the Wechsler Intelligence Scale for Children–Revised (WISC-R) (Wechsler, 1974) at 78 and 96 months, were examined. Although scores on the McCarthy Scales of Children's Abilities administered to the children at 84 months were also available and were included in the full longitudinal analysis reported earlier, they were not included here to minimize possible artifacts due to differences between instruments in this more limited analysis. The means and standard deviations for the Wechsler test scores earned by the four school-age groups are given in Table 8.4.

The analysis model was a 2(Preschool Groups) × 2(School-Age Groups)

2 For the longitudinal set of intelligence test scores, repeated measures multivariate analysis of variance showed a significant between subjects effect for Group ($F_{(1,83)} = 17.93, p < .0001$), a multivariate effect for time ($F_{(3,81)} = 18.88, p < .0001$), and a Group × Time interaction ($F_{(1,83)} = 6.86, p < .0004$). Significant linear ($F_{(1,83)} = 38.31, p < .0001$), and cubic ($F_{(1,83)} = 31.00, p < .0001$) trends were observed across the two groups. There were Group × Time interactions in tests of the quadratic ($F_{(1,83)} = 9.54, p < .002$) and cubic terms ($F_{(1,83)} = 9.58, p < .003$).

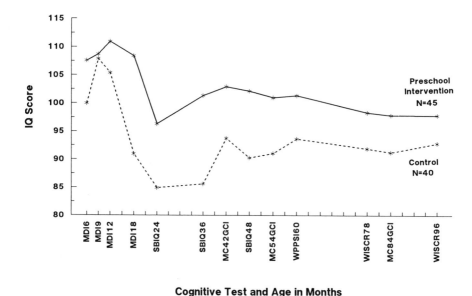

Cognitive Test and Age in Months

Figure 8.2. Intellectual competence results from the experimental phase of the Carolina Abecedarian Project.

× Time multivariate analysis of variance for repeated measures because no directional a priori hypotheses were stated concerning the durability of IQ performance as a function of intervention history. (Complete Wechsler test data exists at all three ages for 87 children.) Planned contrasts showed a significant difference between the preschool groups on mean IQ scores across the three occasions $F_{(1,83)}$ = 6.90, $p < .01$. There was no significant effect for school-age group, and no significant Group × Time interaction. The results did show a significant multivariate effect for time $F_{(2,82)}$ = 4.51, $p < .02$, which accounts for the approximately 2-IQ-point drop from age 5 to age 8 when averaged across all groups. Thus, for the 60-, 78-, and 96-month subset of scores, children who had preschool intervention scored significantly higher than those who did not. The difference was persistent across the first three years of public school with no evidence for a preschool fade-out effect. However, educational intervention that began during the primary grades was not associated with positive effects on IQ performance.

Academic achievement

Even more than scores on standardized intelligence tests, academic outcomes during the primary grades represent a critical test of the practical success of the educational interventions. Achievement in two basic subjects, reading and mathematics, was considered most important because they had been the

Table 8.4. *Mean Wechsler full-scale, verbal, and performance IQ scores at 60, 78, and 96 months by school-age group*

Group	N		60-month WPPSI Mean IQ (SD)	N	78-month WISC-R Mean IQ (SD)	N	96-month WISC-R Mean IQ (SD)
Control	23	Full scale	94.48 (13.83)	22	92.77 (11.47)	22	95.09 (12.69)
		Verbal	94.00 (13.09)		93.23 (10.46)		93.09 (13.01)
		Performance	96.04 (13.82)		94.04 (14.47)		98.09 (13.76)
School-age only	21	Full scale	92.76 (13.75)	21	91.71 (12.32)	20	91.40 (12.13)
		Verbal	93.62 (14.40)		93.95 (11.61)		92.10 (13.25)
		Performance	93.29 (12.79)		90.67 (13.40)		91.95 (12.29)
Preschool only	24	Full scale	102.50 (7.25)	22	98.86 (8.71)	23	97.78 (10.43)
		Verbal	103.46 (9.30)		99.36 (12.92)		96.91 (10.49)
		Performance	100.96 (7.38)		93.68 (12.89)		99.61 (12.21)
Preschool plus follow-through	25	Full scale	100.40 (13.69)	25	98.08 (14.86)	25	97.88 (13.09)
		Verbal	101.92 (13.25)		97.76 (16.43)		98.80 (13.28)
		Performance	98.56 (13.81)		94.76 (17.90)		97.60 (13.03)

primary focus of the Home/School intervention program, and they are the skills to which teachers and school administrators pay particular attention. Both age-referenced and grade-referenced measures were used to compare academic outcomes among the four experimental groups. The age-referenced measure held years of exposure to school constant when children were tested and consisted of age-referenced standard scores for reading and mathematics on the Woodcock–Johnson Psychoeducational Battery, Part 2: Tests of Achievement (Woodcock & Johnson, 1977), which was individually administered to all children by project staff at the end of three years in school. The grade-constant measures were either actual or projected[3] reading and math-

3 Between 1980 and 1983, the state of North Carolina administered the criterion-referenced Prescriptive Reading Inventory and the Diagnostic Mathematics Inventory to children completing second grade; from these instruments, the test manufacturer projected California

Table 8.5. *Means and standard deviations of age-referenced Woodcock–Johnson standard scores and percentiles and grade-referenced California Achievement Test standard scores and percentiles for reading and mathematics achievement by group*

	Woodcock–Johnson			California Achievement Test		
Group	N	Standard score	Percentile	N	Standard score	Percentile
			Reading			
Control	20	82.80	19.10	19	92.00	32.32
		(12.43)	(18.66)		(9.64)	(21.15)
School-age only	20	86.30	23.25	19	95.37	40.05
		(11.14)	(20.49)		(10.51)	(21.99)
Preschool only	23	92.17	34.87	21	96.24	42.57
		(13.69)	(27.62)		(10.88)	(21.89)
Preschool plus follow-through	24	95.75	41.46	24	102.08	53.25
		(12.87)	(27.75)		(12.90)	(26.33)
			Mathematics			
Control	20	91.20	32.60	19	96.63	43.11
		(14.16)	(28.18)		(11.55)	(25.29)
School-age only	20	92.80	37.20	19	99.37	50.32
		(14.89)	(29.12)		(12.12)	(23.56)
Preschool only	23	94.96	39.09	21	106.81	63.14
		(11.07)	(24.67)		(14.71)	(26.73)
Preschool plus follow-through	25	100.28	51.16	25	105.36	60.60
		(13.11)	(28.69)		(13.88)	(27.06)

ematics scores from the California Achievement Test (California Achievement Test, 1978), which was group administered by school system personnel to all pupils at the end of second grade. The California Achievement Test scores became part of each child's permanent record and were released to the project investigators by the children's parents. Children not retained in kindergarten or first grade had both measures administered the same year; retainees of either year had the California Achievement Test after four, not three, years' exposure to school. Both instruments yielded age-referenced or grade-referenced percentiles or age-referenced or grade-referenced standard scores with means of 100 and standard deviations of 15.

Table 8.5 gives the age-referenced means and standard deviations for standard scores for reading and mathematics and percentiles earned by the four groups of high-risk children on the Woodcock–Johnson assessment at

Achievement Test percentile ranks that were reported along with other scores for each child. From 1984 on, the California Achievement Test itself was administered to children completing second grade.

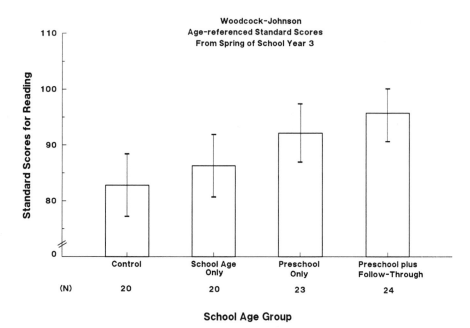

Figure 8.3. Means and standard errors of the mean for age-referenced reading achievement by group. Linear trend $F_{1,79} = 11.09$, $p = .001$.

the end of three years in school and their grade-referenced standard scores and percentiles from the California Achievement Test at the end of second grade. The standard score results for age-referenced performance are presented graphically in Figures 8.3 and 8.4. The grade-referenced achievement data are presented in Figures 8.5 and 8.6 for reading and mathematics respectively. The smaller group sizes resulting from the change to a four-group design for the school-age phase of the Abecedarian study led to the use of a different statistical strategy for examining academic achievement outcomes in order to maximize statistical power. A hierarchical order of scores was hypothesized, that is, a linear trend with academic achievement scores hypothesized to vary positively across the four experimental groups from low to high as the length of educational intervention increased. The first analysis of academic achievement outcomes consisted of a multivariate procedure in which this model was tested across all four sets of standard scores. The results showed a significant multivariate trend across groups for the grand mean of the four sets of scores ($F_{(4,76)} = 3.32$, $p < .02$). Separate univariate analyses were then conducted for each individual set of achievement scores.

The test for the Woodcock–Johnson reading scores showed that, with exposure to school constant, there was an overall linear trend in the means related to treatment amount ($F_{(1,79)} = 11.09$, $p < .001$). The same finding held for the Woodcock–Johnson mathematics scores; performance increased

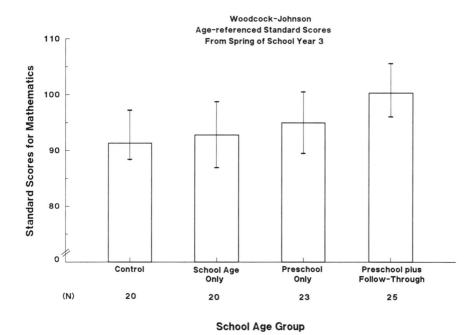

Figure 8.4. Means and standard errors of the mean for age-referenced mathematics achievement by group. Linear trend $F_{1,79} = 4.05, p = .05$.

as a function of the amount of intervention ($F_{(1,79)} = 4.05, p < .05$). Similarly, the univariate test of the California Achievement Test standard scores for reading revealed a significant linear trend as years of educational intervention increased ($F_{(1,79)} = 8.18, p < .005$) and so did the California Achievement Test standard scores for mathematics, ($F_{(1,79)} = 7.13, p < .009$). Thus, all four sets of academic achievement measures showed a significant trend for the mean scores to increase as a linear function of the amount of educational intervention.

Our conclusion with respect to scholastic achievement is that the hypothesized trend across groups from lowest to highest scores as a function of increasing amounts of intervention is seen for both reading and mathematics achievement whether one examines the outcomes holding child exposure to school or grade level constant. The average percentile rank on Woodcock–Johnson reading scores ranged from a low of the 19th percentile for the control group to a high of the 41st percentile for the preschool plus follow-through group. On the California Achievement Test for reading the comparable percentile ranks were 32 and 53.

With respect to mathematics achievement, the control group scored at the 33rd percentile on the Woodcock–Johnson test, and the most intensively treated group scored slightly above national average at the 51st percentile.

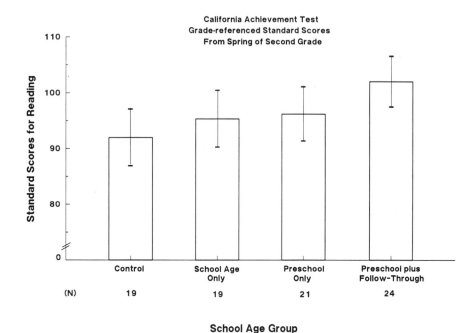

Figure 8.5. Means and standard errors of the mean for grade-referenced reading achievement by group. Linear trend $F_{1.79} = 8.18, p = .005$.

Similarly, on the California Achievement Test for mathematics, the control group was at the 43rd percentile while the preschool intervention plus follow-through group was the highest scoring group, at the 61st percentile.

The mean standard scores and percentiles both indicated that the children in this study scored slightly higher on mathematics than on reading. The findings also indicate that preschool intervention plus follow-through can result in groups of very high-risk children scoring at or above the national average at the end of the primary grades on tests that are either individually administered or group administered.

Retention in grade

In the elementary schools attended by Abecedarian children, the most likely response when a child had serious academic difficulty was retention in grade, especially in the early years. As a result, many of the high-risk children in the study were held back at some point during the first three years. Figure 8.7 shows the percentage of children in each treatment group retained in grade across the first three years in public school. Previously reported by Horacek, Ramey, Campbell, Hoffmann, and Fletcher (1987), these data show that the control group high-risk children overall fared much worse than the

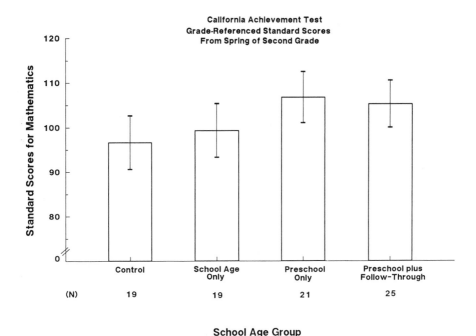

Figure 8.6. Means and standard errors of the mean for grade-referenced mathematics achievement by group. Linear trend $F_{1,79} = 7.3$, $p = .009$.

local systemwide average for retentions in the early grades, confirming the high-risk status of this sample, which was determined at birth.

Comparing the grade-retention rate among the high-risk groups in Figure 8.7, we found that the highest failure rate occurs in the control group and the lowest rate in the preschool plus follow-through group. In fact, the rate for the preschool plus follow-through group is very similar to that for the local population base rate of 13%. The group that received the school-age intervention only had a somewhat more favorable experience than the control group but less favorable than the group that received the more intensive and prolonged preschool intervention alone. Thus, the failure rate exhibits a decreasing pattern with increase in duration and intensity of intervention. A statistical test for this pattern of association was undertaken with the Spearman Rank Correlation statistic for ordered categorical data (Landis, Heymann, & Koch, 1978). Its result ($X^2 = 6.49$, 1 df, $r_s = -0.27$) was significant ($p = 0.01$). Also, specific tests were undertaken for each of the components of the intervention with the Mantel-Haenszel statistic (Mantel, 1963). With this method the preschool intervention was found to have the stronger effect ($X^2 = 4.78$, 1 df, $p = 0.03$), with the school-age effect being nonsignificant ($X^2 = 1.71$, 1 df, $p = 0.19$) but still in the positive direction.

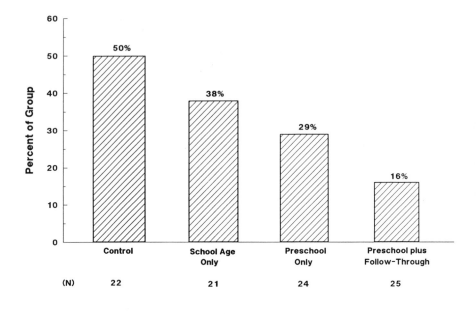

Figure 8.7.   Percent of school-age intervention groups retained in grades kindergarten, 1, or 2.

Teacher ratings of classroom behavior

One measure of social adaptation to the classroom was obtained by having teachers rate the children's behavior in each of the first three years in elementary school using the Classroom Behavior Inventory (CBI) developed by Schaefer, Edgerton, and Aaronson (1977). This inventory contains 10 scales designed to measure three factors: Considerateness versus Hostility, Academic Competence, and Introversion versus Extraversion.

To learn whether the varying degrees of intervention experienced by the high-risk children had any effect upon teacher perceptions of the children's adaptation to the classroom, teacher ratings made in the spring of the third year in school were analyzed. The analysis strategy was to test for a linear trend across intervention groups as was done with the academic achievement scores. Ratings on three scales, representing the three dimensions of positive school adaptation, were analyzed. For the bipolar dimensions, Considerateness versus Hostility and Extraversion versus Introversion, the scales describing the considerateness and extraversion poles were chosen for analysis, and a scale labeled Verbal Intelligence represented the teachers' ratings of Academic Competence.

Means for these ratings across groups are given in Table 8.6. The academic

Table 8.6. *Means and standard deviations of teacher ratings on selected classroom behavior inventory scales and mean t-scores from parent ratings on the child behavior checklist for four experimental groups*

Group	Preschool plus follow-through Mean (SD)	Preschool only Mean (SD)	School-age only Mean (SD)	Control Mean (SD)
	Teacher ratings on Classroom Behavior Inventory			
	N = 24	N = 23	N = 20	N = 20
Verbal	13.63	13.26	12.15	11.80
intelligence	(3.95)	(3.82)	(4.03)	(3.83)
Considerateness	15.17	14.70	17.00	16.45
	(4.56)	(4.53)	(3.97)	(3.69)
Extraversion	19.58	18.22	19.20	19.40
	(3.69)	(3.55)	(3.82)	(3.52)
	Parent ratings on Child Behavior Checklist			
	N = 22	N = 21	N = 20	N = 23
Activities *t*-scores	47.68	48.33	45.25	45.87
	(6.65)	(5.69)	(7.85)	(7.29)
Social *t*-scores	49.82	48.33	45.45	49.35
	(4.65)	(6.56)	(7.69)	(7.34)
Academic *t*-scores	43.14	45.38	42.65	40.70
	(11.06)	(9.61)	(8.73)	(9.10)
Total problem	56.68	56.62	57.20	58.22
t-scores	(12.05)	(8.01)	(11.95)	(9.61)

competence scores showed a marginally significant positive linear trend across intervention groups as a function of the number of years of intervention ($F_{(1,83)}$ = 3.09, p = .08). Thus, children who had greater amounts of educational intervention were perceived as more competent than children who had lesser amounts of intervention. There was not a linear relationship between teachers' ratings of extraversion and considerateness as a function of increasing amount of intervention.

Parent ratings of child behavior. Parents completed the Child Behavior Checklist (Achenbach & Edelbrock, 1979) after the children had completed three years in public school. This instrument provides ratings of the child's adjustment or adaptation in four categories: range of activities, social adjustment, academic progress, and problem behaviors. Ratings in each category may be expressed as *t*-scores with a normative sample mean of 50 and a standard deviation of 10. Analysis showed no statistically significant relationship between the amount of intervention and parents' descriptions of the children's behavior as measured by their responses to the Child Behavior Checklist. Applying the same linear model already described to Child Behavior Checklist t-scores, no significant linear trends were found across the four groups. Moreover, all mean t-scores were within normal limits indicating that for the primary school years these children as groups were not seen by their parents as at high risk for behavior problems.

Comparison with other preschool intervention programs

The Perry Preschool Project and the Milwaukee Project. It is instructive to compare the outcomes of the Abecedarian program with those of other intervention programs. Two other programs are particularly relevant because of their previous impact on public policy and because they are different from the Abecedarian program in important and systematic ways. The first, the Perry Preschool Project, was targeted, beginning in 1962, at 128 socioeconomically disadvantaged urban 3- and 4-year-olds who had pretest IQs between 70 and 90. Approximately half were assigned to receive a 2½-hour per day preschool education program coupled with a weekly family education home-visit program (Schweinhart & Weikart, 1989). Thus, this program was less intensive than the Abecedarian program and was remedial in nature rather than preventive. The other half of the sample served as completely untreated control subjects.

The second program, the Milwaukee Project, began in 1966, was set in an urban ghetto area, and provided intensive early intervention in an educational day-care setting for 17 socioeconomically disadvantaged children, beginning in early infancy. The children's mothers participated in an intensive family education and employment program. The sample children's development was compared to that of 18 completely untreated control children. In addition, the Milwaukee program required that the children admitted have mothers with IQs of 75 points or lower (Garber, 1988). Thus, the Milwaukee Project was preventive in nature and focused on a more intellectually restricted high-risk sample than the Abecedarian Project.

All three programs found significant differences between treated and untreated children's IQs at age 5. The Milwaukee study, however, reported much greater differences in IQ levels at age 5 between treated (mean = 120) and untreated children (mean = 94), a difference of 26 IQ points, compared with a difference of 11 points for children in the Perry Preschool Project (mean = 94 for treated and 83 for controls) and 8 points for Abecedarian Project 5-year-olds (mean = 101 for treated and 93 for controls). Similarly, the Milwaukee Project reported much larger group differences in IQ at age 8 for treated (mean = 103) and control subjects (mean = 83), approximately 20 points (Garber, 1988), than existed between Abecedarian preschool intervention (mean = 98) and control subjects (mean = 93) (approximately 5 points). By age 8, children in the Perry Preschool Project did not differ in IQ as a function of preschool intervention (mean = 88) in comparison to controls (mean = 87).

The three preschool programs varied in intensity, in duration, and also in the children's ages at entry into the programs. However, from the intellectual competence outcomes of the three studies taken together, one would infer that intervention for disadvantaged children is more effective and lasts longer if it begins in early infancy and is very intensive. Although IQ gains were demonstrated when intervention began at age 3, the gains were better maintained and treated children scored at significantly higher IQ levels in those programs that began intervention in infancy.

It is difficult to explain the discrepancy in the amount of difference between treated and untreated subjects in the Milwaukee and Abecedarian studies. The programs were comparable with respect to length of preschool intervention provided; both began in infancy, and both provided full-day programs for treated children. Recent re-analyses of the Abecedarian preschool data by Martin, Ramey, and Ramey (1990) have suggested that one reason for the apparent difference in outcomes for the two projects lies in the restriction of the Milwaukee sample to children with very low maternal IQs. Examining the differences in IQ between educationally treated and untreated Abecedarian children whose mothers had IQs within the retarded range (IQ < 70), Martin, Ramey, and Ramey (1990) found a difference of 21 points on the General Cognitive Index of the McCarthy Scales of Children's Abilities when children were 4½ years of age. This result is consistent with the results from the Milwaukee Project's difference of 26 points at age 5 and raises important questions about differential response to treatment by subgroups of poverty-level children. When, in the present study, the 96-month IQs for a continuing-to-participate subset of these children were compared, there was a difference between treated and untreated children of 13 points on the WISC-R full-scale IQ. The remaining 6 children of retarded mothers in the preschool intervention group had a mean IQ of 93.67 (*SD* = 7.00) at 96 months whereas the 5 such remaining children in the control group had a mean IQ of 80.20 (*SD* = 16.24). Because the numbers of subjects who actually had retarded mothers was so small, this finding, even though statistically significant, must be interpreted with caution, but it does suggest that had the initial groups of subjects in the Milwaukee Project and the Abecedarian study been more comparable with respect to maternal IQ level, the overall relative discrepancy between treated and control children's intellectual test performance might have been more similar in the two studies. Put another way, it appears that high-risk children of low-IQ mothers may be particularly responsive to intensive, high-quality preschool intervention and particularly vulnerable without it.

In none of the three longitudinal studies did the intellectual test scores of children in the preschool control groups display the trend usually reported from cross-sectional studies of disadvantaged children, that is, a gradual and continuing trend downward as child age increases (Heber, Dever, & Conry, 1968). The Abecedarian longitudinal data for the preschool control group indicated a rather sharp drop from above average in tested intellectual level after the infancy period, followed by a gradual recovery toward national average at age 8 years. A slight rise in test performance when control children entered public school has been found in the present study, in the Milwaukee Project, and in the Perry Preschool Project. Thus, the introduction of systematic education is associated with increased intellectual competence in high-risk children.

The rise in intellectual competence for the Abecedarian control children actually began after the age of 3 years, before school entry (see Figure 8.2). Of particular importance is the fact that after the age of 3 years, many of the high-risk control children entered other preschools and day-care centers and thus also had the benefit of some preschool education (Burchinal, Lee, & Ramey, 1989). An active Head Start program and other high-quality preschools with scholarships for low-income children were available to and used by many Abecedarian control group preschoolers. From reports of the historically earlier Perry Preschool Project and the Milwaukee Project it does not seem that such programs were available to their control group subjects during the preschool years, which may account for the beginning of the rise in their control children's intellectual competence coincident with the onset of public school in their projects and for the earlier rise in the Abecedarian Project's control group. Neither were the Perry or Milwaukee control subjects provided with nutritional supplements or family supports. Thus, the results from the Abecedarian Project may be particularly conservative given the preschool services provided to its control subjects by the project and by the control group's participation in other preschool programs, particularly after the age of 3.

Scholastic achievement outcomes. When scholastic achievement is compared, all three studies reported significant effects of intervention on achievement test scores. Direct comparison of the three programs is difficult because of differences in the way outcomes are reported: The Milwaukee Project and the Abecedarian Project report outcomes in terms of standard scores and percentiles, but the Perry Preschool Project gives scholastic outcomes in terms of percentage of test items passed. It is possible to compare the significance levels of reported group differences for tests on reading and mathematics. The results, however, are based upon different test instruments and different procedures of data collection: The Perry Preschool program used California Achievement Test scores individually administered by project personnel; the Milwaukee study used Metropolitan Achievement Test scores administered by the city; and the Abecedarian scores are based upon school-administered statewide standardized tests. The results are shown in Table 8.7.

Both the Abecedarian study and the Perry Preschool Project report end-of-second-grade preschool experimental versus control group differences. The Milwaukee p value is derived from an F test of the group differences in achievement data summed across the first four years of school. With these caveats, the generalization is that the Abecedarian preschool intervention group differed significantly from its control group in both reading and mathematics at the end of second grade. The Milwaukee experimental and control groups differed significantly in mathematics across four years but not in reading (Garber, 1988, p. 267), and the Perry Preschool experimental children differed marginally significantly ($p < .10$) on mathematics but not on reading at the end of second grade (Weikart, Bond, & McNeil, 1978, p. 49).

From data presented by Garber (1988), it is possible to compare post-second grade reading and mathematics percentile ranks for children in the Abecedarian and Milwaukee studies. (Comparable data are not available for the Perry Preschool Project to our knowledge.) These figures, given in Table 8.8, show that Abecedarian children who had preschool educational intervention earned higher percentile scores in both subjects than did the experimental group Milwaukee Project children. Differences existed, however, not only in the instruments upon which these percentile scores are based but also in the experimental procedures, which makes it difficult to know the best way to compare percentile scores across the two studies. For example, Abecedarian children, with one exception, entered public school kindergarten at age 5, whereas Milwaukee experimental children remained in their preschool program that year and entered public school as first graders. Milwaukee experimental group children had a summer tutorial in reading and mathematics after they had completed first grade. Not all treated Abecedarian children had summer tutorial programs, only those in the school-age intervention groups. Thus, it is difficult to know whether it is more relevant to compare the Milwaukee experimental group children with the Abecedarian preschool only group or with the Abecedarian preschool plus follow-through group. However, inspection of the Abecedarian California Achievement Test percentiles and the Metropolitan Achievement Test results reported by Garber (1988) shows that Abecedarian children earned higher percentile scores no matter which comparison is made.

On standardized tests of reading achievement at the end of second grade, children in the Abecedarian preschool only intervention group earned a mean score at the 43rd percentile, and those in the preschool plus follow-through group scored at the 53rd percentile, compared to the 25th percentile scored by children in the Milwaukee experimental group. In mathematics, the Abecedarian preschool only children scored at the 63rd percentile, and those in the preschool plus follow-through group scored at the 61st percentile, com-

Table 8.7. *Reported significance levels for treatment/control differences in reading and mathematics achievement in early elementary school in three early intervention studies*

	Subject	
Study	Reading	Mathematics
Abecedarian[a]	Preschool intervention > control $p = .03$ School-age intervention > control $p = .08$	Preschool intervention > control $p = .01$ School-age intervention > control $p = NS$
Perry Preschool[b]	Experimental > control $p = NS$	Experimental > control $p = .08$
Milwaukee[c]	Experimental > control $p = NS$	Experimental > control $p = < .05$

[a]Based on a 2(preschool groups) 2(school-age groups) ANOVA on post-second grade California Achievement Test percentile scores.
[b]Based on Group × Sex × Wave analysis of variance of California Achievement Test subtest raw scores.
[c]Based on total subject percentile scores from the Metropolitan Achievement Test across years 1–4.

Table 8.8. *Comparison of third school year academic achievement percentile ranks for Abecedarian and Milwaukee Project children*

Subject	Group				
	Abecedarian[a] preschool plus follow-through	Abecedarian preschool only	Milwaukee[b] experimental	Abecedarian control	Milwaukee control
Reading	41.5	34.9	25.1	19.1	15.6
Math	51.2	39.1	22.6	32.6	10.4

[a] Abecedarian scores are age-referenced percentiles from the Woodcock–Johnson Psychoeducational Battery, Part 2 (Woodcock & Johnson, 1977).
[b] Milwaukee scores are percentiles from the Metropolitan Achievement Test, as reported in Heber (1988).

pared to the 22nd percentile for Milwaukee children. Thus, the higher IQ test scores earned by the experimental group children in the Milwaukee Project, relative to those in the Abecedarian study, were not associated with a comparable superiority in scholastic achievement.

It is difficult to interpret these Milwaukee–Abecedarian relative differences in scholastic achievement with confidence because the children were in dissimilar school systems. Garber (1988) described the neighborhood schools where his experimental group children would have been enrolled as "obviously poor" (p. 256), and he arranged to have most of the children enrolled in schools with better records of success. Nevertheless, the schools were still in the inner city. In contrast, the Abecedarian children were in a university town with a predominantly upper middle-class, highly educated population, which was reflected in classroom composition and academic expectations. The level of academic competition faced by Abecedarian children in their classrooms was high and persistent. Abecedarian children entered schools in which the typical child was intellectually about 15 IQ points above the national norm, and thus their classrooms were likely to have been stimulating and cognitively challenging. The public schools in Chapel Hill, North Carolina, also provided many resources for all pupils having academic difficulties. Because of such confounding factors, specific differences in academic outcomes between the two studies cannot be interpreted with full confidence. Clearly, this is an area where additional research is essential if the mechanisms of program impact are to be understood scientifically.

The Consortium for Longitudinal Studies. Having treated the relative outcomes from the Perry Preschool Project, the Milwaukee Project, and the Abecedarian Project in some detail, it is of interest also to compare the Abecedarian outcomes with those from the Consortium for Longitudinal Studies (Lazar et al., 1982), which summarized the long-term effects of early education from 11 different projects. The Perry Preschool Project was one of these programs and one of the four projects given special emphasis as "more nearly randomized designs" (see Lazar et al., 1982, pp. 21, 41, for a fuller description).

A major conclusion of the consortium was that "early education significantly improved the ability of low-income children to meet their school's requirements for adequate performance, as reflected in reduced rates of assignment to special education and retention in grade" (Lazar et al., 1982, p. 55). "For the projects which reported random assignment to groups . . . 29.4% of the Control group children were placed in special education classes compared to only 5.3% of the program group children" (p.33). "For the projects with more nearly randomized designs, the median grade-retention rate was 25.8% in the program group compared to 36.6% for the Control group" (p.34).

The Abecedarian results with respect to retention in grade support this basic conclusion and show a somewhat stronger effect by reducing the likelihood that a child would be retained in the first three years of school from 50% for the control groups to 16% for the preschool plus follow-through group, 29% for the preschool only group, and 38% for the school-age only group. No statistical differences were found for special education placement by the Abecedarian endpoint evaluation, however. The total number of placements was small (10) and fairly evenly distributed across the four groups so there is very low statistical power to detect differences given the small numbers of children placed in special education (11%). It remains to be seen whether longer term follow up of the subjects, comparable to that of the consortium's, will tend to confirm the consortium finding of fewer rather than more placements as a result of preschool intervention. One caveat, however, is that the more affluent Chapel Hill school system, with its relatively advantaged pupils, may make referrals to special classes using different criteria from those that were used in the consortium's historically earlier studies, which were predominantly set in poor, inner-city areas. Further, the ABC Home/School Teachers were advocates for special education where that seemed to offer children additional and needed resources. Only additional time will reveal the impact of such forces.

We cannot yet compare the long-term Abecedarian effects of preschool intervention on intellectual competence assessed by IQ tests with those obtained in the consortium projects because not all of the Abecedarian children are yet of comparable age to those reported by Lazar et al. (1982). Based on its 11 studies, the consortium concluded that the effects of early intervention persisted for at least the first three or four years after the early intervention program ceased, but that longer term follow-ups, when children were 10 to 17 years of age, suggested that earlier differences eventually eroded. We are currently following up the subjects to learn if our endpoint group differences persist through age 12.

The consortium also found across all studies that "program graduates in general performed better than their controls [on school-administered academic achievement tests]" (Lazar et al., 1982, p. 56). The Abecedarian results support these basic conclusions from the consortium with respect to academic achievement in both reading and mathematics. Finally, the Abecedarian and consortium results complement one another with respect to differential effects on children with different backgrounds. Whereas both sets of results indicate a broad positive intellectual and scholastic response to preschool programs with respect to such variables as the child's gender, maternal education, and composition of home, the Abecedarian Project does indicate that economically disadvantaged children of low-IQ mothers may be especially responsive to this form of intervention (Martin, Ramey, & Ramey, 1990). This finding could have obvious implications for future selection criteria for high-risk infants.

Timing of intervention

These data allow us to speculate about optimal timing of interventions for disadvantaged children. Insofar as positive effects on intellectual development and academic accomplishment are concerned, the outcomes suggest that earlier and longer treatments have a more powerful influence on IQ and scholastic success than special treatment begun at school entrance and continued through the primary grades.

The higher levels of intellectual competence demonstrated by Abecedarian children receiving preschool intervention seems a likely explanation for their better achievement in early elementary school, particularly in light of the higher teacher ratings of academic competence for children receiving intervention. If, however, the differences in academic accomplishment were attributable primarily to the supplemental curriculum provided in the school-age intervention, then after three years' exposure to public school the follow-through only children should have performed at about the same level as those in the preschool plus follow-through group, for they attended the same schools and both groups had the benefit of a special and intensive school-age intervention for all three years. This was not the case for reading, however. Children in the preschool plus follow-through group significantly outscored school-age only children in reading, being about 7 standard score points higher on the Woodcock–Johnson reading assessments.

A second interesting comparison is of the relative academic achievements for children who had preschool intervention alone and for those who had school-age intervention alone. Whether one examines Woodcock–Johnson or California Achievement Test mean scores for these two groups, the scores always favor the preschool intervention group. Individual *t* tests indicate that none of these differences attain the .05 level of significance. It is important to remember, however, that the school-age program did have consistently beneficial effects, as shown by the significant linear relationship found between the number of years of educational intervention and scholastic accomplishment.

Conclusions

The Abecedarian experiment and several other carefully designed interventions demonstrate that early educational intervention can significantly benefit children at high risk for academic failure. Early childhood education can enhance intellectual growth and improve later school performance. Taken together with results from similar experiments with disadvantaged children, our results suggest that educational intervention should begin early in the life span and continue at least into the primary grades. Children who appear to benefit most are those born to low-IQ, impoverished mothers. To put it another way, those children who need intervention the most appear to benefit the most.

Intensive intervention during early elementary school in the form of supplemental academic experience at home does undergird increased scholastic achievement but, by itself, appears to be less effective than preschool intervention as a preventive measure against intellectual lags and school failure. We are continuing to pursue questions about the long-term effects of the interventions, the factors associated with such effects, and the processes and mechanisms undergirding the development of disadvantaged children. Follow-up studies of the Abecedarian subjects at age 12 and age 15 are underway to learn to what extent the effects of the earlier interventions might still be apparent at later ages. This follow up also will permit us to examine psychosocial mechanisms at the levels of the child, family, and school that might plausibly sustain or diminish school performance.

One fact is clear: Disadvantaged children face enormous odds even in high-quality, affluent, and socially aware public school systems. Children from low-resource families require intensive and long-lasting educational efforts if they are to reach their full academic potential (see Ramey & Ramey, 1990, for an elaboration of this point relevant to public policy). In our opinion, the primary task for public policy makers is to develop sufficiently supportive mechanisms to maximize the availability of effective and innovative programs. Short and inexpensive programs are not likely to have much practical educational impact.

As a nation, we are now armed with more useful knowledge about the amelioration of the devastating consequences of poverty than ever before. The challenge is to find the leadership and the motivation to convince the public that intergenerational poverty and undereducation is a preventable disease that the United States cannot afford.

Summary

The effectiveness of three forms of educational intervention for high-risk children from low-income families is reported from a longitudinal randomized experiment. The intervention included a preschool plus follow-through program, a preschool only program, a school-age only program, and an educational control condition. Positive effects of intervention are reported on children's intellectual competence, academic achievement in reading and mathematics, and reduction of retention in grade. No significant differences were found in parents' perceptions of problem behaviors, which were of low frequency in all groups. The positive effects of intervention on outcomes are proportional to the amount of intervention. For example, 50% of control children were retained in the primary grades in comparison to 38% of school-age only children, 29% of preschool only children, and 16% of preschool plus follow-through children. Results from the Abecedarian Project are compared and contrasted with results from the Perry Preschool Project, the Milwaukee Project, and the Consortium for Longitudinal Studies. These comparisons suggest that more intensive and longer lasting programs are associated with greater positive educational impact for high-risk students. We conclude that practically significant educational gains will require systematic and intensive interventions even in affluent, progressive, and resourceful school systems.

References

Achenbach, T. M., & Edelbrock, C. S. (1979). The Child Behavior Profile: II. Boys aged 12–16 and girls aged 6–11 and 12–16. *Journal of Clinical and Consulting Psychology, 47*, 223–233.

Baroff, G. S. (1974). *Mental retardation: Nature, cause, and management.* Washington, DC: Hemisphere Press.

Berrueta-Clement, J. R., Schweinhart, L. J., Barnett, W. S., Epstein, A. S., & Weikart, D. P. (1984). *Changed lives: The effects of the Perry Preschool program on youths through age 19* (Monographs of the High/Scope Education Research Foundation, 8). Ypsilanti, MI: High/Scope Press.

Blank, M. (1982). Language and school failure: Some speculations about the relationship between oral and written language. In L. Feagans & D. Farran (Eds.), *The language of children reared in poverty* (pp. 75–93). New York: Academic Press.

Breitmayer, B. J., & Ramey, C. T. (1986). Biological non-optimality and quality of environments as co-determinants of developmental outcomes. *Child Development, 57*, 1151–1165.

Brooks-Gunn, J., & Furstenburg, F. F., Jr. (1986). The children of adolescent mothers: Physical, academic, and psychological outcomes. *Developmental Review, 6*, 224–251.

Burchinal, M., Lee, M., & Ramey, C. T. (1989). Type of daycare and preschool intellectual development in disadvantaged children. *Child Development, 60*, 128–137.

California Achievement Tests. (1978). Monterey, CA: CTB/McGraw-Hill.

Campbell, F. A., Goldstein, S., Schaefer, E., & Ramey, C. T. (in press). Parental beliefs and values related to family risk indicators, educational intervention, and child academic competence. *Early Childhood Research Quarterly.*

Farran, D. C., Burchinal, M., Hutaff, S. E., & Ramey, C. T. (1984). Allegiances or attachments: Relationships among infants and their daycare teachers. In R. Ainslie (Ed.), *The child and the daycare setting* (pp. 133–158). New York: Praeger.

Furstenberg, F. F., Jr. (1976). *Unplanned parenthood: The social consequences of teenage childbearing*. New York: Free Press.

Garber, H. L. (1988). *The Milwaukee Project: Preventing mental retardation in children at risk*. Washington, DC: American Association on Mental Retardation.

Gordon, A. (1984). Adequacy of responses given by low-income and middle-income kindergarten children in structured adult–child conversations. *Developmental Psychology, 20*, 881–892.

Greenberg, P., & Epstein, B. (1973). *Bridges to reading*. Morristown, NJ: General Learning Corporation.

Heath, S. B. (1983). *Ways with words*. Cambridge: Cambridge University Press.

Heber, R., Dever, R., & Conry, J. (1968). The influence of environmental and genetic variables on intellectual development. In J. J. Prehm, L. A. Hamerlynck, & J. E. Crosson (Eds.), *Behavioral research in mental retardation* (pp. 1–23). Eugene, OR: University of Oregon Press.

Henderson, F. W., Gilligan, P. H., Wait, K., & Goff, D. A. (1988). Nasopharyngeal carriage of antibiotic resistant pneumococci by children in day care. *Journal of Infectious Diseases, 157*, 256–263.

Horacek, H. J., Ramey, C. T., Campbell, F. A., Hoffmann, K. P., & Fletcher, R. H. (1987). Predicting school failure and assessing early intervention with high-risk children. *American Academy of Child and Adolescent Psychiatry, 26*, 758–763.

Hunt, J. McV. (1961). *Intelligence and experience*. New York: Ronald Press.

Jencks, C. (1972). *Inequality: A reassessment of the effect of family and schooling in America*. New York: Basic Books.

Labov, W. (1970). The logic of non-standard English. In F. Williams (Ed.), *Language and poverty: Perspective on a theme*, (pp. 153–189). Chicago: Markham Publishing.

Landis, J. R., Heymann, E. R., & Koch, G. G. (1978). Average partial association in three-way contingency tables. *International Statistical Review, 46*, 237–254.

Lazar, I., Darlington, R., Murray, H., Royce, J., & Snipper, A. (1982). Lasting effects of early education: A report from the Consortium for Longitudinal Studies. *Monographs of the Society for Research in Child Development, 47* (2–3, Serial No. 195).

Mantel, N. (1963). Chi-square tests with one degree of freedom: Extensions of the Mental Haenszel procedure. *Journal of the American Statistical Association, 58*, 690–700.

Martin, S. L., Ramey, C. T., & Ramey, S. L. (1990). The prevention of intellectual impairment in children of impoverished families: Findings of a randomized trial of educational daycare. *American Journal of Public Health, 80*, 844–847.

McCarthy, D. (1972). *McCarthy Scales of Children's Abilities*. New York: Psychological Corporation.

McGinness, G., & Ramey, C. T. (1981). Developing sociolinguistic competence in children. *Canadian Journal of Early Childhood Education, 1*(2), 22–43.

Ramey, C. T., Bryant, D. M., Campbell, F. A., Sparling, J. J., & Wasik, B. H. (1988). Early intervention for high-risk children: The Carolina early intervention program. In H. R. Price, E. L. Cowen, R. P. Lorion, & J. Ramos-McKay (Eds.), *14 ounces of prevention* (pp. 32–43). Washington, DC: American Psychological Association.

Ramey, C. T., Bryant, D. M., Campbell, F. A., Sparling, J. J., & Wasik, B. H. (1989). Early intervention for high-risk children: The Carolina early intervention program. *Journal of Prevention and Human Services, 7*, 33–57.

Ramey, C. T., & Campbell, F. A. (1984). Preventive education for high-risk children: Cognitive consequences of the Carolina Abecedarian Project. *American Journal of Mental Deficiency, 88*(5), 515–523.

Ramey, C. T., Farran, D. C., & Campbell, F. A. (1979). Predicting IQ from mother–infant interactions. *Child Development, 50*, 804–814.

Ramey, C. T., MacPhee, D., & Yeates, K. O. (1982). Preventing developmental retardation: A general systems model. In J. M. Joffee & L. A. Bond (Eds.), *Facilitating infant and early childhood development* (pp. 343–401). Hanover, NH: University Press of New England.

Ramey, C. T., McGinness, G., Cross, L., Collier, A., & Barrie-Blackley, S. (1981). The Abecedarian approach to social competence: Cognitive and linguistic intervention for disadvantaged preschoolers. In K. Borman (Ed.), *The social life of children in a changing society* (pp. 145–174). Hillsdale, NJ: Erlbaum.

Ramey, C. T., & Ramey, S. L. (1990). Intensive educational intervention for children of poverty. *Intelligence, 14,* 1–9.

Ramey, C. T., & Smith B. (1977). Assessing the intellectual consequences of early intervention with high-risk infants. *American Journal of Mental Deficiency, 8*(4), 318–324.

Ramey, C. T., Stedman, D. S, Borders-Patterson, A., & Mengel, W. (1978). Predicting school failure from information available at birth. *American Journal of Mental Deficiency, 82,* 525–534.

Ramey, C. T., Yeates, K. O., & Short, E. J. (1984). The plasticity of intellectual development: Insights from preventive intervention. *Child Development, 55,* 1913–1925.

Schaefer, E., Edgerton, M., & Aaronson, M. (1977). *Classroom behavior inventory.* Unpublished. (Available from Earl Schaefer, Department of Maternal and Child Health, University of North Carolina at Chapel Hill, Chapel Hill, NC 27599.)

Schweinhart, L. J., & Weikart, D. P. (1989). The High/Scope Perry Preschool study: Implications for early childhood care and education. *Prevention in Human Services, 7,* 109–132.

Sparling, J. J., & Lewis, I. (1981). *Learningames for the first three years: A program for parent / center partnership.* New York: Walker Educational.

Tough, J. (1976). *Listening to children talking.* London: Ward Lock Educational.

Wallach, M. A., & Wallach, L. (1976). *Teaching all children to read.* Chicago: University of Chicago Press.

Wechsler, D. (1949). *Wechsler Intelligence Scale for Children.* New York: Psychological Corporation.

Wechsler, D. (1955). *Wechsler Adult Intelligence Scale.* New York: Psychological Corporation.

Wechsler, D. (1967). *Wechsler Preschool and Primary Scale of Intelligence.* New York: Psychological Corporation.

Wechsler, D. (1974). *Wechsler Intelligence Scale for Children–Revised.* New York: Psychological Corporation.

Weikart, D. P., Bond, J. T., & McNeil, J. T. (1978). The Ypsilanti Perry preschool project: Preschool years and longitudinal results. *Monographs of the High/Scope Educational Research Foundation.*

Woodcock, R. W., & Johnson, M. B. (1977). *Woodcock–Johnson Psychoeducational Battery. Part 2: Tests of academic achievement.* Boston: Teaching Resources.

9   Educational acceleration for at-risk students

Henry M. Levin

A national educational crisis looms before us in confronting the education of at-risk students. Such students lack the family and community resources to succeed in schools as schools are currently constituted (Levin, 1986). They enter schools unprepared to take advantage of the standard curriculum and fall farther and farther behind in academic achievement. Their test scores indicate that they are two years behind other students by grade 6 and four years behind at the end of grade 12, if they reach that level. About half do not graduate from high school, which is a minimum requirement for productive entry into the U.S. labor force.

At-risk students are drawn heavily from poverty populations, minority groups, immigrant and non-English-speaking populations, and single-parent families. They represent about one-third of all students in elementary and secondary schools (Levin, 1986; Pallas, Natriello, & McDill, 1989), a proportion that is rising rapidly because of the substantial immigrations from impoverished and rural areas of Asia and Latin America and because of high birth rates among these populations.

Unless we are able to intervene successfully, there will be dire economic consequences for higher education, the labor force, and the cost of public services from this growing at-risk student population. Larger and larger numbers of educationally disadvantaged students will mean that public institutions of higher education will have to become more restrictive in their admissions criteria or more devoted to remedial academic work. Restrictive admissions not only will be politically contentious at a time of increasing population growth and political power of disadvantaged populations but it also may restrict the supply of college-educated workers below that needed by the economy. Alternatively, increasing numbers of remedial courses and students will raise costs substantially to both the colleges and universities and to the students who must forgo earnings for a longer period in order to get a college education.

A further consequence of the expansion of disadvantaged student populations will be a serious deterioration of the future labor force. As the numbers of educationally disadvantaged students grow and these students continue to

222

experience low achievement and high dropout rates, a larger and larger portion of the labor force will be unprepared for available jobs. Even clerical workers, cashiers, and salespeople need basic skills in oral and written communication and in computation and reasoning, skills that are not guaranteed among the educationally disadvantaged. A 1976 U.S. government study found that whereas 13% of all 17-year-olds were classified as functionally illiterate, the percentage of illiterates among educationally disadvantaged populations was about half (National Assessment of Educational Progress, 1976). Without successful interventions to improve the plight of the educationally disadvantaged, employers and the economy will suffer lagging productivity, higher training costs, and competitive disadvantages as well as lost tax revenues. This will be especially so in those states, regions, and localities containing the largest disadvantaged labor forces, but there will be a national impact as well.

These economic losses will come at a time of rising costs of public services for populations that are disadvantaged by inadequate educational attainments. More and more citizens will need to rely upon public assistance for survival, and increasing numbers of undereducated teens and adults will pursue illegal activities to fill idle time and obtain the income that is not available to them through legal pursuits (Berlin & Sum, 1988, pp. 28–30). A further point for consideration is that economic analyses of educational investments in behalf of at-risk students suggest that the financial value of the benefits to society far exceed the social costs (Levin, 1989).

Are we on the right track?

What is clear is that we are not on the right track for meeting the challenges of educationally at-risk students, despite educational reforms for the general population (e.g., National Commission on Excellence in Education, 1983; U.S. Department of Education, 1984). These reforms have not really addressed the specific needs of educationally at-risk students. The reforms stress raising standards at the secondary level, without providing additional resources or new strategies to assist the disadvantaged in meeting these higher standards (National Coalition of Advocates for Students, 1985).

Thus it is not surprising that the status of at-risk students has not advanced under the latest reforms. Any strategy for alleviating the educational plight of at-risk children must begin at the elementary level and must be dedicated to preparing children for doing high-quality work in secondary school. Simply raising standards at the secondary level without making it possible for at-risk students to meet the new standards is likely to increase the students' rate of dropping out (McDill, Natriello, & Pallas, 1985).

How to produce educational failure. Disadvantaged students begin school with a learning gap in those areas valued by schools and mainstream economic and social institutions. The existing model of intervention assumes that the disadvantaged students will not be able to maintain a normal instructional pace without prerequisite knowledge and learning skills. These youngsters, therefore, are placed in less demanding instructional settings (either they are pulled out of their regular classrooms or their regular classrooms are adapted to their "needs") in order to provide them with remedial or compensatory educational services. This approach appears to be both rational and compassionate, but it has exactly the opposite consequences.

First, this process reduces the learning expectations held by both the children and the educators who are assigned to teach them, and it stigmatizes both groups with a label of inferiority. Such stigma undermines social support for the activity, imparts a low social status to the participants, and promotes negative self-images for the participants. The combination of low expectations and low social status is tantamount to treating educationally disadvantaged students as discards who are marginal to the mainstream educational agenda. Thus, the model creates the unhealthiest of all possible conditions under which to expect significant educational progress. In contrast, *an effective approach must focus on creating learning activities that are characterized by high expectations and high status for the participants.*

Second, the usual treatment of the educationally disadvantaged is not designed to bring these students up to the level that enables them to benefit from mainstream instruction and perform at grade level. There exist no timetables for doing so, and there are rarely incentives or even provisions for students to move from remedial instruction into the mainstream. In fact, because students in compensatory or remedial situations are expected to progress at a slower than "normal" pace, a self-fulfilling prophecy is realized as they fall farther and farther behind their nondisadvantaged counterparts. As a result, once a disadvantaged student is relegated to remedial or compensatory interventions, that student will be expected to learn at a slower rate, and the achievement gap between that disadvantaged student and advantaged students will grow. *A successful program must set a deadline for closing the achievement gap so that, ultimately, educationally disadvantaged children will be able to benefit from mainstream instruction.*

Third, in deliberately slowing the pace of instruction a heavy emphasis is placed on endless repetition of material through drill and practice. As a consequence, the school experience of the disadvantaged lacks intrinsic vitality, omits crucial learning skills and reinforcement, and moves at a plodding pace that reinforces low expectations. In the primary grades exposure to concepts, analysis, problem solving, and interesting applications is largely proscribed in favor of decoding skills in reading and arithmetic operations in mathematics on the premise that these fundamentals must be learned before anything more challenging can be attempted. Mechanics are stressed over content. Such a joyless experience contributes to the child's negative feelings about school and diminishes the possibility that the child will view school as a positive environment in which learning progress can be made. *An effective curriculum for the disadvantaged not only must be fast paced and actively engage the interests of these children in order to enhance their motivation, but it also must include concepts, analysis, problem solving, and interesting applications.*

Most compensatory educational programs do not involve parents sufficiently or draw adequately upon available community resources. Parents are either not viewed as a potentially positive influence on their childrens' learning or not utilized as such. Furthermore, the professional staff at the school level are usually omitted from participation in making the important educational decisions that they ultimately must implement. Their omission means that teachers are expected to dedicate themselves to the implementation of programs that do not necessarily reflect their professional judgments, a condition that is not likely to spur them to great enthusiasm. *The design and implementation of educational programs that successfully address the needs of the educationally disadvantaged will require the involvement of parents, the use of community resources, and the extensive participation of teachers in formulating the interventions.*

An effective approach to educating disadvantaged children must be characterized by high expectations for these children, deadlines by which these children will be performing in grade-level range, stimulating instructional programs planned by the educational staff who will offer the programs, and the employment of all available resources, including the parents of students. In addition, it should utilize instructional strategies that are particularly appropriate for the disadvantaged and make better use of the students' time. Most important of all, the approach should incorporate a comprehensive set of strategies that mutually reinforce each other in creating an organizational push toward raising the achievement of students to grade level.

Accelerated schools for at-risk students

The Accelerated Schools Program at Stanford University was designed as an alternative to present practice. This program builds on the knowledge base that argues in favor of a different set of assumptions for achieving school success for at-risk students (Edmonds, 1979; Levin, 1987, 1988). At its heart is the notion of doing for at-risk students what we presently attempt to do for gifted and talented students, that is, striving to accelerate student progress rather than slowing it down. The goal of the Accelerated Schools Program is to speed up the learning of at-risk students so that the children are able to *perform at grade level by the end of elementary school.* Although this goal leads to the use of standardized tests to assess grade-level performance, we should not be constrained by the tests. Rather, we must ask what children should know at this level in order to be academically able and assess results accordingly. In the longer run, we expect to develop new assessment instruments that are broader and more nearly valid than the present standardized tests with their multiple-choice format.

Acceleration is supported by recent approaches to the definition of intelligence and giftedness (Chase, in press; Gardner & Hatch, 1989) as well as by experimental evidence supporting accelerated programs for at-risk students. Peterson (1989) randomly assigned low-achieving seventh graders who normally have been given remedial instruction to three different instructional settings: remedial, average, and pre-algebra for accelerated students. He found that the remedial students assigned to the accelerated, pre-algebra classes showed significant gains in achievement in all three areas in which they were tested, computation, problem solving, and mathematical concepts.

To accomplish academic acceleration systematically in all subjects for at-risk students, schools need to be restructured completely. Restructured schools are characterized by high expectations on the part of teachers, parents, and students; deadlines by which students are expected to meet particular educational requirements; stimulating instructional programs; planning by the educational staff; and the use of all available resources in the community, including parents, senior citizens, and social agencies. Over the last two and one-half years, some 40 of these schools have been established, most of them within the last year.

By effectively closing the achievement gap in elementary school, accelerated schools are designed to enable at-risk students to take advantage, by the seventh grade, of mainstream or accelerated middle school or secondary school instruction. These schools are expected to reduce the number of dropouts, the use drugs, and the number of teenage pregnancies by creating in those students who now feel rejected by school and frustrated about their abilities a strong sense of self-worth and educational accomplishment. Specific attributes of the accelerated school follow.

Organization

The entire organization of the accelerated school focuses on the goal of having students achieve at or above grade level by the time they leave sixth grade. Central to the accelerated school strategy is the placement of curriculum and instructional decisions in the hands of the instructional staff of the school. Classroom teachers know the children best. They understand the children's learning needs, styles, and capabilities in ways that most administrators and program specialists cannot. If desired changes in student achievement are to be realized, teachers must have both the responsibility and the authority to design curriculum and instructional programs in ways that are compatible with the teachers' unique classroom perspective.

To facilitate this process, in each accelerated school are task forces composed of teachers, other school staff, and parents and an overall steering committee. The principal, who serves on the steering committee along with parent and task force representatives, is the instructional leader, coordinating and guiding the planning process. The school's staff work together to set out a program that is consonant with their strengths and the strengths of the district and with student needs. Information, technical assistance, and training are provided by district personnel. In these ways, the reform is a "bottom-up" approach in which those educators who are providing the instruction make the decisions as to its implementation and evaluation. These broad features of the accelerated school make it into a total institution for increasing the educational progress of the disadvantaged rather than just leave it as a conventional school onto which compensatory or remedial classes have been grafted.

We believe that this approach to the education of disadvantaged students has a high probability of ultimate success. The characteristics contributing to the success of this approach are its emphasis on the instrumental goal of bringing students to either grade level or above by the completion of sixth grade; its stress on the acceleration of learning, on critical thinking, and on high expectations; its reliance on a professional model of school governance that is attractive to educators; its capacity to benefit from instructional strategies already shown to have had good results for the disadvantaged within existing models of compensatory education; and its ability to draw upon all of the resources available to the community, including parents and senior citizens.

Emphasis is placed on the school as a whole rather than on a particular grade, curriculum, approach to teacher training, or other, more limited, strategy. Underlying the organizational approach are three major assumptions:

1. The strategy enlists a unity of purpose among all of the participants.
2. The strategy "empowers" all of the major participants and raises their feelings of efficacy and of responsibility for the outcomes of the school.
3. The strategy builds on the considerable strengths, rather than decries the weaknesses, of the participants.

Unity of purpose refers to agreement among parents, teachers, and students on a common set of goals for the school that will be the focal point of everyone's efforts. Clearly, these goals should focus on bringing children into the educational mainstream so that the students can benefit fully from their further school experiences and their later adult opportunities.

Empowerment refers to the ability of the key participants to make important decisions at the school level and in the home in order to improve the education of students. It is based upon breaking the current stalemate among administrators, teachers, parents, and students in which they tend to blame each other, as well as other factors "beyond their control," for the poor educational outcomes of disadvantaged students. Unless all of the major actors are empowered to seek a common set of goals and to influence the educational and social processes that can achieve these goals, it is unlikely that the desired improvements will take place or be sustained.

An accelerated school must build upon an expanded role for all groups, encouraging them to participate in and take responsibility for the educational process and educational results. This approach requires a shift to school-based decision making with its extensive involvement of teachers and parents and development of new administrative positions.

Building on strengths refers to the utilization of all of the learning resources that students, parents, school staff, and communities can bring to the educational endeavor. In the quest to place the blame for the schools' inability to improve the education of the disadvantaged, it is easy to exaggerate the weaknesses of the various participants and ignore their strengths. For example, among the considerable advantages that parents have in serving as positive influences on the education of their children are their deep love for their children and desire that their children succeed. Teachers are capable of insights, intuition, and teaching and organizational acumen that are lost when they are excluded from making educational decisions. Both parents and teachers are largely underutilized as sources of talent in the schools.

The strengths of disadvantaged students too are often overlooked. The students are perceived as lacking the learning behaviors associated with middle-class students rather than as having unique assets that can be used to accelerate their learning. These assets often include curiosity about oral and artistic expression and the ability to learn through the manipulation of appropriate materials, to become engrossed in intrinsically interesting tasks, and to learn to write even before attaining the competence in decoding skills that is prerequisite to being able to read. In addition, students can serve as enthusiastic and effective learning resources for other students through peer tutoring and cooperative-learning approaches (Slavin, 1983).

School-based administrators also are underutilized, placed in "command" roles and required to meet the directives and standard operating procedures of districts rather than to work creatively with parents, staff, and students. And communities have considerable resources, including youth organizations, senior citizens, businesses, and religious groups, that should be viewed as major assets for schools and children. These participants can be important resources for creating accelerated schools.

Curriculum and instructional strategies

The instructional program in accelerated schools is based upon a curriculum designed to bring all children to grade level or higher in core areas (i.e., to score at the 50th percentile or above on norm-referenced standardized achievement tests in reading comprehension, language, and mathematics computation and applications). Significant curriculum aspects include a heavily language-based approach, even in mathematics. Language is emphasized across the curriculum, with early introductions to writing and reading for meaning and to the development of critical literacy. The curriculum presents to students interesting applications of new tools to everyday problems and events, stressing the usefulness of what is being taught and learned and introducing a problem-solving orientation. Active learning approaches based upon students' discovery and testing of ideas represent a response to student curiosity and enables students to benefit from learning by doing rather than having to learn just by listening.

Other features include the implementation of an extended-day program in which rest periods, physical activities, the arts, and a period for independent assignments or homework are provided. During this study period, college students and senior-citizen volunteers work with individual children to provide learning assistance. Because many of the students are latchkey children, the extension of the school day is attractive to parents. Instructional strategies also include peer tutoring and cooperative learning, both of which have been shown to be especially effective with disadvantaged students (Slavin & Madden, 1989).

Parent involvement

Parent involvement is necessarily a central focus of the accelerated school. Epstein (1987) has shown that research on parental and family involvement supports the important potential role of their families in raising the educational accomplishments of students. The accelerated school builds on parental involvement in several ways.

Parents or guardians are expected to affirm an agreement that clarifies the goals of the accelerated school and the obligations of parents, students, and school staff. The agreement is explained to parents and translated, if necessary. Parents agree to support the program through, for example, ensuring that their children go to bed at a reasonable hour and attend school regularly and punctually. Parents are asked to set high educational expectations for their children, to talk to their children regularly about the importance of school, and to take an interest in their children's activities and in the materials that the children bring home from school.

Parents are expected to encourage their children to read on a daily basis and to ensure that independent assignments are addressed. They are also expected to respond to queries from the school. The importance of the parental role is emphasized through the dignity of an agreement that is affirmed by all parties. Students and school staff also have obligations appropriate to their roles. It is generally understood that the accelerated school will succeed only if all three parties work together.

Parents participate in the governance structure of the school through their membership on task forces and the steering committee. They also are given opportunities to be part of the school program and to interact with school staff through an open-door policy and a parent lounge. Parents may also receive training so that they can actively assist their children. Such training includes not only the skills necessary for working with a child but also many of the academic skills necessary to understand what the child is doing. In this area, close contact with agencies offering basic adult education can help provide the parental foundation. The parental dimension can improve the capacity of and effort made by the child to learn. It also can increase the time that the child devotes to academic learning and can provide additional instructional resources in the home.

Evaluation

Progress is evaluated by an assessment system that monitors student performance to ensure that the children are on the appropriate learning trajectory. Periodic evaluations on wide-spectrum, standardized achievement tests as well as on tailored assessments created by school staff for each strand of the curriculum are essential ingredients. These evaluations emphasize the students' acquisition of higher order thinking and reasoning skills in core curricular areas. Unfortunately, assessment instruments that are presently available are not suitable for these purposes. Accordingly, this dimension is the focus of a major developmental effort.

Accelerated schools in action

At the heart of the accelerated school is the emphasis on on-site responsibility for the educational process and outcomes (Goodlad, 1984). This focus means that there must be an appropriate decision-making structure that will support the school's unity of purpose and that there must be an appropriate process to develop the school's capacity to identify challenges, examine these challenges and potential solutions, and implement and evaluate solutions.

Governance structures

We have found that three levels of participation in school governance are necessary to address the range of issues in a democratic but productive way. These structures encompass the school as a whole, the steering committee, and task and policy committees.

The school as a whole (SAW) refers to the school principal, teachers,

teachers' aides, and other instructional and noninstructional staff and to parent representatives as well as student representatives. The SAW is required to approve all important decisions on curriculum, instruction, and resource allocation that have implications for the entire school. At the opposite extreme, in terms of group size, are the task and policy committees. These small groups are organized around particular areas of concern for the school, such as classroom subject matter, school personnel, or specific school challenges. Where the concern is a continuing one, such as personnel selection and evaluation, learning assessment, or parent participation, a policy committee is formed. In cases where the concern is episodic, such as the planning of new facilities, an ad hoc committee is formed for the duration of the task. The major guidelines for forming committees are to create as few as possible, to look for ways to combine related responsibilities, and to dissolve committees that are no longer needed.

The task and policy committees are the groups that do most of the school's analytic and preparatory work, such as defining specific problems and searching for and implementing solutions. These groups capitalize on the camaraderie, ease of communication, and motivations associated with small teams that work together on a regular basis. Before implementation begins, recommendations of task and policy committees must be approved by the steering committee and, in some cases, by the school as a whole.

The steering committee consists of the principal and representatives of the teachers, aides, other school staff, and parents. The purpose of the steering committee is to appoint the task and policy committees, to monitor their progress, and to develop a set of recommendations for consideration by the school as a whole. The steering committee can have elected members, or it can have a rotating membership of representatives of the smaller committees in order to give all persons a chance to serve. Committees are expected to meet on a weekly basis, the steering committee on a biweekly basis, and the school as a whole on a quarterly basis or as needed. For all of these entities, the agenda must be on public display at least 24 hours in advance of a meeting and the minutes on display within 48 hours following a meeting.

Clearly, the principal in the accelerated school plays a different role than a principal in a traditional school. In the accelerated school, the principal is responsible for coordinating and facilitating the activities of decision-making bodies as well as for obtaining the logistical support necessary in areas such as information, staff development, assessment, implementation, and instructional resources. A good principal in the context of the accelerated school is an active listener and participant who can identify and cultivate talents among staff, can keep the school focused on its mission, and can work effectively with parents and the community. Such a principal also is dedicated to the students and their success, can motivate the various actors and marshal the necessary resources, and is as well "the keeper of the dream." In this last role, the principal is the person who always must remind participants of the "dream," especially when they encounter disappointments.

School districts need to fulfill a greater service role for individual schools than they normally do. Instead of being a regulator, issuing rules, mandates, and policies that ensure the compliance of school activities with some centralized plan, the school district must provide support services to help the accelerated school succeed in its mission. Central office staff must assist task committees and the steering committee in identifying challenges, obtaining information on alternative solutions, implementation, staff development, and evaluation. The Central office staff also must assist the schools in working with parents and helping families sponsor activities in the home that support the educational progress of their children.

Although schools for at-risk students need considerable resources (Levin, 1989), the transformation of a traditional school to an accelerated school is one qualitative change that can be done largely within existing resources. The major resource need is additional released time for staff for meetings, staff development, discussion, reflection, planning, and exploration of alternatives. Our pilot schools have been successful in using various school district resources, grants from foundations, and changes in school organization to accommodate some of these time requirements. In addition, expertise is needed from either the district's central office or outside consultants to assist the school in building its capacity to accelerate the education of its students.

Building school capacity

Existing schools can be transformed structurally through devolution of decision making to school sites, but they will not function as accelerated schools without enlarging the capacity of the schools to establish a unity of purpose, to make responsible decisions, and to build on strengths. Certainly, school staff have not been trained to function in this way, nor have they been expected to function in this way in traditional schools (Keith & Girling, 1990). Much of the capability to become an accelerated school comes directly from practice, or from learning by doing. As school staff and community work at it, they become experts at the process. But in order to get the process started, there are a number of steps that must be taken.

It is usually necessary to provide staff with some training in making decisions within groups. Principals, teachers, and school staff in traditional schools rarely have had this experience. Meetings in traditional schools tend to be highly structured and to be run in a routine, often authoritarian, fashion. Teachers, in particular, consider meetings a waste of time. School staff usually do not view meetings as having the potential to be productive and to accomplish major goals in behalf of the school. Accordingly, school staff need experience in working together, with special attention being paid to group process and participation, sharing of information, and working toward decisions. In addition, staff need exposure to inquiry-oriented processes that help to identify and define challenges, look for alternative solutions, and implement possible solutions.

Involvement in the accelerated school process is itself an important part of building capacity. This process is initiated in four steps. In the first phase, the school is asked to establish baseline information on itself. School staff are asked to assemble, for discussion among all site participants, a report that includes a history of the school; data on students, staff, and school facilities; information on the community and cultures of the parents; reference to particular strengths of the school; data on attendance, test scores, and other measures of student performance; and a discussion of the major challenges faced by the school. Some of this information will be quantitative, although much of it will be descriptive. Thus, the accelerated school process begins through self-examination and preparation of a written record of the school's status with which to compare later progress. The process of collecting, reporting, and discussing the baseline information is completed over several weeks.

The second phase of the capacity-building process is to establish a vision that will be the focus of change for the school. In a series of meetings both of the school as a whole and of smaller components of staff, the participants focus on building a description of a school that will work for students, staff, and community. The accelerated school transition can be expected to take about six years. The process of establishing a new vision of their school can be carried out in a single day if staff members prepare for it in informal discussions in the days preceding this meeting.

The third phase involves comparison of the vision with the baseline report. Clearly, there will be a large gap in almost every aspect between the vision and the existing situation. School staff are asked to set out all of the things that must be done in order to realize the vision for the school. Often 40 to 50 major alterations are cited.

The fourth phase takes the list of what needs to be accomplished and reduces it to a small number of initial priorities, which will become the immediate focus of the school. No organization can work effectively on more than three or four major priorities at a time. The task facing the staff is to select these three or four priorities. This exercise can generate animated discussions that get to the heart of staff concerns. This discourse is useful because through it the staff realizes that they are responsible for changing the school and for choosing those areas in which to begin. Staff agreement on priorities is followed by the establishment of the first task committees – the small groups that will work on these priorities – and the assignment of staff to each group, usually through self-selection, as well as the establishment of a steering committee to coordinate planning and decisions.

At this point the school is ready to adopt the full accelerated process. This process, however, requires the support of the principal, steering committee, and school district as well as of a trained staff. Task committees need to know how to take a broad challenge, for example, the mathematics performance of students, and refine the focus in order to identify the specific concerns. They then must be able to translate these concerns into hypotheses for further exploration. Once staff can narrow the problem to a particular cause or causes, they can seek out alternative ways to address it. Finally, the staff must select a solution or strategy, implement it, and evaluate the results. For this reason it is necessary to provide all task groups with training and guidance in problem solving and the implementation of decisions.

Present status of accelerated schools

The Accelerated School Program at Stanford University began its implementation of the accelerated school process two and a half years ago with the selection of two pilot schools in the San Francisco Bay Area. Since that time, another 35 schools have begun the six-year transition to accelerated schools, including statewide networks of 25 schools in Illinois and 9 schools in Missouri. The purpose of the two pilot schools is to implement the principles of accelerated schooling; simultaneously, these schools provide a basis upon which we can increase our knowledge of how to apply the program in collaboration with practitioners.

It is important to note again that our estimate of the time required to make the transition from a conventional school to an accelerated one is about six years. This fact means that neither pilot school has implemented the full program at this time. However, each school has been able to set its initial priorities and is working to achieve these and, as the initial goals are met, to undertake additional objectives.

Because only two of the six years required for a full transformation of our pilot schools have passed, we have not undertaken a summative evaluation. However, many changes are observable. Parent participation in the two schools has increased dramatically. In the pilot school for which we have longitudinal data, parent attendance at back-to-school night increased from 17 persons prior to the intervention to about 450 persons at the beginning of the third year. Participation at parent conferences increased from less than 40% to almost 95% in the same period. Student discipline problems have declined precipitously, and attendance patterns have improved. School staff report substantial improvements in the school environment.

New programs, selected by school staff, have been introduced to help students learn language arts and mathematics and to raise student self-esteem. In the year following the designation of mathematics as a priority area and the search for and implementation of school-based solutions to the students' poor performance in mathematics, the mathematics scores of sixth graders rose from the 10th to the 27th percentile on statewide norms of the California Assessment Program. Other accelerated schools have had the largest achievement gains in their school districts and have gotten their students to achieve at grade level. Finally, there is evidence in the pilot schools of reduced grade repetition, resulting in considerable savings to school-funding sources.

This is not the only approach to acceleration that shows promise. James Comer (1980) and his associates at Yale University have designed and implemented school programs that draw upon strong parental involvement, the use of a problem-solving approach to meet school challenges, and the provision of mental health service teams to increase the school's capacity to address its problems. The application of the Comer model to elementary schools in New Haven, Connecticut, in the seventies showed powerful results in raising the achievement of inner-city black students to grade level and maintaining that performance in subsequent years (Comer, 1987).

The Success for All Program associated with Robert Slavin and his colleagues at the Johns Hopkins University uses a variety of integrated approaches to advance the progress of at-risk children (Madden, Slavin, Karweit, & Livermon, 1989). It was first implemented in an inner-city black elementary school in Baltimore in 1987–1988 and in other schools in Baltimore and Philadelphia in 1988–1989. This approach places heavy emphasis on tutors, on daily 90-minute reading periods with about 15 students in each class, on a specially constructed reading program, on family involvement, and on changes in school governance. Improvements in achievement have been dramatic.

The program Higher Order Thinking Skills (HOTS), developed by Stan Pogrow of the University of Arizona, has shown extraordinary accomplishments for at-risk students (Pogrow, 1990). The HOTS program is based upon a two-year curriculum in which children in grades 4 through 7 spend 35 minutes daily for four days each week in problem-solving discourse and activities. The content and instructional strategies of this program are highly sophisticated and suggest that students can learn content more effectively through problem-solving approaches than through direct study of the material. This type of program is highly compatible with a more fully accelerated curriculum.

The Reading Recovery Program, which is based upon the work of the New Zealand educator Marie Clay (1979, 1987) also has shown powerful results in raising the reading achievement of at-risk students in U.S. schools (Boehnlein, 1987). This program consists of intensive tutoring by specially trained tutors for 30 minutes daily for 15 to 20 weeks, or 30 to 40 hours of instruction.

Research results from Columbus, Ohio, show that 90% of the children whose pretest scores on reading were in the lowest 20% of their class were able to catch up to or exceed their class average, and it appears that they maintain this position in subsequent years. The program is now being replicated throughout Ohio and elsewhere, and it is also being tested in accelerated schools in the Illinois Accelerated School Network.

What is the cost?

The evidence suggests that we have the knowledge base to accelerate the education of at-risk students, but it is important to understand the magnitude of the national investment that is necessary to accomplish this task. The difficulty in estimating the price tag is due to lack of precise figures on the number of at-risk students, data on the cost of achieving success under the more promising models, and agreement on an appropriate time frame in which to achieve success (Levin, 1989). However, on the basis of certain assumptions, estimates of the cost can be made. If we assume that half again as much money must be spent on the education of at-risk students over their elementary and secondary careers as is presently spent on the education of average students, this would amount to an additional $2,000 per at-risk student in 1988–1989. With an estimate of about 13 million at-risk students (Levin, 1986), the investment for 1988–1989 would be about $26 billion. But the combination of both Chapter I of the Education Consolidation and Improvement Act (ECIA), the major federal appropriation for at-risk students, and the various state support programs for such children is not likely to exceed $5 billion per year, of which Chapter I accounts for about $4 billion. The result is that an additional $21 billion of funding would be needed, or a fourfold expansion in additional spending for at-risk students. The necessary increase would account for only about a 10% increase in overall elementary and secondary educational funding.

Additional funds for at-risk students would need to come from all levels of government. The federal government should provide the bulk of the funding for several reasons. First, failure to address the educational needs of at-risk students will have national repercussions for the nation's economy; second, equality of opportunity has been a foremost commitment at the federal level; and third, the federal government will receive most of the additional tax revenues generated by the income created by educational investments. About 60% of all public revenues are collected at the federal level, but only about 6% of the cost of elementary and secondary education is paid for by the federal government. In contrast, over 90% of the cost of education is paid for by state and local governments even though they receive only 40% of the tax revenues generated by educational investments.

Much of this spending could come from reallocating the billions of dollars wasted in military and other government programs characterized by fraud and incompetence. For example, the federal "bailout" of savings and loans institutions is likely to cost more than $100 billion over the next few years, and recent losses from fraud and political manipulation at the Department of Housing and Urban Development account for at least several billion dollars. Arguments that budgetary deficits and spending stringencies make it impossible to increase federal educational funding for at-risk students are simply statements of political and value priorities. Such assertions tend to pale alongside the possibilities for reallocations from weapons systems that do not work, taxpayer-insured savings and loan bailouts, poorly monitored student loan programs, and bloated health care programs. It is a matter of where we place our priorities, and judicious cuts from each of these programs are unlikely to have an adverse effect on public welfare relative to the benefits that would result from additional spending on at-risk students.

States also must expand their funding of the education of at-risk students. The states are responsible for education, and they will benefit from the increased tax revenues and improved economies associated with raising the productivity and life chances of at-risk students. In addition, such investments in the education of at-risk students should reduce state expenditures on public assistance and the criminal justice system.

Local jurisdictions are most likely to be handicapped in raising additional funds for the education of at-risk students. But at the local level greater accountability for obtaining results is possible, and it is easier to coordinate existing resources to focus more intensely on the needs of at-risk students. Voluntary agencies, such as churches, scouts, and YMCAs, as well as public social service agencies need to coordinate their efforts to assist families in becoming self-sufficient and in contributing to the education of their children. Local communities also need to take greater advantage of local businesses and senior citizens who, by providing financial assistance, tutoring, and other types of support, can help in the effort to achieve better schools.

Building a political coalition

Both the moral imperative and the economic, social, and political rationales for major investments in the education of at-risk students are compelling. Rising inequalities attributable to a growing at-risk population will threaten the ability of a democratic society to function effectively. The gains from educational investments will be more than compensated for by increases in economic productivity and tax revenues. Moreover, the benefits of such a program are diffused so widely that the following constituencies clearly have something to gain:

1. *Business.* Business will gain from a more productive work force and less crime. Also, less money will be needed for the criminal justice system and public assistance so taxes will be lower.
2. *Taxpayers.* Taxpayers will gain because higher tax revenues can be derived from a more productive population. Taxes will be lower because less money will have to be spent on noneducational services for at-risk students as well as on the criminal justice system and public assistance.
3. *Parents.* Parents will gain because their children will attend better schools. More orderly school environments will mean less disruption of education while students are being disciplined. Schools will be able to focus more on academics.
4. *Cities.* With more productive schools and citizens, cities will become more attractive places.
5. *Teachers.* Teachers have much to gain from the additional instructional resources and from the setting of a high priority on educating at-risk students.
6. *Families.* Both the formation of families and their maintenance will gain from a more productive and orderly educational system that attends to the needs of at-risk students and provides them with the skills to gain employment and raise their own stable families.

This list could go on because there are so many constituencies that would benefit from an improvement in the status of at-risk students and few that would be undermined. Moreover, these are the major groups dominating public policy, especially educational policy. A coalition has not yet come together that melds these groups into a powerful force for change. Although some attention has been focused on at-risk students in recent years, it has not been concentrated or sustained with the intensity that is needed. The major political challenge is to mobilize the diverse groups interested in improving the status of at-risk children into a unified political force capable of marshalling the necessary public investments. At the very least, this effort will require a much wider awareness of what is at stake and what public investments and school restructuring can do to improve outcomes in behalf of both at-risk students and the entire society.

Summary

This chapter addresses the educational needs of at-risk students – students who lack the family and community resources to succeed in schools as schools are currently constituted. These students enter school unprepared to take advantage of the standard curriculum and fall farther and farther behind in achievement. They often drop out before completing high school. There are severe consequences to school failure not only for these students and their families but also for the economy, higher education, and the cost and provision of public services that support those individuals who lack the education needed to succeed in conventional ways.

This chapter presents the case for accelerating the education of at-risk students much as we do that of gifted and talented students. It proposes the establishment of accelerated schools that will bring these pupils into the educational mainstream by making them academically able by the end of elementary school. Accelerated schools are described in terms of their organizational and decision-making dimensions, their curriculum, and their instructional strategies.

The final sections of this chapter describe a nascent effort at establishing accelerated schools in the United States and some early results. Issues of financing such schools and obtaining political support for them are also explored.

References

Berlin, G., & Sum, A. (1988). *Toward a more perfect union: Basic skills. Poor families and our economic future* (Occasional Paper 3). Ford Foundation Project on Social Welfare and the American Future. New York: Ford Foundation.

Boehnlein, M. (1987, March). Reading intervention for high-risk first graders. *Educational Leadership, 44*(6), 32–37.

Chase, C. (in press). Releasing the gifted potential of "at-risk" students. In H. M. Levin (Ed.), *Accelerating the education of at-risk students*. New York: Falmer Press.

Clay, M. (1979). *Reading: The patterning of complex behavior*. Exeter, NH: Heinemann.

Clay, M. (1987). Implementing reading recovery: Systematic adaptations to an educational innovation. *New Zealand Journal of Educational Studies, 22*(1), 35–58.

Comer, J. J. (1980). *School power*. New York: Free Press.

Comer, J. J. (1987). New Haven's school-community connection. *Educational Leadership, 44*(6), 13–18.

Edmonds, R. (1979). Effective schools for the urban poor. *Educational Leadership, 37*(1), 15–24.

Epstein, J. L. (1987). Parent involvement: What research says to administrators. *Education and Urban Society, 19*(2), 119–136.

Gardner, H., & Hatch, T. (1989). Multiple intelligences go to school: Educational implications of theory of multiple intelligences. *Educational Researcher, 19*, 4–10.

Girling, K., Girling, S., & Girling, R. H. (1990). *Education: Management and participation.* Boston: Allyn & Bacon.

Goodlad, J. I. (1984). *A place called school*. New York: McGraw-Hill.

Keith, S., & Girling, R. H. (1990). *Education: Management and participation*. Boston: Allyn & Bacon.

Levin, H. M. (1986). *Educational reform for disadvantaged students: An emerging crisis*. West Haven, CT: National Education Association Professional Library.

Levin, H. M. (1987). Accelerating schools for disadvantaged students. *Educational Leadership, 44*(6), 19–21.

Levin, H. M. (1988). Accelerating elementary education for disadvantaged students. In Council of Chief State School Officers (Ed.), *School success for students at risk* (pp. 209–226). Orlando, FL: Harcourt Brace Jovanovich.

Levin, H. M. (1989). Financing the education of at-risk students. *Educational Evaluation and Policy Analysis, 11*(1), 47–60.

Madden, N. A., Slavin, R. E., Karweit, N. L., & Livermon, B. J. (1989). Success for all: Restructuring the urban elementary school. *Educational Leadership, 46*(5), 14–20.

McDill, E. L., Natriello, G., & Pallas, A. (1985). Raising standards and retaining students: The impact of the reform recommendations on potential dropouts. *Review of Educational Research, 55*, 415–434.

National Assessment of Educational Progress. (1976). *Functional literacy and basic reading per-*

formance. Washington, DC: Department of Health, Education and Welfare, U.S. Office of Education.

National Coalition of Advocates for Students. (1985). *Barriers to excellence: Our children at risk.* Boston: Author.

National Commission on Excellence in Education. (1983). *A nation at risk: The imperative for educational reform.* Washington, DC: U.S. Department of Education.

Pallas, A. M., Natriello, G., & McDill, E. L. (1989). The changing nature of the disadvantaged population: Current dimensions and future trends. *Educational Researcher, 18*(5), 16–22.

Peterson, J. M. (1989). Remediation is no remedy. *Educational Leadership, 46*(5), 24–25.

Pogrow, S. (1990). Challenging at-risk students: Findings from the HOTS program. *Phi Delta Kappan, 71*(5), 389–397.

Slavin, R. E. (1983). *Cooperative learning.* New York: Longman.

Slavin, R. E., & Madden, N. A. (1989). What works for students at risk: A research synthesis. *Educational Leadership, 46*(5), 4–13.

U.S. Department of Education. (1984). *The nation responds: Recent efforts to improve education.* Washington, DC: U.S. Government Printing Office.

10 Cost-benefit and cost-effectiveness analyses of interventions for children in poverty

Henry M. Levin

The true measure of the humanity of an affluent society is not how the society treats its wealthy but how it treats its poor. Sadly, the poor are still with us, rising substantially as a proportion of the total population in the last decade. Especially vulnerable to poverty are the nation's children, with some one-quarter of children under 6 years living in a poverty setting. As the chapters in this book amply demonstrate, child poverty translates into child malnutrition, untreated health and dental problems, poor housing, and inadequate educational progress. These handicaps mean not only that the conditions of child poverty are harsh but that the lack of supportive conditions for human development will limit adult productivity and attainment.

Social investments in health, nutrition, housing, and education can improve the lives of children in poverty as well as increase the possibilities that these children will experience productive adult lives. But even within each of these areas the choice of activities is great, and available resources are far from infinite; the needs of children in poverty compete with those of many other constituencies. The search for effective social policies for poor children, therefore, requires a search for programs or interventions that can use resources in the most efficient way.

In this chapter, I explore the use of cost-benefit and cost-effectiveness analyses as tools with which to select from a large number of competing programs that would address the needs of children in poverty. Emphasis is on the role of these analyses and on how they might be made more useful to the task. In the first section, I provide a brief review of cost-benefit and cost-effectiveness analysis to show how each might be used. In the second section, I present examples and raise particular questions about the use of these tools of analysis. In the final section, I suggest ways of ensuring that alternatives for improving the welfare of children in poverty will be analyzed for policy purposes.

What are cost-benefit and cost-effectiveness analyses?

Both cost-benefit and cost-effectiveness analyses have the somewhat unique distinction of being used in policy discussions far more than they are used in policy analysis. Decision makers often claim that they are searching for cost-effective solutions to problems or that a particular choice is cost-effective without presenting any formal analysis to support these claims. Because the terms *cost-benefit* and *cost-effectiveness* are used so freely, they often lose meaning in daily usage. Accordingly, it is important to define and differentiate the two tools before proceeding.

Both cost-benefit analysis and cost-effectiveness analysis refer to approaches for comparing the costs and outcomes of various alternatives under policy consideration. Presumably, those alternatives that have the best outcomes relative to costs are the ones that should be adopted. In this way, a given set of resources can be used for maximal effectiveness relative to the alternatives. But such an approach requires that we have methods to conceptualize, measure, and compare costs and effects or costs and benefits.

Cost-benefit analysis

Cost-benefit analysis compares the costs and benefits of various alternatives in monetary terms. Costs are determined by setting out the monetary value of all of the resource requirements, and benefits are derived by estimating the monetary values of the outcomes for each alternative. For example, the costs of a preschool program would be determined by accounting for the market or market-related value of all of the resources that were required for the program, including those that were provided in-kind. Benefits would be determined by the value of outcomes of the program, such as the savings from reducing the need for later remediation of or grade repetition by children. Because costs and benefits often occur in different time periods, adjustments are required to make their social values comparable. These details will be discussed later.

Cost-benefit analysis has two major features for policy makers. First, it is possible to compare the costs with the benefits of a decision directly. Hence, decision makers can limit their choices to programs or interventions whose benefits exceed their costs. They can select that set of alternatives with the highest benefit to cost ratio or the largest net benefits (benefits minus costs). This process ensures that, within any program area, the combination of programs selected will make the largest contribution to social welfare for any given cost.

Second, cost-benefit analysis enables a decision maker to compare the productivity of investments in one area, such as health, with investments in any other area, for example, housing, education, transportation, or nutrition.

Thus, one can allocate scarce resources among major areas of social investment as well as to specific programs within these areas by using cost-benefit calculations.

The weakness of cost-benefit analysis is that it requires information that is often difficult to obtain. That is, it is not always possible to convert the outcomes of social interventions into monetary benefits. Benefits of alternative activities are most easily calculated when the activities have produced savings in the costs of other activities or when they have produced outcomes that can be valued in the market. Thus, a benefit of early childhood intervention for nutrition and health might be the savings in later health costs that are avoided by preventive measures. A market outcome of such an intervention might be the higher earnings associated with better nutrition and health. The variety of issues raised by benefit-cost studies are found in Gramlich (1981), Levin (1983), and Mishan (1976).

Cost-effectiveness analysis

Although cost-benefit results provide advantages in the search for efficient use of social resources, there are many situations in which monetary values of benefits are difficult to calculate. For example, the goals of some social interventions will be to improve the present welfare of children in poverty regardless of future consequences. Child malnutrition, child abuse, substandard housing, inadequate schooling, and chronic health problems are all subjects of social concern about children, even when the future benefits of alleviating these conditions cannot be readily ascertained and quantified. In these cases, we recognize that improving present child welfare is important as a goal in itself, even in the absence of future implications. Of course, in many instances such improvement will also enhance the future prospects of the affected children, but we are unable to foresee or measure these future effects.

In such cases, the decision maker will wish to choose those programs that provide the highest levels of effectiveness relative to their costs within an area, where effectiveness is measured by criteria specific to that domain. For example, the effectiveness of nutritional programs might be measured by how well they meet the dietary needs of children. Schooling programs can be evaluated by gains in student achievement. Reductions in child abuse, chronic health problems, and substandard housing also can be evaluated directly. In each case, we can compare the costs and effectiveness of programs to address a particular problem such as poor nutrition. The costs and effectiveness of different nutritional programs can be compared to see which program can provide a given level of results at the least cost. Similar analyses can be carried out for other areas of social concern.

Cost-effectiveness analysis compares programs or interventions that share similar goals in order to ascertain which ones have the highest effectiveness relative to cost for an outcome that is consistent with these goals. The results of such an analysis are usually expressed as cost-effectiveness ratios that show the cost per unit of result. Cost-effectiveness studies cannot compare programs with different objectives as cost-benefit studies can for the obvious reason that the former must measure effectiveness using area-specific criteria. The latter can convert outcomes into monetary measures of benefits, which can be compared across highly diverse phenomena. Thus, cost-effectiveness for a reading program can be compared only to that of other reading programs; cost-effectiveness for improved child nutrition can be compared only to that of other nutritional programs. These and similar issues are discussed in Levin (1983).

Measuring costs

Cost-benefit and cost-effectiveness studies differ in their measurements of outcomes but not of costs. The costs of an intervention are defined as the value of the resources that are given up by society to effect the intervention. The resource requirements are referred to as the *ingredients* of the intervention, and it is the social value of these ingredients that constitute its overall cost. At a later stage one can assess the distribution of these costs among the decision-making agency and other entities. Accordingly, the method sets out systematically to identify the ingredients and to ascertain the value of the ingredients required for each alternative under consideration.

The ingredients approach to cost estimation entails three distinct phases: (1) identification of ingredients; (2) determination of the value, or cost, of the ingredients and of the overall costs of an intervention; and (3) analysis of the costs in an appropriate decision-oriented framework.

Identification of ingredients. The first step is to ascertain which ingredients are required for an intervention (Levin, 1983, chap. 3). Most social interventions in behalf of children are labor intensive, so that one initial step is to account for the number and characteristics of personnel. Clearly, we are concerned with whether personnel are part time or full time and the types of skills or qualifications that they need. Beyond personnel matters we need to identify the facilities, equipment, materials, and other ingredients or resources that the the intervention requires.

Identification of ingredients calls for a level of detail that is adequate to ensure that all resources are included and are described adequately in order to place cost values on them. For this reason, the search for ingredients must be systematic rather than casual. The primary sources for data are written reports, observations, and interviews. Written reports usually contain at least a brief history and description of the intervention. Some also provide a detailed list of personnel and other resources. These reports can be used to construct the basic list of required ingredients. My experience suggests that the information in reports is often incomplete and lacks sufficient detail on qualitative aspects of the ingredients. For example, the report may list a number of teachers, coordinators, and other personnel, without stipulating their levels of experience, training, education, or other special personnel qualifications.

Accordingly, other sources of information must be used to corroborate and supplement data on ingredients from evaluations and descriptive reports. If the intervention is present at a nearby site, it may be possible to visit and gather additional data on ingredients through observation. Interviews are a third valuable source; present or former personnel are asked to identify resources from among a number of classifications. The three principal types of information – reports, observations, and interviews – can be used to assure the accuracy of the data by comparing the findings from each source and reconciling differences, the process of triangulation.

Determining costs. Once the ingredients have been identified and stipulated, one must calculate their costs (Levin, 1983, chap. 4). All ingredients, including donated or volunteer resources, are assumed to have a cost. That is, the resources have a cost to someone, even if the sponsoring agency did not pay for them in a particular situation.

Ingredients can be divided into those that are purchased in reasonably competitive markets and those that are obtained through other types of transactions. In general, the value of an ingredient for costing purposes is its market value. In the case of personnel, market value may be estimated by determining what the costs would be for hiring a particular type of person. Such costs must include not only salary but also fringe benefits and other employment costs that are paid by the employer. Many of the other inputs can also be costed by using their market prices. These ingredients include equipment, materials, utilities, and leased facilities.

Although the market prices of some ingredients such as personnel often can be obtained from accounting data for educational enterprises, such data are not reliable sources for deciding overall program costs. The accounting systems that are used by schools were designed for ensuring consistent reporting to state agencies rather than for providing accurate and consistent cost data on educational interventions. For example, school accounting systems either omit completely or understate the cost of volunteers and other donated resources. Capital improvements are charged to the budgets and accounts during the year of their purchase even when the improvements have a life of 20 to 30 years. Normal cost accounting practices would amortize the *annual* costs of such improvements by spreading them over their useful lives through an appropriate method (Levin, 1983, pp. 67–71). Thus, data from accounting and budgetary reports must be used selectively and appropriately and cannot be relied upon for all ingredients.

There exist a variety of techniques for determining the value of ingredients that are not purchased in competitive markets. For example, the method for estimating the value of volunteers and other contributed ingredients is to determine their market value if the personnel had to be hired or the resources had to be purchased. The value of facilities can be determined by estimating their lease value. The annual value of facilities and equipment can be estimated through a relatively simple approach that takes into account depreciation and interest forgone by the remaining capital investment. Details of these techniques are found in Levin (1983, chap. 4).

Analysis of costs. Once each of the ingredients is costed, the costs can be added to obtain a total for the intervention. The next stage entails the use of these costs in an analytic framework (Levin, 1983, chap. 5). The two most important questions for cost summary and analysis are what is the appropriate unit for expressing costs and who pays the costs.

The appropriate unit for expressing costs depends upon how effectiveness is measured. The effectiveness of social interventions is usually measured as the average outcome per participant, such as achievement gains per student. In this case, total costs must be converted to a cost per participant for comparing alternative interventions. Cost-effectiveness ratios are typically based upon the average effects and costs per participant. However, it is possible to do an analysis based on total project or program costs and effects. In some cases the additional or marginal costs versus additional or marginal effectiveness may be the subject of scrutiny. For example, we may want to analyze the number of additional students who will graduate from high school relative to the additional costs of alternative approaches for reducing dropouts.

Average cost-effectiveness data are likely to vary according to the scale or magnitude of an intervention. Programs that require a large amount of fixed investment for facilities and equipment will generally experience declining average costs as utilization of the program increases. Those that are personnel intensive will not generally be as sensitive to differences in scale because personnel can be altered according to the number of clients or participants. Accordingly, cost-effectiveness comparisons of alternatives should take into account the scale of the program rather than assume that cost-effectiveness differences will pertain at all levels of scale.

A different issue is who pays the costs. The overall cost-effectiveness ratio may be irrelevant to a decision maker who pays only part of the costs for one intervention but the full cost of an alternative of equal effect. Assume that the total cost of the first intervention is twice as high as the cost of the second. In this case, we would say that the first is only half as cost-effective as the second. But what if the first alternative attracts contributed facilities and volunteers so that most of its cost is "paid" by constituencies external to the decision maker, whereas all of the costs of the second alternative will be borne by the decision maker? In this case, the decision maker is likely to choose the first alternative, with its high subsidies, even though it is less cost-effective in the use of society's total resources.

For this reason, in cost-effectiveness analysis it is important to separate out those costs that are borne by the decision maker in considering different alternatives. However, because different decision-making units have different opportunities to obtain volunteers and contributed resources, we should not assume any particular cost subsidy to the decision maker. The basic estimate of costs that is used for all subsequent cost analyses is the overall cost of the intervention. Later analyses can distribute the costs among those who will bear them in order to predict the implications of that distribution for decisions.

Some examples

Several recent reviews of economic analyses of educational interventions provide an overall summary of the strengths and weaknesses of the field (Barnett & Escobar, 1987; Levin, 1988). Barnett and Escobar (1987) present an especially useful review of studies of the economics of early childhood education with attention to both cost-benefit and cost-effectiveness analyses.

Barnett (1985) undertook a cost-benefit analysis of the Perry Preschool Project. Students who had been enrolled in the preschool project were followed until they reached age 19. Relative to a matched control group, enrollees in the project experienced better school achievement, educational placement, educational attainment, and employment. Benefits were calculated for the value of child care during the program; reduced school expenditures for remediation, special services, and grade repetition; reduced costs to combat crime and delinquency and reduced welfare costs; and higher earnings and employment.

The benefits exceeded the costs by a large margin, under a wide range of assumptions about the level and duration of benefits. The one-year program showed benefits of $7.00 for every dollar of costs, a benefit–cost ratio of about 7:1, and the two-year program showed a benefit–cost ratio of about 3.6:1 (Berrueta-Clement, Schweinhart, Barnett, Epstein, & Weikart, 1984, p. 90). About 80% of the net benefits were received by taxpayers in the form of higher tax contributions and lower expenditures on education, the criminal justice system, and welfare and by potential crime victims in the form of lower costs for property loss and injuries.

Further analysis of the benefits of compensatory preschool education by Barnett (1989) suggest that even when the preschool gains in IQ for children in such programs tend to diminish or disappear in the early elementary years, the overall educational and social benefits are sustained. For example, both of the studies that Barnett located in which achievement test data were collected beyond the elementary years found advantages for students who had received compensatory preschool experiences. Of the 10 studies with data on special education or grade retention at grade 3 or later, 8 showed statistically significant advantages, always in favor of the group with preschool education. That is, such students were less likely to be retained in grade or placed in special education, saving considerable social resources. Finally, 3 of the 4 studies that followed students up to age 18 showed that students in compensatory preschool programs were more likely to graduate from high school.

Another benefit-cost study was designed to estimate the cost to the nation of high school dropouts (Levin, 1972). Estimates were made of the additional lifetime earnings and tax revenues that would accrue if all members of the cohort of 25- to 34-year-old males in 1970 had graduated from high school. The total loss in lifetime earnings for this group was estimated to be about $238 billion; in contrast, estimated costs for a minimum of high school completion for all members of the cohort were about $40 billion. Thus, the net expected benefits (benefits minus costs) were about $200 billion or a benefit–cost ratio of about 6:1. The additional lifetime income would have generated about $71 billion in government revenues, so the taxpayers would have received net benefits of about $30 billion or about $1.75 for each dollar invested in raising high school completions. The study also estimated that inadequate education was contributing about $6 billion a year to the costs of welfare and crime. Other studies have applied a similar method for Texas (Ramirez & del Refugio Robledo, 1987) and for Los Angeles (Catterall, 1986).

These studies suggest that investments in educationally disadvantaged and poor children yield high returns to society. That is, such social investments are highly worthwhile in that their benefits exceed their costs, and, furthermore, the margin by which benefits exceed costs is competitive with or superior to other highly productive investments. Nevertheless, these facts have not stimulated large increases in such social investments, an issue that will be addressed later in this chapter.

Cost-effectiveness studies of early childhood programs are also prominent. For example, the National Day Care Study (Ruopp, Travers, Glantz, & Coelen, 1979) found that several program interventions that had little influence on cost had positive effects on such measures as the Preschool Inventory and the revised Peabody Picture Vocabulary tests. These interventions included small group size and teacher training in early childhood education. In contrast, differences in the teacher–child ratio within the range of 1:5 to 1:10 were not related to observed quality of programs or test-score gains, despite the fact that such ratios are the most important determinants of the cost of child care and preschool programs. If these findings are valid, approximately twice the number of children could be accommodated in such programs at the higher ratio without added costs or a loss of effectiveness. This finding

Table 10.1. *Estimated cost and effectiveness of four educational*
interventions in months of additional student gain per year of instruction

	Annual cost per student per subject	Effectiveness in estimated months of achievement gain	
		Mathematics	Reading
Longer school day	$ 61	0.3	0.7
Computer-assisted instruction	119	1.2	2.3
Cross-age tutoring			
Peer component	212	9.7	4.8
Adult component	827	6.7	3.8
Reducing class size			
from *to*			
35 30	45	0.6	0.3
30 25	63	0.7	0.4
25 20	94	0.9	0.5
35 20	201	2.2	1.1

Source: H. M. Levin (July 1986). Are larger school sessions a good investment? *Contemporary Policy Issues,* *4*(3), 72.

has important implications for preschool programs, such as Head Start, that are unable to accept more than a small fraction of eligible children.

In the search for cost-effective programs for early childhood education, a number of cost-effectiveness comparisons have been made. Levin, Glass, and Meister (1984, 1987) compared cost-effectiveness ratios for raising the reading and mathematics achievement of elementary school students who were drawn largely from at-risk populations. Four alternatives were chosen for comparison: computer-assisted instruction, peer tutoring, extended school day, and smaller class size. Computer-assisted instruction consisted of the drill-and-practice curriculum of the Computer Curriculum Corporation. Peer-tutoring estimates were based upon a very successful model used in Boise, Idaho, and disseminated by the Joint Dissemination and Review Panel of the U.S. Department of Education. The longer school day refers to adding one hour, to be divided equally between mathematics and reading instruction. Class-size reductions were evaluated in 5-student decrements from 35 students down to 20 students as well as for a full 15-student decrease.

Table 10.1 shows the estimated cost and effectiveness of the four educational interventions in months of student gain per year of instruction. Costs varied from $827 for adult tutoring and $212 for peer tutoring to only $61 per subject for a longer school day and $45 per subject for a reduction in class size from 35 students to 30. Effectiveness also varied considerably, with almost a full-year gain (10-month school year) for peer tutoring in mathematics

Table 10.2. *Estimated annual cost to obtain an additional month of student achievement per year of instruction*

	Mathematics	Reading
Longer school day	$203	$ 87
Computer-assisted instruction	100	52
Cross-age tutoring		
Peer component	22	44
Adult component	123	218
Reducing class size		
from *to*		
35 30	75	150
30 25	90	158
25 20	104	188
35 20	91	183

Source: H. M. Levin (July 1986). Are larger school sessions a good investment? *Contemporary Policy Issues, 4*(3), 73.

to only .3-month gain for the same subject for a longer school day. Differences in the effectiveness of the interventions for reading are almost as dramatic.

The results in Table 10.1 are combined in Table 10.2 to provide cost-effectiveness ratios as reflected in estimated annual costs to obtain an additional month of student achievement per year of instruction. These differences are substantial, ranging from only $22 for an additional month of student-achievement gain in mathematics through peer tutoring to over $200 for the same gain from a longer school day. The differences in cost-effectiveness among approaches for reading are more modest. The policy implications are profound. For obtaining equivalent gains in mathematics achievement, increasing the school day is about nine times as costly and reducing class size or introducing computer-assisted instruction are about four times as costly as peer tutoring. In reading, the results for peer tutoring and computer-assisted instruction are relatively similar, but both are more cost-effective than a longer school day or reduced class size.

Small effects can be important

Another way in which cost-benefit studies can be helpful in evaluating social interventions, whether for children in poverty or for other populations, is by providing a different criterion for success than is provided by a standard evaluation. The conventional evaluation examines how effective a program is in achieving its objectives without reference to costs. Presumably, if a program shows relatively small effects, it is considered to be a weak candidate for consideration or for further expansion and diffusion.

But, as we have seen in the previous cost-effectiveness example, some alternatives that show large effects are also associated with large costs that make them inefficient in resource use. Thus, the adult component of tutoring in Table 10.1 showed additional student gains of almost seven months in mathematics and four months in reading beyond what normally might be expected in a year of instruction. These effects are about 6 times and 1½ times those of computer-assisted instruction in mathematics and reading respectively. But the costs of adult tutoring are about 7 times as great as those of computer-assisted instruction. When costs and effects are combined, it appears that the computer-assisted instruction is about 25% more cost-effective for mathematics and 4 times as cost-effective for reading. That is, a given budget could provide 4 times the reading gains if allocated to computer-assisted instruction relative to adult tutoring.

Thus, programs or interventions that appear to be highly effective may be relatively poor choices from an economic perspective. This point – that the "most effective" may not represent the most efficient use of resources – typically is lost in evaluations of social programs. Indeed, programs that normally might be discarded from consideration because of their apparent low effectiveness may represent, in reality, very efficient allocations of social resources.

A smoking cessation program, for example, that induced only 5% of its participants to stop smoking usually would be viewed as ineffective. But if this result could be obtained at an exceedingly low cost, the program would be highly cost-effective, or have large benefits relative to its costs. Weiss, Jurs, Lesage, and Iverson (1984) studied a smoking cessation program in which participants met for two 1½-hour sessions a week for four weeks. During these sessions, participants were made aware of the reasons why they smoked, learned techniques of behavior modification to assist them in quitting, and had their nonsmoking reinforced. On the basis of follow-up data, the authors concluded that the percentage of participants who stopped smoking completely may have been as low as 16%, although about three-fourths of the others did reduce their smoking.

The modest nature of this intervention, however, meant that costs were low, only about $30 per participant for the direct instructional costs and from $46 to $117 for lost wages, depending upon the participant's job. Benefits to the firm that sponsored the cost included savings on its insurance for fire, life, health, and workman's compensation as well as reductions in absenteeism and lost productivity associated with smoking. Depending upon the gender and age composition of the workers as well as the assumptions about success rates in their stopping smoking, the benefit-cost ratio varied from 1.3:1 to over 12:1, or net benefits per class of 20 participants from $2,700 to over $30,000. Even if only a single person out of the 20 gave up smoking, the ratio of benefits to costs was favorable.

These examples show the value that such studies would have for analyzing the effectiveness of alternative programs for improving the welfare of children in poverty. (1) Cost-benefit analysis could establish which programs are good social investments in terms of the degree to which their benefits exceed costs. This information could be used to persuade Congress, state legislatures, and appropriate government agencies to invest in these programs. (2) Cost-effectiveness analysis could determine which interventions and projects represent the most efficient use of agency and program resources. This information could be used to choose the combination of programs that would provide the largest impact using available resources.

Comparability of studies

This outlook would argue both for cost-analysis as a standard part of the evaluation of programs that address child poverty and for an accumulation of such evaluations in order to assist decision makers in choosing among programs. Policy makers could compare the cost-effectiveness of programs with similar goals and the cost-benefit findings for programs with either similar or diverse goals when benefits could be converted into monetary terms. Indeed, present policy could build on such findings to the degree that they already exist in the literature. However, the accumulation of evaluation results reflected by meta-analysis (Glass, McGaw, & Smith, 1981) does not lend itself to cost-effectiveness analysis for reasons that are discussed in Levin (1987, pp. 88–90).

Unfortunately, there are three major obstacles to capitalizing on the existing cost-benefit and cost-effectiveness literature. First, few persons engaged in the evaluation of social programs generally or of those that serve children in poverty in particular have the background and training in techniques of economic analysis to take advantage of this literature. Such training rarely is provided in the preparation either of evaluators or of persons engaged in social interventions. Also, social scientists outside economics do not feel comfortable in seeking to master the techniques of economic analysis, even though it has been argued that these tools to a large extent can be learned readily by nonspecialists (Levin, 1987).

Second, the data that do exist vary enormously both in quality and in the sources of cost estimates for each of the resource ingredients. Many studies take a very casual approach to estimating costs with respect to the qualitative dimensions of the data. They simply request information from whoever is responsible for financial accounting or take data, whether appropriate or inappropriate, from available budgetary documents. Both of these approaches are unlikely to provide the accurate cost accounting that is necessary to obtain appropriate costs for all of the ingredients that are used in social interventions (Levin, 1983, pp. 50–51). In their comprehensive review of economic analyses of early childhood educational interventions, Barnett and Escobar (1987) found that many studies failed to provide any information on how costs were calculated, or they estimated only a portion of costs. Only 5 of 20 studies that they reviewed had complete cost information. Cost figures that are provided with no details are equivalent to reports of intervention effectiveness with no details about methods.

Even when competent researchers estimate costs, however, the results may differ *between two different assessments of the same intervention* because costs differ from place to place and over time. If similar studies were conducted in two different regions of the country, even if at the same time, the costs probably would vary with regional prices. The cost of a teacher, a nurse, or some other professional of a given quality can differ substantially both across the country and within a state (Chambers, 1980). In the case of divergent assessments of the same intervention, therefore, differences in costs may be due to differences in the prices of the same resource ingredients from one place to another rather than to intrinsic differences in costs.

The same problem can occur with differences in costs over time. Because costs of individual ingredients or of all of the ingredients taken together can change over time, cost studies done at different times will show different results, even for the same program ingredients. In order to make studies comparable, the costs must be evaluated for the same time period and for the same set of prices for the ingredients. This evaluation can be accomplished if researchers use a "standard" set of costs or of prices for each ingredient in the comparison of studies. For example, it may be advisable to use national (or, when pertinent, regional or local) averages for the costs of ingredients for a particular, recent year in order to provide a common basis for cost calculations among studies. When studies have been carried out in different years, a careful specification of ingredients will enable researchers to convert the costs to a common base for comparability.

Information on the date and place of a study are usually available, so an informed audience at least can identify these as factors that may account for differences in outcomes of different cost studies. A more insidious problem is that different researchers will make different implicit assumptions in areas where a judgment is merited.

Consider the following dramatic example from Ribich (1968). In the 1960s the federal government sponsored training programs in different parts of the country under the Area Redevelopment Act of 1961 and the Manpower Development and Training Act of 1962. Underlying these training programs was the assumption that much unemployment was due to surpluses of potential workers in some occupations and shortages in others. Underemployed and unemployed persons in the surplus areas could be retrained to work in areas of shortage, with benefits for both the retrained individuals and the local economies in which they were located.

Table 10.3. *Estimates of benefits and costs of retraining, per worker, in independent studies in three states*

Study	Benefits	Costs	Benefit–cost ratio
Connecticut	$29,965	$218	137.3
Massachusetts	4,299	698	6.1
West Virginia	8,990	693	12.9

Source: Ribich (1968, 46).

Table 10.4. *Adjusted estimates of benefits and costs of retraining, per worker, presented in Table 10.3*

Study	Benefits	Costs	Benefit–cost ratio
Connecticut	$6,852	$ 680	10.1
Massachusetts	9,805	2,361	4.2
West Virginia	9,034	602	15.0

Source: Ribich (1968, 49).

From the federal perspective, it was desirable to invest in programs with the highest benefit–cost ratios. Thus, federal administrators were keen on obtaining benefit–cost ratios for the different programs to use as investment guidelines. Ribich (1968, pp. 38–50) reviewed three studies that had estimated the costs and benefits of retraining in three states during the same time period. In Table 10.3 the estimates of benefits and costs from each study as well as the resultant benefit–cost ratios are shown. All of the studies suggest benefits that exceed costs, but a ranking of studies according to benefit–cost ratios places Connecticut at the top by a wide margin, followed by West Virginia and Massachusetts. Presumably, a given investment in the Connecticut project would yield 11 and 23 times the benefits respectively produced by the same investment in West Virginia or Massachusetts.

Ribich (1968, pp. 38–50) decided to inquire into the causes of such large discrepancies among studies. To his surprise, most of the difference was due to different computational procedures rather than to actual variations in costs and benefits. The discrepancies were attributable to the use of different discount rates for making future benefits and costs comparable with present ones (Levin, 1983, pp. 97–98; Mishan, 1976, chap. 27, pp. 30–34) and to variations in the treatment of pretraining earnings. Ribich selected what he considered the "most reasonable" set of computational rules and applied them to each of the independent studies in order to gain consistency.

Table 10.4 shows the estimates of benefits and costs of retraining, per worker, of the same projects that were evaluated by separate researchers in Table 10.3. By applying a consistent set of computational procedures across studies, drastic changes in the rank ordering and magnitude of the results were produced. All three studies still suggest that the benefits markedly exceed costs, but West Virginia's benefit–cost ratio is now ranked ahead of that for Connecticut. Moreover, the benefit–cost ratio for Connecticut has been reduced from an astronomical 137:1 down to a healthy 10:1. The reason for much of this change was the Connecticut researcher's assumption that the trainees had zero earnings prior to training; he failed to subtract actual pretraining earnings from posttraining earnings to calculate the benefits of training.

Most decision makers neither are sufficiently knowledgeable nor have access to underlying data with which to explore carefully the procedures in different cost-benefit studies in order to see if the computational techniques across studies are comparable and appropriate. They are disempowered from evaluating the results. It is not surprising that there is a certain degree of skepticism among policy makers and decision makers when they are informed of cost-benefit results.

The same problems are true of cost-effectiveness results derived from different studies. For example, Lockheed and Hanushek (1988) compiled a useful summary of educational interventions in developing countries. Their presentation, however, includes a comparative display of costs and cost-effectiveness measures for a number of interventions that violates virtually all of the guidelines that were set out earlier. The methods of estimating costs in each study are not addressed despite the large number of independent studies and their authors. It should not be expected that the bases for computation among such studies are even remotely comparable. Further, the costs reflect studies done in different countries and at different times over a decade, and the specific years are not identified. Nor is the reader cautioned about the potential vagaries of the cost data that are presented. Unfortunately, the naive reader may believe that the results are comparable, when they are not.

Some proposals

Earlier in this chapter, I asserted that cost-benefit and cost-effectiveness analyses can be useful policy tools for making decisions within a framework of limited resources. Cost-effectiveness analysis can inform choices among alternative programs with the common goal of improving the status of children in poverty. Cost-benefit analysis can be used to compare the benefits with the costs of different alternatives within programs addressing the needs of children in poverty as well as to compare investments in these programs with potential social investments in other areas. To the degree that investments in children show high benefits relative to costs, these analyses also can persuade policy makers of the social priority of such investments.

I have also emphasized three obstacles to using these tools more widely to address the needs of children in poverty. First, most decision makers are unfamiliar with the mechanics of and the assumptions underlying these analyses. They can be misled by a self-serving analysis dressed in the garb of technical sophistication because they do not know what to look for in validating such a study. Second, most evaluators of social programs are not proficient in cost-effectiveness or cost-benefit analysis. Hence, such studies are unlikely to be forthcoming in any substantial numbers. Finally, different studies employ different assumptions and data bases with respect to the construction of benefits and costs so that comparisons among studies are hazardous at best and misleading at worst. What can be done about these obstacles?

Educating the decision makers

The first barrier to employing cost-benefit and cost-effectiveness analyses might be addressed by educating decision makers regarding the purposes and elements of these analyses. It is unlikely that decision makers would rely on results from economic studies unless they understood the data's value and felt comfortable with the method. Decision makers might be educated through a combination of specially designed written materials and staff-development workshops lasting one or two days. It is of particular importance to demonstrate to decision makers how economic studies are constructed and how the basic data are evaluated to create the bottom-line results. Decision makers also need to be taught how to read a cost-benefit or cost-effectiveness study, and they should be given a checklist of questions that they might raise when systematically reviewing such reports (Levin, 1983, pp. 138–140).

Educating applied social scientists

Applied social scientists who focus on the problems of children in poverty hope to make their mark on society by finding policies that will alleviate the undesirable conditions in which these children live. In carrying out their work, these researchers are preoccupied with the effectiveness, or the effect sizes, of different programs or interventions and show little concern for the cost-effectiveness, or the relations between costs and benefits. But decision makers cannot make decisions strictly on the basis of predicted effects because they are always operating in a context of limited resources. The resource or cost implications of decisions must always be taken into account at the policy level.

Professionals who work in the applied social sciences should have at least some exposure to cost-effectiveness and cost-benefit analyses in their formal training. Their training should go beyond the practical familiarity recommended for decision makers; applied social scientists need a fuller understanding of the underlying concepts and methods. Although most professionals will not themselves engage in cost-effectiveness or cost-benefit studies, they should be prepared to work jointly with economists who are trained to do such studies.

These goals can be met largely through exposing professionals who work in the applied social sciences to cost-benefit or cost-effectiveness training in evaluation or policy courses. Such courses would have the advantage of integrating these tools both with social science evaluations and with the various components of policy formation. Economics departments and schools of public policy might be called upon to assist in this endeavor. Finally, the collection of cost data should be a standard part of the evaluation design of any social program in order to provide a basis for later calculations.

Establishing standard methods

A final proposal calls for the establishment of standard methods for constructing cost-benefit and cost-effectiveness studies in order to ensure better comparability. All studies should use the ingredients method, which represents a sound economic approach to the estimation of costs and also provides the underlying information on the specific ingredients and their costs so that overall costs can be reconstructed under other assumptions. All studies should have enough information so that the costs can be standardized for a given year and place in order to compare them with the results of other standardized studies.

Key assumptions in all studies should be highlighted as a matter of course so that the reader can determine if differences in outcomes are a derivative of different premises. Sensitivity analyses should be undertaken for a variety of contingencies that might affect outcomes to see how dependent the results are on the assumptions and to enable comparisons of results among studies employing the same premises. For example, Ribich (1968) demonstrated how differences in discount rates for equating future benefits and costs with present ones and how different assumptions about pretraining earnings can create a broad range of results for the same basic interventions. Just as there are general evaluation standards established for psychological and educational measurement and for educational evaluation (American Educational Research Association, 1986; Joint Committee on Standards for Educational Evaluation, 1981), there ought to be general evaluation standards established for cost-benefit and cost-effectiveness analyses.

Summary

This chapter explores the use of cost-benefit and cost-effectiveness analyses for selecting interventions among a large number of competing possibilities that address the needs of children in poverty. The initial section of the chapter provides a brief review of cost-benefit and cost-effectiveness analyses to show how each might be used in this area. This section also addresses the methodology of cost measurement, an endeavor that is often carried out incorrectly in the literature.

The second section presents specific examples of applications of these tools. These applications include cost-benefit studies of early childhood educational interventions and dropout prevention as well as cost-effectiveness programs of child care and four educational interventions to improve mathematics and reading achievement at the elementary level.

The third section focuses on the necessity to make studies comparable in order to compare results among alternatives. It illustrates the various ways in which studies use different assumptions and methods, thus confounding any comparisons. The concluding section of the chapter provides proposals for improving the use of cost-benefit and cost-effectiveness analyses in evaluating alternative programs for children in poverty. Special emphasis is placed on the provision of better training of both policy makers and researchers as well as the establishment of agreement on standard methods of analysis.

References

American Educational Research Association, American Psychological Association, National Council on Measurement in Education. (1986). *Standard for educational and psychological testing*. Washington, DC: American Psychological Association.

Barnett, W. S. (1985). Benefit-cost analysis of the Perry Preschool program and its long-term effects. *Educational Evaluation and Policy Analysis, 7*(4), 387–414.

Barnett, W. S. (1989). *Benefits of compensatory preschool education*. Philadelphia: Center for Research in Human Development and Education.

Barnett, W. S., & Escobar, C. M. (1987). The economics of early childhood intervention: A review. *Review of Educational Research, 57*(4), 387–414.

Berrueta-Clement, J. R., Schweinhart, L. J., Barnett, W. S., Epstein, A. S., & Weikart, D. P. (1984). *Changed lives: The effects of the Perry Preschool program on youths through age 19* (Monographs of the High/Scope Education Research Foundation, 8). Ypsilanti, MI: High/Scope Press.

Catterall, J. S. (1986). *On the social costs of dropping out of school* (No. 86-SEPI-3). Stanford, CA: Stanford University, Stanford Education Policy Institute.

Chambers, J. G. (1980). The development of a cost of education index. *Journal of Education Finance, 5*(3), 262–281.

Glass, G. V., McGaw, B., & Smith, M. L. (1981). *Meta-analysis in social research*. Beverly Hills, CA: Sage.

Gramlich, E. (1981). *Benefit-cost analysis of government programs*. Englewood Cliffs, NJ: Prentice-Hall.

Cost-benefit and cost-effectiveness analyses 259

The Joint Committee on Standards for Educational Evaluation. (1981). *Standards for evaluations of educational programs, projects, and materials.* New York: McGraw-Hill.

Levin, H. M. (1972). *The costs to the nation of inadequate education.* Report prepared for the Select Senate Committee on Equal Educational Opportunity. Washington, DC: U.S. Government Printing Office.

Levin, H. M. (1983). *Cost-effectiveness: A primer.* Beverly Hills, CA: Sage.

Levin, H. M. (1987). Cost-benefit and cost-effectiveness analyses. In D. S. Cordray, H. S. Bloom, & R. J. Light (Eds.), *Evaluation practice in review* (New Directions for Program Evaluation, No. 34, 83–99). San Francisco: Jossey-Bass.

Levin, H. M., (1988). Cost-effectiveness and educational policy. *Educational Evaluation and Policy Analysis, 10*(1), 51–69.

Levin, H. M., Glass, G. V., & Meister, G. R. (1984, May). *Cost-effectiveness of four educational interventions* (Project Report No. 84-A11). Stanford, CA: Stanford University, Institute for Research on Educational Finance and Governance.

Levin, H. M., Glass, G. V., & Meister, G. R. (1987, February). A cost-effectiveness analysis of computer-assisted instruction. *Evaluation Review, 11*(1), 50–72.

Lockheed, M. E., & Hanushek, E. (1988). Improving educational efficiency in developing countries: What do we know? *Compare, 18*(1), 21–38.

Mishan, E. J. (1976). *Cost-benefit analysis.* New York: Praeger.

Ramirez, D., & del Refugio Robledo, M. (1987, April). The economic impact of the dropout problem. *IDRA Newsletter.* San Antonio, TX: Intercultural Development Research Association.

Ribich, T. I. (1968). *Education and poverty.* Washington, DC: Brookings.

Ruopp, R., Travers, J., Glantz, F., & Coelen, C. (1979). *Children at the center: Summary findings and policy implications of the National Day Care Study.* Cambridge, MA: Abt Associates.

Weiss, S. J., Jurs, S., Lesage, J. P., & Iverson, D. C. (1984). A cost-benefit analysis of a smoking cessation program. *Evaluation and Program Planning, 7,* 337–346.

11   Effective programs for children growing up in concentrated poverty

Lisbeth Bamberger Schorr

New knowledge, derived from the last 20 years of research and experience in a variety of domains and disciplines, provides the basis for designing significant new programs and policies to improve the futures of children growing up in poverty and disadvantage. A new national commitment to improve the programs and institutions that serve these children and their families would result in reduced rates of school dropout, adolescent childbearing, delinquency, long-term welfare dependency, and perhaps drug abuse. Coupled with economic reforms, the widespread improvement of services early in the life cycle could be a powerful force in breaking the intergenerational cycle of disadvantage.

It is important to emphasize at the outset that an underlying assumption of this chapter is that economic measures are central to any broadscale attack on intergenerational poverty. More jobs, jobs that pay better, expanded job training, more sensible housing policies, and a welfare system that provides effective income supports while helping more recipients to become productively employed, are as important as changing the institutions that provide services and supports. But especially for the persistently poor, neither an economic strategy nor a services strategy will work alone. Even if economic opportunities are expanded, they cannot be seized by young people whose health has been neglected, whose education has failed to equip them with the skills they need, and whose early lives have left them devoid of hope and without the capacity to persevere.

My conclusions are based on a study that identified

1. through literature reviews and consultations, the risk factors that precede and interact to produce adverse outcomes;
2. through informal consultations with researchers, policy makers and analysts, and administrators and practitioners, programs that (a) intervene early, (b) serve children and families at risk, (c) use methods consistent with theoretical findings in the field, and (d) have been able to document successes over time;
3. the commonalities among successful programs across a variety of fields; and
4. the obstacles to more widespread implementation of successful programs and strategies through which these obstacles might be overcome.

This chapter will take up each of these points in turn.

260

Risk factors that lead to adverse outcomes

Damaging outcomes ranging from adolescent childbearing to school failure and delinquency are preceded by a strikingly overlapping cluster of risk factors (Schorr, 1988). They include

1. growing up in persistent or concentrated poverty and in a family of low social class;
2. being born unwanted or into a family with too many children born too close together;
3. growing up with a parent who is unemployed, a teenager, a school dropout, or illiterate, a parent who is impaired (as the result of alcoholism, drug addiction, or mental illness), and/or a parent who is without social supports;
4. growing up in a family or neighborhood with such a high level of social disorganization as to leave a young child unprotected from abuse and violence, and with little exposure to healthy role models;
5. growing up outside one's family, especially in multiple foster care or institutional placements; and
6. growing up with the sense that one has bleak prospects for good employment or a stable family life and little power to affect one's own destiny and that one is not valued by the outside world.

The research on the impact of these risk factors on later outcomes reflects an extraordinary degree of convergence. The findings from studies of animals and of infants and from the longitudinal studies of children as they grow up, all suggest that when it comes to such complex outcomes as school failure or delinquency, it is the interaction between constitution and environment that is critical (Beckwith & Parmelee, 1984; Escalona, 1982; Leiderman, 1983).

> In a University of Wisconsin study by Suomi, rhesus monkeys who were found by physiological measures to be unusually anxious at birth, grew up to be perfectly normal *if* they were cared for in "socially rich and stable" environments. But when these congenitally vulnerable monkeys were subjected to chaotic caretaking in infancy, 80% neglected or abused their first offspring. (Suomi, Mineka, & DeLizio, 1983)

> In a group of babies born in 1955 on the Hawaiian island of Kauai and followed by Werner and Smith for twenty years, those with moderate neurological problems during the first year were not handicapped when they got to school if they came from middle class families. Early biological problems, by contrast, were exacerbated in children from impoverished and uneducated families, and, typically were reflected in troubled elementary school careers. (Werner & Smith, 1982)

> At Boston Children's Hospital, Levine found no correlation between nervous system deficits and later delinquent behavior until he analyzed the data in clusters. Then he found that when health problems occurred together with socio-economic disadvantage, the chances of delinquency were significantly increased. (Levine, 1985)

The research also shows that the more risk factors are present, the greater the damaging impact of each. But the impact is not just additive – risk factors multiply each other's destructive effects. In England, psychiatrist Michael

Rutter found that children who encountered only one risk factor were no more likely to suffer serious consequences than children experiencing no risk factors at all. By contrast, when two or more stresses occurred together – such as being born prematurely *and* into poverty – the chance of a damaging outcome went up at least fourfold, and when four risks were present, the chances of later damage increased by a factor of ten (Sameroff & McDonough, 1984; Sameroff & Seifer, 1983).

The evidence of the multiplicative effect of risk factors is summarized in Rutter (1980), *Changing Youth in a Changing Society*. Eisenberg (1982) provides further corroboration of the interaction of risk factors by calling attention to research findings that very poor nutrition early in life can lead to mental retardation but apparently only when combined with poor rearing conditions. "In a fashion yet to be understood, appropriate stimulation in the home appears to be able to protect against the deleterious effects of undernutrition on mental development" (Eisenberg, 1982, p. 63).

These findings make clear that the prevention of damaging outcomes in adolescence is not a matter of all or nothing. This point has critical implications for social policy at a time when the income gap between the richest and the poorest one-fifth of the nation has reached a 40-year peak (Congressional Budget Office, 1988) and when social and economic changes have had a devastating effect on employment opportunities for the unskilled (Wilson, 1987) and have markedly decreased the number of poor children growing up in stable two-parent families (U.S. House of Representatives, 1987). If it is possible to reduce the incidence of low birth weight or of uncorrected vision defects, if the isolated mother can be helped to become more responsive to her difficult infant, if more children come to school better prepared to master academic skills – by achieving these attainable goals it is possible to weaken the grip that poverty and social class have on future prospects.

Identifying successful programs

Because my purpose was to assemble the information that could provide a knowledge base for social action, this understanding of risk factor interaction led me to focus on those risk factors that, on the basis of present evidence, are most amenable to change. I therefore sought out programs using a variety of interventions, all of which had actually succeeded in changing the futures of children growing up at risk by changing adverse outcomes or their antecedent risk factors.

Early intervention

I concentrated on early interventions because so many of the determinants of adverse outcomes in adolescence are established well before they occur.

Poor school performance and truancy *as early as third grade* are among the most reliable predictors of adolescent childbearing, delinquency and dropout (Bachman, O'Malley, & Johnston, 1978; Dryfoos, 1983; Elliot, Ageton, & Canter, 1979; Furstenberg, Brooks-Gunn, & Morgan, 1987; Kaplan & Luck, 1977; Klerman, Weitzman, Alpert, & Lamb, 1984; Loeber & Dishion, 1983; Phipps-Yonas, 1980; Robins, 1978; Seitz, Apfel, & Rosenbaum, 1983; Stroup & Robins, 1972). Moreover, trouble at third grade is frequently preceded by being unwanted, being born at low birth weight, lacking bonds with a caring adult, and entering school without language skills, without having learned consistent connections between cause and effect, or with untreated health problems (Bee, Van Egeren, Streissguth, Nyman, & Lackie, 1969; Hess & Shipman, 1968; Institute of Medicine, 1985; Kagan, 1984; Kohn, 1969; McCarton, 1986; Neubauer, 1976; Richmond, 1970; Rutter, 1982; Schorr, 1988; Segal & Yahraes, 1979; Tizard & Hughes, 1984) – all factors that we know how to change with good services. By the time adolescents actually drop out of school, become pregnant too soon, or are in serious trouble with the law, helping them to change course is a daunting task. Of course, it is possible to help adolescents in trouble to make a successful transition to adulthood, but earlier help is more effective and more economical. Failure and despair do not have as firm a grip, and life trajectories are more readily altered.

Programs serving children and families at risk

I looked for programs that served populations at risk, either by targeting services exclusively at such groups or by providing services explicitly designed to meet the distinctive needs of high-risk groups as part of a universal program. I used a definition of children at risk that included the following characteristics: growing up in persistent or concentrated poverty and social dislocation; growing up with an isolated, mentally ill, alcoholic, or drug-addicted parent; and at risk of neglect, abuse, or removal from home.

Methods consistent with theory

I looked for programs that used methods that were consistent with the theoretical findings in the field in order to eliminate programs that might have achieved their successes through flukes.

Documentation of effectiveness

I found documentation of improved outcomes in health programs, social services and family support, child care and preschool education, and elementary school reform. (See Table 11.1.) A few examples:

Table 11.1. *Examples of quantified effects of selected interventions*

Intervention	Outcome		
School-based health clinic, St. Paul, MN St. Paul-Ramsey Co. Medical Center 1973–present	Childbearing among female students in first two participating high schools decreased by more than 50% within three years		
School-related health clinic, Baltimore, MD, serving junior and senior high school with all black, low-income student bodies totaling over 1,700 students Johns Hopkins University School of Medicine 1982–1984	Among 695 female respondents (of whom about three-quarters were sexually active), the proportion of sexually active 9th- to 12th-grade girls who became pregnant declined by 25%; rate in comparison school went up 58% in same period		
Augmented, comprehensive prenatal care for 7,000 low-income women in 13 California counties California State Department of Health 1979–1982	LBW (< 2,500 g) rate among participants: among comparison group: VLBW (< 1,500 g) rate among participants: among comparison group:	4.7% 7.0% 0.5% 1.3%	
Augmented, comprehensive prenatal care for 744 school-aged pregnant girls, mostly black and single, all poor, Baltimore, MD Johns Hopkins University School of Medicine 1979–1981	LBW (< 2,500 g) rate among participants: among comparison group: VLBW (< 1,500 g) rate among participants: among comparison group:	9.9% 16.4% 1.9% 3.9%	
Home visiting to 305 pregnant teenagers by lay "Resource Mothers" in rural South Carolina South Carolina State Health Department 1981–1983	LBW (< 2,500 g) rate among participants: among random controls: VLBW (< 1,500 g) rate among participants: among random controls:	10% 13% 1% 4.5%	
Homebuilders intensive in-home crisis and family-preservation services, Tacoma and Seattle, WA Catholic Children's Services and Homebuilders 1974 to present; evaluation 1983–1985	In 88% of families in which removal of child was imminent when intervention began, family was intact and child had not been removed one year later		

Table 11.1 (*cont.*)

Intervention	Outcome

Comprehensive health, child care, and social services for 18 infants aged 0 to 2½ and their families, New Haven, CT
 	
Yale University Child Study Center
 	
1968–1972
	At 10-year follow-up:
	
	Av. years of education completed by mother:
	  participants: 13.0
	  comparison: 11.7
	Av. no. of children in family:
	  participants: 1.67
	  comparison: 2.2
	Proportion of families self-supporting:
	  participants: 86%
	  comparison: 53%
	Children with serious school problems:
	  participants: 28%
	  comparison: 69%

Nurse home visiting of high-risk mothers during pregnancy and for two years after birth, Elmira, NY (comparison with randomly assigned controls)
 	
University of Rochester Medical School
 	
1978–1983
	Among poor, unmarried women ($N = 110$):
	
	Returned or completed school, 10 months postpartum
	  participants: 75%
	  controls: 50%
	Subsequent pregnancy, 4 years postpartum:
	  Half as many among participants as among controls
	Abuse or neglect of children
	  participants: 4%
	  controls: 19%
	Among 14- to 16-year-olds: Participants ($N = 28$) had babies 395 gms heavier than controls ($N = 17$)
	Among mothers who smoked: Premature births
	  participants: 2%
	    ($N = 78$)
	  controls: 10%
	    ($N = 64$)

Summer preschool education; weekly home visits during remainder of year for black 3- to 5-year-olds and their mothers, Murfreesboro, TN (The Early Training Project) Peabody Teachers College 1962–1965	At age 21, one-third more dropouts in comparison group than among participants; control children placed in special education classes at 6 times the rate of participating children

Table 11.1 (*cont.*)

Intervention	Outcome
Preschool education and weekly home visits over two-year period for 3- and 4-year-old randomly assigned poor black children, Ypsilanti, MI (The Perry Preschool Project) High/Scope 1962–present; evaluation of 1962–1964 participants	Of 121 (N = 123) responding at age 19:

Of 121 (N = 123) responding at age 19:

	Partic. (%)	Controls (%)
Employed	59	32
HS Grad.	67	49
Post-HS ed.	38	21
Arrested	31	51

Of 112 (N = 123) responding: Years in special education

participants	16%
controls	28%

Among 49 females: Teenage Preg.

participants	32
controls	59

Intervention	Outcome
Preschool education and enriched classes through 3rd grade for 750 Harlem 4-year-olds; active parent support and participation Institute for Developmental Studies, New York University 1963–1969	At age 21, twice as many participants as random controls were employed, one-third more had high school diplomas or GED certificates; 30% more had obtained post-high school education or training
Changing elementary school climate through applying principles of child development and basic management; new relationships among principal, teachers, parents, New Haven, CT Yale University Child Study Center 1968–present	At outset, intervention schools ranked 32nd and 33rd of 33 New Haven elementary schools in reading, math, attendance, and behavior; 15 years later, with no change in SES of students, demo. schools ranked 3rd and 5th in test scores and had no serious behavior problems. One had best attendance record in city 4 of previous 5 years

Note: These effects are from interventions described in L. B. Schorr (1988).

In St. Paul, Minnesota, and in Baltimore, Maryland, school-based health clinics have reduced the rate of teenage childbearing. (Brann et al., 1979; Edwards, Steinman, & Hakanson, 1977, 1980, 1986; Kirby, 1984; P. J. Porter, personal communication, 1986; Zabin, Hirsch, Smith, Streett, & Hardy, 1986; Zabin, Streett, Hardy, & King, 1984)

In 13 California low-income counties, and among teenagers in Maryland and in rural South Carolina, comprehensive prenatal care has resulted in a lower rate of babies born at low birth weight. (Gregory, Hausner, & Solarz, 1984; Hardy, King, & Repke, 1986; Korenbrot, 1984; Lennie, Klun, & Hausner, 1985; McManus, 1985; Piechnik & Corbett, 1985; Schorr, 1988; Unger & Wandersman, 1985)

In Elmira, New York, New Haven, Connecticut, and Tacoma, Washington, nurse home visiting and family support programs have resulted in fewer low birth weight babies, fewer children having to be removed from home, and lower rates of welfare dependence and of child abuse and neglect. (Edna McConnell Clark Foundation, 1985; Haapala & Kinney, 1979; Kinney, 1978; Kinney, Madsen, Fleming, & Haapala, 1977; Olds, 1981, 1982; Olds, Henderson, Chamberlin, & Tatelbaum, 1986; Olds, Henderson, Tatelbaum, & Chamberlin, 1986a, 1986b; Provence & Naylor, 1983; Schorr, 1988; Seitz, Rosenbaum, & Apfel, 1985; Trickett, Apfel, Rosenbaum, & Zigler, 1981)

Head Start and other comprehensive preschool programs in 14 cities that kept track into adulthood of their 3- and 4-year-old participants found that compared to control groups their graduates included fewer children needing remedial education, fewer dropouts, fewer delinquents, fewer girls who became pregnant as teenagers, and fewer youngsters who were unemployed. (Berrueta-Clement, Schweinhart, Barnett, Epstein, & Weikart, 1984; Consortium for Longitudinal Studies, 1983; Deutsch, 1985; Gray, Ramsey, & Klaus, 1983; Lazar & Darlington, 1982; Schorr, 1988)

Commonalities among successful programs

The programs that have succeeded in changing outcomes for children at highest risk of later damage differ, in fundamental ways, from prevailing services (Schorr, 1988). Successful programs *see the child in the context of family and the family in the context of its surroundings.* The clinician treating an infant for recurrent diarrhea sees beyond the patient on the examining table to whether the child's health is threatened by circumstances that require a public health nurse or social worker to help the family obtain nonmedical services. The successful school mobilizes parents in collaborative efforts to give children reasons to learn. Successful programs in every domain offer support to parents who need help with their lives as adults before the parents can make good use of services for their children. Successful programs, whether they begin with a focus on children or on their parents, generally evolve into programs that explicitly adopt a *two-generational* approach. Many programs, in fact, find they must work with three generations at once in order to be most effective.

Programs that are successful in helping high-risk children and their families are *comprehensive.* They typically offer a *broad spectrum of services.* They know that social and emotional support and concrete help (with food, housing, income, employment, or anything else that seems to the family to be an insurmountable obstacle) may have to be provided to enable a family to make use of other services, from antibiotics to advice on parenting.

To respond to their clients' or patients' complex array of needs, staff make sure that services are *coherent and integrated.* When necessary, staff cross traditional professional and bureaucratic boundaries. These programs rely only rarely on referrals to other agencies. They take special pains to maintain continuity in relationships and to assume responsibility for assuring that child and family needs are in fact met regardless of bureaucratic or professional compartmentalization. No one says, "This may be what you need, but helping you get it is not part of my job or outside our jurisdiction."

Most successful programs find that services cannot be rigidly routinized. Staff members and program structures are fundamentally *flexible*, and services are rendered *ungrudgingly* and often at a *high level of intensity*. Professionals are able to exercise discretion about meeting individual needs (which new mother needs three home visits every week and which needs only one during the first month), and families are able to decide what services to utilize (whether and when to enroll their child in the available day-care program) and how they want to participate (whether to work in their child's school as a library volunteer, a paid aide, or a member of the parent advisory body). Professionals in these programs tend to take a collaborative posture, listening to parents, exchanging information rather than instructing, and always ready to help parents to act more effectively on behalf of their own children.

Professionals in successful programs are perceived by those they serve as people they can *trust*, people who *care* about them and *respect* them. Virtually without exception, leaders of successful programs emphasize the importance of *relationships*. They know that *how* services are provided is as important as *what* is provided. Some program leaders explain their emphasis on relationships as based on mental health principles, some talk about child development principles, some stress that they provide through formal mechanisms the supports that more fortunate families obtain informally, and some come to it entirely pragmatically – that it is simply what they do to make their program work.

Staffs of these programs tend to be highly skilled. Most emphasize how much training, support, and time it takes to establish the kind of relationships that actually bring about change. Many human service programs have been successful in utilizing paraprofessionals who receive training, supervision, and support of high quality and consistency; however, experience suggests that effective help to families in the most marginal and stressed circumstances may require a level of skill, maturity, and judgment most often found among well-trained professionals.

In successful programs, *professionals are able to redefine their roles* and to find ways to escape the constraints of a professional value system that confers highest status on those who deal with issues from which all human complexity has been removed.[1] These professionals venture outside familiar surroundings to make services available in nontraditional settings, including homes, and often at nontraditional hours. The program does not ask families to surmount

1 Sociologist Andrew Abbott (1978) has written that within a given profession, the highest status professionals are those who deal with issues defined by colleagues in such a way as to remove human complexity, whereas "the lowest status professionals are those who deal with problems from which the human complexities are not or cannot be removed" (p. 819).

formidable barriers, unassisted, before they can get what they need. It makes sure that payment arrangements and eligibility determinations do not pose insuperable obstacles. It does not set preconditions, such as keeping a series of fixed appointments in faraway places or a display of adequate "motivation," that may screen out those most in need. On the contrary, successful programs try to reduce the barriers of money, time, fragmentation, and geographic and psychological remoteness that make heavy demands on those with limited energy and organizational skills. Instead of waiting passively to serve only those who make it through the daunting maze, these programs persevere to reach the most inaccessible people who are likely to benefit the most.

In sum, the programs that succeed are never narrowly categorical and always seek to *adapt the content of their services to the distinctive needs of the population they serve.* Health care that is adequate for monitoring the pregnancy of a healthy middle-class woman may bypass totally the most pressing needs of an undernourished, depressed, drug-using pregnant teenager. The parent support component of a preschool program, occasionally helpful to middle-class participants, is often essential for high-risk families. Intensive, comprehensive, individualized services with aggressive attention to outreach and to maintaining relationships over time may be frills for more fortunate families, but they are rock-bottom necessities for high-risk populations, whose level of energy and tolerance for frustration may be low, who are likely to have more than one problem at a time, and whose experiences in searching for help are likely to leave them profoundly discouraged and unable to use services as customarily offered.

The distinctiveness of the characteristics of programs that succeed in helping children and families surrounded by concentrated poverty and social dislocation suggests a fundamental contradiction between the needs of these children and families and the traditional requirements of professionalism and bureaucracy. This contradiction helps to explain why programs that work for these high-risk populations are so rare and why less effective programs are so much more prevalent. It is a contradiction that future attempts to build on successful programs must take carefully into account.

The prevalence of ineffective programs

Just as programs that have proven successful have many common attributes, patterns can be discerned in past failures. Many failures have resulted from a mean-spirited unwillingness to help those most in need. Many have resulted from a lack of understanding of the nature of the problem – a lack of understanding of how important intensiveness, flexibility, coherence, and comprehensiveness are in making interventions effective and of how much help is enough for the seriously disadvantaged. And some of our failures result

from a lack of understanding of how promising programs can be widely replicated.

For children with many strikes against them, *damage cannot be prevented by simplistic, one-pronged approaches* of any kind. Because narrowly defined interventions aimed at circumscribed problems make for ready measurement, assessment, and replication and because it is easiest to mobilize political support to fight one simple evil with one simple remedy, we are left with half-way programs that fail to ameliorate profound social problems. Complex, deeply rooted tangles of troubles cannot be successfully attacked with isolated fragments of help.

The recent history of human services is replete with examples of those in greatest need, when they obtain services at all, receiving services that are too fragmented and too meager to accomplish their purpose. This failure not only wastes money but it also creates an overwhelming managerial burden for depleted families. The lessons of successful models are ignored, whereas mistakes of the past are perpetuated; failures that might have been predicted on the basis of current knowledge are erroneously interpreted as evidence that high-risk families are beyond help.

Even when children's advocates succeed in expanding *access* to medical care, the *content* of services frequently remains unmatched to the needs of the underserved. Consider Gail, a 13-year-old who stabbed a boy on the school playground, possibly as a result of a psychomotor seizure that might have been averted had she received proper medical attention. Gail had been seen at the local hospital more than 30 times during the preceding year. But because of the fragmented, episodic nature of much of the care that poor families get, Gail had never had a proper workup until after she had killed her schoolmate (Lewis & Balla, 1976; Lewis & Shanok, 1979; Lewis et al., 1979).

Extreme fragmentation of services and a consistent "pattern of failed con-nections" were the critical weaknesses in children's mental health services identified in a broad review by the Children's Defense Fund (Knitzer, 1982, 1984). The study showed that children's problems and their need for services were often identified early, and sometimes repeatedly. But the services them-selves seldom materialized. A similar finding of "failed connections" emerged from a review of case records of children who had died or been seriously injured as a result of child abuse in Massachusetts during 1984 (Knitzer, 1984). All of the children were known to social agencies. Even children and families with extensive agency contacts were not getting the services they needed. Across the country, caseworkers with direct reponsibility for vulnerable chil-dren often experience "impossibly large caseloads, excessive and meaningless paperwork, no time to get to know the children for whom they make decisions, no time to visit families, and no training to deal with complex family problems

(Edna McConnell Clark Foundation, 1985; Knitzer, McGowan, & Allen, 1978; Uhlig, 1987).

Sister Mary Paul, of Brooklyn's Sunset Park Center for Family Life, has said that the most troubled families in her community do not get much help from the local mental health center, which "can't get involved with the family or the school or the legal system – only the individual client, sitting there in the office." As long as this is true, she added, the center's services will remain largely irrelevant to families in greatest need (M. Paul, interview, April 2, 1985).

Conventional parent education, which brings helpful child-rearing information to many middle-class parents, is another intervention that is often quite irrelevant to socially isolated and otherwise seriously disadvantaged parents (Polansky, 1979; Polansky, Chambers, Buttenweiser, & Williams, 1981). The mother who needs the most help with parenting because she is alcoholic, depressed, under serious economic stress, or, perhaps, was profoundly neglected during her own childhood, is unlikely to find the information offered by most parenting classes very useful. She may need direct support for her own needs before she can successfully nurture her child.

Many interventions have turned out to be ineffective not because seriously disadvantaged families are beyond help but because we have tried to attack multiple, intertwined troubles with isolated fragments of help, with help rendered grudgingly in one-shot forays, with help designed less to meet the needs of beneficiaries than to conform to professional or bureaucratic convenience, with help that may be useful to middle-class families but is often irrelevant to families struggling to survive. With all the experience now amassed of success and failure in working with high-risk families and children there is no basis for believing that some single, simple, one-shot intervention is bound to work and produce a quick payoff if only we could find just the right one.

Even with proven models, the temptation to make services more widely available by watering down a successful program is ever present. Agonizingly familiar is the story of a successful program continued or replicated in a form so weakened that the original concept is destroyed. Dr. Heather Weiss, of the Harvard Family Support Center, has said that she has seen it happen many times: "You put a lot of resources into a demonstration, and try and deliver a model program. You show your effectiveness with a strong evaluation, and you think you've succeeded. The program is continued. But either you're asked to do the same thing with sharply reduced funds, or you have the same level of funds and are asked to expand your services" (H. Weiss, personal communication, April 1987).

The Prenatal/Early Infant Program of nurse home visiting to high-risk mothers in Elmira, New York, which placed a high value on the development of relationships between nurses and families over time, documented such dramatic reductions in low birth weight and child abuse that the local health department agreed to continue the program when the original university-sponsored demonstration ended. On the day that the health department took over, it cut by two-thirds the period that the nurses could continue with the family and doubled the nurses' caseloads (Schorr, 1988).

Especially when funds are scarce, there are powerful pressures to dissect a successful program and select some one part to be continued in isolation, losing sight of the fact that it was the sum of the parts that accounted for the demonstrated success. Dilution and mechanistic replication without careful preparation and planning will continue to threaten the spread of successful programs until there is greater understanding that the intensity and comprehensiveness of these programs are almost invariably the very essence of their success and until enough resources flow to high-risk populations to obviate the need to choose between an elegant program that works for a few or a diluted version that serves many – inadequately.

Other failures have their origins in the unsupportive state and national policies that can threaten the survival of valuable local programs and undermine the chances of successful replication. Failure to recognize this fact will lead to repeated disappointments, for even the most valiant local efforts cannot, over the long term, flourish in the face of financing and regulations that do not take the needs of deprived populations into account.

Reimbursement arrangements of public and private third-party payors that do not reflect the complexities of effective interventions undermine the stability of well-designed local programs. When services such as outreach, counseling, and support are not paid for by Medicaid and private health insurers, then hard-pressed health programs will not provide them, no matter how essential they are to the program's purposes. When reimbursement definitions do not reflect the higher costs of providing service to poor, multiproblem families, then programs that provide the poor with the care they need cannot survive. This is why there is no correlation between a program's survival over time and how successful it is in achieving improved outcomes for families at risk.[2] In the provision of social services, the extreme and irrational fragmentation of both tasks and clientele that is typical (Kamerman & Kahn, 1986) means that attempts to coordinate services at the local agency level and make

2 A classic study of the factors that accounted for financial survival of rural health clinics found that the more laboratory tests a clinic provided, as a proportion of total services, the more likely it was to become self-sufficient. The more outreach services it provided, the more likely it was to shut down when grant funding came to an end (Feldman, Deitz, & Brooks, 1978). Social welfare researchers Sheila Kamerman and Alfred Kahn of the Columbia University School of Social Work arrived at the same conclusion with regard to social services: "There is no relation between survival of agencies and either need or impact" (Kamerman & Kahn, 1986).

them available to families in some coherent way are so time-consuming, costly, and difficult that they are unlikely to succeed.

It is no coincidence that programs with demonstrated success in changing outcomes for disadvantaged children have developed, for the most part, in unusual conditions. They have been able for a variety of reasons to operate free of "normal" outside constraints (Schorr, 1988). With some exceptions, most of these programs were funded initially with private seed money or with government grants that did not flow through ordinary channels or carry the usual encumbrances. In almost all cases, these programs originated in circumstances that were somehow idiosyncratic. Several programs began under the auspices of a university with a mandate to conduct service experiments; some had a specific charge from the federal government's War on Poverty; some had explicit mandates from state legislatures or governors; many began when the special circumstances of the moment allowed an effective leader to insulate the program from normal political and bureaucratic pressures.

That successful programs have come out of unusual circumstances does not negate their significance, if only because it is important to know that there *are* programs that have succeeded in solving seemingly intractable social problems. Even if they are idiosyncratic in origin, model programs provide a vision of what can be achieved. But as Weatherly, Klerman, and their colleagues have shown, when proven programs performing vital functions are available in only a few isolated places, relying on unique talents and commitments to prevail in the face of perverse incentives is, at the most fundamental level, poor public policy.[3]

Overcoming obstacles to large-scale implementation

Having identified the uncommon and often elusive attributes of programs that succeed in helping high-risk families and having seen that simple remedies often turn out to be ineffective and that local efforts cannot long survive in the absence of supportive state and federal policies, we reach the critical

---

3 R. A. Weatherly and his colleagues came to this conclusion after surveying comprehensive programs for pregnant and parenting adolescents: "The development and survival of local programs during the past decade is nothing less than phenomenal considering the obstacles" they face. They "stand as a testimony to the vibrancy, resourcefulness, and responsiveness of local effort" (Weatherly, Perlman, Levine, & Klerman, 1985, p. 251). The researchers pointed out that the exemplary programs and services they found were exceptions and "must inevitably remain so in the absence of basic policy changes." The difficulties at the local level that must be overcome in developing and operating good programs, and the cumbersome strategies that must be devised to overcome prevailing constraints, favor "the development of services in relatively few fortunate [resource-rich and better-served] localities." They conclude by asking whether "the encouragement of a cottage industry [is] an appropriate response to . . . a serious, widespread social problem" (Weatherly et al., 1985, p. 251).

question of how effective interventions can be widely implemented. The first and most obvious answer is that, to begin, *programs already working successfully on a large scale must be expanded to cover all those who are at high risk and can benefit.* Examples are Head Start, Special Supplemental Food Program for Women, Infants and Children (WIC), and Medicaid. Second, existing policies and practices at all levels of government must be modified to *remove the obstacles that interfere with or provide disincentives to the operation of programs* that improve long-term outcomes for children growing up at risk.

The third challenge is to devise the multiple strategies that will *encourage the widespread implementation of successful programs*, a challenge as great as devising successful interventions in the first place. The development of such strategies involves the give-and-take of many minds, many interests, many disciplines, and many levels of practical experience as well as theoretical insights. This quest must receive a much higher priority than it has today from academics, philanthropists, administrators, and policy makers. Specifically, it is essential to find new and improved ways of

> developing and encouraging the use of more appropriate methods of evaluating program effectiveness and of assuring program accountability;
> attracting, training, and supporting talented personnel; and
> gentling the heavy hand of bureaucracy.

Improved methods of evaluation and accountability

The reasonable demand for evidence that something good is happening as a result of the investment of funds – especially if they are public funds – often exerts unreasonable pressures to convert both program input and outcomes into whatever can be readily measured. This rush to quantify, engaging funders, policy makers, academics, policy analysts, and program administrators alike, drives programs into building successes by ducking hard cases and diverts energy into evaluation research that asks trivial questions and sacrifices significance (cf. Campbell, 1987).

As Donald Campbell (1987) has agreed, we must make sure that judgments and decisions are based on "a cumulation" of wisdom. No single study, no single set of statistics, no single piece of evidence should be the basis of decisions to fund or not to fund, to abandon, or to replicate a project. Judgments about what works must be based on a thoughtful appraisal of the many kinds of evidence available. This means relying not only on quantitative but also on qualitative information, not only on the evaluations of "objective" outsiders but also on the experiences of committed practitioners, not on isolated discoveries but on understanding how consistent the findings are with other knowledge. Relying on common sense, prudence, and understanding in interpreting evidence does not mean sacrificing rigor in dealing with available information. But numbers can obscure as well as illuminate. (For example, although practitioners agree that time spent on developing relationships is critical, budget officers measure success by how high a number of "encounters" each professional racks up in a day.) The application of human intelligence may bring us closer to policy-relevant conclusions than reliance on numbers that utimately conceal basic ignorance of what is really going on.

Attracting, training, and supporting talented personnel

Effective programs require competent, caring, and flexible professionals. If successful interventions aimed at high-risk populations are to become widely available, the training of professionals, and the value systems within which they work, must take better account of the special needs of disadvantaged children and their families.

In the hierarchy of values in health, social services, and education, disadvantaged populations rank low and preventive services rank low, and, in medicine, the nontechnological services essential to many successful interventions rank low. When it comes to professional status and economic compensation, the direct provision of basic services to the least powerful has little prestige. Even the development of better methods to accomplish such important public purposes as reaching hard-to-reach populations with effective services is rarely prized.

At the level of theory and research, the solution of problems with multiple causes, best addressed by combining talents from several disciplines, receives little support in most academic settings. At the level of the practitioner, narrowly drawn boundaries that limit what is expected of a professional are the very essence of professionalism for many (Schorr, 1988, p. 178). Some professionals work in settings where they see unmet needs so overwhelming that they can only continue functioning by looking away from matters beyond the confines of their own specialties.

In most fields, professionals who are trained to work with children are not also trained to work with parents. They are trained to respond to isolated problems but not to a combination of problems. When these professionals encounter difficulties that extend beyond their expertise, they are inclined to retreat to what is more familiar rather than to mobilize the help of others. The limits of their training set the limits of their practice. Both practice and training reflect the low priority assigned to the special needs of the poor.

Dr. John Conger, former dean of the University of Colorado Medical School, has said, "We train people for what they like to do, which is related to what is socially valued and well reimbursed, rather than for what needs to be done" (Conger, 1986). Yale University psychiatrist and researcher Dr. Donald Cohen has made virtually the same point: "Professionals go where the money is, where success is most likely, and where it's easy to provide their services. That's why the problem doesn't get defined in terms of family or social needs, but in terms that work for the professionals" (Cohen, 1985). Many more professionals would be willing and able to work more effectively with high-risk children if their training equipped them with the requisite skills and exposed them to relevant experiences and if they worked in a setting that assigned higher rewards for doing so.

In addition, in a more encouraging national climate many more professionals would be available to work in these programs. In the early days of the War on Poverty, when the word went out that federal support was available to establish comprehensive health centers in forsaken rural areas and inner-city slums, health professionals in the hundreds appeared. They left their private practices and their laboratory benches to respond to the challenge (Schorr, 1988). Child development professionals did the same to get Head Start going (Sugarman, 1979). At many times in our history gifted and committed people in all walks of life have responded to articulated human need. With thoughtful planning, inspiring leadership, and serious resolve, this response could happen soon again.

Gentling the heavy hand of bureaucracy

Making a good program work amid harsh bureaucratic realities may be the hardest task of all. Clearly, the replication of any initiative on a broad scale involves a certain amount of bureaucratization. Agency boundaries and massive paperwork requirements develop willy-nilly. Regulations that may reflect a legitimate need for accountability and for some measure of standardization to prevent abuse and to assure high quality may at the same time discourage the flexibility and creativity that are central to a program's successful operation.

The bureaucratization that inevitably accompanies large-scale replication raises the most acute problems for the fragile attributes of effective interventions for high-risk populations. The first remedy is to achieve greater recognition and understanding of the problem. It is astonishing, after all the literature on fragmentation of services and on the tragedies that result when referrals fail and services do not reach those who need them most, that so many public officials and program administrators still seem uninterested in the day-to-day functioning of their human services agencies. Professionals, politicians, advocates, and caring citizens must all make the detailed questions of how bureaucracies actually deal with people their continuing concern. They must recognize that when it comes to health, social services, and education for high-risk families, how people are treated is central to whether the service works.

After understanding comes action. As governors, county executives, and mayors come to appreciate how poorly agency boundaries correspond to family needs, these public officials must take responsibility for building bridges across agency and jurisdictional lines. Outside monitoring is essential for programs serving primarily the poor – programs that not only are complex but also may be administered by people who believe that they are dealing with an "undeserving" clientele and that these programs ought to be at least tough and perhaps punitive. Essential too is training in the skills that allow people in large organizations to continue to see the importance of personal human connections.[4]

Conclusion

The state of our knowledge, and society's high stakes in acting on this knowledge, beckons voters and taxpayers, labor and business, professionals and philanthropists, administrators and politicians to join in a new commitment, specific in its objective, broad in its scope, and enduring in its staying power, to reallocate resources, to find new funds, and to eliminate obstacles to widespread implementation on behalf of children and families at risk. We must work together to repeal the "inverse care law"[5] that holds that those who need high-quality services the most will get the least and the worst. We must recognize that investments in preventive interventions are a bargain compared to the cost of our current failures and that self-interest and social justice require us to build boldly on the foundations of the rich new knowledge now available.

References

Abbott, A. (1978). Status and status care centers. *American Journal of Public Health, 68*, 981–987.

Bachman, J. G., O'Malley, P. M., & Johnston, J. (1978). *Adolescence to adulthood: Change and stability in the lives of young men.* Ann Arbor, MI: University of Michigan, Institute for Social Research.

Beckwith, L., & Parmelee, A. H. (1984, April). *Infant sleep states, EEG patterns, caregiving and 5 year IQs of preterm children.* Paper presented at the International Conference on Infant Studies, New York.

Bee, H. L., Van Egeren, L. F., Streissguth, A. P., Nyman, B. A., & Lackie, M. S. (1969). Social class differences in maternal teaching strategies and speech patterns. *Developmental Psychology, 1*, 726–734.

Berrueta-Clement, J. R., Schweinhart, L. J., Barnett, W. S., Epstein, A. S., & Weikart, D. P. (1984). *Changed lives: The effects of the Perry Preschool program on youths through age 19* (Monographs of the High/ Scope Education Research Foundation, 8). Ypsilanti, MI: High /Scope Press.

4 Obstacles to widespread implementation of successful programs, and how they might be overcome, are examined in greater detail in Schorr, 1988.
5 "Inverse care law" is the phrase of the British philosopher of health care organization Tudor Hart (Hart, 1971).

Brann, E. A., Edward, L., Callicott, T., Story, E. S., Berg, P. A., Mahoney, J. A., Stine, J. L., & Hixson, A. (1979). Strategies for the prevention of pregnancy in adolescents. *Advances in planned parenthood, 14*, 68–76.

Campbell, D. T. (1987). Problems for the experimenting society in the interface between evaluation and service providers. In S. L. Kagan, D. R. Powell, B. Weissbourd, & E. Zigler (Eds.), *America's family support programs: Perspectives and prospects.* New Haven, CT: Yale University Press.

Cohen, D. (1985, January 15). Comments at a meeting of the Panel on Mental Health of Children and Adolescents, Institute of Medicine, National Academy of Sciences, Washington, DC.

Conger, J. (1986, May 16). Comments at a meeting of the Board on Mental Health of the Institute of Medicine, National Academy of Sciences, Washington, DC.

Congressional Budget Office. (1988). *Trends in family income: 1970–1986.* Washington, DC: U.S. Government Printing Office.

Consortium for Longitudinal Studies. (1983). *As the twig is bent. . . Lasting effects of preschool programs.* Hillsdale, NJ: Erlbaum.

Deutsch, M. (1985). *Long-term effects of early intervention: Summary of selected findings.* Report from the Institute for Developmental Studies, New York University.

Dryfoos, J. G. (1983, October). *Review of interventions in the field of prevention of adolescent pregnancy.* Preliminary report to the Rockefeller Foundation.

Edna McConnell Clark Foundation (1985). *Keeping families together: The case for family preservation.* New York: Author.

Edwards, L. E., Steinman, M. E., & Hakanson, E. Y. (1977). An experimental comprehensive high school clinic. *American Journal of Public Health, 8*, 765–766.

Edwards, L. E., Steinman, M. E., & Hakanson, E. Y. (1980). Adolescent pregnancy prevention services in high school clinics. *Family planning perspectives, 12* (1), 6–14.

Edwards, L. E., Steinman, M. E., & Hakanson, E. Y. (1986). *Contraceptive continuation in adolescents.* Paper presented at the annual meeting of the American Public Health Associaton, Las Vegas.

Eisenberg, L. (1982). Conceptual issues on biobehavioral interactions. In D. L. Parron & L. Eisenberg (Eds.), *Infants at risk for developmental dysfunction* (pp. 57–68). Washington, DC: National Academy of Sciences, Institute of Medicine.

Elliot, D. S., Ageton, S. S., & Canter, R. J. (1979). An integrated theoretical perspective on delinquent behavior. *Journal of Research in Crime and Delinquency, 16*, 3–27.

Escalona, S. K. (1982). Babies at double hazard: Early development of infants at biologic and social risk. *Pediatrics, 70*, 670–676.

Feldman, R., Deitz, D. M., & Brooks, E. F. (1978, October). The financial viability of rural primary health care centers. *American Journal of Public Health, 68*(10), 981–987.

Furstenberg, F. F., Jr., Brooks-Gunn, J., & Morgan, S. P. (1987). *Adolescent mothers in later life.* Cambridge: Cambridge University Press.

Gray, S. W., Ramsey, B. K., & Klaus, R. A. (1983). The early training project, 1962–1980. In Consortium for Longitudinal Studies, *As the twig is bent. . . Lasting effects of preschool programs* (pp. 33–69). Hillsdale, NJ: Erlbaum.

Gregory, M., Hausner, T., & Solarz, A. (1984). *Final evaluation of the Obstetrical Access Pilot Project, July 1979–June 1982.* Sacramento, CA: State of California Department of Health Services.

Haapala, D. A., & Kinney, J. M. (1979). Homebuilders approach to the training of in-home therapists. In S. Maybanks & M. Bryce (Eds.), *Home-based services for children and families* (pp. 248–252). Springfield, IL: Charles C. Thomas.

Hardy, J. B., King, T. M., & Repke, J. T. (1986, January, revised). *The Johns Hopkins Adolescent Pregnancy Program.* Baltimore: Johns Hopkins University School of Medicine and the Johns Hopkins Hospital, Departments of Pediatrics and Gynecology and Obstetrics.

Hart, J. T. (1971). The inverse care law. *Lancet, 1*, 405–412.

Hess, R. D., & Shipman, V. (1968). Maternal influences upon early learning: The cognitive environments of urban pre-school children. In R. D. Hess & R. M. Bear (Eds.), *Early education* (pp. 91–103). Chicago: Aldine.

Institute of Medicine, Committee to Study the Prevention of Low Birthweight, Division of Health Promotion and Disease Prevention. (1985). *Preventing low birthweight*. Washington, DC: National Academy Press.

Kagan, J. (1984). *The nature of the child*. New York: Basic Books.

Kamerman, S. B., & Kahn, A. J. (1986, November). *Social services for children, youth and families*. A proposal to the Annie E. Casey Foundation, New York.

Kaplan, J. L., & Luck, E. C. (1977). The dropout phenomenon as a social problem. *Educational Forum, 42*, 41–56.

Kinney, J. M. (1978). Homebuilders: An in-home crisis intervention program. *Children Today, 1*, 15–35.

Kinney, J. M., Madsen, B., Fleming, T., & Haapala, D. A. (1977). Homebuilders: Keeping families together. *Journal of Consulting and Clinical Psychology, 45*, 667–673.

Kirby, D. (1984). *Sexuality education: An evaluation of programs and their effects*. Santa Cruz, CA: Network Publications.

Klerman, L. V., Weitzman, M., Alpert, J. J., & Lamb, G. A. (1984). School absence: Can it be used to monitor child health? In D. K. Walker & J. B. Richmond (Eds.), *Monitoring child health in the United States: Selected issues and policies* (pp. 143–152). Cambridge, MA: Harvard University Press.

Knitzer, J. (1982). *Unclaimed children: The failure of public responsibility to children and adolescents in need of mental health services*. Washington, DC: Children's Defense Fund.

Knitzer, J. (1984). Mental health services to children and adolescents. *American Psychologist, 39*(8), 905–911.

Knitzer, J. (1984, November). Report presented at a meeting of the Working Group on Early Life, Harvard Division of Health Policy Research and Education, Boston.

Knitzer, J., McGowan, B., & Allen, M. L. (1978). *Children without homes*. Washington, DC: Children's Defense Fund.

Kohn, M. L. (1969). *Class and conformity: A study in values*. Homewood, IL: Dorsey Press.

Korenbrot, C. C. (1984). Risk reduction in pregnancies of low income women. *Mobius, 4*, 34–43.

Lazar, I., & Darlington, R. (1982). Lasting effects of early education. *Monographs of the Society for Research in Child Development, 47*, Serial No. 195.

Leiderman, P. H. (1983). Social ecology and childbirth: The newborn nursery as environmental stressor. In N. Garmezy & M. Rutter (Eds.), *Stress, coping, and development in children* (pp. 133–159). New York: McGraw-Hill.

Lennie, A., Klun, J., & Hausner, T. (1985, November). *Low birth weight reduced by OB Access Project*. Paper presented at the annual meeting of the American Public Health Association, Washington, DC.

Levine, M. D. (1985). A study of risk factor complexes in early adolescent delinquency. *American Journal of the Diseases of Childhood, 139*, 50–56.

Lewis, D. O., & Balla, D. A. (1976). *Delinquency and psychopathology*. New York: Grune and Stratton.

Lewis, D. O., & Shanok, S. (1979). A comparison of the medical histories of incarcerated delinquent children. *Child Psychiatry and Human Development, 9*(4), 210–214.

Lewis, D. O., Shanok, S. S., Pincus, J. H., & Glaser, G. H. (1979). Violent juvenile delinquents. *Journal of the American Academy of Child Psychiatry*, 307–319.

Loeber, R., & Dishion, T. (1983). Early predictors of male delinquency: A review. *Psychological Bulletin, 94*, 68–99.

McCarton, C. M. (1986). The long-term impact of a low birth weight infant on the family. *Zero to Three, 6*(4) 6–10.

McManus, M. (1985). *Evaluation of interventions to reduce racial disparities in infant mortality.* Prepared for the DHHS Infant Mortality Task Force.

Neubauer, P. (1976). *Process of child development.* New York: New American Library.

Olds, D. L. (1981). Improving formal services for mothers and children. In J. Garbarino & S. H. Stocking (Eds.), *Protecting children from abuse and neglect* (pp. 173–197). San Francisco: Jossey-Bass.

Olds, D. L. (1982). The prenatal/early infancy project. In J. Belsky (Ed.), *In the beginning* (pp. 270–285). New York: Columbia University Press.

Olds, D. L., Henderson, C. R., Chamberlin, R., & Tatelbaum, R. (1986). Preventing child abuse and neglect: A randomized trial of nurse home visitation. *Pediatrics, 78,* 65–78.

Olds, D. L., Henderson, C. R., Tatelbaum, R., & Chamberlin, R. (1986b). Improving the delivery of prenatal care and outcomes of pregnancy. *Pediatrics, 77,* 16–28.

Olds, D. L., Henderson, C. R., Tatelbaum, R., & Chamberlin, R. (1986b). *Improving the life-course development of socially disadvantaged parents.* Unpublished report.

Phipps-Yonas, S. (1980). Teenage pregnancy and motherhood: A review of the literature. *American Journal of Orthopsychiatry, 50,* 403–431.

Piechnik, S., & Corbett, M. A. (1985). Reducing low birthweight among socio-economically high risk adolescent pregnancies. *Journal of Nurse-Midwifery, 30,* 88.

Polansky, N. A. (1979). Isolation of the neglectful family. *American Journal of Orthopsychiatry, 49* (1), 149–152.

Polansky, N. A., Chambers, M. A., Buttenwieser, E., & Williams, D. P. (1981). *Damaged parents, An anatomy of child neglect.* Chicago: University of Chicago Press.

Porter, P. J. (1985). St. Paul: Facing teen pregnancy. *Healthy children* (pp. 4–11). Boston: Harvard University, Division of Health Policy.

Provence, S., & Naylor, A. (1983). *Working with disadvantaged parents and their children: Scientific and practice issues.* New Haven: Yale University Press.

Richmond, J. B. (1970). Disadvantaged children: What have they compelled us to learn? *Yale Journal of Biology and Medicine, 43,* 127–144.

Robins, L. N. (1978). Sturdy childhood predictors of adult antisocial behavior: Replications from Longitudinal Studies. *Psychological Medicine, 8,* 611–622.

Rutter, M. (1980). *Changing youth in a changing society: Patterns of adolescent development and disorder.* Cambridge, MA: Harvard University Press.

Rutter, M. (1982). Prevention of children's psychosocial disorders: Myth and substance. *Pediatrics, 70,* 883–894.

Sameroff, A. J., & McDonough, S. (1984). The role of motor activity in human cognitive and social development. In E. Pollitt & P. Amante (Eds.), *Energy intake and activity* (pp. 331–353). New York: Alan R. Liss.

Sameroff, A. J., & Seifer, R. (1983, April). *Sources of continuity in parent–child relations.* Paper presented at a meeting of the Society for Research in Child Development, Detroit.

Schorr, L. B. (1988). *Within our reach: Breaking the cycle of disadvantage.* New York: Doubleday/Anchor.

Segal, J., & Yahraes, H. (1979). *A child's journey: Forces that shape the lives of our young.* New York: McGraw-Hill.

Seitz, V., Apfel, N. H., & Rosenbaum, L. E. (1983, April). *School-aged mothers: Infant development and maternal education outcomes.* Paper presented at the biennial meeting of the Society for Research in Child Development, Detroit.

Seitz, V., Rosenbaum, L. K., & Apfel, N. K. (1985). Effects of family support intervention: A ten-year follow-up. *Child Development, 56,* 376–391.

Stroup, A. L., & Robins, L. N. (1972). Elementary school predictors of high school dropouts among black males. *Sociology of Education, 45,* 212–222.

Sugarman, J. M. (1979). Head Start, a retrospective view. In E. Zigler & J. Valentine (Eds.), *Project Head Start: A legacy of the War on Poverty* (pp. 114–120). New York: Free Press.

Suomi, S. J., Mineka, S., & DeLizio, R. D. (1983). Short- and long-term effects of repetitive mother–infant separations on social development in rhesus monkeys. *Developmental Psychology, 19,* 770–786.

Tizard, B., & Hughes, M. (1984). *Young children learning*. Cambridge, MA: Harvard University Press.

Trickett, P. K., Apfel, N. H., Rosenbaum, L. K., & Zigler, E. F. (1981). A five-year follow-up of participants in the Yale child welfare research program. In E. F. Zigler & E. W. Gordon (Eds.), *Day care: Scientific and social policy issues* (pp. 200–222). Boston: Auburn House.

Uhlig, M. A. (1987, November 9). Many child-abuse deaths come in cases where risk is known. *The New York Times.*

Unger, D. G., & Wandersman, L. P. (1985). Social support and adolescent mothers. *Journal of Social Issues, 41*(1), 29–45.

U.S. House of Representatives. (1987). *U.S. children and their families*. Washington DC: U.S. Government Printing Office.

Weatherly, R. A., Perlman, S. B., Levine, M. H., & Klerman, L. V. (1985). *Patchwork programs: Comprehensive services for pregnant and parenting adolescents*. Report prepared for the U.S. Department of Health and Human Services, U.S. Public Health Service, Office of Population Affairs.

Werner, E. E., & Smith, R. S. (1982). *Vulnerable but invincible: A longitudinal study of resilient children and youth*. New York: McGraw-Hill.

Wilson, W. J. (1987). *The truly disadvantaged: The inner city, the underclass, and public policy*. Chicago: University of Chicago Press.

Zabin, L. S., Hirsch, M. B., Smith, E. A., Streett, R., & Hardy, J. B. (1986). Evaluation of a pregnancy prevention program for urban teenagers. *Family planning perspectives, 18* (3), 119–126.

Zabin, L. S., Streett, R., Hardy, J. B, & King, T. M. (1984). A school-, hospital- and university-based adolescent pregnancy prevention program. *The Journal of Reproductive Medicine, 29* (6), 421–426.

Aletha C. Huston

We began this volume with three sets of questions. First, why are so many children in the United States growing up poor? How and why has the economic status of children deteriorated during the last 20 years? Second, how does poverty affect the physical, cognitive, and social development of children? Third, what role can public policy and policy research play in preventing or alleviating the damaging effects of poverty on children? In this chapter, I attempt to summarize and integrate some of the answers presented by the contributors to this book and to put policy issues in a broader context of social values and assumptions.

Why has children's poverty increased?

Greg Duncan's chapter summarizes the major social and economic changes that have led to increases in children's poverty during the last 20 years. These include changes in the economy, in family structure, and in government benefits for families with children.

Economic changes leading to low parent earning power

The U.S. economy has shifted from manufacturing and producing goods to providing services. Relatively unskilled but high wage jobs in such industries as automobile and steel production have declined in numbers. The new jobs created in service industries typically pay low wages, have few benefits, are not "career" jobs, and are unlikely to be covered by union contracts. Those individuals who suffer most from these changes are people without college educations, particularly minorities.

  People who have children early are more disadvantaged today than they were in earlier generations because a high school education is no longer enough to enable many young people to enter a reasonably stable and even modestly lucrative occupation. Between 1976 and 1988, the median wage of 25- to 34-year-old men with only a high school education dropped from $24,000 to $21,000; for college graduates in this age group it rose from $28,000 to $30,000 ("Jobs and Insecurity," 1988). The disadvantage of growing up poor has increased as higher education has become more important for occupational opportunity. Among affluent families, children are no longer expected to be financially independent at age 18. They often require a longer period of economic dependency and familial support to obtain the skills and credentials that will open the doors of stable and lucrative employment.

At a time when higher education has become more critical for occupational success, the percentage of whites completing high school has declined (Glazer, 1986). Among blacks, the percentage of high school graduates going on to college dropped during the 1980s, in part because many colleges and universities did not maintain the momentum of the 1970s for recruiting and providing financial support for minority students.

The groups hit hardest by these economic changes are young blacks. The increased opportunities afforded by antidiscrimination and affirmative action programs have indeed helped to increase the numbers of blacks in professional and managerial jobs. However, the decline in manufacturing jobs has left black men and black women without an important source of job opportunities. The result is a growth in the black middle class but a swelling of the black underclass as well. The percentage of black men who are in the labor force (i.e., employed or looking for work) has declined steadily since the 1940s. In 1985, 64% of black men over age 20 were in the labor force; the figure for white men was 76% (Malveaux, 1988). Unemployment was also higher among black men who were in the labor force than it was among whites; young black men had especially high rates of unemployment. Full-time wages for black men who were employed were about 75% of the average for white men (Danziger, Haveman, & Plotnick, 1986; Glazer, 1986; Malveaux, 1988; Wacquant & Wilson, 1989; Wilson, 1987).

Black women historically have worked at the bottom of the wage scale, and they continue to suffer higher rates of unemployment and lower wages than white women. In 1985, unemployment rates were 12.6% for black women and 5.4% for white women. Although the average occupational status for the two groups was similar, black women's earnings were 92% of those of white women (Malveaux, 1988).

Still another important labor market change has been the increasing employment of women. The increase has occurred primarily for white women; historically, black women more often have worked for wages. In two-parent families, women's employment has served to counteract the effects of other economic changes. Many families maintain sufficient income only because there are two earners (Congressional Budget Office, 1988; Hernandez, 1989).

Economic and labor market forces have increased the gap between the affluent and the poor for both blacks and whites. Between 1970 and 1986 real incomes of those persons in the lowest 20% (many of whom had children) declined whereas the incomes in the top 20% rose considerably (Congressional Budget Office, 1988). Income and opportunity for individuals in the higher echelons of education and occupational status have improved, but the opportunities in the middle and lower levels have declined.

Single-parent families

Single-parent families headed by women are at much higher risk of being poor than two-parent families or father-only families. The total family incomes for children in married-couple and mother-only families are shown in Figure 12.1. During the 1970s, increases in the number of single-mother families contributed to rising children's poverty; in the 1980s, increases in children's poverty have been due more to declining income for single mothers than to increments in their numbers (Bane & Ellwood, 1989).

Children's economic fate is closely tied to the the economic position of women. Impoverishment of children is inextricably bound to the feminization of poverty. In a time when many families survive by having two full-time earners, a family with one earner is at a disadvantage, particularly when that earner experiences gender and race inequalities in earnings. Median earnings in 1985 for white women were $264 per week and were $242 per week for black women. Both groups earned less than men, white or black. Median earnings were $324 per week for white men and $287 per week for black men (Malveaux, 1988).

Single parents also face conflicts between employment and child-rearing responsibilities. During the time they are on the job, their children usually must have care from someone other than a parent. As a result, single parents frequently find it difficult or impossible to work full time. When they do, the cost of child care reduces the net income that they receive from their wages. That cost is 20% to 30% of a woman's earnings; it is not insignificant (Phillips, this volume).

Still another reason that single parenting leads to poverty is the absence of effective social and legal obligations for nonresident parents to provide care or support for their children. Children of single mothers typically receive little or no financial support from their fathers. About half of those children have no court-ordered child support; for those who are supposed to receive support, about half actually receive the court-ordered amounts in full (Weitzman, 1985). Despite the recent push for joint custody and increased father involvement, nonresident fathers typically do not take any regular responsibility for child care; many have little or no contact with their children (Furstenberg, Peterson, Nord, & Zill, 1983).

According to an analysis by Bane (1986), increasing fathers' obligations would reduce poverty among white families but would not substantially change

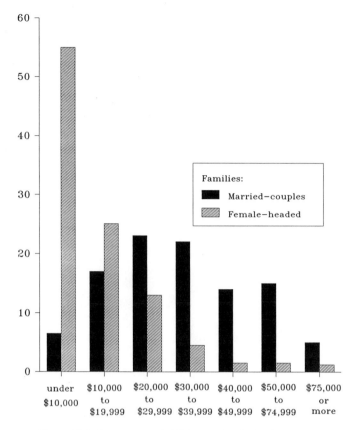

Figure 12.1. Percentage of children under 18 by family income for married-couple families and female-headed families in 1985. From *Youth Indicators: 1988. Trends in the Well-being of American Youth* by the U.S. Office of Education, 1988, Washington, DC: U.S. Government Printing Office.

the economic position of black families. If financial resources of fathers and mothers were allocated equitably according to need, about 15% of white families' poverty would be alleviated, but black poverty would not be changed substantially. Many black families are poor before a marital split; many fathers who never marry their children's mothers are also poor.

Single parenting is an outcome as well as a cause of poverty. Girls who grow up in poverty are at risk for early childbearing (often during adolescence), births outside marriage, and truncated education. All of these circumstances in turn contribute to the likelihood that a woman will remain poor because she has few skills with which to earn a living, she has child care responsibilities, and she has a relatively low probability of marrying someone with better skills than her own or of remaining married (Furstenberg, Brooks-Gunn, & Morgan, 1987; Klerman, this volume).

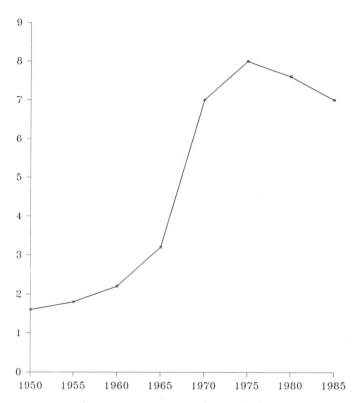

Figure 12.2. Number of children (in millions) receiving Aid to Families with Dependent Children from 1950 to 1985. From *Youth Indicators: 1988. Trends in the Well-being of American Youth* by the U.S. Office of Education, 1988, Washington, DC: U.S. Government Printing Office.

Reduced government benefits

A third major reason for increases in poverty, especially in the 1980s, was reduced expenditures on virtually all federal programs benefiting children. Between 1981 and 1984, the federal outlays on 25 programs affecting children declined by 11% (Garwood, Phillips, Hartman, & Zigler, 1989). The erosion had begun earlier, however, with reduced value of cash benefits and reduced numbers of children declared eligible. The total number of children receiving Aid to Families with Dependent Children (AFDC) peaked in 1975 and dropped sharply in the early 1980s despite the increased number of poor families (see Figure 12.2). Most cash benefit programs, such as AFDC, were not indexed to inflation during the 1970s and 1980s, so payment rates did not keep pace with increasing costs of living. For instance, between 1971 and 1983, the real value (i.e., buying power) of food stamps and AFCD declined by 22% (Ellwood & Summers, 1986).

Both one- and two-parent families have been affected by changes in the tax system. The real value of the personal exemption on federal income taxes was reduced by one-half between 1950 and 1983 (Blank & Blinder, 1986). In 1948, the exemption was $600, about 42% of per capita income. In 1984, the same percentage of per capita income would have been $5,600; if the 1948 benefit had been indexed by the Consumer Price Index, it would have been $2,589 in 1984 (Moynihan, 1986). As more two-parent families rely on two workers, they suffer the "marriage penalty," that is, higher tax rates than two unmarried workers would pay on the same income. Finally, the payroll tax, which is borne disproportionately by lower income wage earners, increased greatly over this period. These changes were partly counteracted for working parents by instituting an Earned Income Tax Credit enabling working parents to receive up to $550 a year in credits or payments (Moynihan, 1986; Rodgers, 1988).

In the 1980s, some federal dollars were shifted from direct benefit programs to indirect benefits, such as tax credits and deductions. The result was a shift from helping the poor to helping the nonpoor. For instance, the amount spent on the child care tax credit tripled from 1981 to 1986 whereas direct spending on child care decreased by 14.5% in the same period (Garwood et al., 1989).

The net result of all these changes was smaller cash benefits for poor nonworking parents and some reductions for poor working parents. Noncash benefits, such as food stamps and Medicaid, did not decline as much as cash benefits, and the number of families served remained fairly level during this period (see Figure 12.3).

Contrasts with other countries. Duncan in this volume summarizes poverty rates and benefit programs in several other Western industrialized countries. With the exception of Australia, all have poverty rates for children that are substantially below the United States, and almost all spend more on cash transfers to families with children. In several instances, such cash transfers to families result in significant reductions in childhood poverty. Sweden, the country that is often viewed as a model welfare state, reduces children's poverty by 58% through cash transfers. In many of these countries, programs for children and families are universally available rather than being restricted to the poor. Many nations have child allowances, universal health care, maternity or parental leaves for childbirth, and free or inexpensive child care. Such universal programs help to reduce poverty just as Social Security and Medicare help to reduce poverty among the elderly in the United States.

Links among economic conditions, family structure, and government benefits

Economic conditions, family structure, and government programs have all contributed to increases in children's poverty since the early 1970s. Family

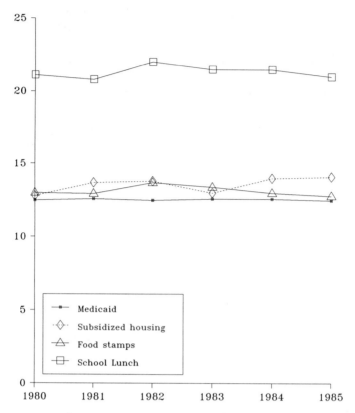

Figure 12.3. Percentage of households with children under 18 receiving noncash benefits from 1980 to 1985. From *Youth Indicators: 1988. Trends in the Well-being of American Youth* by the U.S. Office of Education, 1988, Washington, DC: U.S. Government Printing Office.

structure changes were more important influences during the 1970s; the percentage of single-parent families began to level off in the 1980s. In the 1980s, the more important factors were macroeconomic – unemployment and reduced income due to the recession of the early 1980s – and governmental – large reductions in spending on social programs during the administration of President Ronald Reagan (Bane & Ellwood, 1989). Several scholars have proposed causal links among some of these factors.

Effects of government benefits on family structure. Charles Murray (1984) argued that generous government benefits begun during the 1960s War on Poverty increased poverty by reducing the incentive to work and increasing the incentive to form single-mother families. His thesis generated heated debate and persuasive rebuttals (see Ellwood, 1988; Jencks, 1985; Moynihan, 1986; Steiner, 1981; Wilson, 1987; Zimmerman, 1988). Ironically, the best counterargument was provided by the Reagan administration's efforts to implement Murray's recommendations for massive reductions in social programs in the 1980s. Reduced benefits did not lead young people to enter the labor market in larger numbers or to have more children within marriage.

Effects of labor market conditions on family structure – male joblessness. From a different vantage point, Wilson (1987) proposed that the large increases in single-mother families among blacks were due partly to male joblessness. The core of his thesis was that when young black men cannot find jobs, they are unlikely to marry or to support children. Wilson argues for an association between marriage rates and the percentage of "marriageable" males to females. Marriageable males are defined as men with jobs; all females are apparently assumed to be marriageable. From a woman's point of view, a man without a job is a liability rather than an asset. He is one more family member for her to support. I am reminded of a young black woman undergraduate who was about to return to her native Cleveland. She remarked that she was wary about getting attached to any young man because young men often just wanted to move into a woman's apartment and "mooch off of you." From either vantage point, the root cause rests in the labor market that does not offer employment opportunities to young black males.

Wilson's arguments are persuasive, but their focus on labor market conditions affecting males appears to be one-sided. Unemployment rates among black women are almost as high as those for black men, and wages for women who are employed are considerably lower (Malveaux, 1986). It would be unfortunate if policies were targeted to improving the employment prospects of black men without corresponding efforts on behalf of women.

Effects of labor market conditions on family structure – women's independence. The thesis that male joblessness contributes to single-mother families clearly does not apply to whites. Single-mother families have increased among whites despite good labor market conditions for white men. An alternative hypothesis is based on women's increasing economic independence as they have entered paid employment in large numbers. With an independent income, they may be freer to dissolve an unhappy marriage or to remain single. However, their economic prospects without a male partner remain limited. In effect, relatively low-wage jobs may provide many women with just enough power to move away from an aversive relationship but not enough to become fully equal earners.

How poverty affects children

At first glance, it is difficult to imagine any way in which poor children have an advantage over affluent children. The many impediments to children's development imposed by poverty are obvious. However, the simple view that poverty is bad must be tempered by two considerations. First, there is a tradition in American literature and myth that children (and adults) can be strengthened by adversity; that having few material goods induces maturity, unselfishness, ambition, and family solidarity. Second, in developmental psychology, many investigators have identified "resilient" children – those children who prosper despite disadvantageous environments (Werner & Smith, 1982). A young black woman whom I knew several years ago is an example. At age 20, she supported herself and her 3-year-old son by working while attending a university full time. She was remarkably mature, efficient, well organized, and goal oriented for someone so young. She received crucial support from an older woman friend who cared for her child, but she was otherwise almost entirely self-sufficient.

Black scholars have also argued forcefully that early discussions of "cultural deprivation" incorrectly implied that poor blacks were incompetent and inadequate. Many poor communities have a viable, adaptive culture that helps to sustain them in difficult circumstances (Slaughter, 1988, p. 4). This point of view has important implications for understanding the effects of poverty on children's development. Although admitting that poverty can create serious psychosocial stress, it also suggests that the outcomes occur in the context of a cultural milieu in which different skills and competences may be valued. The cultural context must be understood in order to generate reasonable and effective policies for change (Ogbu, 1988).

Nonetheless, children living in persistent poverty are at risk for problems in health, cognitive and social development, school achievement, and future job prospects. The word *risk* is used to signify that not all poor children have poor health, low school performance, and other negative outcomes. The effects are not all-or-none. Just as high blood pressure, obesity, and smoking raise the probability that a person will have heart disease, poverty raises the probability of problem outcomes for children. Not every obese smoker has a heart attack, and not every child in poverty drops out, becomes delinquent, or has a baby at age 16. By the same token, policies should be evaluated according to changes in probabilities rather than according to the expectation that they will solve problems for every child.

Persistent poverty

The risks associated with persistent poverty begin before birth. The poor have high rates of infant mortality and low birth weight largely because of inadequate or nonexistent prenatal care, bad nutrition, and maternal health problems (Klerman, this volume). During infancy and childhood, poor children run a relatively high risk of acute and infectious diseases. Poor children miss more school due to illness and spend longer times in hospitalization than more affluent children. In surveys, low-income families say that their children are in "fair" or "poor" health more often than higher income families do (Butler, Starfield, & Stenmark, 1984; Klerman, Chapter 6 in this volume). Poor children also have more mental health problems than the affluent (McLoyd & Wilson, this volume). These health problems result largely from social and environmental conditions, including dangers in the physical environment (e.g., lead poisoning), unhealthy life-styles, lack of access to appropriate medical care, lack of knowledge about health care, and family stress (Butler, et al., 1984; Klerman, Chapter 6 in this volume).

Poor children are also at risk for delayed intellectual development and behavior problems during infancy and the preschool years. When they reach conventional school age, they often enter elementary school with fewer academic skills than advantaged children, and their average school achievement levels lag farther and farther behind as they move through elementary and high school. They are more likely than other children to be retained in a grade or to be placed in special classes for slow learners (Levin, Chapter 9 in this volume; Ramey & Campbell, this volume).

Although the problems associated with persistent poverty begin in early life, the effects become especially visible in adolescence. Children from poor homes are at risk for dropping out of school. Even if these children finish high school, their chances for higher education are considerably lower than those of other children. They have high rates of unemployment; the jobs they get are apt to be poorly paid positions with little possibility for advancement. They are at risk for crime and delinquency. Adolescent pregnancy, often outside of marriage, may accompany low education and low wages, making it difficult for young women to move out of poverty.

There is little doubt about the risks of persistent poverty. The difficult questions arise in attempting to determine which social conditions associated with low income are the most crucial contributors to negative outcomes for children. Is income per se the major ingredient, or are such associated factors as low parent education, substandard housing, poor nutrition, adolescent parenting, single-parent family structures, dangerous neighborhoods, and inadequate schools more important?

Income per se is important. In general, low income predicts negative outcomes in health, education, and later occupational attainment even when other factors such as parent education and occupational status are controlled. For instance, family income is a strong predictor of children's health status even when maternal education is controlled (Butler et al., 1984). Similarly, the high rates of educational failure among children of single-mother families are attributable in large measure to low income (Garfinkel & McLanahan, 1986). Family income during childhood and adolescence predicts adult occupational attainment even when education and occupational status of parents are controlled (Duncan, this volume). On the other hand, income is a less clear predictor of early childbearing, and its relation to mental health and behavior problems has not been studied extensively (Garfinkel & McLanahan, 1986; McLanahan, Astone, & Marks, this volume).

At a more individual psychological level, parental stress and family integration mediate many of the effects of poverty, both persistent and transitory, on children's development. Being poor, single, and vulnerable to discrimination all contribute to psychological stress and distress for parents. As a result, poor parents' interactions with children are sometimes punitive or nonsupportive and occasionally abusive. When poor mothers are able to cope with financial problems and avoid sharing financial worries with their children, the children appear to be shielded to some degree from psychological distress (McLoyd & Wilson, this volume).

Many persistently poor children grow up in families, schools, and neighborhoods where opportunities and achievements are limited. As they grow into adolescence, their expectations and hopes for the future are eroded by what they observe around them and by their own experiences, especially if they are black. National surveys of black young adults (ages 19 through 28) document a dismal picture of frequent unemployment, discouragement, and hopelessness about job prospects (Bowman, 1990).

Transitory poverty

Although children in transitory poverty are not at risk for the multiple health problems and early developmental delays associated with persistent poverty, family income losses can lead to behavioral and emotional problems as well as to reduced aspirations and attainment. Sudden drops in family income are most common when a parent loses a job or parents are divorced. Studies of the Great Depression of the 1930s and the recessions of the 1980s show that when fathers lose their jobs, children and adolescents experience psychological stress, increased risk of behavior problems, and reduced educational attainment. Similarly, many of the effects of divorce and single parenting on children are a function of income loss; women's family incomes after divorce average roughly half their predivorce family incomes.

Economic stress affects children partly through the reactions of their parents; that is, children are most apt to show problem behavior when their parents become punitive and nonsupportive (Elder & Caspi, 1989; Emery, Hetherington, & DiLalla, 1984; McLoyd, 1989; McLoyd & Wilson, this volume). Income loss also may force families to move to less expensive housing and poorer schools. When recessions affect whole communities, the entire school system loses revenues, and schools reduce enrichment programs and support services (Flanagan, 1990).

Rural poverty

Persistent and temporary poverty have long existed in rural as well as urban areas. In many respects, the impact of poverty on children's development is similar regardless of whether they live in the city or the country. Many persistently poor people in rural areas, however, have less access to public assistance and services, in part because the rural poor are concentrated in states with scant public services.

The farm crisis of the 1980s produced a wave of income losses for farmers that are in some ways analogous to job loss among urban workers. For farmers and their families, a way of life that appeared secure and lasting no longer produced a living wage, and many people were threatened with losing land that had been in their families for generations. Children and adolescents in farm families experienced some of the same stresses as those whose parents lost urban jobs, but they also experienced a more lasting change in their expectations and hopes for the future (Van Hook, 1990).

Conclusion

Understanding how poverty influences children's development requires a conceptual model in which the individual and family are placed in the ecological contexts of neighborhood, school, culture, and economic conditions. Economic circumstances affect children by influencing their families, schools, neighborhoods, and available services. The problems of poverty need be attacked at several levels ranging from the individual to the society as a whole.

Public policy and children's poverty

Despite the myth that deprivation breeds strength, poverty clearly places children at serious risk for problems in physical, academic, emotional, and behavioral development. Many families and cultural groups have evolved modes of coping and mutual support to deal with poverty, but the stresses imposed by persistent lack of money cannot be questioned. Children are often the losers when their families suffer unemployment, depression, violence, health problems, or marital disruption.

Before 1960, poverty among children and adults was common but virtually invisible in the mass media or in political discussion and decision making. Lyndon Johnson's War on Poverty was based on implicit faith that the problem could be quickly conquered. When poverty did not disappear within a few years, some people concluded that it was intractable to any known political remedy – that "throwing money" at social problems was ineffective. In the meanwhile, the numbers of women and children living in poverty began to increase as early as 1970 with very little public notice. Children's poverty was rediscovered by popular media sometime in the mid-1980s.

When the damaging effects of poverty are known so well, why did we allow more and more children to slip into poverty? The answer given by such conservatives as Murray (1984) was that the policies of the 1960s and 1970s failed; government programs could not solve the problem. The authors in this book disagree. They and many other recent commentators arrive at remarkably consistent conclusions about what policies would reduce if not eradicate poverty among children. As Schorr (this volume) aptly states, the problem is not that we do not know what to do, but that we do not have the will to do it. In part, our lack of will is a result of some basic values and social role expectations in American society.

Barriers to effective intervention

Individualism and the privacy of the family. Americans pride themselves on being individualist, independent, and self-sufficient. We prize autonomy; we believe in the value and the virtue of work; we think that help should go to those who help themselves; and we believe that rewards should be based on merit (Ellwood, 1988; Phillips, this volume; Wilensky, Luebbert, Hahn, & Jamieson, 1985). Although we recognize that disaster can overtake anyone, we think people have control over their own destinies. If they try hard enough, they will succeed. Psychologists call this assumption "internal locus of control" – the belief that one's actions have an effect on one's environment or that consequences are a result of one's own actions rather than of chance, luck, or other forces beyond one's control.

Such values and beliefs feed an explicit or implicit distinction between the deserving and undeserving poor. People who are clearly *unable* to work (e.g., the disabled) and those who have worked (e.g., the elderly) are deserving, but anyone who is young and physically able is suspected of being lazy and unwilling to work. They are the "undeserving" whose poverty is at least partly their own fault and who could become self-sufficient if they tried hard enough. For many people, "welfare mothers" fall into this category. Widely held stereotypes of conniving women who cheat the government and produce babies in order to get a welfare check are ample evidence of the negative public image of mothers on welfare. Although one might expect children to be classed as "deserving" because they cannot be expected to be self-sufficient, attitudes about children of the poor are mixed. The children are tainted with the stigma of their parents.

Americans believe in the privacy of the family and in individual parental responsibility for children (Ellwood, 1988; Grubb & Lazerson, 1988). Parents have an almost exclusive *right* to make decisions, teach values, and apply discipline as well as the full *responsibility* for nurturance and support. An anecdote illustrates the norm by contrast. An American friend living in Paris often sat in a park where children came to play. She was struck by the fact that any adult who was present might correct a child's misbehavior. It seemed to be taken for granted that strange adults had the right, and perhaps the obligation, to socialize children. In the United States, an adult who corrected a strange child might well be told to mind her or his own business.

Although the state has some obligation to assure protection, nurturing, and basic quality of life for children, the balance between community and parental responsibility is weighted more heavily toward parents than in many other industrialized countries. In the United States, the society provides universal education, but little else. The state intervenes only when the family fails – when children are abused, neglected, or abandoned. As a consequence, services (e.g., health care) and income transfers are targeted to those families who fail to provide for themselves rather than being universal benefits for all children (Grubb & Lazerson, 1988). Perhaps a more fundamental consequence is that no level of government formulates a coherent child or family policy (Steiner, 1981). Government policies pertaining to families are suspect as infringements on individual rights and privacy. Yet countries that have family policies have more programs to serve children's needs than those that do not (Kahn & Kamerman, 1983).

Short-run economic criteria in policy decisions. In Chapter 1, I contrasted social-economic bases with child-centered developmental criteria for policy decisions. Most policy analysts and policy makers stress economic rationales for policies and programs affecting poor children. For instance, the debate surrounding the federal welfare reform legislation passed in 1988 was couched almost entirely in a framework weighing the costs of welfare against the costs of education and training that could lead to employment. This view leads to attempts to provide child care "on the cheap" and gives little attention to the possibility that getting a mother into the labor force may not benefit her child if that child is left in unsuitable care or is unsupervised after school.

Schorr (this volume) points out repeatedly the futility of policies designed to do a quick fix. The social and economic assumptions guiding many policy analyses as well as the realities of the political process make it easy to rely almost exclusively on short-term economic criteria in policy making. Without a balance of direct concern for children's welfare, these criteria often fail to lead to the most effective policies and programs to alleviate the effects of poverty for children.

Family roles. A third barrier to effective public policy is a disjunction between idealized family roles and current reality. In "traditional" families, fathers are responsible for providing material goods to the family, and mothers are full-time homemakers and child caregivers. Our images of motherhood derive from the 19th and early 20th centuries – an ideal of a mother who devotes her time and emotional energy to her family (Scarr, 1986). In fact, there was never a time when the majority of families fit the ideal of a breadwinner father and stay-at-home mother (Hernandez, 1989), but we as a society have always expected women to take the primary responsibility for care of their children (Fraser, 1987).

In the last part of the 20th century, mothers have taken on the provider role as well as the nurturing role. The majority of mothers in two-parent families are employed at least part-time from very early in their children's lives. Women's income is essential for many families to attain an acceptable standard of living. And, of course, increasing numbers of single mothers provide the sole economic support for their children.

Although women have entered the marketplace, they have not left the home. Society continues to expect women to nurture children, and women continue to accept that responsibility. Approximately 90% of the children who live in single-parent families live with their mothers, a figure that has remained remarkably stable over many years. In most two-parent families, even when the mother is employed she is responsible for the children. Family needs are expected to take priority over women's jobs or careers. Mothers typically arrange for child care, stay home when the children are ill, and supervise their children's whereabouts.

In short, recent social changes have created a conundrum. Employment and parenting often generate conflicting demands on women's time and energies. They cannot be wage earners and 24-hour parents simultaneously. Women are subjected to two sets of social expectations, each loaded with emotion. On the one hand, we emphasize the primacy of motherhood and express hostility toward working mothers in such pejorative terms as "latchkey children." On the other hand, we criticize as lazy a woman who fails to be "self-sufficient," that is, to support herself and her children. Mothers are held largely responsible for their children's day-to-day care yet are expected to spend their time in the labor force at considerably lower wages than men. Poor mothers are stigmatized and blamed if they fail to care adequately for their children, but they are also castigated if they fail to earn a living.

Ironically, as women have entered paid employment, their traditional activities as homemakers and mothers have become devalued. Policy makers and the public continue to assume that women should take responsibility for children, but they no longer think child rearing is a full-time job. The rhetoric of welfare reform illustrates the change. From the 1930s, when Aid to Dependent Children was established, until the 1960s, the avowed purpose of the program was to allow single mothers to stay home to care for their children. In the 1980s, politicians advocated programs to get AFDC recipients into the paid work force with the argument that middle-class women were not staying home with their children, so there was no need for welfare clients to do so. In other words, it was no longer worthwhile to pay a woman to be a full-time mother.

The value of child rearing. Finally, the political and economic institutions of the United States have not adjusted to the fact that the "job" of child care is rapidly moving from unpaid labor performed by women in their homes to labor that is part of the money economy. "Women's work" traditionally has had little economic value. It was awarded no wages and therefore was not counted in such conventional economic indices as the Gross National Product. An economics professor who taught a friend of mine in the 1950s referred facetiously to his wife's labor as the "household self-feeding factor." However, when dollar value was assigned to women's home labor for purposes of insurance claims or research, it was high. One economist estimated that if married women's work at home were compensated in dollars, it would raise family income by 60%. "The value of housework [including child rearing] is so great that when the wife joins the labor force, the loss of her home production is almost equal to her increased money earnings" (Duncan, 1984, p. 23).

Although the theoretical value of women's unpaid labor was high, its practical economic and social value was low, at least partly because no money was involved. Policy-oriented economists often take as a premise the marketplace notion that people's values and preferences can be inferred from their allocation of resources. The more money or other resources one is willing to invest toward a goal, the more important or valued that goal is (Rhoads, 1985). By that criterion, child care has had little value in American society.

The shift of child care into the money economy has occurred especially rapidly in the last 15 to 20 years, as large numbers of women with infants and preschool children entered the labor market.[1] For the most part, fathers have not taken on more responsibility (Hoffman, 1989). Instead, the duties of child care have shifted to people other than the parents – to either extended family members or paid caregivers.

The budgets of government, businesses, and private citizens were not prepared for the very large cost of child care once it was translated into real money. The current crisis in child care reflects the dislocations created by rapid changes in women's employment. Child care costs are prohibitive for many families; the needed appropriations from government are large. Yet

---

1 Married women entered the labor market in large numbers from the 1940s on, but the bulk of those entering employment in the early part of this period had older children. During the 1970s and 1980s, the largest increases in percentages of married women entering the labor force occurred for women with children under age 6.

the profession of child care is dismally financed. A recent study of child care staffing in several U.S. cities demonstrates the problem dramatically. The average child care worker in 1988 was a woman earning $5.35 per hour. Her level of education was well above the national average for women workers, but her wages were less than *half* the average woman's wage and less than *one-third* the average wage for comparably educated men (Whitebook, Howes, & Phillips, 1989).

As the low dollar value of child care becomes more evident, American society is confronted with an increasingly glaring conflict between its professed priority for children's welfare and its low valuation of children and their needs. In all likelihood, the trend toward nonparental care of young children will continue for some time. One of the major tasks of public policy is to find ways to provide resources for that care and give child care the value it deserves. A society that devalues the work of raising children devalues its children.

Summary. In short, several barriers to effective child policies exist in American society. We prize individual responsibility of parents and the privacy of the family, and we are reluctant to exercise societal responsibility for children's welfare and development. Policy analysis and policy making rely too exclusively on economic criteria without a counterbalancing concern for the welfare of children. We maintain an ideal that women should be full-time mothers while at the same time expecting women to be self-sufficient providers for their families. Society has not yet evolved new forms to fulfill its increased responsibility for the care and nurturing of children, nor has it come to grips with the costs of replacing women's traditionally unpaid labor. The children of the late 20th century are falling in the cracks, and, of course, poor children suffer most of all from these social and economic changes.

Effective child policies

Policies to deal effectively with the problems of child poverty require some changes in these basic assumptions. We[2] are not proposing values and views that are diametrically opposite to those just described, but a reorientation of emphasis and perspective. Rapid social changes often leave gaps between beliefs and reality; our society needs some adjustments to encompass the current social realities of children's lives.

Community responsibility for children. The most central change is a shift in the balance of parent and societal responsibility for children's welfare. We

---

2 I use the word *we* here because what follows is a direct outgrowth of the discussion at the conference; it represents the ideas of the group as well as those of this author.

propose that children be defined as a category of citizens who deserve social insurance just as the elderly and the disabled do. Society, as represented by different levels of government and community, should become a partner and a support for parents in order to meet children's basic needs for food, housing, health care, education, and physical safety. Both humanitarian and human capital rationales support this proposal. Children merit categorical treatment because they are not able to be self-sufficient. They deserve a reasonable quality of life. Moreover, the society has an interest in promoting the development of children into productive, independent citizens. Categorical benefits for children should be regular and continuing, along the lines of public education and child allowances. Although some benefits must be based on need, they should not be defined only as a temporary expedient to be implemented when families fail to provide for their children.

Policy goals should be defined according to developmental as well as economic criteria. Evaluations of policies should include indices of children's physical and mental health, academic progress, and social development as well as indices of family income and parental labor force participation. This recommendation is especially important for policy researchers. The sequels to the income maintenance experiments of the 1970s and the welfare reform experiments of the 1980s need careful and extensive measurement of outcomes for children as well as for parents.

Perhaps the most startling implication of shared social and parental responsibility is a challenge to "self-sufficiency" for parents, especially single parents, as the only goal of antipoverty programs. Most poverty policies for the last 30 years have been designed to induce economic self-sufficiency among the poor by providing education, job training, small business opportunities, and other means to enable people to become self-supporting.

Direct financial aid and such in-kind programs as food stamps are intended as temporary expedients in times of crisis. In the 1980s, the entire social welfare system was popularly described as a "safety net," designed to provide temporary assistance during unavoidable losses of income. Most people believe the system has failed when adults of working age become long-term recipients of welfare. By contrast, the elderly and the handicapped are acknowledged as groups who require continuing assistance because they cannot be expected to work. Mothers used to fall in this class because they needed to care for children at home, but the changes in role expectations for women have placed mothers in the category of people who are expected to provide for themselves and their families.

Morris and Williamson (1986) argue congently that policies aimed at teaching poor people to be economically self-sufficient have limited potential to reduce poverty. In order for education and training programs to succeed, for example, the individuals must change *and* the economy must provide the needed opportunities. Evaluations of job-training programs in the last 25 years support the contention that such programs have important, but limited, potential for reducing poverty (Bassi & Ashenfelter, 1986). The education and training programs aimed at parents receiving AFDC in the 1980s produced between 3% and 8% increases in employment for women. They had no impact on father's employment in two-parent families receiving AFDC. Even when job-training programs lead to increased employment, participants may not earn enough to lift them out of poverty. The total increase in earnings for the average AFDC recipient in a San Diego training program was $700 in 15 months; in Baltimore, 12-month earnings increased by $176 (Gueron, 1987; Wiseman, 1988).

Direct assistance, whether cash or in-kind, has more demonstrable effects on family income than policies intended to produce self-sufficiency. In the United States, direct aid is most acceptable when it occurs in the form of social insurance rather than need-based assistance. Social Security is the prototype, and this program has been more successful than any other in reducing poverty; 34% of the individuals who would be poor without government support are raised above poverty incomes by Social Security. By contrast, AFDC raises fewer than 4% out of poverty (Morris & Williamson, 1986). There are a host of reasons why Social Security is not stigmatized as "welfare," but the point in this context is that we as a society accept the premise that certain categories of people (the elderly in this case) can and should be supported by payments from the government. The program is not considered a temporary safety net but rather a long-term system for maintaining a minimum decent standard of living.

Categorical programs for children are consistent with human capital rationales as well. The development of healthy, skilled, emotionally stable citizens is worth an investment, not just to give aid to poor parents but to yield benefits for the entire society. The same contrast appeared in recent debates about farm subsidies. Some politicians proposed restricting subsidies to farmers with incomes below $100,000. Opponents of the plan pointed out that subsidies are not welfare for individual farmers in need; they are intended as investments in a resource that is needed by the nation as a whole.

If children are to be raised out of poverty, our society must begin to think of them as another group that can and should be provided with social insurance to guarantee a decent standard of living. Virtually all industrialized countries already take this approach through universal child allowances, medical care, child care, and other benefits that are considered rights of all children. So long as we continue to treat the problems of poverty as temporary failures that can be reversed by changing individual parents, we will fail to provide for many children. Many parents cannot or will not become self-supporting. Even if all parents could become economically self-sufficient, their children would not always benefit. Successful prevention of poverty and its ill effects on children will require a wide range of programs designed to avoid or reduce the effects of persistent poverty and to cushion the impact of transitory poverty.

Family structure and women's roles. A second major reorientation is needed to encompass changes in family structure and women's roles. The movement of mothers into the labor market and the increases in single parenting are not likely to be reversed in the near future. Effective policies for children need to be designed to fit these new social realities.

Because single-mother families are highly vulnerable to poverty, policy analysts sometimes talk as if the solution were to get more people to marry and stay married. That notion is central to Moynihan's (1986) focus on family instability and Wilson's (1987) argument that job opportunities for black men would reduce poverty among black children by increasing the pool of marriageable men. Implicit in these discussions is a vision of the traditional family in which the man is the primary wage earner and the woman cares for the children perhaps while earning some supplementary income at considerably lower wages than her husband.

Few would disagree that children benefit from living in a stable two-parent family for many reasons, including income, and that policies ought to encourage, or at least not discourage, family stability.[3] However, marital instability is a fact in modern society; it occurs among the affluent as well as the poor and among whites as well as blacks even though white men have plenty of job opportunities. It is essential to develop policies that assure support for children in a variety of family forms and that embrace different cultural patterns (Washington, 1988).

Moreover, whether or not mothers are married, most of them will spend much of their lives in the paid labor force. Instead of deriding the working mother, we as a society need to build policies that buttress her efforts to combine paid employment with parenting. Once we accept the idea that it is "natural" and "expected" that many mothers will combine parenting with earning a living, policies for the workplace, paternal responsibility, and child care will follow more naturally. Once we accept that it is natural and expected for young children to be cared for by people other than their parents, the job of child care can acquire the economic value it deserves.

---

3 Although marriage may not be the solution in many cases, policies that encourage marital dissolution could be eliminated. For instance, only about half of the states currently allow Aid to Families with Dependent Children to be paid to two-parent families with an unemployed head (AFDC-U). If that program were extended to all states, there might be less pressure to dissolve a marriage in order to make the family eligible for aid.

Policy proposals

These broad assumptions are incorporated in a wide range of specific policy proposals offered by the authors in this volume. These fall under three major rubrics: (1) family income maintenance; (2) health care; and (3) education and child care. Throughout the book, we have distinguished between persistent and transitory poverty, and some of the policy proposals offered are specific to one of these subgroups. Ellwood (1988) delineated three subgroups for whom different policies were needed: two-parent working families, single-mother families, and families in urban ghettos. These classifications overlap with ours in that black, single-mother families are at especially high risk for persistent poverty. The rural poor are still another important subgroup, but we like others have not addressed the possibility that they may have different needs than the urban poor. Instead, we point to the need for attention to the rural poor by policy analysts and policy makers.

Maintaining family incomes

Increased earnings by parents. The bulk of most families' incomes is acquired from parents' earnings; in poor families, parents either have no jobs or work at jobs that pay insufficient wages to support a family. In recent welfare policy, the primary emphasis has been placed on job search and job training. Planners seem to assume that jobs are available for qualified candidates, but most of the evaluation data show that such programs are successful primarily for getting participants with little work history into entry-level jobs, many of which do not supply enough income to rise above the poverty level. An equally critical problem is the lack of jobs that pay nonpoverty wages. In the 1980s, poverty increased among two-parent families, often with one full-time worker. Women and minority men continue to be especially concentrated among the low-wage earners and the unemployed.

Several steps could improve poor parents' earning power and shrink the widening gap between the rich and poor. Economic planning to provide jobs is one solution advocated by Wilson (1987). Raising the minimum wage would make it more likely that a full-time worker could earn enough to rise above the poverty level. It is equally important to maintain strong affirmative action policies to assure that women and minorities have access to all jobs.

Workplace policies that reduce the conflicts between job and parenting are increasingly important for two-parent families with two workers as well as for single parents. The United States should join the rest of the industrialized world in providing paid leave for childbirth or family illness as well as more opportunities for flextime and part-time employment (Stipek & McCroskey, 1989). Such policies are particularly important for women workers, but their extension to men might encourage more paternal involvement in children's care.

Universal child allowances. We have argued already that the society should share responsibility for children with their parents; we should define children as a group entitled to social insurance. Most industrialized countries provide this social insurance through a universal child allowance. The closest parallel in the United States is a tax exemption for dependents, which benefits high-income families more than low-income families. For example, in 1989, a married couple with an income over $75,000 received a tax reduction of $660 per child; a couple with an income below $30,000 received $300 per child; families who did not owe taxes got no benefit at all. Ideally, a child allowance would be paid like Social Security with a monthly check, but it might be more politically feasible to convert the current tax exemption to a refundable tax credit that would be more equitable. Every child would receive an equal amount under this plan. The major drawbacks for poor families are that it is delayed and would require them to file a tax return even with no earnings.

Guaranteed child support for single parents. In their chapter, McLanahan et al. outline a Child Support Assurance System, currently being implemented in Wisconsin, that is designed to provide a guaranteed minimum level of support to children in single-parent families. It combines several elements: (1) a fixed percentage standard of the nonresident parent's income for child support awards, (2) automatic withholding of child support from the nonresident parent's wages or income, and (3) a guaranteed minimum payment provided by the state in cases where sufficient support cannot be collected from the nonresident parent. The last component is accompanied by a custodial parent surtax that requires well-off custodial parents to pay back the state subsidy.

This plan has several advantages over the current systems of child support and welfare for families in both persistent and transitory poverty. It reduces the uncertainties and risks of nonpayment of child support by nonresident parents. It does not provide disincentives for work because custodial parents do not lose benefits when they earn money. The benefit plus earnings lifts many families out of poverty. Perhaps most important, benefits are not for the poor alone but are more akin to social insurance to which all children eligible for child support are entitled (Garfinkel, McLanahan, & Wong, 1988). These benefits are not considered just a temporary safety net or a sign of parental failure but a continuing part of the state's obligation to its children. Moreover, the program is direct aid rather than being designed to change individual parents, and it is, therefore, more likely than most current welfare reform efforts to alleviate children's poverty (Morris & Williamson, 1986).

Despite these differences the cost of this program is estimated to be comparable to that of AFDC (Garfinkel et al., 1988).

Services for the poor. The policies described thus far are designed to produce public and private transfers of income and in-kind benefits. A wealth of evidence exists showing that income alone is related to children's health, educational progress, and other indices of development (Duncan, this volume; McLanahan et al., this volume). But is it enough to bring family incomes to an acceptable level? For many children whose poverty is transitory, the answer is probably yes.

Schorr and others argue, however, that some persistently poor parents and children are beset with multiple problems that require services and interventions that go well beyond money alone. Parents who themselves have grown up in persistent poverty, who have little education and no job experience, and who live in neighborhoods with high unemployment, to name only a few risk factors, need additional services to alleviate the effects of poverty. They are the group that benefits from education and job-training programs, particularly if they are young and have little or no job experience. They are also the group at greatest risk for long-term poverty and welfare dependency.

Health care

Children living in persistent poverty suffer a myriad of health risks beginning before birth. Those children in transitory poverty are less apt to be exposed to long-term health risks but often may be temporarily exposed to poor nutrition and unhealthy living conditions. They probably also go without personal health services for problems such as ear infections that are not life-threatening but that can interfere with normal development.

Klerman's recommendations for health policy summarize the proposals offered by several authors. Public health and prevention are at least as important as personal health services. Children's health could be significantly improved by improving family living conditions so that children get adequate food, clean housing, and safe neighborhoods. For most families, supplying adequate income will achieve this goal. For others, such in-kind benefits as subsidized housing and food stamps are needed. Government can also intervene with such preventive regulations as requirements for automobile safety restraints, fire-resistant child clothing, and no-lead paint.

The personal health care system in the U.S. had reached a highly visible level of crisis at the end of the 1980s. Klerman proposes a reorientation of the personal health service system to provide universal health care, probably through a combination of government-funded insurance and private insurers. As a result, health care would be available for everyone, and the beneficiaries would include two-parent families and working-poor families not currently eligible for Medicaid. It would also enable some single parents to support their families on their earnings; at present, the loss of eligibility for Medicaid can be a major obstacle to leaving welfare for employment. Klerman also proposes targeting low-income families by increasing eligibility for Medicaid and other means-tested programs and by making them available to families who are not on welfare.

Improved public health and access to personal health services are not specifically targeted to any subgroups of the poor. They would benefit a wide range of the population. Both Schorr and Klerman argue, however, that for multiproblem families among the persistently poor, expansion of services and targeted programs is needed to overcome a variety of barriers to physical and mental health for children. These include prenatal care, adolescent pregnancy prevention services, early screening and evaluation, routine immunization, and nutritional services (WIC) – all programs with well-documented records of success. Such services are most successful when personnel are trained to be sensitive to the needs of multiproblem families and when facilities are convenient and comfortable for families to use.

Family planning services for all poor women and adolescent pregnancy prevention are especially critical for breaking the cycle of intergenerational poverty. Comparisons of the United States with several European nations demonstrate that the rates of adolescent sexual activity are roughly equivalent, but the rates of pregnancy in the United States are dramatically higher. Klerman (this volume) and Schorr (1988) both provide documentation that health services, including access to contraception and abortion, reduce the rates of adolescent pregnancy and childbearing, particularly if the services are convenient and tailored to adolescents' needs. Educational programs stressing life goal setting and other skills also contribute to lowered pregnancy rates. If poor women of all ages are enabled to control their own fertility, fewer will bear children at a very early age, and more children will be born to parents who want them. Intervention at this crucial point in women's lives can have especially important consequences.

Child care and education

Both social-economic and developmental rationales for policy indicate the importance of child care and education from infancy on. As Phillips points out, however, children will not benefit (nor will the society in the long run) if child care policies are based primarily on the short-term goal of providing custodial care for children in order to free mothers for paid employment. Whether one emphasizes children as human capital or stresses children's optimal development as a goal in its own right, the importance of quality care and appropriate education is glaringly clear.

I discuss child care with education deliberately in this context because there is no clear separation between the two, at least during the years from infancy through age 6. The prototype of "developmental child care" described by Phillips is Head Start, an early education program. Intensive early stimulation and education programs such as the Abecedarian program are child care. Infancy and early childhood are extremely important periods for fostering healthy social-emotional development and optimal cognitive development. There is ample evidence that early education programs have short-term and long-term effects on the development of children, particularly children from economically deprived homes.

Policy makers in the United States have debated a variety of child care plans, but their efforts are often described as ways of helping parents with something that is essentially an individual and private problem, a reflection of the assumptions discussed earlier. Shared community and parent responsibility implies that society has a direct obligation to provide for the care of young children. Public education provides a good parallel. A little over 100 years ago, it was assumed that education was a private parental prerogative to be obtained if one had enough money. Universal public education represented an important restructuring of such views and a recognition that the society had an interest in creating an educated citizenry as well as an obligation to provide for children's fundamental needs. At the end of the 20th century, this view needs to be extended to children from zero to 6 for the same two reasons. Early child care should become a regular feature of social programs available to all children, particularly to those from families who are headed by single parents or who are poor.

The specifics of federal child care policies were hotly debated during the 1980s (see Phillips, this volume). Although a wide range of programs would be consistent with the philosophy we propose, some general guidelines are clear. First, adequate care requires government aid for both the supply of child care (direct funding of child care providers) and the demand (aid to parents paying for child care). Second, widely accepted standards for evaluating quality of care need to be adopted and enforced. Simply providing funds to parents through tax credits or direct grants does not assure quality care. The National Child Care Staffing Study demonstrated, for example, that for-profit centers were generally of lower quality than nonprofit centers, although the cost for parents was about the same. Centers that met Federal Interagency Day Care Requirements had teachers who were more sensitive to and appropriate with children than centers not meeting minimum requirements for teacher–child ratios, group size, and teacher training (Whitebook et al., 1989). Government agencies need to set and enforce standards for child care as well as provide funds to supply child care.

These proposals deal with the welfare of children whose families are in both persistent and transitory poverty, but, once again, additional targeted programs are needed for multiproblem families in persistent poverty. The

Abecedarian Project described by Ramey and Campbell and the accelerated school model described by Levin are examples of such programs. In each case, the educational programs are intensive and carefully tailored to the populations participating. The preschool interventions have demonstrated long-term benefits for academic achievement and other important outcomes. They are most likely to succeed when they have the kind of flexibility that Schorr discusses in her chapter.

Levin's discussion brings home another point that is sometimes obscured in discussions of early development: Intervention during the preschool years is not enough; it is not a long-term "fix." Discussions of Head Start and other early interventions often assume that the program is worthwhile only if its effects last into adulthood without further intervention. There is indeed some evidence for lasting effects of early intervention, but intervention should not stop at age 5. The children who had participated in the Abecedarian preschool programs did better in school than control group children, but those who had additional intervention in the early elementary grades performed even better. Education at every level needs to be innovative and responsive to the special needs of poor children.

Summary. Adequate income, health services, and educational child care form the cornerstones of policies needed to meet the needs of poor children. If we are to solve some of the problems of children's poverty in this country, all three areas need to be addressed. Some programs for children will need to be shifted from temporary, means-tested "welfare" to continuing social insurance. One result of such a change probably would be greater economic self-sufficiency among many families, especially single-mother families. Under the present system, mothers who earn a modest amount lose not only their AFDC and food stamps but also their eligibility for Medicaid and child care assistance. Most of the education and training programs for people on AFDC phase out medical and child care benefits within a year after the mother becomes employed. The result can be large costs for health and child care that tip the balance; a parent whose income is barely sufficient for basic living costs cannot absorb these added costs and is forced to return to welfare.

Policy action and policy research

This is a book for policy researchers as well as policy makers. A tension between action and research exists in any area of applied scholarship. On the one hand, as Schorr (1988) has argued so well, we have enough knowledge on which to act. The policy proposals offered here were developed from a sound knowledge base about what works. There is a striking similarity among the recent proposals generated by scholars examining poverty issues (e.g.,

Ellwood, 1988; Grubb & Lazerson, 1988; Wilson, 1987). The impetus for action is strong because the need is immediate and great.

On the other hand, the data are woefully inadequate in many domains. We need research to provide a sound basis for policy decisions. As Levin noted, it is a lot less expensive to conduct research than to put new policies into effect. If the knowledge base is uncertain, rushing into policy choices can be wasteful and even harmful to the very people the policy is designed to help.

Most scholars in this area would agree that research and action are not in conflict but should complement one another. In this section, I summarize some recommendations for research. Again, the list is by no means exhaustive, but it includes examples of issues that the authors in this book consider important.

Evaluation. Program evaluation is perhaps the most common type of research. Yet many programs lack solid evaluations. Even those programs that have been subjected to reasonably sophisticated research designs (e.g., experimental controls) often fail to include measures of important features of children's development, including health, cognitive and academic performance, and emotional well-being. Much of the existing research reflects economic assumptions with little attention to developmental issues.

In order to answer questions about the effectiveness of policies for alleviating children's poverty and its consequences, developmental outcomes must be measured. An emphasis on developmental outcomes follows fairly naturally when a program is designed initially with developmental goals. For example, Head Start and other early intervention programs are typically evaluated by examining children's performance on intelligence tests, progress in school, and long-term social adjustment. Educational interventions are assessed using measures of educational progress and academic achievement. Prenatal care is judged by measuring birth weight and infant mortality.

Evaluations of programs designed primarily from an economic perspective typically concentrate on economic outcomes for the adults who participate and the government units that supply funds. We noted earlier that the income maintenance experiments of the 1960s and 1970s and the welfare reform experiments of the 1980s concentrated on participants' labor force participation, earnings, and ability to be economically self-sufficient. Children's health, school progress, and emotional development were measured superficially if at all.

Both economic and developmental criteria can be incorporated in program evaluations. For instance, cost-benefit and cost-effectiveness techniques derived from economics can be applied using outcomes measured in units other than dollars (e.g., amount of school progress, reduction in adolescent pregnancy). One of the most pressing needs for future research is to assure that such techniques are used intelligently, avoiding the pitfalls that Levin (Chapter 10 in this volume) describes. One of these pitfalls is the danger that programs and policies will be directed toward quantifiable, measurable outcomes while neglecting important domains that are difficult to quantify. Some authors, notably Schorr, argue for more qualitative methods to overcome this problem.

Implementation and exportability. Interventions and service programs typically begin in experimental settings on a small scale. Once their efficacy is demonstrated, they are disseminated to other settings on the assumption that the demonstrated outcomes will be transferable. Yet the literature is replete with examples of programs that did not transfer well. The reasons are numerous. Policy makers often water down a program, reducing its funding and personnel well below the levels of the successful demonstration. Implementation can vary considerably across different bureaucratic structures (Schorr, 1988; this volume).

Very little is known about how to make good programs exportable. One kind of research needed is exemplified by the creators of the Teaching Family model for residential treatment of delinquent adolescents. The initial program was established and evaluated extensively in one model residential program (Achievement Place) in the late 1960s. It was effective in reducing problem behavior and improving school achievement for the young boys in the program. Other residential centers were then established, staffed with trained personnel, and supplied with detailed manuals, but their successes were mixed. As a result, the program originators tried a range of techniques and conducted investigations over many years to determine how the original model could be successfully exported to new settings (Braukmann & Wolf, 1987). They have found the need for both continued quality control and a network of professionals serving in the program. The result is a Teaching Family professional organization, a master's degree program for training teaching parents, a small hierarchy of positions through which personnel can advance, and a continuing system of direct supervision and observation of procedures in all the group homes using the model.

Summary and conclusions

The authors in this volume address three sets of questions. First, why are children at higher risk for poverty than any other age group in the United States, and why has their poverty increased in the last 20 years? Second, what are the processes by which poverty affects children's physical and mental health, cognitive development, academic and occupational achievement, and social development? Third, how can public policy be designed to prevent children's poverty and to counteract its effects?

A major theme of the book is child-centered policy analysis – that is, we take as a focal point and a primary policy goal the healthy development of children. In Chapter 1, child-developmental goals are contrasted with the more usual social-economic goals assumed by policy analysts. As a result, we examine children's physical and mental health, cognitive development, academic achievement, and social behavior as well as parental earnings and labor force participation as important outcomes both of poverty and of antipoverty policies.

Why has poverty increased among U.S. children over the last 20 years? First, macroeconomic changes have resulted in fewer well-paid jobs for young and unskilled workers. The income gap between rich and poor has increased, and many families with children maintain sufficient income only because they have two earners. Second, more children live in single-parent families, usually headed by women. Single mothers are at high risk for poverty because they are often poorly educated; they are subject to gender and race inequalities in earnings; they must provide for child care; and fathers often do not contribute to their children's support. Third, government benefits dropped precipitously, especially in the early 1980s. Expenditures on such means-tested programs as AFDC and subsidized child care declined without corresponding increases in other resources. In most other industrialized countries extensive government benefits for children reduce poverty rates significantly.

How does poverty affect children's development? Children in persistent poverty are at risk for problems in physical and mental health, cognitive development, academic attainment, and social behavior. Children who experience transitory poverty are also at risk for behavior problems and lowered attainment. Family income per se makes a direct contribution to these developmental outcomes. Economic circumstances affect children by influencing the physical environment in which they live, the health conditions into which they are born, their parents' stresses and coping mechanisms, the schools they attend, and the explicit and implicit messages surrounding them about what the future has to offer. Some children and some families are sufficiently resilient to weather economic stresses and even gain strength from them, but they are the exceptions. It is not reasonable to conclude that most of those who are adversely affected could with reasonable effort overcome their disadvantages.

How can public policy alter children's poverty and prevent its damaging effects? There is remarkable agreement among many policy analysts about what policies would be effective; therefore, it appears that the problem may be less that we do not know what to do and more that we lack the national will to do it. Some basic assumptions in American society pose barriers to implementing effective interventions. First, the American value on individualism and the privacy of the family has led to an imbalance between parental and social responsibility for children. Parents are expected to provide almost all resources, except formal education, for socializing children from ages 6 through 18. In other industrialized countries, the society's interest in healthy children is manifested in universal health care, child allowances, paid family leaves for parents, subsidized child care, and a host of other benefits.

Second, policies in this country have been dominated by short-term economic goals (e.g., reducing the welfare rolls) that often do not lead to improved conditions for children. Those programs aimed directly at improving the lot of children (e.g., Head Start, WIC) have been demonstrably successful, but remain chronically underfunded and therefore unavailable to many eligible children.

Third, we as a society have not accepted the new roles of women; we retain an image of a stay-at-home mother who provides unpaid child care while her husband earns a living. New expectations that women should be self-sufficient and able to provide economically for their families have taken root without recognizing the conflict with old images. Hence, women still bear most of the responsibility for child rearing, and their earnings average less than two-thirds of men's wages. There is only grudging recognition of the need to form government and workplace policies that allow women (and men) to provide for their families while being responsible parents.

Finally, the political and economic institutions of this country are suffering shock as the job of child care moves from unpaid labor by women to paid labor that must be included in the overall money economy. Because child care was traditionally unpaid, its practical economic value was low, although its true value was quite large. As a result of the rapid movement into the labor force by women with infants and preschool children, families are confronted with large child care costs while the profession of child care is dismally funded. Wages for child care workers are half those for women workers of comparable education.

Changes in these assumptions are required to bring about truly effective policies to reduce children's poverty. The most fundamental change is to alter the balance of parental and social responsibility for children – to accept the principle that society has a stake in the welfare of children and an obligation to provide for its children. Children should be defined categorically as deserving certain benefits beyond public education, just as the elderly and the disabled are now. Antipoverty policies must move beyond the goal of increasing the economic self-sufficiency of parents; programs to make parents completely self-supporting have limited potential to eliminate children's poverty. We need regular and continuing support for health, early child care, and other basic needs of children. As a natural corollary, short-term economic considerations should be tempered with more long-range concerns for children's development and future economic productivity.

We must also bring our assumptions about women's roles, family structure, and the economic value of child care into line with the major social changes that have occurred over the last 20 or 30 years. Women, whether married or single, rich or poor, are now expected to combine primary responsibility for child rearing with earning a living. Single-parent families and other unconventional family forms are here to stay; policies need to be tailored to a variety of family forms. As child care shifts into the money economy, our social and political institutions need to be adapted to provide for the large real cost of rearing young children. Not only do we need public support for the costs of child care, but the true value of such labor needs to be reflected in adequate earnings for the people who perform it.

Our policy proposals are offered within this general framework. Several policies have potential for maintaining adequate family income:

1. increasing parents' earnings by economic development that will create jobs as well as train workers, increasing the minimum wage, and enforcing affirmative action policies;
2. enabling parents to combine family responsibilities with jobs by providing paid leaves for childbirth and family illness and increasing the possibilities for flextime and part-time employment;
3. converting the current tax exemption for dependents to a refundable tax credit or universal child allowance that is equivalent for every child; and
4. implementing a guaranteed child support program for single parents that combines automatic withholding of child support from a nonresident parent with a guaranteed minimum payment provided by the state.

Health is the second major domain in which changes are urgently needed.

1. Preventive public health measures to assure adequate housing, nutrition, prenatal care, and safe neighborhoods as well as enforcement of regulations about seat belt use, nonleaded paint, and the like could make important contributions to health, especially for persistently poor children.
2. A system of universal health care, involving some combination of private and government-funded insurance is needed to assure adequate personal health services to children.
3. For the persistently poor, health could be improved considerably by increasing eligibility for Medicaid and related programs.
4. Improved access to family planning and abortion services, particularly for adolescents, would allow poor women to decide when to have children.

Finally, new policies are needed for education and child care.

1. Improved funding for early childhood developmentally oriented programs (e.g., Head Start) could make major contributions to the long-term prospects of persistently poor children.
2. Large-scale public funding for child care from infancy through the school years is essential for providing adequate rearing environments for young children.
3. Education throughout the school years can benefit from alternative programs for high-risk children that incorporate staff and parent involvement in decision making, high expectations for students, and flexibility in curriculum.

Policy researchers can contribute to effective policy development by incorporating child-developmental outcomes (e.g., school achievement, mental health) as well as economic criteria into evaluation research. The best research will arise from an integration of disciplines that includes economic analyses and the intelligent use of cost-benefit and cost-effectiveness techniques in conjunction with analyses of the social and psychological factors involved in effective programs and interventions.

I end this chapter with a call for action. American children in the 1990s face high odds of experiencing poverty, violence, family disruptions, drug addiction, and poor schooling. Proposals for new programs are consistently greeted with statements that there is no money, that the national deficit is already out of hand. Yet money is found for crises – the savings and loan bailout and the Middle Eastern military operations of 1990 and 1991 are two salient examples. The welfare of children is also a crisis, and we ignore it at our peril. "Children are ever the future of a society. Every child who does not function at a level commensurate with his or her possibilities, every child who is destined to make fewer contributions to society than society needs, and every child who does not take his or her place as a productive adult diminishes the power of that society's future" (Horowitz & O'Brien, 1989, p. 445). Without major changes in public policies for children, our future will be bleak.

References

Bane, M. J. (1986). Household composition and poverty. In S. H. Danziger & D. H. Weinberg (Eds.), *Fighting poverty: What works and what doesn't* (pp. 209–213). Cambridge, MA: Harvard University Press.

Bane, M.J., & Ellwood, D. T. (1989). One fifth of the nation's children: Why are they poor? *Science, 245,* 1047–1053.

Bassi, L. J., & Ashenfelter, O. (1986). The effect of direct job creation and training programs on low-skilled workers. In S. H. Danziger & D. H. Weinberg (Eds.), *Fighting poverty: What works and what doesn't* (pp. 133–151). Cambridge, MA: Harvard University Press.

Blank, R. M., & Blinder, A. S. (1986). Macroeconomics, income distribution, and poverty. In S. H. Danziger & D. H. Weinberg (Eds.), *Fighting poverty: What works and what doesn't* (pp. 180–208). Cambridge, MA: Harvard University Press.

Bowman, P.J. (1990). The adolescent-to-adult transition: Discouragement among jobless black youth. In V. C. McLoyd & C. A. Flanagan (Eds.), *New directions for child development: Vol. 46. Economic stress: Effects on family life and child development* (pp. 87–106). San Francisco: Jossey-Bass.

Braukmann, C. J., & Wolf, M. M. (1987). Behaviorally based group homes for juvenile offenders. In E. K. Morris & C. J. Braukmann (Eds.), *Behavioral approaches to crime and delinquency* (pp. 135–160). New York: Plenum Press.

Butler, J. A., Starfield, B., & Stenmark, S. (1984). Child health policy. In H. W. Stevenson & A. E. Siegel (Eds.), *Child development research and social policy.* (Vol. 1, pp. 110–188). Chicago: University of Chicago Press.

Congressional Budget Office. (1988). *Trends in family income: 1970–1988.* Washington, DC: Author.

Danziger, S. H., Haveman, R. H., & Plotnick, R. D. (1986). Antipoverty policy: Effects on the poor and the nonpoor. In S. H. Danziger & D. H. Weinberg (Eds.), *Fighting poverty: What works and what doesn't* (pp. 50–77). Cambridge, MA: Harvard University Press.

Duncan, G. (1984). *Years of poverty, years of plenty: The changing economic fortunes of American workers and families*. Ann Arbor, MI: University of Michigan, Survey Research Center.

Elder, G. H., Jr., & Caspi, A. (1989). Economic stress in lives: Developmental perspectives. *Journal of Social Issues, 44*, 25–45.

Ellwood, D. T. (1988). *Poor support: Poverty in the American family*. New York: Basic Books.

Ellwood, D. T., & Summers, L. H. (1986). Poverty in America: Is welfare the answer or the problem? In S. H. Danziger & D. H. Weinberg (Eds.), *Fighting poverty: What works and what doesn't* (pp. 78–105). Cambridge, MA: Harvard University Press.

Emery, R. E., Hetherington, E. M., & DiLalla, L. F. (1984). Divorce, children, and social policy. In H. W. Stevenson & A. E. Siegel (Eds.), *Child development research and social policy* (Vol.1, pp. 189–266). Chicago: University of Chicago Press.

Flanagan, C.A. (1990). Families and schools in hard times. In V. C. McLoyd & C. A. Flanagan (Eds.), *New directions for child development: Vol. 46. Economic stress: Effects on family life and child development* (pp. 7–26). San Francisco: Jossey-Bass.

Fraser, N. (1987, February). *Women, welfare and the politics of need interpretation*. Lecture presented at the University of Kansas, Lawrence, KS.

Furstenberg, F. F., Jr., Brooks-Gunn, J., & Morgan, S. P. (1987). *Adolescent mothers in later life*. Cambridge: Cambridge University Press.

Furstenberg, F. F, Jr., Peterson, J. L., Nord, C. W., & Zill, N. (1983). The life course of children after divorce: Marital disruption and parental contact. *American Sociological Review, 48*, 656–658.

Garfinkel, I., & McLanahan, S. S. (1986). *Single mothers and their children: A new American dilemma*. Washington, DC: Urban Institute Press.

Garfinkel, I., McLanahan, S., & Wong, P. (1988). Child support and dependency. In H. R. Rodgers, Jr. (Ed.), *Beyond welfare: New approaches to the problem of poverty in America* (pp. 66–85). Armonk, NY: M. E. Sharpe.

Garwood, S. G., Phillips, D., Hartman, A., & Zigler, E. F. (1989). As the pendulum swings: Federal agency programs for children. *American Psychologist, 44*, 434–440.

Glazer, N., (1986). Education and training programs and poverty. In S. H. Danziger & D. H. Weinberg (Eds.), *Fighting poverty: What works and what doesn't* (pp. 152–172). Cambridge, MA: Harvard University Press.

Grubb, W. N., & Lazerson, M. (1988). *Broken promises: How Americans fail their children*. New York: Basic Books.

Gueron, J. M. (1987). Welfare to work programs: Lessons on recent state initiatives. *Policy Studies Review, 6*, 733–743.

Hernandez, D. J. (1989, April). *The changing needs of America's children from the Great Depression to the 21st century*. Paper presented at the Biennial Meeting of the Society for Research in Child Development, Kansas City, MO.

Hoffman, L. (1989). Effects of maternal employment in the two-parent family. *American Psychologist, 4*, 282–292.

Horowitz, F. D., & O'Brien, M. (1989). In the interest of the nation: A reflective essay on the state of our knowledge and the challenges before us. *American Psychologist, 44*, 441–445.

Jencks, C. (1985, May 9). How poor are the poor? *New York Review of Books*, 41–49.

Jobs and insecurity increase. (1988, May 1). *New York Times*, pp. F25, F27.

Kahn, A. J., & Kamerman, S. B. (1983). *Income transfers for families with children: An eight-country study*. Philadelphia: Temple University Press.

Malveaux, J. (1988). The economic statuses of black families. In H. P. McAdoo (Ed.), *Black families* (2nd ed., pp. 133–147). Newbury Park, CA: Sage.

McLoyd, V.C. (1989). Socialization and development in a changing economy: The effects of paternal job and income loss on children. *American Psychologist, 44*, 293–302.

Morris, M., & Williamson, J. B. (1986). *Poverty and public policy: An analysis of federal intervention efforts*. New York: Greenwood.

Moynihan, D. P. (1986). *Family and nation*. San Diego: Harcourt Brace Jovanovich.

Murray, C. (1984). *Losing ground: American social policy, 1950–1980*. New York: Basic Books.

Ogbu, J.U. (1988). Cultural diversity of human development. In D. T. Slaughter (Ed.), *New directions in child development: Vol. 42. Black children and poverty: A developmental perspective* (pp. 11–28). San Francisco: Jossey-Bass.

Rhoads, S. E. (1985). *The economist's view of the world: Governments, markets, and public policy.* Cambridge: Cambridge University Press.

Rodgers, H. R., Jr. (1988). Reducing poverty through family support. In H. R. Rodgers, Jr. (Ed.), *Beyond welfare: New approaches to the problem of poverty in America* (pp. 39–65). Armonk, NY: M. E. Sharpe.

Scarr, S. (1986). Cultural lenses on mothers and children. In L. Freidrich-Cofer (Ed.), *Human nature and public policy: Scientific views of women, children, and families* (pp. 202–238). New York: Praeger.

Schorr, L. B. (1988). *Within our reach: Breaking the cycle of disadvantage.* New York: Anchor Press.

Slaughter, D. T. (Ed.). (1988). *New directions for child development: Vol. 42. Black children and poverty: A developmental perspective.* San Francisco: Jossey-Bass.

Steiner, G. (1981). *The futility of family policy.* Washington, DC: Brookings.

Stipek, D., & McCroskey, J. (1989). Investing in children: Government and workplace policies for parents. *American Psychologist, 44*, 434–440.

U.S. Department of Education. (1988). *Youth indicators 1988: Trends in the well-being of American youth.* Washington, DC: Author, Office of Educational Research and Improvement.

Van Hook, M.P. (1990). The Iowa farm crisis: Perceptions, interpretations, and family patterns. In V. C. McLoyd & C. A. Flanagan (Eds.), *New directions for child development: Vol. 46. Economic stress: Effects on family life and child development* (pp. 71–86). San Francisco: Jossey-Bass.

Wacquant, L. J. D., & Wilson, W. J. (1989). The cost of racial and class exclusion in the inner city. *The Annals of the American Academy of Political and Social Science, 501*, 8–25.

Washington, V. (1988). Historical and contemporary linkages between black child development and social policy. In D. T. Slaughter (Ed.), *New directions for child development: Vol. 42. Black children and poverty: A developmental perspective* (pp. 93–108). San Francisco: Jossey-Bass.

Weitzman, L. J. (1985). *The divorce revolution: The unexpected social and economic consequences for women and children in America.* New York: Free Press.

Werner, E. E., & Smith, R. S. (1982). *Vulnerable but invincible: A longitudinal study of resilient children and youth.* New York: McGraw-Hill.

Whitebook, M., Howes, C., & Phillips, D. (1989). *Who cares? Child care teachers and the quality of care in America.* Executive summary of the National Child Care Staffing Study. Oakland, CA: Child Care Employee Project.

Wilensky, H. L., Luebbert, G. M., Hahn, S. R., & Jamieson, A. M. (1985). *Comparative social policy: Theories, methods, findings.* Berkeley, CA: University of California, Institute of International Studies.

Wilson, W. J. (1987). *The truly disadvantaged: The inner city, the underclass, and public policy.* Chicago: University of Chicago Press.

Wiseman, M. (1988). Workfare and welfare reform. In H. R. Rodgers, Jr. (Ed.), *Beyond welfare: New approaches to the problem of poverty in America* (pp. 14–38). Armonk, NY: M. E. Sharpe.

Zimmerman, S. L. (1988). *Understanding family policy: Theoretical approaches.* Newbury Park, CA: Sage.

Author index

317

Subject index

Abecedarian experiment, 16–17, 190–221, 307; description of intervention, 195–200; effects on behavior problems, 209–10; effects on classroom behavior, 208–9; effects on IQ, 200–1, 210–12; effects on reading and math achievement, 201–7; effects on retention in grade, 206–8
abortion, 14, 150; among adolescents, 83, 97
abuse of children, *see* child abuse
academic achievement, 16–18, 190, 266, 291; and Abecedarian experiment, 201–8, 210–17; in accelerated schools, 334–6; cost-effectiveness analysis of, 249–51; effects of early intervention on, 200–8, 210–17
accelerated education, 222–40; parent and community involvement, 225, 229–30
accelerated schools: achievement in, 334–6; cost, 336–337
Accelerated Schools Program, 225–35; capacity building, 332–4; curriculum, 228–9; governance structure, 230–2; instructional strategies, 228–9; parent involvement, 229–30
accountability of social services, 274–5
achievement, academic, 16–18, 190, 266, 291; in accelerated schools, 334–6; cost-effectiveness analysis, 249–51; effects of early intervention on, 200–8, 210–17
achievement gap, between poor and nonpoor, 224, 226
Act for Better Child Care Services, 181
adolescent births: changes over time, 82–4; incidence, 80–2; influences on, 56–67, 69, 91; reasons for concern, 84; to unmarried women, 80–4
adolescent mothers, 9, 12–14, 79–104, 260–1, 263–7; earnings, 87–8; educational attainment, 89–90; paternal support, 87–8, 99; programs for, 13, 98–9; risk to children, 13, 91–3; and welfare, 86, 88
adolescent pregnancy: causes of, 13, 91, 260–1, 291; prevention, 13, 94–8, 263–7, 305; relation to poverty, 13, 84–7, 91, 98–9

adolescent sexual behavior, 80–1, 84; use of contraception, 91
adoption: incidence among adolescent mothers, 81–2; programs to promote, 97
AFDC, *see* Aid to Families with Dependent Children
AFDC child care disregard, 165–7
affirmative action, 70, 283, 302
Aid to Families with Dependent Children (AFDC), 14, 30, 45–7, 73, 79, 85, 88, 89, 99, 101, 116, 148–9, 152, 286–97; and child care, 158, 164, 169, 179; effects on poverty, 299–300, 303, 307; long-term recipients, 171–3
AIDS, pediatric, 139–40, 142
aspiration, educational, in mother-only and step families, 61
at-risk children and education, 222–40
attainment, educational, 12–13, 17; effects of family income, 54–8, 222, 291–2; neighborhood influences on, 63

barriers to effective intervention, 294–8
behavior problems: effects of early intervention on, 208–10
benefit-cost analysis, *see* cost-analysis
benefits, government, 286–7; effects on family structure, 288–9
benefits for children, categorical, 299–301
Berkeley Guidance Study, 35
black families, views about, 52
bureaucracy and social service, 276–7

Carolina Abecedarian Experiment, *see* Abcedarian experiment
categorical benefits for children, 299–301
child abuse, 1, 141–2, 261; prevention, 265, 267, 270, 272
child and adolescent mortality, 138–9
child care, 158–189; as adjunct to welfare reform, 160–2, 167, 175–8; for children of adolescent mothers, 98–9; cost, 16, 71, 163–4; developmental, 16–17, 160–2, 167,

326